Hopewell Ceremonial Landscapes of Ohio

For Lynn

Mark Lynott

(21 January 1951 – 29 May 2014)

Photograph taken at the Society for American Archaeology conference in
Austin, Texas, 24 April 2014, during a poster session on *American Landscapes*
(photo: Michaela Goff, Oxbow Books).

Hopewell Ceremonial Landscapes of Ohio

More than mounds and geometric earthworks

by

Mark J. Lynott

AMERICAN LANDSCAPES

VOLUME 1

American Landscapes is an imprint of Oxbow Books

Published in the United Kingdom in 2015 by
OXBOW BOOKS
10 Hythe Bridge Street, Oxford OX1 2EW

and in the United States by
OXBOW BOOKS
908 Darby Road, Havertown, PA 19083

© Mark Lynott 2014

Paperback Edition: ISBN 978-1-78297-754-4
Digital Edition: ISBN 978-1-78297-755-1

A CIP record for this book is available from the British Library

Printed in the United States by Bang Printing

For a complete list of Windgather titles, please contact:

UNITED KINGDOM
Oxbow Books
Telephone (01865) 241249
Fax (01865) 794449
Email: oxbow@oxbowbooks.com
www.oxbowbooks.com

UNITED STATES OF AMERICA
Oxbow Books
Telephone (800) 791-9354
Fax (610) 853-9146
Email: queries@casemateacademic.com
www.casemateacademic.com/oxbow

Oxbow Books is part of the Casemate Group

*Front cover: Reconstruction of the Hopewell ceremonial complex of the Newark Earthworks by
Steven Patricia. Reproduced by kind permission of the artist.*

*Back cover, left to right: 1. Burned palisade wall at the Pollock Works (photo: R. Riordan); 2. reconstructed
ceramic vessel from Riverside site (photo: Midwest Archeological Center, Lincoln, Nebraska); 3. image
of Fort Ancient during a storm created by CERHAS, University of Cincinnaiti (www.ancientohiotrail.
org); 4. mannequin of a flint knapper crafting a biface, and tool types created with Flint Ridge flint
(photo: Pete Topping).*

Contents

Editors' Preface

The launch of a new series of books is an occasion of great anticipation and excitement. We are delighted to present *Hopewell Ceremonial Landscapes of Ohio* as the first in our new series entitled *American Landscapes*. The aim of this series is to present to a wide audience informed overviews – from a holistic landscape perspective – of the history and changing land use of particular areas/regions or archaeological/historical themes in North America. We aim to present connections, to look beyond the individual site to establish how settlements interacted with their neighbours, discuss their landscape settings, review regional and supra-regional networks, and tell the stories of how people lived in, and moved around, their parts of the North American continent during specific time periods. Each volume will provide a comprehensive and accessible narrative aimed at the informed reader, presenting an up-to-date review of the latest research from archaeology, anthropology, historical studies and the environmental sciences.

Having recognised a possible gap in the market for a series that would complement our highly successful *Windgather* imprint, which publishes studies on the landscape history and archaeology of Britain, one of us (JG) set about promoting the idea. This first involved recruiting the other (PT), also British based but with a longstanding interest in, and knowledge of, North American prehistoric archaeology, as a potential series editor and then pitching it to archaeologists in the US. We began with those who we met on a "Moundbuilders" tour organised and led by PT for the Prehistoric Society (of Britain), in June 2012. Five days of that most excellent tour of the archaeology of the Midwest were spent in Chillicothe, Ohio, in the company of Mark Lynott who, together with colleagues including Bret Ruby, introduced us to the astonishing earthwork complexes built by Hopewell communities in the Scioto–Paint Creek drainage. By the end of the stay Mark, who was shortly to retire from the Midwest Archeological Center, National Park Service, had not only agreed to become a third series editor, but also to write the first volume.

Following his "retirement" Mark quickly threw himself into the dual tasks of drafting this text and promoting the new series to colleagues across the US. Together, we three worked on the remit for the series, produced a "wishlist" of potential subjects and authors, and began commissioning titles. Mark's enthusiasm, knowledge and guidance proved invaluable and he further set about assisting our marketing team in the US, especially in targeting conferences and organisations that could actively promote the series. In April 2014, with several titles confirmed, Oxbow Books presented a very successful poster session at the Society for American Archaeology Annual conference in Austin, Texas, hosted by the three of us and one of our series authors, Bob Birmingham. We came away with several new titles and promises of others, much encouragement, and a strong feeling that the series was going to go very well indeed.

At the conference we achieved a major milestone when Mark handed over the revised draft of this book, his first draft having been completed and peer reviewed in late fall 2013. Over the next few weeks the three of us worked together on tying up the loose ends and little bits of finishing off that are an inevitable feature of any "final" draft text, and eagerly anticipated its publication. But barely a month after returning from Austin came the devastating news of Mark's sudden and untimely death. Like all his family, friends and colleagues we were completely stunned. After several weeks of soul-searching, it became clear that there was strong support all round for his publication to go ahead, as a testament to his research and as his legacy to Hopewell studies. So, with much kind assistance from many friends and colleagues in Ohio and Nebraska, we have worked together to bring this book to press, including, with the generous assistance of Drs Tim Schilling and Mike Allen, completion of the text box "asides" in each chapter that Mark was in the process of composing as the final element of the work. Nevertheless, there undoubtedly remain some small matters that Mark would have liked to improve upon or had a final opportunity to revise.

It is tragic that Mark will not see publication of this book. Proof-reading it has been both a pleasure and a genuine sadness, but we are proud to present it on his behalf as the first *American Landscapes* volume and we are certain that it and the series as a whole, which has benefitted so much from his experience and advice in its establishment, will be a lasting and fitting monument to a good friend, a lovely man and a very fine archaeologist.

Julie Gardiner & Peter Topping

Foreword

Bradley Lepper

Mark Lynott died unexpectedly in May of 2014 before this book was published. It now stands as the culmination of his more than three decades of study devoted to the Hopewell culture. Those of us who knew Mark and had the opportunity to work alongside of him are enormously grateful to have this testament to his hard work and careful thinking about one of North America's most spectacular and intriguing ancient cultures. You, the reader, should be glad, too.

Mark was one of the foremost students of Hopewell archaeology in this century and he is the perfect person to have written this book. He was the manager and Supervisory Archeologist at the Midwest Archeological Center in Lincoln, Nebraska, until he retired in 2013. Between 1995 and 2010, he served as the editor of *Hopewell Archeology*, a newsletter devoted to promoting "interest in the study and interpretation of Hopewell archeology."

He spent much of his career studying the Hopewell culture at the National Park Service sites of Mound City, Hopewell Mound Group, and the Hopeton Earthworks. Using geophysical prospecting and strategic testing he attacked a variety of important questions relating to these classic Hopewell sites.

The results of his work are presented in the following pages, but one of the most important conclusions to come out of his research was the recognition that at least one segment of the earthen walls at Hopeton had been built, or at least

Mark Lynott explaining mound stratigraphy to the Prehistoric Society (of Britain) at Mound City, June 2012 (photo: Pete Topping).

heavily modified, by Late Woodland folks at around AD 1000. That came as a huge surprise to all of us who thought that earthwork construction had ended abruptly with the "collapse" of the Hopewell culture.

The last time I heard from Mark was in an e-mail I received in February of 2014. Mark responded to some comments I had offered on an early draft of the manuscript of this book and then proceeded to discuss all the things we still don't know about the Hopewell culture. He wrote about trying to improve our understanding of the chronology of Hopewell sites by, for example, seeing if we could get archaeomagnetic dates for the so-called "altars" beneath the mounds at the Hopewell Mound Group and Mound City. He supposed that to accomplish this, we would "have to be patient and hope that the tribes will become curious about these issues too." He mentioned having some "really good data on Mound City that is insufficiently developed to fully include in this volume" and then brought up other questions relating to things we would like to know about other Hopewell sites not encompassed in Hopewell Culture National Historical Park. He concluded with an excitement and a sense of wonder that was palpable even through the e-mail – "I am not sure where I will go next."

I am deeply saddened that Mark won't have the chance to follow that sense of wonder to new discoveries at the Hopewell Mound Group and other Ohio Hopewell sites. But I take consolation from knowing that this book will pave the way for others to follow in his footsteps and make those discoveries.

Bradley Lepper
Curator of Archaeology, Ohio History Connection

Acknowledgments

The very last thing that Mark was working on for this volume was the acknowledgements but, regrettably, these had not been completed. We have been able to compile the following from notes and conversations. The list below seems far too short – many colleagues have contributed directly, or indirectly, to the lifetime of research that has led to this book. There are undoubtedly omissions for which we apologize and we offer thanks to anyone who has been unwittingly left out.

We thank, on Mark's behalf, all the colleagues who provided help and support over many years at the Hopewell Culture National Historical Park: Superintendents John Neal, Dean Alexander and Jennifer Pederson Weinberger and their staff; all the current and former staff of the Midwest Archeological Center, Lincoln, Nebraska, especially Jeff Richner, Carrol Moxham, Ann Bauermeister, Bruce Jones and Steve DeVore; and the US National Park Service. The University of Nebraska provided great support in the form of students participating in summer Archaeological Field Schools at Hopeton alongside the expertise of the late John Weymouth. The Milton Hershey School also provided student participants, and the Kansas Geological Survey supported Mark's research at Hopeton.

Among the many other individuals who should be named are: John Barnhart, Bruce Bevan, Kathy Brady, James Brown, Jarrod Burks, Frank Cowen, Rinita Dalan, William Dancey, Dawn W. Gagliano, N'omi Greber, John Hancock, Robert Harness, John Kelly, Brad Lepper, Rolfe D. Mandel, Robert Riordain, Bret Ruby, Tim Schilling, Doug Scott, Katherine A. Spielmann, and David Towel.

The Ohio Historical Society, Hopewell Culture National Historical Park, and Midwest Archeological Center, Lincoln in particular have been extremely generous in allowing the reproduction of many of the images in this book without charge.

Julie Gardiner and Peter Topping would like to thank all those who assisted in tying up the loose ends and encouraged us to bring this book to press. In particular we are grateful to Brad Lepper, Tim Schilling, Bret Ruby, Jarrod Burks, Frank Cowen, John Hancock and Robert Riordain for giving us so generously of their time. Everyone at Oxbow Books has been very supportive in the final stages and we would particularly like to thank Michaela Goff for all her State-side assistance, Sarah Ommanney for completing several unfinished maps, and Val Lamb, who has been responsible for the design and layout of the book.

Perhaps, rightly, the final words of this acknowledgement should go to Mark himself, who said in an acknowledgement he published in 2009:

> *Those of us who have had the privilege of conducting archeological research in Ross County, Ohio truly appreciate the pioneering efforts of Ephraim G. Squier and Edwin H. Davis. More than a century and a half later, their work on the great earthen monuments in this area continues to inspire and encourage our fascination with Ohio Hopewell archeology'.* (Lynott 2009b, i)

1

More than mounds and ditches, an introduction to Ohio Hopewell ceremonial landscapes

During the first five centuries of the Christian era, a remarkable group of small-scale societies built a large and elaborate complex of earthen mounds, walls, ditches, and ponds in the southern flowing drainages of the Ohio River valley. The number, size, and variety of earthen forms make them some of the most impressive earthworks in all of North America. The period from *ca.* AD 1–500 (Middle Woodland period) witnessed the construction of earthen landscape features covering dozens of hectares at many sites and hundreds of hectares at some. The development of the vast Hopewell Culture earthwork complexes such as those at Mound City, Hopewell, Fort Ancient, Turner, and the Newark earthworks was accompanied by the establishment of wide-ranging cultural contacts reflected in the movement of exotic and strikingly beautiful artifacts such as elaborate tobacco pipes, obsidian and flint spearheads, copper axes and regalia, animal figurines, sharks teeth, and delicately carved sheets of mica. These phenomena, coupled with complex burial rituals, indicate the emergence of a powerful ideology of individual and group power and prestige, strong shamanistic influences, and the creation of a vast cultural landscape within which the monument complexes were central to a ritual cycle encompassing a substantial geographical area. What makes these accomplishments so noteworthy, is that the people who participated in this ideological network lived in small-scale societies and maintained substantial local autonomy. The building of all these great ceremonial landscapes was accomplished over four or more centuries, and reflects an amazing level of social stability and societal commitment to monumental and ceremonial construction.

Despite two centuries of archaeological investigation and review of Native American oral histories, we still have many questions about who built these ancient earthworks, why they were built, how they were used, and why the builders allowed the forests of southern Ohio to gradually reclaim these carefully built landscapes. The passage of time, changes in regional populations, and the impact of modern land use practices have served to obscure much of the once vivid archaeological record in this region. Fortunately, recent archaeological research is helping to document the massive scale of landscape construction, and identify some of the geo-engineering and ceremonial principles applied to these

MAP OF OHIO SHOWING DISTRIBUTION OF EARTHWORKS.

Dots—Mounds
x—Enclosures

XI

monumental earthen constructions. The labor needed to build these vast cultural landscapes exceeds population estimates for the region, and suggests that people from near (and possibly far) traveled to the Scioto and other river valleys to help with their construction. Early archaeological research revealed much about the spectacular mortuary rituals associated with Ohio Hopewell burial mounds, but more than a decade of geophysical and geoarchaeological research has produced extensive new datasets with which to re-examine the spectacular and massive scale of Ohio Hopewell earthworks and landscapes and to explore the society that created them (Fig. 1.1).

Fig. 1.1. Map of mounds and enclosures in Ohio prepared by W. C. Mills (1914). The map is multi-period and serves to demonstrate the density of prehistoric sites in the State.

The Ohio River is the largest tributary of the Mississippi River, by volume, and from its origin in the highlands of western Pennsylvania to its mouth near Cairo, Illinois it is 981 miles (1579 km) long. The Ohio River flows in a generally south-westerly direction, and started developing more than two million years ago. The configuration and channels of the Ohio River and its tributaries were greatly influenced by the continental ice sheet that formed and advanced to just north of the main valley. As the glaciers receded north, great volumes of water from the melting ice created large southward flowing valleys that emptied into the Ohio River at what is now the southern boundary of the State of Ohio.

Southern Ohio, the heartland of Ohio Hopewell people, may be characterized as a land of great physiographic and biotic diversity. The flat to gently rolling areas of central Ohio are Till Plains in the Central Lowlands province. These gently rolling landscapes are in sharp contrast to the rocky highlands of what is now south-east Ohio, with its wide range of cliffs, gorges, waterfalls, and deeply dissected valleys. Although south-western Ohio was exposed to impacts of the glaciers, it still exhibits significant rocky uplands and deep valleys, particularly along the northern margins of the Ohio River. The dissected uplands of southern Ohio are the north-west margins of the Appalachian and Allegheny Plateaus. Most of the major rivers valleys in southern Ohio were partially filled with sand and gravel outwash from the giant glaciers that covered northern Ohio and the Great Lakes region. As the glaciers receded northward, southern Ohio experienced a succession of vegetation zones that seem to have generally stabilized several thousand years ago. Many millennia after the glaciers receded north, Ohio Hopewell people built a large number of monumental earthen landscapes in the generally southward flowing tributaries that formed in the glaciated landscapes of southern and central Ohio.

When Europeans entered the Ohio Valley they found dense forests of beech, oak, maple, chestnut, ash, and other hardwood species. The valley bottoms supported varied eco-systems of floodplain swamps, sloughs, and hardwood forests. Rich soils had formed on the alluvial terraces found along the numerous streams and, as the forests were cleared by settlers to open fields for farming, they discovered numerous large earthen fortifications and mounds that were reminiscent of the earth and stone ruins of their ancestral homelands. More earthen features that looked like fortifications were found in the rocky and forested uplands of south-western Ohio.

The amazing earthen constructions of the Ohio River valley generated great curiosity among the scholarly communities in Europe and the developing cities of the eastern seaboard during the 18th century. Prior to discoveries in the Ohio River valley, Spanish explorers who accompanied Hernando de Soto in the Tampa Bay region of Florida were among the first to record the presence of earthen mounds at native villages in the south-east (Silverberg 1968), but only after western expansion proceeded into the Ohio River valley did scholars and writers begin to learn about the number and variety of earthen monuments in that region. Samuel Haven (1856, 3) notes that:

> "the French priests, Franciscan, and Jesuits, who, very early in the 17th century, penetrated to the upper lakes, and thence worked their way through the Valley of the Mississippi to the Gulf of Mexico, would have seen the mounds and inclosures there so frequent, and have been impressed by their numbers and magnitude."

Unfortunately, despite several 17th century French expeditions to explore the Mississippi River valley and Great Lakes regions, little mention is made of the mounds and earthen enclosures we now know to be present in those regions.

The first significant observations about the earthen monuments of the Ohio

River valley appear in the 18th century writings of missionaries and explorers like Jonathan Carver, who noted in his journal that while traveling to Lake Pepin on the Mississippi he observed embankments that appeared to be of a military character, sufficient to protect 5000 men (Haven 1856, 20). Most of the early accounts of earthworks in the Ohio country were written by men living in settled areas along the east coast of North America. They obtained their information from hunters, trappers, and explorers, and the publication of these early accounts helped to fuel speculation about the origin of the ancient earthen features. Daniel Boone and other woodsmen of the 18th century received funds, supplies, and equipment from land companies with an interest in securing the best lands in Ohio and Kentucky when those lands became available for settlement (Morgan 2008). It seems likely that, in addition to noting the valuable land and natural resources in the region, they must have observed mounds and embankments, and their storytelling contributed to the growing curiosity about the ancient monuments.

As the frontier moved west, more literate observers came into direct contact with the mounds and earthworks of the Ohio River valley. The impressive earthworks at Marietta at the mouth of the Muskingum River in Ohio were among the first to be mapped and described (Fig. 1.2). Henry Clyde Shetrone (1930) notes the importance of a map of the Marietta mound group prepared by General Rufus Putnam for the Ohio Company in 1788. Shetrone (1930, 12–13) believes this map:

> "may be regarded as the genesis of the science of archaeology in the United States. General Putnam it will be recalled made an enviable record as an officer in the War of Independence under General Washington. As surveyor and military engineer, he selected the site for West Point and constructed the fortifications there. He was a leader in the Ohio Company, which opened the great Northwest Territory to white settlement, and is credited with preventing the introduction of slavery in the country north and west of the Ohio River".

While Willey and Sabloff (1974) correctly note that the map prepared by General Putnam really did not lead to further archaeological studies, it certainly raised awareness in the scholarly community of the presence of ancient remains in what were then called the western lands of North America.

As explorers and travelers began to reach out to other parts of eastern North America, the presence of earthen architecture in these regions was also noted. John and William Bartram discovered the remarkable mound site of Mount Royal in Florida in 1765, and William Bartram documented numerous earthen monument sites during his 1773 travels through the Carolinas, Georgia, and Florida (Bartram 1996). Shortly after Lewis and Clark returned from their landmark journey to the Pacific Ocean, Henri Marie Brackenridge traveled up the Missouri River with fur trade legend Manuel Lisa and spent 1810 through 1814 in the Missouri–Louisiana country. Particularly noteworthy for archaeologists, Brackenridge (1814) describes mounds and mound groups in the vicinity of St Louis, and provides the first description of Cahokia and what is almost certainly Monk's Mound (Brackenridge 1914, 187–8). On a trip through Ohio, Thomas Joynes described the Spruce Hill Earthwork and mentioned the abundance of mounds in the Paint Creek Valley during a trip in 1810 (Joynes 1902). First-hand observations such as these, combined

Fig. 1.2. The earthworks at Marietta were one of the first recorded Ohio Hopewell ceremonial landscapes in the Ohio River valley. Most of the embankment walls are no longer visible, but some of the mounds were preserved as landscape features within the developing city of Marietta during the 19th century. Map reproduced from *Ancient Monuments of the Mississsippi Valley* (Squier and Davis 1848, pl. xxiv).

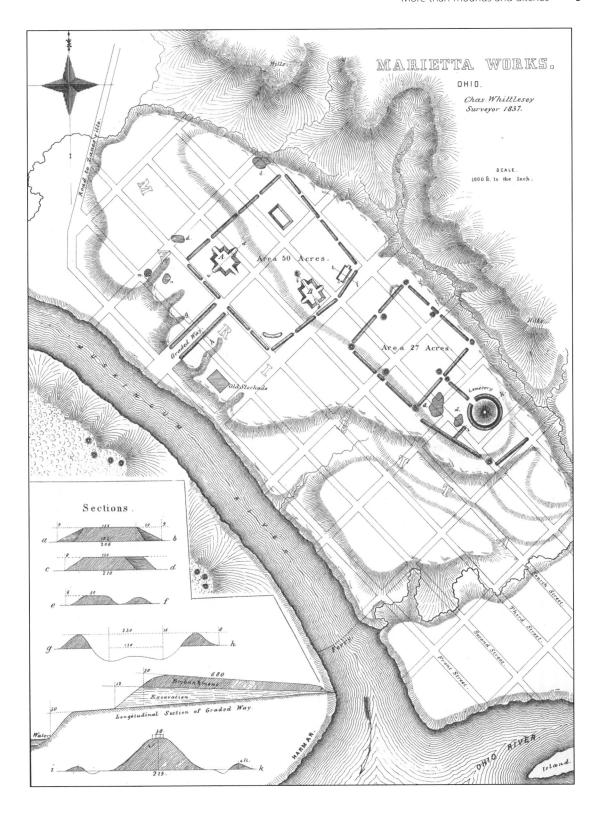

with accounts by military officers in the Ohio River valley were instrumental in bringing the presence of extensive mound and earthwork complexes to the attention of the public (Silverberg 1968).

Early Euro-American settlement west of the Allegheny Mountains followed the Ohio River valley into what was then called the western lands. White settlement was fairly rapid in the years following the American Revolution, and farms and roads began to appear in southern Ohio at the end of the 18th century. This led to Statehood for Ohio in 1803 with Chillicothe, in Ross County, as the first State Capital. Mounds and earthworks were common in this area of Ohio, and eventually systematic study would reveal that this area contained perhaps the highest density and variety of prehistoric mounds and earthworks in all of North America.

Ohio and the beginning of North American archaeology

"Our Antiquities have been noticed by a great number of travelers, few of whom ever saw one of them, or who riding at full speed, had neither the industry, the opportunity, nor the ability to investigate a subject so intricate. They have frequently given to the world such crude and indigested statements, after having visited a few ancient works, or heard the idle tales of persons incompetent to describe them, that intelligent persons residing on the very spot, would never suspect what works were intended to be described.

It has somehow happened, that one traveler has seen an ancient work, which was once a place of amusement for those who erected it, and he concludes, that none but such were ever found in the whole country. Another in his journey sees a mound of earth with a semicircular pavement on the East side of it; at once he proclaims it to the world as his firm belief, that ALL our ancient works were places of devotion, dedicated to the worship of the Sun. A succeeding tourist falls in with an ancient military fortress, and thence concludes that ALL our ancient works were raised for military purposes. One person finds something about these works of English origin, and, without hesitation, admits the supposition that they were erected by a colony of Welchmen. Others again, find articles in and near these ancient works, evidently belonging to the Indians, to people of European origin, and to that Scythian race of men who erected all our mounds of earth and stone. They find, too, articles scattered about and blended together, which belonged not only to different nations, but to different eras of time, remote from each other – they are lost in a labyrinth of doubt. – Should the inhabitants of the Western States, together with every written memorial of their existence be swept from the face of the earth, though the difficulties of future Antiquarians would be increased, yet they would be of the same KIND with those, which now beset and overwhelm the superficial observer" (Atwater 1820, 109–10).

Many people had observed the mounds and earthworks of southern Ohio as the lands in this region were cleared and brought into cultivation. Winthrop Sargent (1799) described the monumental works at Marietta on the Ohio River and prepared a map that he sent in a letter to the American Academy of Arts and Sciences. Unfortunately, accounts like those prepared by Sargent are rare. Curiosity about the origin and contents of the mounds must have been widespread, but only a few writers in the early years of the 19th century offered more than brief descriptions and speculation about these ancient earthen monuments.

That began to change when Caleb Atwater of Circleville, Ohio, began his effort to map and record earthen enclosure sites throughout the region. Atwater's primary contribution was in providing the first extensive maps and descriptions of the Ohio earthworks. His research and interpretations were eventually published by the American Antiquarian Society in 1820. The book is titled *Description of the Antiquities Discovered in the State of Ohio and Other Western States*, and although far from conclusive, it provides the first substantial data about the size, variety, and number of earthen monuments in the Ohio River valley.

When Atwater was conducting his studies in Ohio there were certainly other local scholars who took an active interest in mounds and earthworks, but outlets for scientific publications at that time were based primarily in the populated areas along the east coast (e.g. *American Journal of Science and Arts*; *Transactions of the American Ethnological Society*). In addition to his description of numerous botanical species in the region, C. S. Rafinesque (1824) also mapped and recorded numerous earthworks and mounds in Kentucky. Charles Whittlesey mapped and recorded earthen enclosures as part of his work as a member of the Geological Survey of the State (Ohio) in 1837 and 1838 (Whittlesey 1851). Whittlesey received help in his mapping of the Newark Earthworks in 1836 from a young medical student with an interest in mound studies – Edwin Hamilton Davis (Barnhart 1986).

Edwin Hamilton Davis was born January 22, 1811 in Hillsboro, in western Ross County, Ohio. He was born to a well-educated family and he and two brothers graduated from Kenyon College in Ohio. It is unclear how Davis developed his interest in mounds and archaeology, but it was well established during his stay at Kenyon College where his commencement address was titled "Antiquities of Ohio." With encouragement from Daniel Webster, a member of the American Antiquarian Society, Davis continued his research on the Ohio mounds first from Bainbridge (1835–39) while he pursued his medical education in Cincinnati, and then from Chillicothe, where he practiced medicine (Meltzer 1998). Davis was clearly well recognized for his medical and archaeological expertise in Ross County by 1845 when Ephraim G. Squier moved to Chillicothe and became editor of the *Scioto Gazette*.

Squier was born at Bethlehem, New York, on 17 June 1821. He was largely self-educated and worked as a journalist in Albany, New York and Harford, Connecticut, before moving to Chillicothe, and launching a landmark study of mounds and earthworks in partnership with Edwin Hamilton Davis. Ephraim G. Squier's archaeological career later resulted in research and books on Central America and the mounds of New York State. His life and accomplishments have been detailed in an excellent biography (Barnhart 2005).

The partnership of Squier and Davis was built upon a mutual interest in the study of the mounds and mound-builders. During an intense year of fieldwork, the team and their employees excavated nearly 200 mounds and mapped about 100 earthworks. While their excavation methods fall far short of contemporary standards, their data established a new level of scholarship for archaeology in North America (Fig. 1.3). Subsequent research has documented the shortcomings of the maps they produced, but many of these are still the baseline for research by the current generation of scholars. After considerable anger, argument, and squabbles, their book *Ancient Monuments of the Mississippi River Valley* was published by the Smithsonian Institution in 1848.

Some key players in the early exploration of Hopewell archaeology

Ephraim G. Squier (1821–1888) was born in Bethlehem, New York and studied engineering, but with a downturn in the national economy he took various positions as a writer and journalist and became associated with the Whig political party. Squier became interested in the artifacts and mounds in New York State but moved to Chillicothe, Ohio in 1845/6 to become editor of the *Scioto Gazette*. The move to Ohio put him in the center of the largest concentration of mounds and earthen enclosures in the United States, which brought him in contact with Dr Edwin H. Davis who had been studying Ohio mounds for more than a decade. Their short-term, but highly productive, partnership resulted in the publication of *Ancient Monuments of the Mississippi Valley* in 1848, which was the first publication by the Smithsonian Institution. It quickly became, and remains, one of the most influential books on American archaeology that has ever been published. Squier used the research and personal contacts he developed during his partnership with Davis to write a number of additional books on archaeology. His political contacts earned him a career in the diplomatic field and he was an important participant in the building of the national railroad of Honduras. Davis' later career was spent as a writer in New York, where he was also treated for mental illness. After their bitter quarrel over copyright and royalties, Squier and Davis never reconciled and they died, ironically both in New York, less than a month apart.

Edwin Hamilton Davis (1811–1888) was born in Hillsboro, Ohio. He developed an early interest in the prehistory of Ohio that is reflected in a graduation address he made while a student at Kenyon College. After graduating from Cincinnati Medical College in 1838, Davis established a medical practice in Chillicothe, the first State Capital of Ohio. He married Lucy Woodbridge, raised a family and became a prominent figure in Ross County. Davis continued his studies in archaeology and became well known for his research on Ohio mounds and earthworks before he met Ephraim G. Squier. After publication of their book and the unpleasant dissolution of their partnership, Davis sold the collection of artifacts he amassed during almost two decades of digging in Ohio (see Fig. 1.7). He moved to New York and joined New York Medical College in 1850, where he lived until his death on 15 May 1888. He is buried with his family in Grandview Cemetery, Chillicothe, Ohio.

Warren K. Moorehead (1866–1939) was born in Siena, Italy. His parents were both missionaries and the family moved to Xenia, Ohio, where Moorehead was raised. His interest in the archaeology of Native American peoples began at an early age and he conducted many excavations but, likely largely because he failed to graduate from both Denison University and the University of Pennsylvania, much of his work was quickly dismissed. He earned a living as a writer and worked tirelessly on behalf of living Native Americans, writing many articles condemning the Wounded Knee massacre. Moorehead's excavations in Licking County and the Muskingum Valley caught the attention of Frederic Ward Putnam of Harvard University's Peabody Museum who hired him to conduct excavations at Fort Ancient and the Hopewell Mound Group to obtain artifacts for the Columbian Exposition in 1893. From 1894–97 he was the first Curator of Archaeology for the Ohio Historical Society, excavating sites, acquiring collections for the Society, and compiling data for a map of Ohio's mounds and enclosures that was later used by his successor William C. Mills, for the *Archaeological Atlas of Ohio* (published 1914). Later in his career, as the head of the Peabody Institute in Andover, Massachusetts, Moorehead conducted important excavations at Cahokia in Illinois and Etowah in Georgia.

Henry Clyde Shetrone (1876–1954), shown on the left in this photo, was born in Fairfield County, Ohio. His early career was as a reporter and his interest in archaeology was awakened when he was reporting on William C. Mills' discoveries at the Adena Mound and other Ohio sites. He became friends with Mills who, though he had no formal training in archaeology, hired him as an assistant in 1913 and appointed him as the new Curator of Archaeology for the Ohio Archaeological Society when he (Mills) became its first Director in 1921. Shetrone conducted many major excavations, including those at the Mound City Group, Hopewell Mound Group, and Seip Mound, which he published promptly in the *Ohio Archaeological and Historical Society Quarterly*. His seminal work *The Mound-Builders* was published in 1930. Following Mills's death in 1928 Shetrone succeeded him as Director of the Society where he focused his efforts on preserving archaeological sites and promoting public awareness of Ohio's Native American heritage. He retired in 1947, but continued his activities as Director Emeritus of the Ohio Historical Society, a position he held until his death in 1954.

William Corless Mills (1860–1928), on the right in the photograph, was born and raised on a farm in Montgomery County, Ohio. Though trained as a pharmacist, which he practised for some years, his interest in archaeology began as a boy, collecting Indian artifacts from local farm fields. Mills became the Ohio Historical Society's Curator of Archaeology in 1898 and its first Director in 1921, a position he held until his death in 1928. He conducted major excavations at the Adena Mound, Harness Mound, Mound City Group, the Seip Conjoined Mound, Tremper Mound, and the Baum Village site, establishing an excellent practice of rapidly publishing his results in the *Ohio Archaeological and Historical Society Quarterly* and setting a high standard for promptness and professionalism. He published the *Archaeological Atlas of Ohio* in 1914, drawing on the works of his predecessors such as Warren Moorehead. Mills was responsible for defining and naming the Hopewell, Fort Ancient, and "Intrusive Mound" cultures, though he misunderstood their relative sequence, believing that culture evolved from simple to more complex levels of organization, with the Hopewell representing the culmination of cultural development in the Ohio Valley.

Photos courtesy of Ohio History Connection, except for Davis, courtesy of Ross County Archaeological Society

Fig. 1.3. Squier and Davis worked before photography became readily available. This drawing of the Hopeton Earthworks appeared in E. G. Squier's 1860 two-part paper titled *Ancient Monuments in the United States* published by Harper's magazine in 1860.

After the relatively brief but intense battle over authorship and royalties (Barnhart 2005; Meltzer 1998), the partnership was ended. Although the publication of *Ancient Monuments* failed to produce a significant financial reward for either author, it created for them an important place in the development of American Archaeology. It also established the role of the Federal Government in support of archaeology. The fledgling Smithsonian Institution was established, with funds bequeathed from British scientist James Smithson (1765–1829), as the U.S. National Museum and *Ancient Monuments of the Mississippi Valley* was its first publication. Interest and support for archaeology was strong among leaders of the U.S. National Museum, as can be seen in the early emphasis on archaeological publications (Haven 1856; Lapham 1855; Squier 1847; Whittlesey 1851). Much of which is directly related to the debate about who were the mound-builders.

During the latter half of the 19th century public interest in mounds, mound-builders, and archaeology continued to grow and is reflected in the publication of a range of popular books (MacLean 1879; Peet 1903; Randall 1905; 1908; Thomas 1903). Support for professional archaeological research began to develop in institutions like the Peabody Museum at Harvard, which was founded in 1866 (Brew 1966), and journals such as the *American Antiquarian* (established by Rev. Stephen Peet in 1878) and the *American Anthropologist* (established in 1888). The role of the U.S. National Museum in archaeology and the resolution of the mound-builders question continued to grow, and eventually became firmly established in the Smithsonian Institution Bureau of American Ethnology (later renamed the Bureau of American Ethnology).

The early work of Atwater and then Squier and Davis had firmly established archaeology as a subject of interest among scholars of the 19th century, and the beginning of scientific inquiry can be seen not only in the maps they produced and the artifacts they collected, but also in the types of questions that were being asked about the archaeological record. Many of the questions that were raised about the great Hopewell ceremonial landscapes of Ohio in the 19th century are still very relevant today.

"Yet the great enclosures at Newark, at Marietta, at or near Chillicothe, and in many other localities, with their systems of minor embankments, mounds, and excavations, manifest a unity of design, expressive of concentrated authority and combined physical effort. If those structures were produced by a sudden exertion of these agencies, they would require the presence of large bodies of disciplined men, having experience in such labors, and some regular means of subsistence. If they were gradually formed, or brought to completion by labors at various intervals of time, they imply, in addition to unity of power and action, permanent relations to the soil, and habits inconsistent with a nomadic life.

Many of these works are also such as we should expect to see appropriated to the religious ceremonials of a populous community accustomed to meet for the common observance of solemn and pompous rites. Their arrangements correspond to those of which are known to be applied elsewhere to that use. The consecrated enclosures, the mounts of adoration or sacrifice, the sacred avenues approaching guarded places of entrance, are recognized as common features of semi-civilized worship, or rather as exemplifications of the manner in which the instinct of religious reverence has everywhere a tendency to display itself. The number of works of this character, and the scale on which they are constructed, suggest irresistibly the idea of an organized multitude fond of spectacles and habituated to public displays of an imposing nature" (Haven 1856, 154–5).

Scholarly and public fascination with mounds and earthworks served as motivation for the U.S. Congress to appropriate $5000 in 1881 to the Bureau of Ethnology for archaeological investigations of the mounds and mound-builders (Powell 1894).

Cyrus Thomas was appointed Director of the Division of Mound Exploration and over the next decade, the Division explored over 2000 mounds from Florida to the Red River of North Dakota. "Particular attention has been paid to the mode of construction and methods of burial in the ordinary conical tumuli, because these furnish valuable evidence in regard to the custom of the builders and aid in determining the different archeological districts." (Thomas 1894, 23), The study identified eight districts within the mounds area, and Ohio was distinguished to some extent by the large number and variety of enclosures. Enclosures were recorded in other districts, but the vast number and variety of forms and sizes were unmatched in the Ohio District (south-eastern Indiana, Ohio, West Virginia, and northern Kentucky).

The work of the Division of Mound Exploration in Ohio was less intense than in other parts of the Eastern United States. Thomas notes that due the work of the Peabody Museum at Harvard, Col. Charles Whittlesey, Professor Locke, Squier and Davis, J. P. McLean, and Hempstead in this area, extensive efforts by the Division was not necessary. However, Thomas did send Col. Middleton and Gerard Fowke to conduct investigations in Ohio. Particularly notable are the excellent maps prepared by James Middleton for the Hopeton, High Bank, and Newark Works. These maps were made in 1887, and Thomas notes the goal was to resurvey some of the more important earthworks described by Squier and Davis "to determine the accuracy of the measurements and figures of these authors" (Thomas 1894, 440). The excellent maps produced by the Division provided evidence about the inaccuracy of the published maps of Squier and Davis (1848). The nature and extent of the problems with some of the Squier and Davis maps is well illustrated at the Hopeton Earthworks (Chapter 3), and is likely due to the rapid pace of work conducted by the pioneering archaeologists during their two year partnership. Thomas published a detailed report of the Division's survey in 1889 titled "Circular, Square and Octagonal Earthworks of Ohio." The maps from these studies are particularly important because they were made at a time when these earthen monuments could still be readily seen. However, a comparison of the sites reported by Squier and Davis in 1848 against those mapped by Thomas and his Division three to four decades later document the heavy impact of agriculture on even the largest earthen features (Fig. 1.4).

Fig. 1.4. This 1938 aerial photograph by the U.S. Department of Agriculture is one of the earliest aerial photos of the Hopeton Earthworks. All of the major earthwork elements – large rectangular enclosure, large circular enclosure, two small sacred circles, and the long parallel walled trackway – are still visible at this time. Note that the parallel walls and small sacred circles are increasingly less visible than in 19th century maps and accounts.

Through the efforts of the Division of Mound Exploration, thoughts about a lost race of mound-builders were largely erased. The study by the Bureau had been so extensive and thorough and its publication by an agency of the U.S. government (Thomas 1894) established with certainty that the mounds and earthworks were built by the ancestors of the American Indians. Due to the diligence of this program, it is likely that few if any major earthworks were unknown after the work of the Bureau was completed (see Thomas 1891). The distribution of known mound sites in Ohio would eventually be published as the Mills (1914) *Archaeological Atlas of Ohio*. A similar volume was produced by Hinsdale (1931) for Michigan.

Until relatively recently, archaeological research at earthen enclosure sites was limited largely to mapping and excavation of associated mounds. This was in part due to the relatively low number of artifacts found associated with earthen walls but also because, until the development of geoarchaeology, very little meaningful data could be obtained by excavating earthen walls. By the beginning of the 20th century there was a decline in interest in earthen enclosures, and archaeologists shifted their attention to mortuary mounds and their contents.

Mortuary mounds and artifacts

Westward expansion brought more and more farmers and settlers into the rich, wide valleys of central North America. As they cleared the forests for farms, roads, and towns, the presence of more and more mounds and embankment walls came to light. Doubtless, many undocumented excavations in these earthen features were undertaken. This is illustrated in the comment of Thomas R. Joynes in his 1810 account of travel in southern Ohio:

"There are likewise a large number of circular mounds, some of which are on the summits of the highest hills, and are generally about 20 feet [6.1 m]) high and 150 feet [45.7 m] in diameter. These appear to have been burying places for the dead, as great numbers of bones have been found upon opening them." (Joynes 1902, 227)

The few more detailed records that have survived to document these early excavations note the presence of remarkable artifacts associated with human burials. Copper artifacts and mica mirrors, along with other amazing objects, were found. The discovery of these remarkable artifacts seems to have diverted attention from the large embankment walls and enclosure sites and focused interest on mounds and their contents.

Dr S. P. Hildreth of Marietta, Ohio, wrote to Caleb Atwater with a first-hand account of a burial that was found when a mound associated with the Marietta earthworks was excavated in June 1818:

"Lying immediately over, or on the forehead of the body, were found three large circular bosses, or ornaments for a sword belt, or a buckler; they are composed of copper, overlaid with a thick plat of silver. The fronts of them are slightly convex, with a depression, like a cup, in the centre, and measure two inches and a quarter across the face of each. On the back side, opposite the depressed portion, is a copper rivet or nail, around which are two separate plates by which they were fastened to the leather. Two small pieces of the leather were found lying between the plates of one of the bosses; they resemble the skin of an old mummy, and seem to have been preserved by the salts of the copper." (Hildreth, July 19, 1819 as quoted in Atwater 1820, 168–9)

Hildreth also collected several broken pieces of a copper tube that was filled with iron rust. He believed these pieces were part of the "lower end of a scabbard, near the point of the sword. No sign of the sword itself was discovered, except the appearance of rust above-mentioned." (Atwater 1820, 169). In concluding his letter to Atwater, Hildreth notes that the evidence found with this burial demonstrates that the people who built the mound had knowledge of metalworking.

In a somewhat later letter, Hildreth documented a burial in a mound on the Little Muskingham River which had fragments of a copper helmet buried with it (Hildreth 5 Nov. 1819, in Atwater 1820: 174–6). Hildreth also included information in this correspondence that he has been told "by an eye witness, that a few years ago, near Blacksburgh in Virginia, eighty miles [129 km] from Marietta, there was found about half of a steel bow, which, when entire, would measure five or six feet [1.5–1.8 m]" (p. 176). He also reports "I have been told from good authority, that an ornament, composed of very pure gold, somewhat similar to those found here, was discovered a few years since in Ross county, near Chillicothe, lying in the palm of a skeleton's hand, in a small mound" (p. 176).

Observations of advanced metalwork, artwork, and gold contributed to speculation that the mounds were built by a society that was far more advanced than the Indians who inhabited the Ohio River valley. Speculation about the origin of mound-builders ranged from the Toltecs, to refugees from the lost continent of Atlantis, to the Lost Tribes of Israel. The origin of the mound-builder myth and all the factors that fueled its development have been thoroughly covered by

Silverberg (1968) and, although the myth was not universally accepted by scholars of the 19th century (e.g. Haven 1856), it certainly had a large following, including Atwater and Squier and Davis.

Through their extensive investigation of Ohio mounds, Squier and Davis established a higher standard for reporting the results of their mound excavations. Although their shaft-like excavation units are crude by modern standards, they did observe and report the structural character of the mounds they excavated. Their mound profile drawings and descriptions provide some of the first substantive data about the internal character of Ohio Hopewell mounds. They document that many of the mounds were built in stages with multiple types of material. They demonstrated that the mounds are not simply piles of earth heaped on top of graves, but carefully selected soils that were also carefully placed in layers of varying thickness (Fig. 1.5).

While Squier and Davis were establishing a new and higher standard for reporting the structure of Ohio mounds, it was the features and artifacts they found under the mounds that were drawing all the attention. On clay platforms that had been hardened by fire, which Squier and Davis called "altars", there were human remains and an amazing variety of artifacts and materials sometimes accompanied by human remains. These included copper "celts", breast-plates, head-dresses, and ornaments in the shapes of animals or geometric forms. There were large mirrors made from mica and animal and human forms cut from mica sheets. Squier and Davis found a variety of cut and carved shell objects and ornaments made from conch shells, and other materials from the Gulf Coast region. Lithics included exotic flint materials and large obsidian objects, but most amazing were the pipes. In Mound 8 at Mound City, Squier and Davis uncovered almost 200 fragmentary small stone pipes. These were delicately carved in the forms of birds, reptiles, mammals, and people. The high quality of these objects and the exotic nature of the material they were made from contributed to the belief that these were the remains of a lost race of mound-builders (Fig. 1.6).

Despite great acclaim for their research, it had been a considerable challenge finding a publisher and bitterness developed between the Squier and Davis over authorship credit and distribution of proceeds from the sale of the book (Barnhart 1986; 2005; Meltzer 1998). In the end, both men abandoned the study of Ohio archaeology for other fields and they became highly bitter toward one another.

In an effort to recoup some of the funds he expended for the Ohio research, Davis and a commissioned artist prepared a catalog of the objects in his possession and offered them for sale. Despite sincere efforts to find a museum in the United States to purchase the collection, Davis finally sold the artifacts to William Blackmore, who shipped the collection to England and built a museum to house the objects in his hometown of Salisbury (Fig.

Fig. 1.5. Squier and Davis were not the first people to excavate mounds in the central Ohio River valley, but the mound profiles they incorporated into *Ancient Monuments of the Mississippi River Valley* provide some of the earliest images of Ohio Hopewell mound structure and the arrangement of certain burial deposits. This drawing shows multiple construction layers in Mound 7 at Mound City (Squier and Davis 1848, fig. 41).

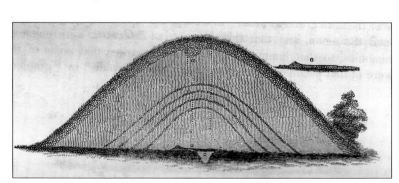

Fig. 1.6. Looking east at Mound City at dawn, June 2005 (photo: author).

1.7). E. T. Stevens, museum curator and brother-in-law of Blackmore, prepared an illustrated guide to the collections (Stevens 1870).

The loss of this famous collection to an international rival sparked considerable discussion among scholars and learned people in the United States and demonstrated the need for a museum dedicated to New World archaeology (Brown 1949). Although the Smithsonian Institution had supported numerous important archaeological publications, it is a museum of natural history and used its resources for a broader field of study. With this in mind, philanthropist George Peabody donated a substantial sum of money to Harvard University to create a museum of archaeology and ethnology. The Peabody Museum of Archaeology and Ethnology was established in 1866 with Jeffries Wyman as its first curator.

The Peabody Museum at Harvard University became involved in the study and preservation of Ohio mounds in 1874, when Frederick Ward Putnam became Curator. Under his direction the Peabody Museum conducted excavations at a number of Ohio mounds and mound groups (Putnam 1883; 1886; 1887a; 1887b, 1890a, 1890b; Willoughby and Hooten 1922). Putnam became particularly impressed with the Great Serpent Mound in Adams County, Ohio. After several visits to the site, he became terribly alarmed by the vandalism and rampant excavation by visitors to this impressive earthen monument. With assistance from Alice Fletcher and Zelia Nuttall, funds were solicited from woman's organizations in the Boston area to purchase and protect this important site (Brown 1949, Putnam 1887a; 1890b). The Peabody Museum purchased the site and surrounding grounds in 1887 and donated the landmark to the Ohio Archaeological and Historical Society in 1900, which certainly represents one of the earliest deliberate efforts to preserve an archaeological site in the United States (Fig. 1.8).

Despite expanding his archaeological interests and the influence of the Peabody Museum well beyond the Ohio River valley, Putnam maintained a strong interest in mound and earthwork sites of Ohio. He and the Peabody staff conducted excavations at the Turner Mound Group, Madisonville site, Edwin Harness Mound in Ross County (Putnam 1887b), the Connett Mound, Wolf Plain (Putnam 1882), and various other locations near Cincinnati (Putnam 1887a).

Putnam's influence and skills at organization contributed greatly to the expansion of archaeology in the United States, and he helped establish the Field Museum of Natural History in Chicago, the Anthropology Department at the University of California at Berkeley, and the Anthropology Department of the American Museum of Natural History in New York (Browman 2002). In 1890, Putnam was appointed Chief of Department M (Anthropology) for the World's Columbian Exposition in Chicago. To secure specimens to display at the Exposition,

Putnam hired archaeologists and ethnologists to conduct fieldwork in different areas of North and South America. In Ohio, he hired Warren King Moorehead, who conducted excavations at Fort Ancient in Warren County (Moorehead 1890; 1908), and the Hopewell Mound Group in Ross County (Moorehead 1896; 1897a 1897b; 1922).

Moorehead began excavations at Fort Ancient with a team of 11–12 men. After four to five months of digging he was disappointed that most of the graves they excavated did not contain many artifacts and moved his team to the Hopewell Mound Group near Chillicothe in Ross County, Ohio. Moorehead was convinced by Squier and Davis' (1848) data from what was then called Clark's Works, that this was "one of the principal if not actually the largest, settlement of the Scioto Valley mound-building tribe" (Moorehead 1922, 80). Moorehead and his team were the third archaeological group to study the Hopewell mound group, having been preceded by Caleb Atwater (1820) and then Squier and Davis (1848). Atwater published the first map and description of the site, and Squier and Davis prepared another map and conducted excavations in several of the mounds. By the time Moorehead began excavations at the Hopewell Mound Group it is likely that the site had been cleared and cultivated for close to a century.

Moorehead excavated many of the mounds at the Hopewell site, and quickly learned that few burials were present in the earthen fill of the mounds. Most of the burials were placed on floors beneath the mounds that permitted him to excavate the mounds using scrapers pulled by horse or mule teams. Although a few of the mounds he excavated contained only fragmentary human burials, most provided substantial evidence of the rich mortuary remains associated with the people who built the Hopewell Mound Group.

These excavations produced some of the first photographs of Ohio Hopewell ceremonial and mortuary remains, and documented the rich diversity of mortuary treatment and associated artifacts (Fig. 1.9). Artifacts collected for exhibit include sheets of mica, copper and mica sheets cut into a wide range of ornamental shapes, carved stone pipes, shell cups, carved bone, copper, shell and pearl beads, perforated animal teeth (shark, bear, fox, elk, and wolf), galena, and copper beads, ear spools, bracelets, breast-plates, head-dresses, and celts. The collection also included more than 7000 Wyandotte flint disks from Mound 2, and a number of large obsidian ceremonial spear-points. The sophisticated character and artistic nature of these objects had tremendous appeal to both the public and museum curators and provided substantial incentive for more mound excavations across southern Ohio.

Although popular accounts and short papers about the work at the Hopewell Mound Group were published shortly after the excavations were completed (Moorehead 1892; 1893; 1896; 1897a), the full excavation report was not completed until 29 years later. Moorehead (1922, preface) notes that Putnam

Fig. 1.7. William Henry Blackmore (1827–1878) was an English lawyer, born in Salisbury, Wiltshire. He made a number of trips to America where he invested in land, amassed (and ultimately lost) a fortune, and became interested in archaeology. In 1867 he founded the Blackmore Museum in Salisbury to house the recently purchased Squier and Davis collection and much other archaeological and ethnographic material from around the world with the purpose of 'exhibit[ing] the earliest known work of man and to show the ubiquity of stone implements'. This photograph, one of very few surviving images, shows the museum's original curator, E. T. Stevens, leaning on a case of Danish flint implements. Unfortunately, the collections of the Blackmore Museum were later dispersed to other museums with the Davis collection ultimately being curated by the British Museum (photo courtesy of Salisbury Museum).

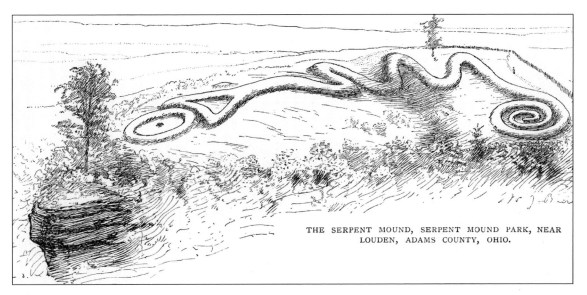

THE SERPENT MOUND, SERPENT MOUND PARK, NEAR
LOUDEN, ADAMS COUNTY, OHIO.

Fig. 1.8. The Serpent Mound of Ohio is one of the most impressive earthworks in all of North America, now thought to have been constructed by Fort Ancient communities around AD 1030 and, therefore, several centuries after the end of the Hopewell period. Frederick Ward Putnam of the Peabody Museum at Harvard University raised funds to purchase the site and donate it to Ohio for preservation. This drawing appeared in "The Serpent Mound of Ohio" (Putnam 1890b).

originally intended to write and publish the results of the 1890–91 excavations, but his busy schedule never permitted it. Charles C. Willoughby prepared a report based upon his analysis of the artifacts Moorehead collected. This manuscript was published with editorial notes by N'omi B. Greber and Katharine C. Ruhl in 1989. With funding from the Field Museum in Chicago, Moorehead was finally able to complete a summary report that was published in 1922. However, he also laments that in the intervening years, the loss of important field notes and records combined with the lapse of time since the work was done meant that information and observations were omitted that might have been remembered if the report had been undertaken in the years immediately following field investigations.

Moorehead conducted excavations at sites from the southern plains to Maine, but he is best known for his research in his native Ohio. He served as Museum Director at the Ohio Archaeological and Historical Society from 1894 to 1897. During his tenure in this position, excavations were focused on mounds and resulted in a number of important publications (1892; 1897b; 1899). Many of the mounds he excavated were Hopewell mounds, including the Porter mounds at Frankfort (1892), Slate Mills mounds (1892), the Edwin Harness mound at the Liberty Works (1897), and the Carriage Factory mound at Chillicothe (1899). All of these excavations, and many others conducted by Moorehead during this era, added information about the nature of Hopewell mortuary and ceremonial deposits.

At the turn of the century, Gerard Fowke prepared a summary of what was known about the archaeology of Ohio, particularly the mound and earthwork remains that had been the subject of much investigation and speculation in the preceding century. Fowke began archaeological work in Ohio through the Bureau of Ethnology program of mound research. His *Archaeological History of Ohio* (Fowke 1902) was written for a wide audience and published by the Ohio Archaeological and Historical Society. The book summarizes the state of knowledge about Hopewell scholarship and reflects the scale and pace of archaeological research relating to mounds and earthworks in Ohio.

The Ohio Archaeological and Historical Society was established in 1885, and grew out of an impressive exhibition of antiquities for the Ohio Centennial Exposition (Read and Whittlesey 1877) that highlighted the prehistory of the State. In the first 20–30 years of the 20th century: "the Ohio State Museum was the dominant center for archaeology west of the Appalachians and east of the Rocky Mountains" (Griffin 1985, 268). Excavations under the direction of Moorehead, William C. Mills, and Henry C. Shetrone occupied

Fig. 1.9. Warren K. Moorehead excavated at the Hopewell Mound Group in 1891 and 1892. The photographs from his work are the earliest images of this great Ohio Hopewell earthwork. This image shows the northern embankment at Hopewell with the trees cleared (photo courtesy of the Field Museum, Chicago).

significant numbers of pages in the annual journal of the Ohio Archaeological and Historical Society. Their work continued to focus on the mounds, with Mills excavations of Adena (1902a; 1902b), Edwin Harness (Mills 1907), Seip (Mills 1909a; 1909b), Tremper (Mills 1916), and Mound City (Mills 1922a; 1922b) and Shetrone's excavations at Ginther (Shetrone 1925), Seip (Shetrone *et al.* 1931), and the Hopewell Mound Group (Shetrone 1926). The spectacular discoveries from these excavations continued to focus attention on the archaeological record of southern Ohio, and ultimately led to the definition of the Hopewell Culture, a name that has become synonymous with spectacular mounds, earthworks, and incredible artifacts.

One of the first of many spectacular discoveries came from the Adena mound, on the Worthington Estate west of Chillicothe in Ross County (Mills 1902a; 1902b). The site and nearby lands had been purchased from the Worthington Estate and the new owner wished to put the land into cultivation. William C. Mills led a team from the Ohio Archaeological and Historical Society in excavation of the site in 1901. At that time, the mound was 26 ft (7.82 m) high on the south side and 26 ft 9 in (8.05 m) high on the north side, with a circumference of 445 ft (135.6 m). Excavations were conducted in 5 ft (*ca.* 1.5 m) vertical sections starting at the top of the mound.

Mills observed that the mound was built in two stages. The original mound was 20 ft (6.1 m) high and 90 ft (27.4 m) in diameter and composed of dark sand. The second stage covered all of the original mound surface but it was also expanded in height and width to the north (see Fig. 1.10). The fill for stage two differed from stage one and was a mixture of light colored sand and loamy soil from the surrounding area.

Mills found that all of the burials in the original mound were located near its base. They had all been wrapped in bark and placed inside log tombs (Mills calls these "sepulchers"). The timbers used to build these crypts were unhewn, and ranged from 3 in to 17 in (*ca.* 7.6–43.2 cm) in diameter. Logs were placed over the crypt to enclose it, and crypts were generally 8–9 ft (*ca.* 2.4–2.7 m) long, 5–7 ft (*ca.* 1.5–2.1 m) wide, and 18–30 in (*ca.* 45.7–76.2 cm) high. In a few instances, these sepulcher rooms were large enough to stand in. Grave goods were found in all sepulcher burial chambers.

Fig. 1.10. The Adena Mound as seen during W. C. Mills 1901 excavation. The photo shows the top of the original mound surface in profile. The original mound was enlarged with the addition of large amounts of earth (Mills 1902b , fig. 3).

Mills observed that while all burials were placed near the base of the original mound, they were placed throughout the fill and added to enlarge the mound. Objects had been placed with all but one of the burials in the original mound, but many of the burials in the enlarged mound contained no associated mortuary objects. There was no difference in the types of ornaments and objects associated with burials in either part of the mound, but they were far more numerous in the original mound.

One burial (Skeleton 21) was particularly noteworthy. It was found on one side of the mound in a log sepulcher. The skeleton was laid with its head to the east on bark that covered the bottom of the tomb. Many objects were placed in the tomb, including 500 shell beads, 500 bone and pearl beads, large shell beads near the left knee, and a raccoon effigy made of shell. On the right side of the head were three antler spear points, seven projectile points and three knives of Flint Ridge Flint. Three more projectile points of Flint Ridge Flint were at the right hand. Near the left hand was a unique effigy pipe that is now believed to represent a dwarf.

Mills description of the unique discovery observed that the effigy pipe was found near the left hand of Skeleton 21:

> "The pipe which is 8 inches [*ca.* 20.3 cm] in length, is composed of clay, resembling the fire clay found in Scioto County, which further south be in the same valley. The pipe is tubular in form, the hole extending the entire length of the body, the large opening between the feet having a hole ⅝ inch [15.9 mm] in diameter. Within an inch of the top of the head it begins to narrow down to a very small aperture ⅛ inch [3.2 mm] in diameter. The mouthpiece formed a part of the headdress of the image. The front part of the pipe is light gray color, while the back part is of a brick red. The specimen is covered with a deposit of iron ore, which appear in small blotches over the entire surface of the specimen, the one side of the face and body being more densely covered with it than the other part of the pipe. The effigy represents the human form in the nude state with the exception of the covering around the loins. This covering extends around the body and is tied in the back. The ends of the covering hang down and serve as ornaments. On the front of this covering is a serpentine or scroll line ornamentation. From the lobe of each ear is hung an ear ornament that is quite large in proportion to the ear and resembles very much the button-shaped copper ornaments that are so frequently found in the mounds of the Scioto Valley. However, none of these ornaments have been found in this mound, but quite a number have been taken from mounds in the immediate vicinity. In looking at this specimen one is struck with the close resemblance to the Mexican and Central American art." (Mills 1902b, 146–9)

In addition to the excavations at the Adena Mound, the first three decades of the 20th century witnessed the excavation of mounds across much of Ohio.

Many of these excavations produced impressive artifacts in association with complex mortuary deposits, but the spectacular character of the mortuary remains in the Scioto River Valley attracted the greatest attention and became the signature for Ohio Hopewell archaeology. Incredible artifacts and features exposed during major mound excavations at the Seip (Mills 1909a; 1909b) and Seip-Pricer (Shetrone *et al.* 1931) mounds at the Seip Earthworks, the Tremper mound (Mills 1916), the Hopewell Mound Group (Shetrone 1926), and Mound City (Mills 1922a; 1922b) created a narrow view of Ohio Hopewell archaeology that survived for decades.

Fig. 1.11. Moorehead excavated Mound 25 at the Hopewell Mound Group by stripping it with mule teams and scrapers. Mound 25 was the largest of all Hopewell mounds and this type of excavation was common in the 19th century. Excavators have exposed a large cache of copper objects on the floor of the mound (photo. courtesy of the Field Museum, Chicago).

Throughout the 19th and early 20th century, archaeologists focused on mortuary mounds but struggled in their efforts to place these data into meaningful spatial and temporal contexts. Cyrus Thomas (1894), in his report on the work of the Mounds Exploratory Division of the Bureau of Ethnology, published an impressive map showing the distribution of mounds in eastern North America. In Ohio, Charles Whittlesey (Reid and Whittlesey 1877) began to address the spatial context of Ohio Hopewell mounds and earthwork complexes through a statewide survey program to document the distribution of these monumental earthen sites. The project was continued under the direction of Warren K. Moorehead (1897a) and William C. Mills, who published and impressive atlas depicting the location of mound and earthwork sites from every time period within each Ohio County (Mills 1914).

Throughout most of the first half of the 20th century, Ohio Hopewell research continued to fixate on mounds and mortuary artifacts (Fig. 1.11). Within this context, scholars began to fixate more attention on the chronological position of Ohio Hopewell and its relationship to other mound-building complexes in the Eastern United States. Although today, Ohio Hopewell is universally included in the Middle Woodland period and is believed to date generally from about AD 1 to AD 500, this understanding of chronological placement did not develop until the widespread application of radiocarbon dating in the period after the 1960s. Prior to the development of radiocarbon dating, archaeologists relied extensively on the stratigraphic sequences at sites to place artifacts and features into chronological order. The absence of meaningful chronological stratigraphy in mortuary mounds made it extremely difficult to seriate the various mound sites that were built throughout the Woodland period (*ca.* 1000 BC–AD 1500) in the Ohio River valley.

Mound excavations continued well into the 1950s, but the once excellent record of publication began to falter. Certainly, the history of North American archaeology is checkered with excavations that were regrettably never fully reported and published. However, the number of Ohio mound excavations that fall into this category began to increase after the administrations of William C. Mills and Henry C. Shetrone at the Ohio Archaeological and Historical Society came to an end.

The last episode of significant mound excavations was conducted in the 1960s and 1970s. At Mound City, the National Park Service took over management of the site following World War II and began a program of mound exploration and restoration. A desire to restore the site to its "Squier and Davis era" appearance led the National Park Service to fund a major project that examined the south-east and south embankment walls, discovered the south-east borrow pit, and re-examined Mounds 10 and 13 in a level of detail that had never previously been entered into in Ohio Hopewell archaeology in the Scioto River valley. James A. Brown directed a team of largely untrained laborers, and this project introduced a much higher level of field data recording than had previously been common in the region. The accomplishments of this research have been described elsewhere (Brown 2012; Brown and Baby 1966), but it is important to note that the study demonstrated that although nearly all of the mounds at the site had been obliterated by a combination of U.S. Army demolition and archaeological excavation, there was still a great deal of information preserved at the site. Unfortunately, subsequent efforts to relocate sub-mound structures were less well organized, badly executed, and generally poorly reported (Fig. 1.12).

Much of what we have learned about what we now call Ohio Hopewell Great Houses is derived from N'omi Greber's (1983a; 1983b) excavation of the Edwin Harness Mound in 1976–1977. After several previous excavations under the direction of Squier and Davis (1848), Putnam (1887b), Moorehead (1897a), and Mills (1907), the Harness family decided to level the mound to better facilitate management of their farm for agriculture. Recognizing that potentially important archaeological deposits might remain in the basal remnant of the mound, Robert Harness provided permission and time for a multi-season excavation of the mound base. Two seasons of excavations revealed the presence of more than 100 mortuary and ceremonial features along with evidence for a large and substantial timber-built structure. The structure was formed by several rooms and hallways and was roughly 147 ft 6 in (45 m) long and 65 ft 6 in (20 m) wide. The two main rooms of the building are unequal in size though built using the same number of major support posts. The location and number of support posts suggest there may have been an upper floor or balcony. Portions of these massive timber-built Great Houses have been identified in early excavations of other large mounds in the Scioto-Paint Creek area, but the superb work by Greber and her colleagues has given us a sense of the size and scale of these major structures and their immediate surroundings. Like most Ohio Hopewell mounds, the initial soil mantel covering the floor of the building was only the first of several

Fig. 1.12 In 1963 the Ohio Historical Society, under the direction of James A. Brown, excavated the reconstructed versions of Mound City Mounds 12 and 13. Brown's careful excavation provided considerable details about the placement of objects on the floors of the sub-mound structures, and resulted in the recovery of an array of small objects that were often ignored by earlier Hopewell mound excavations (photo courtesy of Hopewell Culture National Historical Site).

layers of soil that were eventually added to the mound. It is important to remember that these Great Houses likely dominated the ceremonial landscape for some time before the building was dismantled and earth and gravel layers were placed over the floor to build the mound.

Ohio Hopewell archaeological research has never been conducted in a vacuum. Excavation of mound sites in other areas, particularly the Illinois River Valley, documented that people living in much of the Eastern United States made similar artifacts and buried their dead in mounds that had at least general similarities to Ohio Hopewell sites. Very few of the mound excavations outside southern Ohio came close to meeting the spectacular character of the mortuary deposits seen at Mound City, Hopewell Mound Group, Seip, Tremper and other sites in the Scioto river drainage, but the similarity gave the impression that the people who built these earthen features had wide influence in prehistoric Eastern North America.

Expanding research interests in earthworks and ceremonial centers

Throughout most of the 19th century, archaeological scholars lacked any meaningful method to chronologically order the mound-building cultures in the archaeological record of eastern North America. In his landmark study of the mounds and earthworks for the Bureau of Ethnology, Cyrus Thomas recognized eight districts based upon the character of the mounds and earthworks and their geographic distribution. Thomas (1889a) believed that the mound-builders were ancestors to the Cherokee, and the Shawnee and Delaware were descended from the people who build the stone box graves along the Ohio River. While some attention was paid to the contents of the mounds, Thomas completed his summary paper (1894) before W. H. Holmes had finished his study of the ceramics from the Mississippi Valley.

In the early years of the 20th century, an increase in the number and quality of mound excavations produced an increasingly detailed record of the material culture associated with mounds. As this information became available in museum collections and in publications, efforts to classify mounds and their contents into spatial-temporal groups began in earnest. Definitions for the Hopewell, Adena, and Fort Ancient cultures were initially developed almost entirely from the contents of burial mounds. This focus on mounds and mortuary evidence would continue through the first half of the 20th century, and that singular emphasis on mortuary practices and associated artifacts has limited our understanding about the people we now call Ohio Hopewell to the present day.

The temporal placement of Ohio Hopewell and the sites that comprise that unit of the archaeological record have been the subject of discussion and debate since the mounds and earthworks were first discovered by Euro-American explorers. Prior to the development of radiocarbon dating, the best approach to estimating the age of the ancient earthen monuments was to count the rings of trees growing upon them (Moorehead 1934; Neuman 1962). The focus on mound excavations negated the use of stratigraphy to order archaeological complexes, because mounds

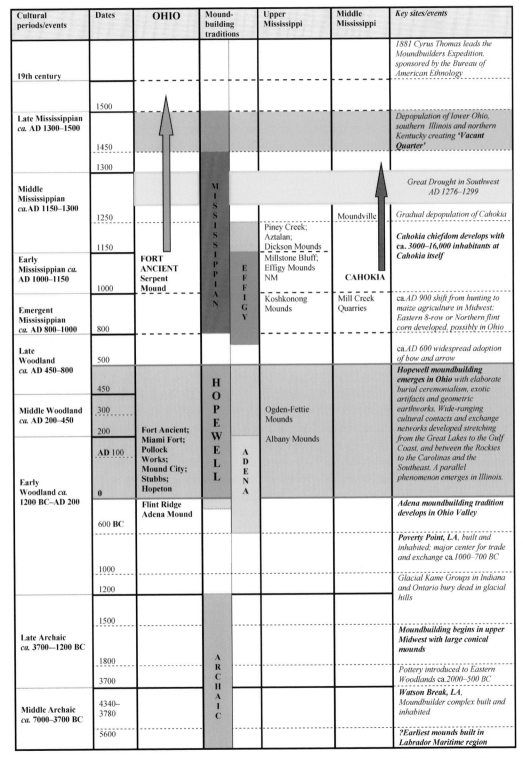

Fig. 1.13. Timeline chart showing cultural development in Ohio against other major cultural groups, areas and events (illustration by Pete Topping).

tend to have been built by a single cultural group. So even as classificatory names we use today were becoming commonplace (i.e. Adena, Hopewell, Fort Ancient), the temporal relationships between these units were proposed via little more than educated guesses.

In 1903 William C. Mills identified the differences between Ohio Hopewell and Fort Ancient cultures and gave each their respective names. Moorehead (1909) recognized the validity of these classifications and added Glacial Kame as a third group. It should be noted that after excavating the Adena site, type-site for the Adena culture in the Scioto-Paint Creek region, Mills believed that Adena was an early stage of Hopewell. Not all of his contemporaries agreed with merging Adena into Hopewell, and this debate continues to some extent even today (Brown 2005; Clay 2002; 2005; Greber 2005a; Mainfort 2005).

In an important effort to sort out the spatial and temporal relationship of archaeological complexes in Ohio, H. C. Shetrone (1920) published a paper on his observations. Shetrone said there was no connection between the historic tribal occupants of Ohio and the mound-builders. He believed that the native Algonquian people of Ohio were pushed out of the region by the Iroquois Confederacy. He observed that while most of his contemporaries distinguished Hopewell from Fort Ancient on the basis of the large and complex earthen enclosure sites associated with Hopewell, the Fort Ancient culture has produced Serpent Mound and the Fort Ancient site itself. Shetrone felt that the cultural traits associated with Fort Ancient culture were unlike those of historic Algonquian people, but more likely Iroquois. Shetrone disagreed with Mills about the relationship between Adena and Hopewell, and viewed them as separate and distinct entities. He also thought that Hopewell, Fort Ancient, and stone box grave people were contemporaneous.

This confusion about the sequence of archaeological complexes in Ohio continued even after the beginning of radiocarbon dating. The publication of *Archaeology of Eastern United States*, edited by James B. Griffin (1952a) marked the first orderly and defensible attempt to utilize radiocarbon dates to interpret the Ohio archaeological sequence. In a paper from this volume Griffin (1952b) proposed the same order of archaeological complexes that we recognize today, but his age estimates are skewed by the less accurate early radiocarbon dates that were available to him.

A few years later Griffin (1958) reviewed the radiocarbon evidence for all Hopewell sites throughout the Eastern United States. He reported 14 radiocarbon dates for Adena sites in the Ohio River valley and although the dates spanned from 830 BC to AD 782, Griffin believed that any dates after AD 200–300 were too young for Adena. Unfortunately, at that time there were only four radiocarbon dates for Ohio Hopewell sites, so the age of the complex was not yet fully understood. In this important paper, Griffin distinguished three stages within the Hopewell culture of Illinois, mainly on the basis of ceramic evidence. In this and other papers (Griffin 1941; 1945; 1946) he argues that the Illinois and Ohio Hopewell ceramics are completely independent from one another.

It would be several years and many radiocarbon dates later until the chronological details of Hopewell would become "more clear." The growth of radiocarbon dating has most certainly produced better age estimates for all the regional complexes now attributed to Hopewell (Fig. 1.13). However, even today the radiocarbon evidence derived from Ohio Hopewell features and artifacts is insufficiently precise to answer many important questions about the relative contemporaneity of sites or duration of Hopewell activity at individual sites. Although archaeological science has come a long way since the speculative writing of 19th century scholars, we still lack the tools to make the precise chronological estimates to evaluate most of our anthropological models and hypotheses about inter-site contemporaneity and the chronology of the Ohio Hopewell world. This is a serious obstacle to continued development of interpretations about all aspects of the Ohio Hopewell archaeological record, and will receive further attention throughout this volume.

One of the most impressive characteristics of Ohio Hopewell archaeology is the variety and vast quantities of artistic objects that are made from raw materials that are not found in the Ohio River valley. Particularly notable are obsidian and grizzly bear teeth from the Rocky Mountains, copper from the northern Great Lakes, mica and quartz crystals from the Appalachian mountains, and a range of shark teeth, barracuda jaws and conch shells from the coast of Florida. Early archaeologists recognized the exotic nature of these materials, even if they were uncertain as to their origin. As scientific data became available indicating how far these items had travelled, the general assumption developed that the items were obtained through trade. Ideas about Hopewell and trade became formalized when Joseph R. Caldwell (1964) published an influential paper in which he explained the movement of exotic items to Ohio as part of the Hopewell Interaction Sphere. The advantage of this argument is that it helped explain "Hopewellian" sites found at intervals throughout eastern North America. This exchange network linked peoples living great distances from Ohio with the amazing earthen architecture, ceremonialism and mortuary remains of the sites in Ohio. The nature of the interaction between groups living great distances from one another is still being discussed today, but the paucity of exotic items like obsidian at archaeological sites between the Rocky Mountains and Ohio have led many scholars to abandon the idea of trade in favor of more long-distance movement of people.

Since scholars no longer believe trade was the mechanism that brought all the copper, mica, obsidian, and other exotic material to the Ohio River valley during the Hopewell era, how were these materials transported such great distances? Two models have been offered to explain how this might have worked, and both offer meaningful insights into the social and ideological network that created the vast ceremonial landscapes in southern Ohio.

Katherine Spielmann (2002; 2009) has documented several instances where small-scale societies have intensified economic activities to sustain demand for individual and communal ceremonial obligations. Using examples from Melanesia, Spielmann has shown that prestige goods are not limited to societal elites, and socially valued goods are often abundant in small-scale societies. She has proposed that members of these societies undertook power quests that involved long distance travel, or hazardous activities to acquire raw materials (Helms 1988; 1993). The shaping of these objects into forms that were symbolic of important societal beliefs would serve to further enhance the prestige of the item and owner who held it. The significance of these socially valued goods was related to the spatial and temporal scales in which they circulated. While these ideas have merit for the larger field of anthropology, Spielmann has provided many examples of how they relate to the Ohio Hopewell archaeological record, and may also explain how exotic raw materials may have arrived in the Ohio River valley.

Bradley Lepper (1995; 2006) has suggested another mechanism by which exotic raw materials may have been brought to the Ohio River valley. Lepper has found evidence that Hopewell people may have built a ceremonial road linking the giant center at Newark with the dense area of ceremonial landscapes in the Scioto-Paint Creek area of south-central Ohio. He proposes that the road served as a ceremonial pathway for pilgrims who traveled to the region to participate in the construction of the landscapes and associated ceremonial activities. These pilgrims may have brought exotic raw materials with them and contributed the materials and their labor to the construction of the landscapes.

Perhaps both types of movement – of people and exotic objects – helped to develop the vast geographic sphere of influence or at least communication that we recognize as Hopewell in the archaeological record of eastern North America. If individuals from the Ohio River valley traveled to the Rocky Mountains, Gulf Coast, or northern Great Lakes, people they encountered would have heard about the ceremonial and social activities being conducted by Ohio Hopewell people. Not only would the traveling Ohio people bring back exotic materials they encountered in their travels, they would return with important information about the peoples and natural world along their path. Many of the people along those paths may have been encouraged by meeting the people from Ohio and inspired by the stories of landscape construction. This would have led some of them to make pilgrimages to participate in the monumental earthen constructions and generate bonds with the Ohio Hopewell people. The archaeological record indicates that these activities persisted over several centuries and during this time information about places and people throughout North America was flowing into the Ohio River valley. Sites with artifacts and/or earthen architecture that is similar to what is found in Ohio have been documented across a wide area of eastern North America. The relationship of these sites to Ohio Hopewell is discussed in greater detail in Chapter 2.

It is unclear what generated the burst of landscape construction in southern Ohio that is the subject of this volume. Arguments can be made for world renewal ceremonies (Byers 2004), recognition of astronomical events (Hively and Horn 2006; 2010; Romain 2000), or perhaps even the rise of influential and talented people. It was almost certainly a combination of many factors that generated the cultural forces that created a society of landscape builders in southern Ohio. However, it is important to remember that whatever forces led to the beginning of these activities, it also generated sufficient stability for numerous small-scale societies living in this region to continue to build (probably with outside help) dozens of very large monumental earthen landscapes and hundreds of small earthen monuments.

The monumental ceremonial centers are certainly the most visible aspect of the Ohio Hopewell archaeological record, but current research is also investing considerable time and energy into better understanding the nature and character of Ohio Hopewell habitation localities. Lewis Henry Morgan (1881) long ago proposed that the embankment walls at High Bank Earthworks were the foundation for pueblo-like buildings that were built around a central plaza. Early excavations at major sites like the Hopewell Earthworks (Moorehead 1922), Fort Ancient (Moorehead 1890; 1908), Baum (Mills 1906a; 1906b), and Turner (Putnam 1886; Willoughby and Hooten 1922) identified dense habitation debris and/or cemeteries that they assumed were the villages associated with the large monumental earthen enclosures. Subsequent study has shown that some of these "village" remains are likely the product of subsequent peoples who used these places well after the Hopewell people abandoned the sites. More recent work has led to the widespread belief that the large Hopewell ceremonial centers did not have major permanent residential populations (Prufer 1964), and may have been used only for special events like the ancient Maya ceremonial centers.

William Dancey and Paul Pacheco (Dancey 1991; 2005; Dancey and Pacheco 1997; Pacheco and Dancey 2006) have generated a model that builds on Prufer's (1964) vacant ceremonial center model. Their model proposes that Ohio Hopewell people lived in dispersed sedentary communities, consisting of single or extended families living in single-family farmsteads or small hamlets that were occupied over multiple generations. The model suggests these households were clustered around earthen enclosures or mound centers and spaced along river valleys to maximize resource availability. The people living around the earthworks, and mound centers practised hunting and gathering and they would have cleared small fields for cultivation of native, starchy seed plants.

Other scholars have argued that Hopewell societies were more mobile. Richard Yerkes (2005; 2006) and Frank Cowan (2006) have proposed that the Hopewell achieved considerable cultural complexity through organizational flexibility without food surpluses, specialized production, or permanent residences. Cowan (2006) observes that with the exceptions of blade cores and bladelets, Hopewell lithic technology focused on the manufacture and use of bifaces. Although biface manufacture represents a greater initial effort, bifaces are multi-functional tools that effectively serve the needs of mobile hunting and gathering societies. The mobile Hopewell model proposes that Ohio Hopewell societies relied on a diverse range of subsistence resources including wild foods supplemented by starchy seeds. Proponents of this model argue that the construction and use of earthen enclosures served to socially bind together dispersed members of mobile societies.

This ongoing debate has been unnecessarily contentious at times and, in the end, it is possible that both sides of this argument may prove to be correct. Across the broad expanse of southern Ohio and within this large span of time, it seems unlikely that Hopewell settlement and subsistence practices remained static. There is good evidence that the collection and cultivation of starchy seeds was a hallmark of the Middle Woodland era in this region. The historic ethnographic record in North America has many examples of societies that planted crops and still maintained a mobile lifestyle for at least part of the annual cycle. It seems possible that even within a single generation, an individual family unit might be sedentary for a few years and more mobile in others. It is also possible that people living around a major hilltop enclosure like Fort Ancient may have remained more mobile than people living around the geometric enclosures in the Scioto

River valley. Although social organization, subsistence, and settlement practices are not the focus of this volume, they are critical to understanding how the large ceremonial landscapes were built and used.

There are many long-held assumptions about human societies that simply do not fit our understanding of Ohio Hopewell societies. For example, Lewis Henry Morgan (1881) wrote that population densities sufficient to build all the Ohio Hopewell enclosures would have had domestic animals and/or cultivation to support the populations. Archaeologists have generally linked large public-works type constructions to sedentary populations with established hierarchical leadership. This notion is no longer widely held, because Warren DeBoer (1997) has reported on the Chachi of coastal Equador who have built earthen ceremonial centers during seasonal gatherings that serve to reinforce their group identity. In another example, Katherine Spielmann (2002; 2009) has argued persuasively that even small-scale societies accumulate large quantities of socially valued items including materials obtained at long distances by generating small surpluses at the household or community level. These and other contemporary perspectives are helping to broaden perspectives relating to Ohio Hopewell ceremonial landscapes.

Ohio Hopewell constructed landscapes and the digital revolution

Through the 19th and most of the 20th centuries, the vast size and complex nature of many Ohio Hopewell enclosure sites served as a deterrent to serious archaeological inquiry. While archaeologists in the later 20th century debated the merits of sampling to obtain a representative sample of the archaeological record, the great Ohio Hopewell enclosure sites were often so large, that any attempt to fully sample a site with test units might take dozens of field seasons. This is not meant to imply that the archaeological study of large enclosure sites was abandoned, but archaeologists tended to intensively excavate only small sections of any extremely large site. While these excavations produced detailed information about activities in one part of a very large site, evidence relating to how other parts of the site might have been built or used remained generally lacking.

More careful collection and analysis of surface data provided some better information about the broader nature of constructed Ohio Hopewell landscapes. Particularly notable were the efforts of William Dancey and his students at Ohio State University. They utilized surface distributions of artifacts to seek and interpret habitation sites associated with Ohio Hopewell mound and enclosure sites. This approach clearly produced evidence about the relative intensity of artifacts across the landscape, but it was and still is hampered by issues of surface visibility, differential erosion and deposition, and the difficulty of distinguishing temporally diagnostic artifact types associated with Ohio Hopewell activities.

In a particularly valuable study of the Liberty Works in Ross County, Sean Coughlan and Mark Seeman (1997) studied a carefully collected sample of artifacts from the farm of Robert Harness. Mr Harness' family had established the farm in the early years of the 19th century and their constant presence on the land gave them considerable insight into the nature of the earthworks and the distribution of artifacts that were exposed by cultivation. Mr Harness, with encouragement from another dedicated avocational archaeologist, Alva McGraw, began recording the location where individual and groups of artifacts were collected on his property. Coughlan and Seeman's study of the Harness Collection is indeed a rare opportunity to look at the distribution of artifacts across a major Ohio Hopewell enclosure site.

The development of digital technology did not introduce large numbers of new methods and techniques into archaeology's arsenal of tools. For the most part, digital technology permitted archaeologists to do many of the things they had already been doing faster and more accurately. Personal computers have become an element of daily life for most researchers and there is no question that they have increased productivity in writing and data analysis. However, the real advances have come in the form of digital photography, Geographic Positioning Systems (GPS), Geographic Information Systems (GIS), digital/laser mapping, digital geophysical instruments and computer processing, LiDAR and other aerial photographic applications.

Since the European discovery of Ohio Hopewell earthworks in the 18th century, one of the primary means of depicting these large earthen monuments has been through maps or sketches. The earliest accurate maps were made with a compass and pacing distances, or with a survey chain and compass. Highly accurate maps were produced using this method, and all of the maps that appear in Squier and Davis's landmark volume were likely made using some combination of these methods. That is not to imply that all the maps published by Squier and Davis were accurate. Cyrus Thomas (1889b), in his discussion of circular, square, and octagonal enclosure walls in Ohio, dedicates considerable discussion to the inaccuracy of the Squier and Davis maps.

Detailed and highly accurate maps can be made today using a wide range of instruments with digital technology. Transits and total stations that use lasers and digital technology have become standard tools for establishing grids and making topographic measurements. Larger scale topographic mapping can also be accomplished using aerial photography. Although aerial photography was used extensively in British archaeology after the First World War (Crawford and Keiller 1928), Dache Reeves (1936a; 1936b) was the first to use aerial photographs of Ohio Hopewell earthworks to provide a better view of these massive landscapes. Study of aerial photographs even resulted in the discovery of a previously unknown earthwork near Chillicothe in Ross County, Ohio (Anderson 1980).

More recently, application of LiDAR technology has produced impressive images of Ohio Hopewell earthen enclosures (Romain and Burks 2008a; 2008b). LiDAR (Light Detection and Ranging), is a remote sensing technique that incorporates infrared and other laser pulses, a scanner, and a Global Positioning System (GPS) in an airplane or helicopter. In situations with even significant vegetation, LiDAR is capable of detecting very minor topographic variations, such as the remains of a mound or earthwork. Burks (2010) provides examples of a variety of modern resources and techniques. LiDAR is particularly useful in relocating and mapping small and less well known earthen monuments.

Archaeologists have used spatial analysis of surface artifact data to plan subsurface excavations and interpret activity areas at sites for many generations. Systematic surface collections, using grids and computer analysis, were a foundation of spatial analysis and behavioral interpretations. Recent use of portable GPS has permitted faster and more accurate recording of surface artifact locations. In an analysis of the surface artifacts at the Hopeton Earthworks, Jarrod Burks (Burks and Gagliano 2009; Sieg and Burks 2010) plotted the distribution of different artifact types and noted that while the landform on which the site is situated has a scatter of artifacts reflecting multiple temporal stages, Middle Woodland artifacts tend to occur in clusters around the earthworks. He also noted an overall low density of artifacts inside the earthen enclosure, which may reflect "the existence of rules governing the use of space and the deposition of waste." (Sieg and Burks 2010, 65)

The Geographic Information System (GIS) is becoming an essential tool in the study and management of archaeological resources. The National Park Service is using this approach to create accurate mapping overlays of a wide range of data including topography, geophysics, surface artifacts, test units, soil distributions, etc. GIS technology has permitted archaeologists to relocate accurately the military facilities of Camp Sherman that were built on top of the important features at Mound City (Fig. 1.14). This highly accurate mapping and database management system has great potential in the management and interpretation of known resources.

The single most important advance in digital technology for archaeology has come in the area of geophysical prospection. Geophysical applications in archaeology are certainly not new, and have been an important element of archaeological methods in the UK and Europe since Richard Atkinson performed the first soil resistivity survey in 1946 and Martin Aitken began conducting magnetic surveys in 1958 (Clark 1996). A few years later magnetic survey was initiated in North America through a systematic study at Angel Mounds in southern Indiana (Johnston 1964).

In the United States, University of Nebraska physicist John W. Weymouth began using two proton magnetometers to map earthlodge village sites on the Middle Missouri River in the 1970s (Weymouth and Nickel 1979). His success led to

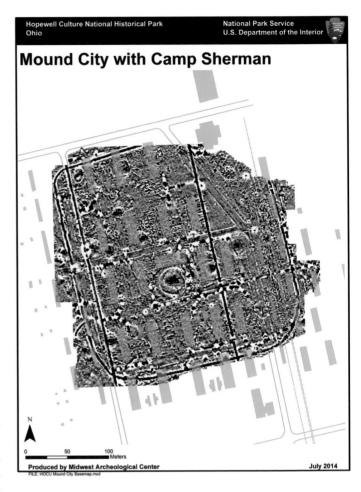

Fig. 1.14. Geographic Information System (GIS) map of Mound City depicting magnetic data and Camp Sherman features (image courtesy of the Midwest Archeological Center, National Park Service, Lincoln, Nebraska).

left: **Fig. 1.15.** John Weymouth in the field at Hopeton Earthworks (photo: author).

Right: **Fig. 1.16.** Geophysical survey and digital technology is transforming archaeology and the study of constructed landscapes. John Weymouth directing a magnetic survey with G858 cesium gradiometer in 1996 at the Wright Brothers Memorial Mound Group, Dayton, Ohio (photo: author).

applications at many other locations across the United States, and contributed to the acceptance of geophysics in North American archaeology (Fig. 1.15). Steven L. De Vore, U. S. National Park Service, began sponsoring workshops on geophysical applications in archaeology in 1991, and has continued that annual program for more than two decades.

For many years, geophysical applications were generally conducted by a small number of specialists, due to the absence of formal training in archaeology programs, the high cost of equipment, and the slow and tedious effort required in data collection and analysis. Prior to the advent of digital technology, geophysical instruments were manually operated and field data was hand recorded. Field data was then transferred by keypunch machine to computer cards for computer analysis. The processing and analysis of data required custom software programs, which were often written by the geophysicist conducting the research. The National Park Service utilized a pair of proton magnetometers throughout the late 1970s and early 1980s. In the field, the two instruments were manually operated and hand recorded, with measurements at 1 m intervals within a 20 × 20 m block. Field collection of a single block of data using this system required approximately two hours, and the collection of four blocks in a day was considered a full day's effort.

John Weymouth conducted one of the first magnetic surveys in Ohio in May 1978. The surveys were conducted at the Seip and Harness sites using two proton magnetometers (one gamma sensitivity) in difference mode, with one unit providing a stationary reference and the other giving readings at 1 m intervals within the grids. Three 20 × 20 m blocks were surveyed at Seip and one block was surveyed at the Harness site. Using soil samples provided by N'omi Greber from feature excavations these two sites Weymouth analyzed the magnetic susceptibility of the samples and used the information to identify anomalies of potential interest in the 1978 magnetic survey data (Weymouth 1979).

In 1996 I led a team of geophysicists and archaeologists in an effort to evaluate the utility of geophysical survey instruments at two earthen mound sites at Wright-Patterson Air Force Base in Ohio (Lynott 1997). The two sites that were studied had seven extant mounds ranging in height from less than 0.5 m to 1.4 m, with diameters ranging from 3 m to 19 m. Six different instruments were used in the study, and several showed significant potential for understanding the structure and content of the earthen features (Fig. 1.16). However, in their analysis of the data, the geophysicists both observed the difficulty of using the current generation of instruments and software on the irregular topography associated with mounds (Bevan 1997; Weymouth 1997). Improvements in software for some instruments have negated this problem and made it possible to create three-dimensional maps of mounds and their contents.

Geophysical survey techniques and the development of digital geophysical instruments attracted the interest of other archaeologists working in the Ohio Hopewell area. Bret Ruby and Stephen Ball conducted resistance surveys at Hopeton in an effort to locate one of the smaller sacred circles on the east side of the large rectangular enclosure (Ruby 1997a). About this same time, R. Berle Clay began using a fluxgate gradiometer in association with a conductivity meter (Clay 2001). As part of a NPS Geophysics Workshop, Clay used these instruments to identify remnants of embankment wall at the Hopeton Earthworks that have not been seen since they were mapped by Squier and Davis in 1846 (Clay 2006).

Digital geophysical instruments began to be used regularly in Ohio Hopewell archaeology in 1996 and 1997 when John Weymouth led a team conducting geophysical studies at the Overly site (Weymouth 1996) and the Triangle site (Weymouth 1998) located near the Hopeton Earthworks in Ross County, Ohio. Both projects were conducted to collect geophysical data to guide excavations to determine whether evidence of Hopewell habitation was present near the Hopeton Earthworks. The geophysical survey at the Triangle site covered 9600 sq.m. using an RM-15 resistance meter, G-858 cesium gradiometer, and Geoscan FM36 fluxgate gradiometer and produced evidence of numerous small anomalies consistent with pits and thermal features (Weymouth 1998). Subsequent excavation and analysis helped develop parameters about the type and size of features using those instruments at 1 m survey intervals (Lynott 2009b).

Weymouth continued work at the Hopeton Earthworks in 2001 when he directed a geophysical survey of the south wall area of the rectangular enclosure. This was one of the first efforts to map Ohio Hopewell earthen enclosure walls using geophysical instruments (Lynott and Weymouth 2001). The study produced conclusive evidence that, despite years of degradation from agriculture, geophysical survey instruments were still able to locate and map the extant wall remains at Hopeton. The surface geophysical survey not only produced accurate maps of the location and extent of the original earthen walls, but showed clearly the position of gateways as depicted by Squier and Davis (1848) and Thomas (1889b). Over the next five years, Weymouth would direct surveys that completely mapped the two large enclosures at Hopeton with a G-858 gradiometer (Weymouth *et al.* 2009). This multi-year project represents the first large-scale use of geophysical survey instruments to map an Ohio Hopewell geometric enclosure site.

The success of using geophysics to map and examine the large geometric enclosures at Hopeton warranted further study, and Bruce Bevan and Rinita Dalan joined the project team to conduct additional geophysical studies. More details about their work is presented in Chapter 3, but it is worth noting at this point that much of their efforts was aimed at developing an understanding of why the geophysical surface survey was so effective in mapping walls that had been degraded by two centuries of agricultural activities. Their work with geoarchaeologist Rolfe Mandel in excavation trenches and test units at Hopeton are the first geophysical studies conducted on subsurface deposits associated with Ohio Hopewell constructed landscapes.

The geophysical research at the Hopeton Earthworks encouraged studies at other Ohio Hopewell sites. Arlo McKee (2005) conducted a multi-instrument survey at Mound 23 of the Hopewell Mound Group. Jennifer Pederson-Weinberger (2007) conducted magnetic and resistance surveys of non-mound areas at the Hopewell Mound Group and located a previously unknown circular ditch feature, and geophysics were an important element of Ann Bauermeister's (2010) research at the Riverbank site. N'omi Greber (2005b; Greber and Shane 2009) launched a multi-year study of the High Bank Works that includes extensive geophysical survey of the octagon and circle. Several different studies have shown that geophysics is even valuable at Mound City, which was leveled and used as a World War I U.S. Army training base (Brady and Pederson Weinberger 2010; De Vore 2010). Jarrod Burks has conducted geophysical surveys with multiple instruments at numerous Ohio Hopewell sites (Burks 2014; Burks and Cook 2011; Burks et al. 2004; Pederson and Burks 2002). His energy in the pursuit of geophysical studies has shown, as John Weymouth (Weymouth et al. 2009) and Rinita Dalan (2007) demonstrated at Hopeton, geophysical survey instruments are capable of detecting ditches and the base of intact walls when those features are not readily visible in surface topography. Jarrod Burks' magnetic survey of the Junction Works near Chillicothe (2014) demonstrated that ditches and other earthen features are still present, although two centuries of cultivation has largely flattened the topography. Burk's magnetic data was instrumental in motivating large numbers of donations to purchase the site when it was threatened by potential development.

The advent of digital technology has made it possible to collect more data at a much faster rate, and instruments of all kinds are being refined to increase sensitivity and simplicity of use. While interpretation of geophysical data still requires considerable knowledge and experience, data collection has become very standardized and computer-literate students find the operation of instruments fairly simple to learn. Due in large part to the development of digital instruments and relatively low cost computers and software applications, geophysical applications are becoming common in all areas of North American archaeology. Unfortunately, few universities still offer formal instruction in archaeological geophysics, but the National Park Service workshops have developed an important network of instructors and mentors who have assisted many archaeologists and archaeology students in learning how to operate instruments and process and interpret geophysical data.

Geophysics has become an extremely important tool in understanding Ohio Hopewell ceremonial landscapes. As instruments and skilled operators are becoming increasingly available, geophysical prospection has now become a standard tool in the study of Ohio Hopewell ceremonial landscapes. The speed, accuracy, and effectiveness of a wide range of instruments make it possible for archaeologists to discover the intact remnants of once great embankment walls, and accurately map the original location, shape, and orientation of enclosures. It is even quite likely that previously unknown earthwork features will be discovered by geophysical surveys.

Ohio Hopewell – an iconic name and iconic sites, but what is it?

The name Hopewell is widely recognized by students of archaeology, but its application and meaning have been used in many different ways. Prior to the advent of radiocarbon dating, chronological distinction between what were perceived to be the different mound-building groups of the archaeological record was based solely on associated artifacts. William C. Mills proposed the name "Hopewell" for one mound-building group based upon the work conducted by Warren K. Moorehead at the Hopewell Mound Group in Ross County, Ohio. He also proposed the name Fort Ancient for cultural remains excavated from the site of that name. This has served to generate some confusion, because the remains at the Fort Ancient site that Mills used to define the Fort Ancient "culture" were from later people who had simply re-used the earthen enclosure built during the Hopewell era as a location for their later village. Mills believed the remains he uncovered within and under the Adena mound were associated with an early phase of Hopewell, however Shetrone (1920) argued that they were the remains of a distinct and separate cultural group.

Since the widespread use of radiocarbon dating, there now seems to be a unanimous agreement that the term Fort Ancient culture applies to a late prehistoric people separated by many centuries from the people who built the Fort Ancient landscape. The relationship between sites that have been called Adena and Hopewell requires a little more examination.

Emerson Greenman (1932a; 1932b), based upon his study of the Coon Mound in Athens County, Ohio, provided the first detailed description of the Adena culture. Definition of archaeological complexes at this time was heavily dependent on identification and comparison of trait lists. This approach is most readily seen in the extensive efforts of Webb and Snow (1945) and Webb and Baby (1957) to further refine the definition of Adena.

After many decades of research and debate, the question still remains as to whether there is a real distinction between Adena and Hopewell, and if so, just what are those differences. This distinction is further complicated because most of what is known about these two archaeological complexes is derived from mortuary or ceremonial contexts associated with conical mounds. From a geographic perspective, more mounds in northern Kentucky are attributed to Adena, while the majority of earthen enclosure sites associated with Ohio Hopewell are found north of the Ohio River. There are a few large and complex earthwork sites in northern Kentucky, but the majority are relatively small circular enclosure walls that surround a conical mound. From a chronological perspective, radiocarbon dating has shown that sites attributed to Adena do tend to be earlier than those attributed to Ohio Hopewell. However, their chronological position within the Ohio River valley is not mutually exclusive.

In a detailed study of the of the two type sites of these complexes, N'omi Greber (1991) found that archival data from the Adena Mound and Hopewell Mound Group indicates both "continuity and contrasts in the social uses of some imported raw materials and in the construction and use of ritual and/or ceremonial spaces." Greber found that, while the two separate archaeological entities are present in the central Scioto River valley, the Early and Middle Woodland local sequences are different to other southern Ohio drainages. Greber also notes that in the lower Hocking Valley of southern Ohio, mound construction that is attributed to Adena continued into Middle Woodland times:

> "The original definition of the term 'Adena' depended upon the existence of two distinguishable entities, one apparently ancestral to the other is a less common sequence. Using the term 'Adena', without modification, to classify cultural remains in regions like the Hocking where Hopewell did not evolve, may confuse different types of culture change." (Greber 1991, 1)

Greber and others are advocating that the larger and more general labels that have been applied to archaeological complexes (e.g. Adena, Hopewell) do not capture the local variation that exists in the different areas of the Ohio River valley. Sufficient work has now been conducted on the construction of mounds, earthen walls and other landscape features to identify some of the variation that exists among and between different earthwork concentrations. While we must acknowledge that the study of landscape feature construction lags far behind other aspects of Ohio Hopewell research, this volume will attempt to illustrate what we have learned about the construction of ceremonial landscapes, and how much there is yet to learn.

2

Current issues in the construction of Ohio Hopewell ceremonial landscapes

In the 18th century, Euro-American explorers pushed into the Ohio River country and began to encounter the giant earthen monuments built by Ohio Hopewell and other prehistoric peoples. The large enclosures, particularly those built on hilltops, were reminiscent of the ancient fortifications of Europe. These early observers assumed the embankment walls were the abandoned fortresses of a more advanced race that had been overpowered by the native people they found living in the region (Silverberg 1968). As settlers entered the Ohio country in the late 18th and early 19th centuries, they cleared the land and the grand magnitude and scope of these earthen constructions became more apparent. This inspired the curiosity of several generations of local scholars who began to map and document these sites.

The first issue that developed in the study of what we now call Ohio Hopewell earthen enclosure sites was the question of their origin. There is a substantial literature about the ideas and attitudes of early scholars who attributed the mounds and the treasures they covered along with the earthen enclosures to people from the lost continent of Atlantis, wandering Welshmen, the lost tribes of Israel, and many other mythological peoples.

As archaeological science has developed and matured, the issues that interest its practitioners continue to grow and diversify. Hopewell archaeology today ranges from very strictly data oriented studies, such as efforts to identify the raw material source locations for artistic objects made of copper (Rapp *et al.* 2000), stone pipes (Emerson *et al.* 2013; Gunderson 2012), and ceramics (Stoltman 2012), to efforts to identify the symbolic meaning of some of the iconographic images that appear on Hopewell objects (Carr and MacCord 2013). Some scholars are attempting to interpret the social organization of Ohio Hopewell people from objects and features found under Hopewell mounds (Carr and Case 2005), while others are documenting the alignment of Hopewell landscape features relative to lunar and solar events (Hively and Horn 2006; 2010; Romain 2000). Still others are working to resolve the basic chronological issues that hinder our ability to make realistic comparison within and between sites (Greber 2003).

Before we examine the evidence that exists relative to the construction of Ohio Hopewell ceremonial landscapes, it is necessary to understand better the issues and current research that affect our understanding of large earthen monuments of southern Ohio. In this chapter, we will discuss some of the issues that affect the methods and interpretations archaeologists are using to study when, how and why Ohio Hopewell people built so many of these large and complicated earthen monuments in the Central Ohio River valley.

Not all Middle Woodland-era (*ca.* AD 1–500) sites exhibit connections with Hopewell, but construction of burial mounds with elaborate mortuary remains and artifacts made from exotic materials are widespread in eastern North America (Griffin 1967). The vast geographic distribution of Hopewellian artifacts and mortuary features was a major factor in the development of the Hopewell Interaction Sphere concept (Caldwell 1964). In documenting the broad geographic distribution, scholars have also recognized that there is great diversity in the local character of Hopewellian sites. Regional Hopewellian manifestations are an important aspect of the Middle Woodland world, and represent strong evidence that Hopewell societies were egalitarian in their organization. Studies of localized settlement and subsistence practices indicate that, while the various regional manifestations of Hopewell likely shared a common ideology, groups maintained local autonomy. This is best reflected in the local variations seen in mortuary practices, including the inclusion of objects made from non-local materials. Scholars working in eastern North America, particularly during the 1920–1960, identified a number of local mortuary variations on the more dramatic and large-scale ceremonial and ritual remains found at the larger earthen monument centers. The brief discussion that follows is not intended to inventory the scope and diversity of all Hopewell site complexes in eastern North America, but hopefully will provide a basis for comparison and greater appreciation of the amazing earthen landscape construction associated with the Ohio Hopewell core area.

Hopewell variation and distribution

Hopewell, as defined by the construction of monumental earthen features (mounds, earthen walled enclosures, and other features), complex mortuary and ceremonial patterns (as reflected in features associated with mounds), and elaborate and artistic artifact types and forms, is found across much of eastern North America during the Middle Woodland period (*ca.* AD 1–500). Not all sites, or regional clusters of sites, appear to have participated in the practices that led to the creation of these features and artifacts at the same level of intensity. Research has demonstrated that the largest and most elaborate sites, as reflected in earthen construction, mortuary and ceremonial patterns, and the quantity and sophistication of artifacts, are found in or near the river valleys of southern Ohio.

Sites and site complexes in other regions of eastern North America display some of these same characteristics (Fig. 2.1), but rarely on the same size, scale, complexity, and number as seen among Ohio Hopewell sites. This has led scholars to consider how sites with a few Hopewellian characteristics in other regions may relate to the great Hopewell centers in Ohio. Just how many of these characteristics are indicative of being "Hopewell"? Does a site in northern Michigan with a fragmentary rocker-stamped ceramic vessel indicate Hopewell? There seems to be a fairly strong bias to identification based upon mortuary characteristics or at least

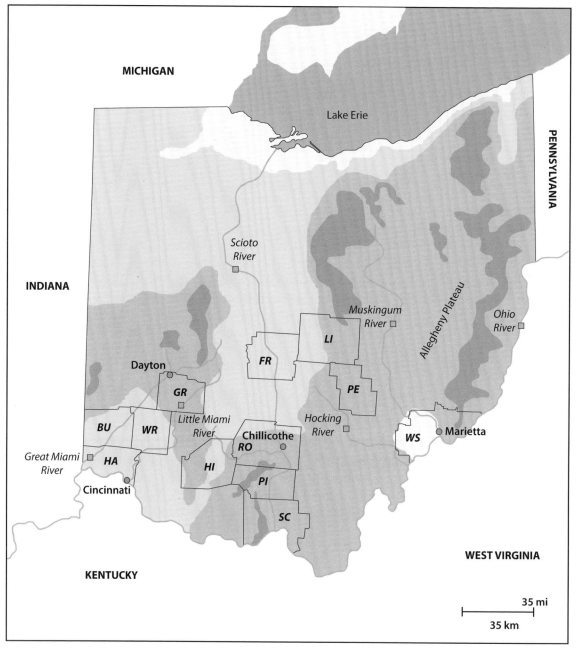

Fig. 2.1. Map of Ohio showing rivers, counties and places of particular importance for Hopewell remains (see Figs 4.1, 4.10, 4.11 and 4.35 for more detailed maps of key areas).

Bu	Butler	GR	Green	HI	Highland	LI	Licking
HA	Hamilton	FR	Franklin	PI	Pike	PE	Perry
WR	Warren	RO	Ross	SC	Scioto	WS	Washington

the presence of socially-valued items that may have been included in sub-mound features or structures. Since this particular volume is about constructed ceremonial landscapes, the focus of this section will be on places where mounds, enclosures, and other earthen features were constructed together. It is not intended to be an inventory of all Hopewell mound sites or a discussion of the Middle Woodland period, but I will attempt to provide background to understand better the massive scale of landscape construction conducted in southern Ohio.

Hopewellian sites are also present in northern Ohio, but they tend to be smaller and associated with only one or a few mounds. In the Cuyahoga Valley, a Hopewell mound associated with a variety of Middle Woodland features has been recorded near the community of Everett (Brose 1974), and the National Park Service has investigated a number of non-mound sites with Hopewellian characteristics nearby (Volf 2000; Richner and Bauermestier 2011; Richner and Volf 2000). Brian Redmond (2007) has documented sophisticated mortuary remains at the Pumpkin site, an inundated Hopewellian site on the shores of Lake Erie in northern Ohio.

Sites associated with the Middle Woodland period are found throughout most of eastern North America. Although Hopewell is the most widely recognized cultural complex during the Middle Woodland period, certainly not all Middle Woodland sites are considered to be Hopewellian. There are large concentrations of Hopewell sites in southern Ohio, Illinois, and parts of southern Indiana. Hopewell sites occur in more localized clusters from south-west Wisconsin south to Louisiana, and from the Kansas City region in Kansas and Missouri on the west to New York and Florida in the east. The discontinuous spatial distribution of Hopewell sites is further complicated by the very strong likelihood that not all of these regional developments were contemporaneous. Radiocarbon dating has done little to resolve concerns about chronological relationships.

Nearly two centuries of study have provided considerable documentation about the geographic distribution of mounds and archaeological complexes with characteristics showing similarities to Ohio Hopewell. Mark Seeman (2011) noted that the late James B. Griffin, one of the most respected of all Hopewell scholars, only used the term "Hopewell" to refer to the archaeological record in the middle Ohio River valley. For him the widespread and roughly contemporary Middle Woodland sites with similar characteristics were, in his mind, "Hopewellian". This distinction is not recognized by everyone, but very few places outside southern Ohio match the combination of large impressive earthworks, complex sub-mound features and the array of prestige objects that characterize Ohio Hopewell.

Beyond Ohio, the greatest concentration of Hopewell mounds and constructed landscapes is in the Illinois River valley of western Illinois. Current radiocarbon dates suggest that the earliest Hopewell manifestations are found in the Illinois River valley, where chronology building has been aided by the recognition of a ceramic sequence for the region. This area was subjected to antiquarian studies throughout the middle and late 19th century, but the richness of the Hopewellian archaeological record in this region was not apparent until Warren K. Moorehead began survey and excavation for the University of Illinois in 1927–1928. Kenneth Farnsworth (2004) provides an enlightening and detailed account of work conducted by Moorehead and his field supervisor, Jay L. B. Taylor, during this seminal period. Published with his synthesis of this work are reprints of the important early papers on Illinois Hopewell mound excavations in this region. The most important of this group is the report of the 1927–1928 work conducted under the supervision of Moorehead (Baker *et al.* 1941), who unfortunately, due to declining health was unable to complete the report himself. James B. Griffin and Richard G. Morgan, both of whom were very familiar with Ohio Hopewell archaeological work, edited the manuscript. Hopewellian manifestations in southern Indiana are associated with the latter phases of the Hopewell era.

Mounds are the most common earthen landscape features associated with Illinois Hopewell sites, and these often occur in clusters of a dozen or more (e.g. Havana, Ogden-Fettie, Morton). Many conical mounds were built on bluff-tops that overlook the Illinois River valley. Habitation debris from associated village sites is also common, often on terraces below the mounds. This pattern of fairly obvious habitation sites with associated mounds is in stark contrast to the situation in Ohio, where the mound and earthen enclosure sites are readily apparent, but associated habitation sites are apparently small and indistinct. Another contrast between the two areas is the nature of sub-mound deposits. In Illinois, mounds usually cover log or stone crypts containing burials. In Ohio, most mounds were built over the floors of buildings that contained mortuary and other ceremonial remains before the buildings were taken down and the mound was built (Brown 1979).

Excavation of mounds at sites like Havana (Baker *et al.* 1941; Taylor 1929), Ogden-Fettie, and Morton (Cole and Deuel 1937) provided substantial and rich details about the character of Illinois Hopewell mortuary practices. More recent studies of Illinois Valley Hopewell mounds have produced significant information about the structure and construction of mounds. Earthen enclosures are rare in association with Illinois Hopewell mounds. The Golden Eagle site, located near the confluence of the Illinois and Mississippi Rivers, consists of at least six mounds surrounded by a large oval enclosure wall (King *et al.* 2013), and is one of the only reported earthen enclosures in this region. An enclosure wall has also been reported at the Ogden-Fettie site (Munson 1967).

Hopewell mounds were also built in the Illinois River floodplain. Floodplain mounds tend to be larger than bluff-top mounds and include loaf-shaped and conical forms. Floodplain mounds may also be built around a plaza. Charles and Buikstra (2002) suggest the large floodplain centers in the Illinois River valley served to integrate larger social communities through their construction, maintenance, and performance of ceremonies, gifting, mate exchange, and games. They propose that the bluff-top mound groups reflect local group identity and contain the remains of all ages and sexes, while the floodplain ceremonial mounds contain largely adult male remains.

The Mound House site is located in Greene County, Illinois in the Lower Illinois River valley (Fig. 2.2). The 5 hectare site is one of the largest Hopewell sites in Illinois and is unusual in that it was built on the floodplain of the Illinois River, rather than on the alluvial terraces or uplands. The site originally included five mounds, but only two are extant. Many years of investigation, including five seasons of excavation by University of Chicago Archaeological Field Schools

Left: **Fig. 2.2.** Overview of excavations at Mound 1, Mound House site in July 2000 (photo: author).

Right: **Fig. 2.3.** Douglas Charles explains stratigraphic profile at Mound 1, Mound House site in July 2000. Geoarchaeological investigations revealed that inverted sod blocks were used in mound construction (photo: author).

(Buikstra *et al.* 1998), have produced important information about the nature of this important Illinois Hopewell site.

Excavation of a 6 × 7 m block in the south side of the Mound 1 provides important information about the construction of the mound (Fig. 2.3). It is worth noting that the mound was built on a locality that had substantial evidence of prior human use, including nine pits and 112 post-holes. While not all of these features could be dated by radiometric methods or their contents, at least some of them contain evidence of Middle Woodland activities, and two of the pits contained turtle carapaces that may have been rattles (Buikstra *et al.* 1998).

Geoarchaeological study of Mound 1 at Mound House (Van Nest *et al.* 2001) indicated that the mound was built on the surface of an existing A horizon, and the core of the mound was constructed of inverted sod blocks. These 3–10 cm thick blocks had been cut from a relatively thin and pedologically youthful soil. Based upon particle size analysis, the researchers were able to determine that the sod blocks were not cut from soils adjacent to the mounds. This type of careful excavation and study demonstrates the potential information that can be derived from the fill of earthen monuments. The authors note that sod blocks are visible in photographs of other Illinois mound excavations, and were apparently used to build vertical walls associated with mound crypts. They suggest that the relatively high energy-cost of obtaining the sod blocks was likely not a requisite of soil engineering, but more probably had important symbolic meaning for the builders of the mounds. Robert Hall (1997) has written about the symbolic importance of soil colors in mound construction.

Hopewellian mounds and a few earthen enclosures have been found on the margins of the Mississippi River valley in what are now Illinois and Iowa. Whittaker and Green (2010) report evidence for earthen enclosures in association with Hopewellian mound groups at Toolesboro and the Gast Farm site south of Davenport, Iowa. Nineteenth century excavations at the Toolesboro Mound Group (Fig. 2.4) produced substantial Hopewellian mortuary deposits (Alex and Green 1995). Hopewellian mound groups are prominent on the bluffs of both sides of the Mississippi River valley in Iowa and Illinois (Alex 2000; Logan 1976; Herold 1970; 1971).

The Wabash River lowlands in south-west Indiana contain a number of large and very important monumental Hopewell landscapes. The Mann site is the largest and probably best known, but scientific study of its earthen features has been fairly limited (Fig. 2.5). This brief summary of the Mann sites is drawn from Kellar (1979), Ruby (2006), and Ruby *et al.* (2005). The site is located about 12.5 miles (20 km) above the confluence of the Wabash and Ohio Rivers. It consists of geometric enclosures built of earthen walls, a variety of mounds in different shapes and sizes, and extensive occupation areas that cover about 432.5 acres (175 ha).

There are two rectangular enclosures near the western margin of the site. Neither of these is complete, with one or more sections of wall missing. One is a rectangular form shaped by three earthen walls, about 600 × 300 m. The open side of the enclosure faces the bottomland to the south. The fourth wall is thus formed by the natural edge of the terrace, and a large loaf-shaped mound is present within the enclosure along this terrace-edge. The other enclosure is square, with each site about 310 m in length. Gateways at the corners and midpoints of the sides are about 15 m wide. Ruby (2006) notes that this is the only square enclosure reported from outside Ohio, and its size is comparable to the tri-partite enclosures in the Scioto River–Paint Creek region.

The central part of the Mann site is dominated by two large flat-topped mounds, two C-shaped enclosure walls, and a large conical mound. None of these landscape features has been scientifically studied, but antiquarian investigations and digs by amateur archaeologists have revealed the presence of at least three stratified activity floors within the fill of the largest mound (Ruby 2006). Those excavations uncovered pits, post-holes, midden, and exotic Hopewellian artifacts on these buried activity surfaces. A radiocarbon date on charcoal from one of the pits suggests that particular activity surface dates about AD 420±45 (Ruby 2006).

The eastern part of the site has about 700 linear meters of embankment wall, five small conical mounds, and a small circular earthen enclosure. Ruby *et al.* (2005) observe that, while the five conical mounds on this end of the site are likely related to mortuary activities, the other landscape features at the site probably had non-mortuary purposes. This is one of the larger ceremonial landscaped located outside the core Hopewell areas of southern Ohio, and it likely was built as an important ceremonial center and almost certainly served a variety of purposes.

Left: **Fig. 2.4.** The Toolesboro Mound Group on the western bluff of the Mississippi River Valley south of Davenport, Iowa. Early excavations revealed elaborate mortuary remains. The site is preserved today as a park (photo: post-card postmarked 1912).

Right: **Fig. 2.5.** Early 20th century aerial photograph of the Mann site, Posey County, Indiana

The Mount Vernon Mound, also sometimes known as GE Mound, came under the scientific spotlight when large numbers and varieties of Hopewell artifacts were illegally removed from private property in 1988 (Ruby 2006; General Electric 1997; Seeman 1995). Cooperation between the landowner, law enforcement agencies, and archaeologists made it possible to reconstruct some information about the large mound that had been partly destroyed for its fill, and was then subjected to wholesale looting by artifact hunters.

The GE Mound was about 125 m long, 50 m wide, and 6 m high. Most people who had seen it thought it was a natural earthen feature, but its original size and shape must have been similar to the Seip-Pricer Mound at the Seip Earthworks in Ross County, Ohio (Ruby 2006). No intact burials were found in the mound, but human bone was certainly present. Most of the looted artifacts were found at or near the floor of the mound. Investigators documented that large quantities of ceremonial artifacts, including silver and copper ear spools, panpipes, copper celts, awls, and beads and pendants, mica cutouts, obsidian, chert and quartz stone tools, and an amazing array of perishable fibers and fabrics had been present (General Electric 1997). Due to the unscientific manner in which it was excavated, little is known about the structure of this giant earthen monument, but it is estimated to have comprised of 11,000 m^3 of soil, making it one of the five largest Hopewell mounds ever recorded.

Much has been written about Hopewellian sites and complexes in the South-east. Robert Thunen (1998) has documented that there are only six Middle Woodland enclosure sites in the Mid-South region, but as this review will indicate, Middle Woodland enclosures are generally rare outside the Ohio River valley area. In another important study of Middle Woodland earthworks in the South-east, James Knight (2001) has provided substantial data to suggest the construction of flat-topped Middle Woodland mounds probably developed in the south-east. These mounds were often the loci of ceremonial activities. Hopewellian mortuary mounds have been recorded across a wide area in the South-east. Some of the better known Hopewellian mounds include Garden Creek in western North Carolina (Keel 1976; Chapman and Keel 1979); Tunacunnhee in north-west Georgia (Jeffries 1976; 1979); Mandeville in south-west Georgia (Keller *et al.* 1962); along with the Bynum mound group (Cotter and Corbitt 1951); Pharr Mound (Bohannon 1972); Ingomar Mounds (Rafferty 1987); and Miller Mounds (Jenkins 1979) in northern Mississippi. Very significant Hopewellian mortuary deposits have also been documented at the Crooks (Ford and Wiley 1940) and Marksville sites (Fowke 1928; Ford and Willey 1940) in Louisiana, and the Helena Crossing site (Ford 1963) in south-east Arkansas.

Although mound construction during the Middle Woodland period is fairly common and well documented in the South-east, evidence for larger landscape construction is more limited. The dates associated with earthwork construction have been debated in regard to most of these sites, but there is now sufficient data to demonstrate that all or some of their earthen features were built during the Middle Woodland era. Either due to the nature of the earthwork construction or the types and styles of artifacts found at the sites, they are all widely accepted as being part of the Hopewellian network. The discussion presented here certainly does not exhaust the list of South-eastern sites that display strong Hopewellian characteristics, but it is intended to provide readers with a sense of monumental earthen construction in the broader Hopewell Interaction Sphere.

The Crystal River site is located on Florida's west-central Gulf Coast (Fig. 2.6). Excavations by C. B. Moore (1903; 1907) in the early 20th century produced a number and variety of artifacts (pottery, copper, shell, and stone) that were similar to materials found in the Hopewell mounds of southern Ohio. William H. Sears (1962) noted that a number of sites on the Florida Gulf Coast have produced Hopewellian artifacts, and he named this phase in Florida prehistory the Yent Complex. Additional research at Crystal River in the 20th century (Bullen 1951; 1953; 1966) produced evidence that some of the earthen features at the site were associated with a later Mississippian occupation. Some writers (McMichael 1964; Ford 1969) thought that Crystal River might represent a colony from Mesoamerica that subsequently stimulated the development of Hopewell in the Midwest. Like many sites Hopewell connections, it has produced more hypotheses than verifiable data. While questions still remain about the relationship between the Crystal River site and Hopewell sites in southern Ohio, more recent research and publications (Weisman 1995; Pluckhahn *et al.* 2010) have produced a more definitive view of this important site on the Florida Gulf Coast.

The most visible landscape features at Crystal River include two flat-topped temple mounds, an extensive shell midden (Fig. 2.7), and two circular earthen embankments, the larger of which also contained a mound made of sand. C. B. Moore (1903; 1907) excavated a large part of the latter feature and noted that the mound itself had three strata: a shell layer at the base was covered by a layer of white sand then a layer of gray sand. Several burials at the base of this mound were found with ornaments and objects that have been found in Hopewell contexts in Ohio and other areas of eastern North America. Two carved stone stelae at the site have contributed to the speculation about Mesoamerican origins.

Recent investigations at the site (Pluckhahn *et al.* 2010) included detailed topographic mapping, geophysical survey, and soil coring. These new data have cast doubt on hypotheses about solar orientation of selected features, produced evidence that the mound and embankment features were built around a plaza, and documented that shell was used as building material for landscape features. Although the radiocarbon dates from Crystal River raise many questions, Pluckhahn *et al.* (2010) make a strong case that the site was first occupied by perhaps 300 BC

Fig. 2.6. Crystal River, Florida: a) Burial Mound F, excavated by C. B. Moore; b) Temple Mound A (photos: Pete Topping).

Fig. 2.7. Moore's 1907 map of burial mound F, part of the main burial complex C–F at Crystal River (Weisman 1995: 44), where Hopewellian artefacts and burials were discovered.

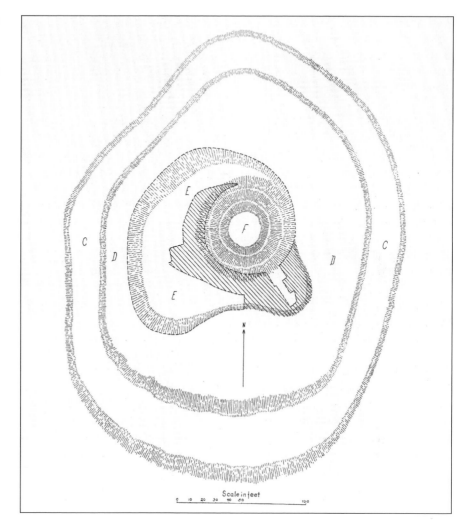

and was used until at least AD 600. The earliest dates correspond with the early Deptford period in the South-east and the earliest phases of ceremonial mound and earthwork construction in the Ohio River valley. The final use of Crystal River would have occurred later than any accepted age for Hopewell anywhere in eastern North America. The importance of Crystal River to Ohio Hopewell scholars rests mainly with the diverse range of sharks teeth, barracuda jaws, conch shells, and other Gulf Coast artifacts that are found at Ohio Hopewell sites, and were likely brought to Ohio from terrestrial fossil deposits in south-west Florida (Colvin 2011).

The Fort Center site in southern Florida is one of the largest ceremonial landscapes in the south-east (Marshall 1996), but at least some of the landscape features were built both before and after the Hopewell era (Thompson and Pluckhahn 2012). The site is located at Lake Okeechobee, just north of the everglades. A recent synthesis by V. D. Thompson and T. J. Pluckhahn (2012) provides a contemporary interpretation of the research conducted largely by

W. H. Sears (1982). Fort Center consists of a complex series of isolated mounds, linear earthen walls, circular walls and ditches, middens, and two artificial ponds that contain extensive human burial deposits. The Great Circle complex is among earliest features at the sites, but dating is based on a single uncorrected radiocarbon date to 800–350 BC (Sears 1982).

West of the Great Circle complex are two substantial mounds and a charnel pond. At about 5.5 m tall, Mound B is the larger of the two mounds. The nearby charnel pond has gained substantial notoriety since investigators removed more than 300 bodies that had been placed on a wooden structure that stood above the pond and was then burned. The bodies and burned scaffolding fell into the water along with a large number of carved wooden effigies. Sears (1982, 164–5) noted that the elaborate burial activities at the pond and adjacent mounds were parallel to the elaborate mortuary deposits at Ohio Hopewell sites. Although there were very few non-local artifacts to connect Fort Center to the Hopewell Interaction Sphere, Sears attributed these features to the Middle Woodland on the basis of a single radiocarbon date. More recent research by Thompson and Pluckhahn (2012) indicates that these features may date as early as the Great Circle complex, but they also report additional radiocarbon dates to document that considerable activity was ongoing during the Middle Woodland period.

Thompson and Pluckhahn (2012) make a convincing argument that Fort Center was an important place for ceremonies and monumental earthen and wooden architecture beginning about the beginning of the Early Woodland period. The site was used throughout the Middle Woodland period and Fort Center continued to be an important ritual landscape until perhaps as late as AD 800–1000 and the appearance of the Calusa chiefdoms.

Hopewellian mounds and burials have also been reported at a number of sites in the Lower Mississippi River Valley (e.g. Ford and Willey 1940; Ford 1963; Cotter and Corbett 1951; Jackson 1998). The Marksville site in central Louisiana is one of the most remarkable Hopewell sites outside of the Ohio River valley. The first map of the site was included in a report by Gerard Fowke (1928), who described two large semi-circular enclosures, assorted mounds of varying shapes and sizes, and eight small circular embankments that he thought were "lodge sites." Fowke, who had considerable experience in Ohio Hopewell archaeology, excavated trenches into several of the mounds, and all three exhibited markedly different structure and contents. The main enclosure is formed by about 3,200 ft (960 m) of earthen wall that varies from 3 ft to 7 ft (0.9–2.1 m) in height (Fig. 2.8). The open end of the enclosure borders on a bluff-edge that overlooks the Old River. Midden areas have been described by different investigators both within and outside this enclosure. A comprehensive synthesis of research at the Marksville site was published by Toth (1974), but a more recent summary research on the small rings or circular enclosures has been published by McGimsey (2003).

Frank Setzler (1933) stressed the stylistic similarity between Marksville and Hopewell ceramics. He also noted that the structure of Mounds 4 and 8 at Marksville differ from Hopewell mounds, and that Marksville artifacts lack the variety of forms and materials found in Hopewell mounds. Setzler's comparison lumped the various Hopewell and Hopewellian manifestations in Ohio, Indiana,

Left: **Fig. 2.8.** Marksville site, Louisiana, enclosure wall (photo: author).

Right: **Fig. 2.9.** Marksville site, Mound 4. The site is preserved today as a park (photo: author).

and Illinois into a single group. He also suggested that Marksville was earlier and served as the inspiration for Ohio Hopewell. Setzler and James A. Ford excavated at Marksville but no report of their work has ever been found.

Works Progress Administration (WPA) excavations made major contributions to archaeology in the south-east, and WPA excavations under Stuart Neitzel in central Louisiana were aimed at unraveling chronological questions about the relationship between Marksville and Coles Creek. Excavations were intended to focus on Crooks (Marksville) and Greenhouse (Coles Creek). Flooding forced the Greenhouse crew to shift to the excavation of Mound 2 at Marksville. Five trenches were excavated and later reported by Vescilius (1957). The trenches produced differing stratigraphy, but two distinct midden levels separated by a layer of sterile loam seem to be confirmed in multiple trenches. Vescilius also reported what he called a house, rectangular in shape and 10 × 8 ft (3 × 2.4 m) in size. WPA excavators investigated one of the "lodge" depressions described by Fowke (1928) but did not find anything.

Mound 4 (Fig. 2.9) was partially excavated by Fowke (1928) and later re-excavated by Setzler and J. A. Ford. Both accounts suggest that the mound was built in several stages and a complex mortuary/ceremonial structure was at the core of the original or primary mound. J. A. Ford in his report on excavations at the Crooks site provides a summary of the central features of Marksville Mound 4:

> "A flat-topped structure about five feet [1.5 m] high had been constructed and allowed to stand for some time. Then the center of the platform had been dug out and a square vault made which was covered with log rafters topped with layers of cane and clay. A number of burials were placed in the vault. Scattered burials were also made in small individual vaults on the surface of the platform. A primary mantle was then piled over the entire platform and its included vault. A few burials were scattered through the soil of the primary mantle. A secondary mantle was added later". (Ford and Willey 1940: 32)

Fowke (1928) dug a trench into Mound 8 and reported the mound fill was comprised of pockets of gray and yellow sandy clay, likely evidence of basketloads. He reported seven graves along with four ceramic vessels. All of the burials were in sub-mound contexts and they had been covered by cane matts. There were no burials in the mound fill.

Fowke (1928) reports that Mound 12 was built in 3 stages. His excavations revealed two floors with features and artifacts, and each had been covered by a layer of mound fill. No burials were found in the mound.

WPA excavators also investigated a village area between Mound 2 and the bluff edge. Toth (1974) reviewed the records for this work and although these records are of poor quality, he suggests Setzler probably excavated several trenches in areas where surface collections were particularly rich. The trenches exposed a "rectangular semi-subterranean outline of a house". The structure was 20 × 25.5 ft (6.1 × 7.7 m) with a central pit, 8.5 × 15 ft (2.5 × 4.5 m). There were post-holes in corners and along the two longer walls. It is unclear what function this building served, but it is probably not a domestic structure.

In 1993 Jones and Kuttruff (1998) conducted test excavations to examine the construction of selected earthen features at Marksville. They observed that despite many years of surface degradation, the core of the original embankment wall forming Enclosure A was still partially intact. They observed that prior to construction of the wall, most of the original A horizon had been removed, although small remnants were still present in places. In the sections of wall that were examined, they concluded that the embankment was built in a single episode, because none of the 30 linear meters of wall they examined "showed any evidence of the weathering or differences in construction-fill deposition that would suggest separate building episodes" (Jones and Kuttruff 1998: 52). The Eastern Circle also appears to have been built in a single episode, and both embankment walls were built with visible basketloads of local A, E, and Bt horizon materials. Much of this material was likely obtained from shallow borrow pits on the exterior side of the Enclosure A embankment.

To the north of the main enclosure, Fowke (1928) reported the presence of low circular enclosures that he thought were the remains of lodges. Thomas Ryan (1975) observed these same features on aerial photographs and excavated part of one. Subsequently, more thorough studies by McGimsey (2003) have shown that these features consist of four architectural elements: an outer ditch, an earthen embankment, a central basin, and a central pit. McGimsey's research has suggested that there are at least eight and possibly as many as 70 of these circular enclosures at Marksville, and they vary in size from 10 m to 30 m in diameter. Due to the paucity of artifacts and domestic refuse, it is apparent that these features are not domestic houses. McGimsey also reports that the central pit in each structure was backfilled with matrix derived from another locality. The backfilling was not sufficient to level the entire feature with the surrounding terrain and no effort was made to backfill the outer ditch. These small circular enclosures are unique in south-eastern archaeology. There are only a few radiocarbon dates from these features, but they indicate the small enclosures to be clearly Middle Woodland in age.

Like so many of the great Hopewell sites in Ohio, much of the fieldwork at Marksville was conducted prior to the development of more modern excavation and recording techniques (Fig. 2.10). Many of the primary excavation records are poor in quality or missing altogether. What little is known about mound structure indicates that at least some of the mounds were built in stages, and there is

Fig. 2.10. Marksville site, Mound 6 (photo: author).

considerable variation between the mounds in terms of their content and structure. Examination of the earthen enclosure walls indicates these features were built in a single event. Even with the limitations on current data, it is apparent that this is a large and complex site that included large and small enclosures, mounds of varying size and shape, and wooden structures that do not appear to be domestic in function. Although the ceremonial artifacts from Marksville lack the number and variety that are characteristic of contemporary sites in Ohio, the number of complete or nearly complete ceramic vessels (Toth 1974) is truly amazing. Additional Middle Woodland enclosure sites in the Yazoo Basin (Spanish Fort, Little Spanish Fort, Leist) are described by Phillips (1970) and Thunen (1998).

Pinson Mounds in western Tennessee is the largest and most complex Middle Woodland ceremonial landscape outside of Ohio. The site includes at least 12 mounds, a large circular earthen enclosure, a small earthen enclosure, and numerous habitation and ceremonial activity areas within about 395 acres (160 ha). The major earthen features at the site occur in three areas separated from each other by small spring-fed stream branches. Research by Robert Mainfort Jr and colleagues have demonstrated that although five of the mounds are flat-topped and rectangular in configuration (Fig. 2.11), shapes that were traditionally attributed to the later Mississippian era, the majority of earthen construction at Pinson dates to the Middle Woodland period (Mainfort 1986; 1988a; 1996; 2013; Mainfort and McNutt 2004). The vast amount of landscape construction is estimated to exceed 100,000 m^3 of earth (Mainfort 1996; Mainfort and Walling 1992). Radiocarbon dates indicate that the Pinson Mounds were built and used from roughly 100 BC through AD 350.

In a recent synthesis of the research at Pinson Mounds, Mainfort (2013) has proposed that the site is comprised of three ceremonial precincts: West, Central, and East. The largest mound at the site (Mound 9, Sauls Mound) is located in the Central Precinct area of the site and is reported to be 22 m high and 100 m wide at the base (Fig. 2.12). The Ozier Mound is another flat-topped rectangular structure. It is about 10 m high and 70 × 73 m at the base, making it the second largest mound at Pinson. Excavations by Mainfort and Walling (1992) revealed that the mound had been constructed in at least six stages, with each temporary mound summit being covered by a layer of pale sand. Several small hearths and a raised clay platform were found on the various mound surfaces. Radiocarbon dates confirm the Middle Woodland age of these features and suggest that all the flat-topped mounds at Pinson were likely built during the Middle Woodland period.

The Twin Mounds, located in the Western Ritual Precinct, are two large conjoined conical mounds. The northern mound is about 26 m in diameter and 7

m tall, and the southern mound is about 30 m in diameter and 8 m tall. Excavation in 1983 of about one-quarter of the northern mound revealed complex stratigraphy and evidence of at least five construction stages (Mainfort 1986; 2013). Individual basketloads of earth were visible in the fill. The 1983 excavation revealed that prior to construction of the mound, the topsoil in this area was removed and the exposed subsoil was flattened. Six tombs along with a large numbers of cremations and several post-holes were excavated into the subsoil. Excavation of four of the tombs revealed substantial variability in construction with evidence for coverings that included combinations of logs, poles, and matting. The tombs and other sub-mound features were covered by a layer of sand and a layer of puddled clay (Mainfort 1986, 51). A circular raised platform with a row of post-holes was built around the perimeter of the burial area. The platform was about 0.5 m tall and 2 m wide and built from mottled sandy clay. The circular interior of the enclosure formed by this platform was then covered with basketfuls of earth to form a primary mound about 2 m high, and capped by a thin (2 cm) layer of sand. Subsequent mound construction stages were also capped with similar sand layers, and evidence of activities was recorded on each of the different mound surfaces. Radiocarbon dates indicate the northern-most of the Twin Mounds was built about AD 100 (Mainfort 1996).

A large circular enclosure wall is associated with the eastern section of the site that is often called the Eastern Citadel (Fig. 2.13). The enclosure is built on a bluff overlooking a tributary of the Forked Deer River. The enclosure is about 180 m in diameter and in places as much as 2 m high. The embankment is a near perfect circle for much of its circumference but takes a slightly oval form in conforming to the bluff edge on which it is built. Mound 29, a flat-topped rectangular mound (3.6 m high, 51 × 49 m at base) is located in the eastern half of the enclosure. A smaller conical mound is located just outside the enclosure along the bluffs overlooking the river.

A 14 m long trench excavated by Morse in 1963 into the northern section of the enclosure wall revealed four stratigraphic levels, with artifacts being present in the upper three (Morse 1986). No evidence for a palisade was observed. Morse observed that where he examined the wall, it had been damaged by plowing

Left: **Fig. 2.11.** Pinson Mounds site, Tennessee: low flat-topped mound (photo courtesy of Bret Ruby).

Right: **Fig. 2.12.** Pinson mounds site: Sauls Mound (photo courtesy of Bret Ruby).

Fig. 2.13. Pinson Mounds site: embankment walls of the Eastern Citadel (photo courtesy of Bret Ruby).

and was 6–9 m wide and 30–100 cm high. Other sections of the enclosure wall were still 2–3 m high. Subsequent testing by Robert L. Thunen (1998) provided substantial evidence of the built-nature of the embankment circle and areas around the mounds. Thunen documented the presence of loaded fills within the enclosure near Mound 29 that are likely remnants of a ramp. He examined the embankment wall in several places and concurred with Morse's observation that its construction was continuous and uninterrupted (Thunen 1998). Mainfort (2013, 178) reports that the embankment fill was placed on top of a Bw horizon.

The Duck's Nest is a small circular embankment located in the Central Ritual Precinct of the site. Excavation of this enclosure was initially conducted by Dan Morse in 1963 (Morse 1986), with subsequent excavations by Mainfort (1986). The earthen enclosure wall is about 13 m in diameter and 1 m high. Morse observed that the embankment was built in three stages. The initial earthen wall was made of light colored sand and stood about 0.5 m high and no more than 3 m wide. The light colored sand was covered by a dark brown sand, up to 70 cm thick, and that was subsequently covered by mottled clayey-sand stratum no more than 55 cm thick. Morse uncovered a conoidal ceramic vessel (Furrs Cord Marked) lying upside down on the topmost stratum just beneath the summit of the wall. Morse also uncovered, but did not excavate, a large charcoal-filled hearth at the center of the circular enclosure.

Mainfort (1986) re-opened the central hearth feature encountered by Morse and discovered that beneath a thick deposit of charcoal and ash was a layer of fire-reddened sand that rested on subsoil. Sherds comprising about half of another cord marked vessel were found in the reddened sand. Three radiocarbon dates from this feature are widely divergent and likely reflect contamination during excavation or the less likely possibility that the feature was in use for many centuries (Mainfort 1986: 27).

Mainfort also conducted excavations nearby and found an area with a high density of artifacts and few features. Ceramics from this area included fragments of at least 47 vessels, a number of which exhibited decorative styles indicative of non-local manufacture. Unfortunately, conflicting opinions about Instrumental Neutron Activation Analysis and petrographic analysis of the potentially non-local sherds has produced differing interpretations (Mainfort *et al.* 1997; Stoltman and Mainfort 2002) that clearly need additional study to resolve. The types of the activities conducted in this area of the site do not appear to be domestic in nature. The Duck's Nest feature complex and associated ceramics are unique among southeastern Middle Woodland landscape features.

Pinson Mounds exhibit some of the same constructed landscape features commonly seen at Hopewell sites across southern Ohio. Research by Mainfort and others demonstrates that the construction of the site involved much more labor and planning than the simple act of scooping up earth and piling it into mounds and walls. Although Mainfort argues that Pinson Mounds served as a center of pilgrimage, artifacts indicative of wider than regional participation (mica, copper, obsidian) are limited at the site. Many questions remain about the sequence and timing of construction, and just as sites in Ohio are revealing remains of stone and timber landscape features in association with mounds and embankments, it is likely that some of these and other features will yet be discovered at Pinson.

There is a variety of Middle Woodland complexes across the Highland areas of the south-east that exhibit Hopewell influence and likely participated in that network. Sites that have been identified include Copena (Walthall 1980) in northern Alabama, and Owl Hollow and MacFarland in southern Tennessee (Faulkner 1988) which produced artifacts that suggest Hopewellian connections. Particularly noteworthy in this region is a site known as Old Stone Fort, near the town of Manchester in south-eastern Tennessee. The site looks much like the hilltop enclosures of southern Ohio, with an enclosure of rock and earth walls built along the perimeter of a hilltop overlooking the convergence of two forks of the Duck River. The walls are not continuous around the perimeter of the mesa, and no evidence of walls coincide with the steepest bluffs of the landform that drop abruptly 80–100 ft (24–30 m) to the river below. The perimeter of the landform is roughly 4,600 ft (1,380 m) in length and encloses about 50 acres (124 ha).

Beyond the speculation of early antiquarians, what is known about the Old Stone Fort is directly attributable to the research of Charles Faulkner (1968). Faulkner excavated seven trenches across the outer walls of the enclosure and nine trenches and three test units across the gateway area and moat. Although there appears to be some variability in material and methods used in building the outer wall, Faulkner found several places where stone was stacked to form an inner and outer wall with soil and stone rubble then being used to fill the space between and above these piles of stone. The outer wall appears to have been 4–5 ft (1.2–1.5 m) high at the time when Faulkner conducted his research, and he notes that earlier visitors and observers often overestimated the wall height. In the gateway area, Faulkner (1968) documented a fairly complex series of walls, earth and stone features, and a moat or ditch. Radiocarbon dates from the 1966 excavations indicate a 3–4 century construction episode, but this may be refined if more samples from better contexts become available for dating with contemporary radiocarbon methods. An overall absence of artifacts from within the enclosure along with the construction methods and morphology of the walls makes this site very reminiscent of several southern Ohio hilltop enclosures.

Hopewell mounds are found throughout much of Prairie Peninsula region particularly along bluff tops of the Mississippi in eastern Iowa, north-west Illinois, and south-west Wisconsin (Figs 2.14 and 2.15). Notable mound groups from the Hopewell era have been reported at Toolesboro (Alex 2000; Alex and Green 1995), and McGregor (Beaubien 1953; Logan 1976) in eastern Iowa, Albany in Illinois (Benchley et al. 1977; Herold 1971), the Trempleau region of south-west Wisconsin (McKern 1929; 1931; Stoltman 2006), and along the Red Cedar River in north-west Wisconsin (Cooper 1933). In most of these areas, the connection with Hopewell is mainly through conical burial mounds, some of which exhibit central crypts built of logs or stone. Burials with objects made of raw materials from the Hopewell

Left: **Fig. 2.14.** Aerial photo of bluff edge mounds in the Effigy Mounds National monument, Iowa, showing the Great Bear Group (left) and Little Bear Group (right) with the Mississippi river in the background (photo courtesy of the Midwest Archaeological Center, National Park Service, Lincoln, Nebraska).

Right: **Fig. 2.15.** Bluff edge Hopewell mound at Five Point Mounds in the Effigy Mounds National monument, Iowa (photo courtesy of the Midwest Archaeological Center, National Park Service, Lincoln, Nebraska).

Interaction Sphere – obsidian, copper, and exotic chert have been documented, but the major connection is Havana-style pottery. Village sites are often found on terraces along the Mississippi River, at mouths of tributaries, and mound sites are found on adjacent bluff tops (Fig. 2.16). Examples of this relationship include the FTD site (Benn 1978) and the McGregor mound complex which are part of Effigy Mounds National Monument in north-east Iowa (Benn and Stadler 2004). Farther south, also on the west side of the Mississippi river, the Wolfe village site (Straffin 1971) is associated with the Malchow and Poisel mound groups (Alex 2000). In an excellent summary of Iowa archaeology, Lynn Alex (2000) points out excavations at the Boone Mound in the central Des Moines River valley revealed the presence of a central crypt that is reminiscent of Hopewellian mounds along the eastern margin of the State.

The Hopewellian occupation of south-west Michigan and north-west Indiana was named the Goodall Focus by George Quimby (1941). The Goodall site in LaPorte County, Indiana was used to define this regional Hopewell manifestation, mainly because, with 22 mounds, it was the largest Hopewell mound group in the region. Based upon limited excavation data, mainly from looted mounds, Quimby recognized that ceramics found in the mounds of this region were similar to the Hopewell sites near Havana on the Illinois River. Quimby and other scholars viewed the small mound groups and associated occupation sites as representing a migration of people from the Illinois River valley to the south-east side of Lake Michigan. The Hopewell character of the Middle Woodland mounds in this region is best documented by excavations at the Norton Mounds in Grand Rapids, MI (Fig. 2.17) by the University of Michigan in 1963–1964 (Griffin *et al.* 1970).

Subsequent research, summarized by Mangold and Schurr (2006), Garland and Des Jardines (2006), and Brashler *et al.* (2006), has provided more details about the material culture and mortuary remains associated with this Middle Woodland occupation. The presence of exotic artifacts and elaborate mortuary deposits provides strong ties to the larger and better-known Hopewell occupations in Illinois. Research has shown that Middle Woodland sites in this region fall into two general periods: AD 1–200, the LaPorte phase, and AD 200–400, the Goodall phase (Mangold and Schurr 2006). Variation between river drainages may be sufficient to further subdivide the Middle Woodland occupation of this region as research continues. While the sites of this region certainly exhibit characteristics that are reminiscent of the Hopewell mounds and occupation sites in the Illinois River valley, they lack the monumental earthen architecture and massive ceremonial and mortuary deposits that have come to define Ohio Hopewell.

The western-most sites associated with Hopewell are found along the Missouri River in the area of Kansas City. Waldo Wedel (1938) recognized the similarity between mortuary remains and ceramic characteristics at the sites he was investigating north of Kansas City and Hopewell sites in the Illinois River valley. Wedel's excavations at the Renner site north of Kansas City revealed a large number of pits containing substantial food remains, along with numerous ceramics, plus stone and bone tools. Wedel recognized that some of the ceramics exhibited decorative treatment that was similar to Illinois Hopewell vessels, and subsequent research in the area (Wedel 1943) provided evidence about additional sites and

associated mounds. The mounds were found to be earthen mantles that covered a central grave pit that was built by piling stones around what was likely a log-lined crypt. The mortuary treatment and associated artifacts are meager in comparison to Hopewellian burials in other areas, but the ceramics and other artifacts found at the sites is indicative of Hopewell influence on the eastern margin of the Great Plains.

Top: **Fig. 2.16.** Bluff edge mounds along the Mississippi Valley, Clinton, Iowa (post-card, titled "Indian Mounds near Clinton, IA", C. D. Hunt Publisher, Germany).

Bottom: **Fig. 2.17.** The Norton Mound Group, Grand Rapids, Michigan. Excavations reported by Griffin *et al.* (1970) produced data to document Hopewell influence in south-western Michigan (post-card titled "Indian Mounds, Grand Rapids, Michigan", Wayne Paper Box & PRTG. Corp, Fort Wayne, IN).

Subsequent research has produced additional data (Johnson 1976; 1979; 1981; B. Logan 1990; 1993) about the distribution and character of the Kansas City Hopewellian sites in western Missouri and north-east Kansas. In a recent synthesis of this information, Brad Logan (2006) has observed that major Hopewellian settlements are found at the mouths of tributaries and specific upland settings in the Kansas City area. O'Brien and Wood (1998) view the Kansas City Hopewell complex as an indigenous development, but Logan (2006) notes that there are no documented local precedents to explain the abrupt appearance about AD 1 of Hopewellian characteristics in the Kansas City area. Logan notes that these characteristics are generally absent in the region, and may be attributed to a westward migration of Hopewellian people from Illinois. Logan (2006) proposes that migration up the Missouri River from Illinois could also explain the presence of other clusters of Hopewellian sites in central Missouri. More detailed analysis of the sites in and around Kansas City, particularly efforts to understand better their chronological placement, is essential to understanding how this western extent of Hopewellian sites relates to other Middle Woodland complexes in the Midwest.

One of the issues that challenged archaeologists for more than a century is how to identify and explain the variation in mound-building societies during the period between 500 BC and AD 500. This temporal-spatial problem is particularly acute in the region from Central Ohio River valley (including northern and central Kentucky) into the Upper Ohio River drainage and into Upstate New York. Within this region, archaeologists have classified most of the Early and Middle Woodland earthwork sites as either Adena or Hopewell. Since these archaeological complexes were originally defined on the basis of traits associated with type sites in the Scioto River–Paint Creek Region of Ohio, it is important to note that Adena and Hopewell do not appear together at any site in stratified context. Originally there was considerable disagreement about their chronological relationship, and the advent of radiocarbon dating has not fully resolved those problems. The situation is further complicated because both archaeological complexes are known primarily from mortuary contexts. Now that numerous radiocarbon samples have been dated from sites in this region (Maslowski *et al.* 1995: Lepper *et al.* 2014), it is generally agreed that Adena mounds, often surrounded by small circular embankments and ditches, appeared prior to Hopewell, but it is unclear whether the end of Adena coincides with the appearance of Hopewell.

Adena mounds and sacred circles are fairly common in northern and central Kentucky and southern Ohio (Fig. 2.18). With the exception of a few large and complex enclosure sites along the south side of the Ohio River at Portsmouth, Ohio, the vast majority of Early/Middle Woodland mound and earthwork complexes in Kentucky seem to be Adena. Adena mounds often cover a log tomb or crypt and may be surrounded by a circular or oval enclosure wall with an associated ditch. Circles of post-holes within some of the sacred circles may represent screens. Identification of Adena as a distinct mound-building complex is due to the work of Emerson Greenman (1932a) who generated a list of characteristics or traits for the Adena culture based upon data obtained from the Adena Mound (Mills 1902a; 1902b) on the Worthington property, north-west of Chillicothe, Ohio. As Griffin has observed, many sites that were classified as Adena shared only a handful of traits with the type-site and the definition of the Adena complex. Expansion of the use of the term Adena was part of an effort to better organize and classify the extensive mound research data collected by William S. Webb and subsequently the complex became widely known and accepted (Webb and Snow 1945; Webb and Baby 1957). More recent work by Berle Clay has helped to expose the great variety of earth and timber architectural characteristics that are

Fig. 2.18. The Miamisburg mound south of Dayton is one of the largest Adena mounds in Ohio and is preserved in a park by the Ohio Historical Society (photo: Pete Topping).

associated with the small circular and oval enclosures associated with Adena in the Ohio River valley (Clay 1986; 1987; 1988; 1998). This research has also led scholars to question whether Adena societies eventually, over time, developed larger and more complex programs of earthen architectural construction as seen in southern Ohio Hopewell, or if some groups south of the Ohio River continued to build the smaller sacred circle earthworks at the same time as the more complex and massive Ohio Hopewell geometric and hilltop enclosures were being constructed (Railley 1996).

In the area around Chillicothe there were quite a few mounds characteristic of Adena. In his original definition, Greenman (1932a) identified 18 mounds in Ross County, Ohio in addition to the type-site (the Adena Mound) as part of his definition of Adena culture. Webb and Snow (1945) identified four additional sites in Ross County in their book *The Adena People*. The Adena Mound was part of a larger mound group of about a dozen mounds located north-west of the city of Chillicothe in the mid-19th century. Greber (1991) calls this the Chillicothe Northwest Group and notes that it included the Miller or Carriage Factory Mound (Fig. 2.19), Story Mound (Fig. 2.20), and the Worthington Group of conjoined mounds. Several of these were excavated by Moorehead (1892; 1897a; 1897b) before Mills began his famous excavation of the Adena Mound itself.

Fig. 2.19. Excavations at the Carriage Factory or Miller Mound, north-west of Chillicothe, Ohio (reproduced from Moorehead 1899, courtesy of the Ohio History Connection).

Nom'i Greber (1991) attempted to unravel the differences between Adena and Hopewell with an analysis of the structure and content of these two type sites, located just a few miles apart in Ross County, Ohio. Her study shows that it is possible to distinguish between the largest and most complex Hopewell ceremonial deposits (Mound 25) and the simpler, but still impressive deposits within the Adena Mound. She notes that her comparative study of sites excavated in the early 20th century is complicated by a number of factors, including differing methods of recovery in the field, differing retention practices of objects between museums, and incomplete inventories and publications of original excavations. Greber's work shows that there is a difference between the structure and content of these two impressive ceremonial/mortuary deposits. She also emphasizes that Early and Middle Woodland people living in the different river drainages in southern Ohio and northern Kentucky were unique and autonomous populations and a clear understanding of the historical evolution of ceremonial practices and landscape constructions must be based upon comparing sequences in individual drainage basins.

Adena mounds and sacred circles are found throughout most of the upper Ohio River drainage, and are more common in West Virginia, Pennsylvania, and into New York. Hopewell mounds are less common but are known from this same

area. Hopewell mounds have been reported from the Moundville (Hemmings 1984) and Gallipolis Locks areas (Clay and Niquette 1992) of West Virginia. Hopewell mounds have also been reported in the Upper Ohio Valley of western Pennsylvania at McKees Rock mound near Pittsburgh (Dragoo 1963). In New York, William A. Ritchie identified a mortuary mound complex that he identified with Hopewell and named it Squawkie Hill after the mound site where it was identified (Ritchie 1938). Working largely before the availability of radiocarbon dating, Ritchie (1969) gave separate phase names to the associated habitation sites of the region. Now that radiocarbon dating has shown the contemporaneity of the Hopewellian mortuary mounds and campsites, Snow (1980) argues convincingly that they should all be part of the Canoe Point phase.

Fig. 2.20. Story Mound, Ross County, one of the largest surviving Adena mounds (photo courtesy of Hopewell Culture National Historical Park).

Time and Hopewell archaeology

Time is an essential element in the study and interpretation of the archaeological record. It is particularly important in the study of Ohio Hopewell archaeology. The mounds and earthworks of southern Ohio have been well known to the scientific community and the interested public for more than two centuries. The large number of large and complex earthen monuments in this region is truly impressive, and understanding their sequence or potential contemporaneity is at the heart of all models interpreting Ohio Hopewell archaeology.

The earliest writing about Ohio Hopewell mounds saw all the mounds as products of a single society, and few writers had any idea about the great time depth associated with the archaeological record of the Americas. In the last half-century, radiocarbon and other dating techniques have gradually shown that construction of mounds and other earthen monuments has a long history in the Eastern United States. We also recognize that there is tremendous diversity in the scale and morphology of these monumental landscapes. We can also hypothesize that not all of the ancient landscapes, particularly those associated with Ohio Hopewell, were built for the same purpose,

The first efforts to build a chronological framework for Ohio Hopewell earthen monuments involved the use of tree-rings. Numerous early writers reported the number of rings they counted on trees growing on earthen features (Moorehead 1934; Neuman 1962). William Henry Harrison even applied his observations about forest succession to argue for the great antiquity of the Ohio Hopewell earthen landscapes (Harrison 1838).

Much of what we believe we know about Ohio Hopewell is derived from excavation of mortuary mounds in the years prior to radiocarbon dating. Early radiocarbon dates on materials excavated by Warren K. Moorehead from Mound 25 in 1891–2 at the Hopewell Mound Group provided the first absolute estimates for the age of Ohio Hopewell (Griffin 1958). Subsequent dating of more recently excavated materials along with radiocarbon dating of additional museum specimens indicates that those parts of the archaeological record of the Eastern United States that is called Hopewell falls into the period between 200 BC and AD 400–450 (Dancey 2005; Neusius and Gross 2007). Unfortunately, this coarse chronological resolution has proven unsatisfactory for interpreting the relationship between the mounds and earthen enclosures that characterize the Ohio Hopewell era.

Stratigraphy is one of the earliest and most basic principles used to build chronological frameworks within the archaeological record. It has been highly effective in building a Middle Woodland chronology for the Illinois River valley. James B. Griffin used seriation of ceramic vessels from mortuary deposits to demonstrate that Illinois Hopewell ceramics developed from Havana ware about AD 1 (Griffin *et al.* 1970). Although few question that Ohio Hopewell represents the "zenith" of Middle Woodland cultural development, the evidence that Illinois Havana Hopewell preceded the same complex in Ohio is quite strong, and there is some evidence that Hopewellian sites in the Lower Valley may be the earliest of all.

Most of the early Ohio Hopewell mound excavations focused energy on exposing burial deposits at the base of mounds. The use of scrapers and horse and mule teams to pull down mound fill in sections offered only limited opportunities to study the earthen construction of the mound itself. This practice began in the 19th century and continued well into the 20th. Although the Mounds Exploration Division attempted to investigate a variety of sites (Thomas 1894), efforts to locate hamlets or village sites with stratified middens or other occupational deposits have been limited. Since much of what we know about Ohio Hopewell is derived from mound excavations, careful analysis of artifacts from these ceremonial and mortuary deposits have produced useful seriations that offer relative ordering of some site deposits.

The most widely accepted seriation study is of copper ear spools. These ornaments are considered a diagnostic characteristic of Hopewell culture throughout eastern North America. Although these are viewed as objects of personal adornment, they are not always found in association with human remains. In some instance they have been found as large ceremonial deposits under mounds without any human remains. Careful study of the construction and style attributes of these objects has produced a number of types that have been tested for temporal and spatial validity (Ruhl 1992; Ruhl and Seeman 1998). Although these types of studies have limited applicability beyond mortuary and ceremonial deposits, they do provide useful options for evaluating the relative temporal placement of mound deposits at major sites like Mound City, Hopewell Mound Group, and Turner.

The presence of obsidian artifacts in the ceremonial deposits at Ohio Hopewell sites has led to efforts to apply obsidian hydration dating to the problem of building an Ohio Hopewell chronology (Hatch *et al.* 1989; Hughes 1992; 2006; Stevenson *et al.* 1992; 2004). Initial scholarly interest in obsidian at Hopewell sites throughout eastern North America focused on determining its original source location. Griffin *et al.* (1969) provided convincing evidence that most of the Ohio Hopewell obsidian was obtained from the Obsidian Cliffs area of Wyoming and Yellowstone National

Park. Variability in the elemental composition of obsidian at Ohio Hopewell sites may indicate that a variety of different sources in the Wyoming area are represented, but it is also possible that the compositional variability from Obsidian Cliffs and nearby obsidian flows is not fully documented.

Obsidian hydration measurements from Mound City, Hopewell Mound Group, and Seip have yielded results that are comparable to radiocarbon dates from these same sites (Hatch *et al.* 1989; Stevenson *et al.* 2004). Interpretation of the obsidian hydration methods is complicated by issues associated with the treatment of the artifacts as part of their burial process. For example, obsidian artifacts at Mound City may have been exposed to extreme temperatures associated with the burning of ceremonial deposits prior to burial. James Gunderson (2012) estimates that some of the stone pipes at Mound City were incinerated at temperatures as high as perhaps 1000°C. Some of the obsidian also appears to have been exposed to high temperatures, which almost certainly affected the hydration of the artifact surface. While this technique may yet be of great value in sorting the ages of artifacts within Ohio Hopewell sites, more research on hydration rates and measurement of more artifacts are needed.

Throughout much of eastern North America, the Woodland and later periods of prehistory are characterized by the presence of ceramics. In many regions ceramic styles and technology have been dated and now serve as horizon markers that may be used to frame regional chronologies and estimate the ages of features and site deposits. Extensive research in the Lower Illinois River valley and the American Bottom areas of south-western Illinois has produced a particularly strong ceramic sequence. Unfortunately, ceramics associated with Ohio Hopewell sites are fairly non-descript and generally lack diagnostic decorative characteristics. It is also worth noting that most Ohio Hopewell ceramic vessels are known mainly from small fragments. Very few relatively complete ceramic vessels have been recovered, making the definition of ceramic types highly dependent upon attribute analysis from sherds.

Definitions of temporally diagnostic ceramic patterns have been difficult to develop. Olaf Prufer (1968) conducted the initial study of Ohio Hopewell ceramics and his broad series types are still generally in use despite widely acknowledged concerns about sampling and quantification. In an analysis of ceramics from the Twin Mounds West site, located in the south-west corner of Ohio, Rebecca Hawkins (1996) observed that ceramics classified in the Miami series (as defined by Prufer 1968) exhibited an increase in cord-marking on the exterior surface of vessels through time, and a corresponding decrease in plain exterior surfaces. This is a pattern that may prove more widespread, but to be truly useful we must know more about the character of complete vessels. In many areas of the Midwestern United States, it is common for vessels to be partially cord-marked, with the remainder of the exterior surface being plain or smooth. There may well be a temporal trend to surface treatment of Ohio Hopewell ceramics, but until more complete individual vessels are collected for study, it is unclear whether this pattern extends beyond this single site.

A number of current scholars have offered models that synthesize and interpret aspects of Ohio Hopewell society (e.g. Bernardini 2004; Byers 2004; Dancey and

Pacheco 1997; Carr and Case 2005; Case and Carr 2008; Romain 2000; Ruby *et al.* 2005; Yerkes 2005). These models offer an impressive array of ideas about social organization, settlement patterns, labor requirements of earthwork construction, the purpose of monumental earthen enclosures, and the Hopewell worldview. All of these models make assumptions regarding the temporal relationship between large Ohio Hopewell earthwork sites. The better-known Ohio Hopewell sites are large, complex, and have been exposed to relatively limited field study since the advent of radiocarbon dating. With the exception of the Pollock Works near Dayton (Riordan 1995; 1996), it is not possible to confidently identify the construction sequence for earthen walls and/or mounds at any single site. Chronological ordering of sites is at the heart of most interpretive models relating to Ohio Hopewell, and yet the assumptions on which chronological ordering is based are generally not substantiated by a solid empirical database.

N'omi Greber (2003, 89) summarizes the problems with the current understanding of Ohio Hopewell chronology:

> "Lack of chronological control in terms of human generations prevents truly evaluating not only models of widespread interactions but, more especially, those of relationships within Ohio Hopewell. How can one evaluate the social effort put into the construction of an extensive enclosure if the length of time it took to build the walls is not known? How can one determine possible changes through time in social structure, community plan, or subsistence base associated with the 'rise' and 'fall' of Hopewell if one cannot distinguish ancestor from descendant in a time frame of human generations? With the current technology, radiocarbon dates cannot determine a single generation, except possibly with large numbers of assays from the same provenience."

In the early days of radiocarbon dating, obtaining a general age from a sample to demonstrate the approximate age of a site was often sufficient. As we continue to ask more sophisticated questions of the archaeological record, the need for more precise dating has become apparent. Ohio Hopewell archaeology suffers from a disarray of radiocarbon results. For many years, archaeologists have simply ignored dates that did not meet their preconceived ideas about what a particular site or feature should date. They have also been too quick to submit a datable sample without considering how that sample was created and how it was deposited in the location where it was collected. Wood charcoal from trash pits and middens has more probability to be derived from another unknown context or event than does charcoal collected from a hearth. Submitting a sample of burned wood will likely produce a radiocarbon age, but if we are uncertain as to the context and origin of the sample, it is often better to simply not process the sample. Extreme care in sampling can produce an accurate radiocarbon chronology, and the problems associated with Ohio Hopewell radiocarbon dates are more often due to uncertain contexts than problems with the process of radiocarbon dating.

The majority of excavations at most of the large Ohio Hopewell ceremonial centers were conducted prior to the use of radiocarbon dating in archaeology. Consequently, many of the dates that have been generated were processed from samples taken from museum collections. Brown (2004, 160) reports nine radiocarbon dates from Mound 10, Mound 13, and Feature 35 under the south-east embankment wall at Mound City. The difficulty with dating macrobotanical remains from older collections is well illustrated in these results. Five dates from Mound 13, three from post- holes and two from features in the floor under the mound, produced uncorrected radiocarbon ages ranging from 1034±123 to 2500±60 BP. It is highly unlikely that this sub-mound-building was in use for more than a millennium, and the five samples are distributed widely within these two extremes. The two dates from Feature 12A under Mound 10 are fairly compatible, but the two dates from Feature 35 under the south-east embankment wall span about 450 years. The relatively large difference between these latter two dates is understandable, because much of the material under the south-east embankment wall was midden that had been collected from another location and placed there to form the base of the embankment wall (Brown and Baby 1966; Brown 1994; 2012).

Brown (2004) observes that of the nine radiocarbon dates from Mound City, four fall within the Middle Woodland period, with a 95% probability that the weighted and corrected average of these dates falls between AD 228 and AD 339. He has clearly documented that the site has some unknown time depth based upon the different orientation of sub-mound structures, presence of time sensitive artifacts, and the incorporation of older Hopewell archeological remains into the south-east embankment wall. Unfortunately, radiocarbon dating objects from older museum collections has not provided much resolution for this problem. To be fair, Lepper *et al.* (2014) have used textile and bark fragments from the central tomb of the Adena mound to effectively date this important feature. In our efforts to unravel the temporal details of the Ohio Hopewell archaeological record, we must also cope with the probability that many of these ceremonial centers are complex sites that may have been used over fairly long periods of time, perhaps even millennia.

There is a very strong tendency to assume that all artifacts and features in close proximity to mounds and earthworks constructed by Ohio Hopewell people were also part of the Ohio Hopewell record. Although recent excavations at many sites have produced evidence that earlier and more recent people used these same landforms, the dramatic presence of monumental earthen architecture has often dominated the analytical thinking of archaeologists. Assumptions about the duration of time associated with construction of a single mound or a geometric earthwork are often lacking empirical support. This will be considered in more detail later in this volume, but there is evidence that mounds and earthen enclosures were built in stages, and may represent multiple generations of participation. There is even evidence at one site that part of a large earthen wall was either rebuilt or repaired by later people. Evidence like this only reinforces the need to base assumptions about the chronology of Ohio Hopewell ceremonial landscapes on some factual evidence.

As research questions about Ohio Hopewell become more sophisticated and specific, the need for more precise chronological controls within sites and between sites becomes more imperative. Virtually all of the current models interpreting aspects of Ohio Hopewell archaeology make assumptions about sequence and/or contemporaneity of various large earthwork sites. The bases for these chronological assumptions range from time sensitive artifacts from mounds associated with the earthworks to the morphological configuration and size of

Hopewell moundbuilders

The tradition of moundbuilding by Native Americans had a very long history. The earliest known mounds date back 7000 years, beginning with the shell middens of the Archaic Period (*ca.* 5600–700 BC (see Fig. 1.13 for a time chart) and extending into the Contact period when Native communities in the south-east, such as the Calusa, first encountered European colonizers in the 16th–17th centuries AD. Throughout that time mounds were constructed by many of the major cultural groupings across a large part of North America, in a myriad of sizes, forms and concentrations, employing various construction techniques which exhibited distinct regional preferences, and can be found with or without burials.

In regions such as the Illinois and Mississippi river valleys Hopewell mounds are most often located on prominent steep spurs overlooking the valley floor. In Ohio, Hopewell mounds are found in a variety of topographic zones and occur in a range of sizes from circular examples just a few feet high to large, elongated types which form an integral part of many of the complex, structured landscapes discussed here. Numbers can vary in any one location from a single example to the 24 mounds recorded within the square enclosure at Mound City.

Ohio Hopewell mounds were placed over a variety of ceremonial features including what have been interpreted as enclosures, charnel houses/crypts made of stone or logs, or complex buildings containing disarticulated and articulated bones. The burial assemblages which accompanied the deceased often included rich, exotic grave goods comprising caches of mica, elaborate ceremonial regalia, copper gorgets and axes, effigy smoking

This photo shows the 1963 excavation of the charnel house found beneath Mound 10 at Mound City (Brown 1979). This building measured 49.5 × 43.3 ft (15.1 × 13.2 m) with an H-shaped group of internal supports. The site was heavily damaged by an army road but one cremation was recovered with parts of a copper headdress; an empty pit; and an oval burial pit containing the cremated remains of an adolescent interred on a bed of charcoal lying upon a bark sheet. This was accompanied by an array of typical Hopewell grave goods including objects of shell, pearl and copper. An unburnt human finger bone was also found suggesting the processing of bodies before cremation in this general area.

This excavation photograph shows part of an altar discovered beneath one of the mounds at Mound City. Altars formed an important element of Hopewell burial ceremonialism and were part of the ritualized cycle through which a body passed on its journey from death to deposition.

A typical log-built crypt found at the Hopewell Mound Group. Crypts are generally much smaller than charnel houses with more limited space for processing bodies, and access is through a removable roof. Crypts also differ from charnel houses in that although both types of site store bodies and grave goods, only the charnel houses normally promote social distinctions through display of the dead.

Stone crypt at the Hazlett Mound, Flint Ridge which lies ca. 1.5 miles (2.4 km) from the main flint quarries. When investigated by Mills in 1918–19 the mound was 85–90 ft (26–27.5 m) in diameter (Mills 1921). A flint wall 6 ft (1.8 m) high enclosed a roughly square area 16 ft (4.8 m) wide which contained the remains of two skeletons, one disturbed by previous explorers. The undisturbed burial, which had been placed on a cloth over bark matting, was accompanied by classic Hopewell artifacts made of copper and shell and an ornament crafted from the lower jaw of a gray wolf. A large hearth in the center of this room and post-molds suggested that the structure had originally been roofed. Overall, this building probably represents the remains of a Hopewell charnel house which had subsequently been buried beneath the mound.

pipes and obsidian artifacts (see text boxes in Chapter 4). Traces of fires in 'crematory basins' are also found. Together these indicate lengthy episodes of burial ceremonialism with the charnel houses/crypts and other structures being revisited and reused on numerous occasions before finally being abandoned and/or demolished and sealed beneath the earthen mounds. Several excavated mounds have revealed over 100 burials. The mounds were usually constructed from a series of different layers of soil, sand and grave, highly variable in texture and color but clearly deliberately chosen, probably to represent symbolically elements of Hopewell cosmology . Artifacts or other features were rarely incorporated in the body of the mound itself, although later people occasionally did bury their dead in the upper levels of Hopewell mounds (the so-called 'Intrusive Mound' Culture).

earthen walls (DeBoer 1997; Byers 2004). When radiocarbon and other dates are available from these sites, they often do not fit the preconceived chronological ideas built into the interpretive model.

This is illustrated in a recent paper on the labor requirements associated with construction of five Ohio Hopewell tripartite earthworks. Bernardini (2004) presents a compelling argument that the amount of labor required to build the large Ohio Hopewell earthworks in the Scioto River–Paint Creek area of southern Ohio could not have been accomplished by autonomous local populations. Bernardini bases his energetic analysis on the amount of labor required to build a large earthwork in ten years or less. Assuming that all the large earthworks in this region were built in less than one generation, and assuming population densities did not greatly exceed those reported by historic Indian groups in the Eastern United States, then the labor pools in the immediate vicinity of the large earthworks would definitely not be sufficient to account for all the mass earthmoving needed to build these monuments. While he does provide some evidence to support the relatively brief episodes of earthwork construction at other sites, there are no radiocarbon dates or geoarchaeological data directly related to construction of any of the five tripartite earthworks that are the subject of his study.

Carr (2005b) argues that the tripartite configuration of these earthwork sites combined with three clusters of burials found under mounds at some of the earthworks reflects social alliances. Carr (2005b: 305) admits that current evidence for the construction and use of tripartite earthworks in this region is insufficient to affirm their contemporaneity, but he argues that the presence of time sensitive artifacts and radiocarbon dates from mortuary structures under mounds at two of the five sites place them between the late AD 200s to the early AD 400s. Greber (1997: 215) estimates that the sub-mound structure under the Seip-Pricer mound, located within tripartite Seip Earthworks, was used for approximately three generations. Thus, both Carr and Greber interpret a somewhat longer period of construction and use for tripartite earthworks in this region than does Bernardini.

Each of these writers offers some interesting and useful ideas about the nature and meaning of these five tripartite earthworks in the Scioto River–Paint Creek region. Unfortunately, at this time we simply lack data to determine whether these sites were built by a single generation, or even if they were built within the same century. We do not know if the mounds were built after the enclosure walls were completed, or as in the case of Mound City, perhaps the construction of the enclosure walls were among the final significant activities conducted at the site in the Hopewell era.

The limitation of the chronological framework for Ohio Hopewell archaeology is a major obstacle to the productive interpretation of all aspects of the record for this period. This was a major consideration as we began plans for a multi-year study of the Hopeton Earthworks in the mid-1990s. We believed that until we could develop a reasonable chronological model for the construction of the monumental earthen features forming a single large geometric enclosure, chronological ordering of the dozens of other large earthen monuments in this region would remain hypothetical. Fortunately, our work at the Hopeton Earthworks has produced enough radiocarbon dates from good archaeological contexts to begin to build a radiometric chronology for the Ohio Hopewell archaeological record in the Scioto River valley.

In a lecture to the Midwest Archaeological Conference, Mark Seeman (2011) reminded us of the multi-scaled character of time in the Ohio Hopewell archaeological record. He observed that there are at least three different temporal concepts that were important to Ohio Hopewell people: daily practices, seasonal cycles, and generational memories and events. All of these temporal scales are used in different interpretations of Ohio Hopewell archaeology, but the differences between them are not always distinguished in interpretive arguments. We may wish to have an absolute chronology that can generate a tightly calibrated culture history for Ohio Hopewell site features and artifacts, but the limitations of radiocarbon and other dating techniques do not permit us to achieve this level of specificity at present.

To effectively interpret the amazing record of Ohio Hopewell archaeology, we must make better use of the techniques and skills available to us. As Seeman (2011) aptly noted, we must obtain scientifically accurate dates from carefully chosen contexts and use them with a wider range of relative dating evidence (geoarchaeology, obsidian hydration, archaeomagnetism) to understand better the generational time scale that current anthropological models require to better interpret the social organization of Ohio Hopewell societies. Our ability to unravel the complexity of Ohio Hopewell ceremonial landscapes is totally dependent upon our ability to obtain accurate dates from clear and well-defined contexts. Radiocarbon dates obtained from charred wood collected from a large deposit of Hopewell artifacts help us understand the general age of Ohio Hopewell culture, but addressing the more complex questions of interest to current scholars requires that we carefully evaluate the context of every artifact and feature we encounter. A more refined Ohio Hopewell chronology will only be obtained from data collected in current and future excavations. Heritage museum collections still have great value (Lepper *et al.* 2014), but very few datable materials were collected from contexts that can tell us how many generations participated in the construction of the Newark Earthworks or any other Ohio Hopewell earthen monument.

Energy analysis: How many people did it take to build Ohio Hopewell ceremonial landscapes

From almost the beginning of written observations about the earthen enclosures of southern Ohio, people speculated about the size of the population that was involved in their construction. Modern anthropologists and archaeologists use energy analysis (Abrams 1989) to calculate how much human labor was required to conduct tasks like earthen monument construction. Obviously, the more that is known about an earthen monument, like the source of materials used in construction, the more accurate the analysis of the human energy output will be.

Gerard Fowke was among the first to attempt to calculate the amount of human labor required for monument building in southern Ohio. Fowke, a native of Ohio, assisted Cyrus Thomas and the Mound Exploration Division, Bureau of Ethnology, with their multi-year study of the mound-builder question. He was hired by the

Bureau of Ethnology as an assistant archaeologist in 1891 and subsequently conducted fieldwork throughout the Eastern United States. Cyrus Thomas (1903) cited him as an authority on mound construction in his overview of American archaeology. Although they worked together on numerous mound investigations in Ohio, Warren K. Moorehead seemed offended by Fowke's critique of earlier writings about Ohio archaeology (Moorehead 1902). He disagreed with Fowke's interpretations that the societies that built the great Hopewell earthworks of southern Ohio were at the same level as historic tribal groups like the Paiutes or Comanches.

In, *Archaeological History of Ohio,* Fowke was strongly critical of early speculation that the mounds and monuments could only have been built by vast armies of workers with strong leadership and hierarchy. Fowke was also highly critical of writers who assumed that building materials for the earthen monuments were acquired at great distances from the location of the monument and carried there to be deposited in walls or mounds. Based upon his direct experience at many Ohio earthen mounds, he says "Neither earth nor stone is ever carried more than a few hundred feet, unless in very small quantities, for a particular purpose; as making an 'altar,' for example." (Fowke 1902).

Early writers speculated about the number of people and the amount of time a population would invest in building large mounds. J. P. MacLean (1879) used the largest mound in Butler County, Madison township, Ohio as an example:

> "Its altitude is forty-three feet [13.1 m] with a circular base of five hundred and eleven feet [155.75 m]. The hypothenuse is eighty-eight feet [26.8 m], the contents being eight hundred and twenty-four thousand four hundred and eighty cubic feet [23,349 m³]. At twenty-two cubic feet [0.62 m³] per load, this gives thirty-seven thousand four hundred and seventy-six wagon loads, which allowing ten loads per day, would take one man twelve years (not including Sundays) to remove the mound say a distance of one mile [1.6 km] (Dr. J. B Owsley)". (McLean 1879: 294)

Fowke argued that these speculative estimates contributed further to the mythology associated with the mound-builders. He tried to make the task for earthen construction understandable in terms of logical estimates for what people could accomplish. Using the same mound considered by MacLean, Fowke observed:

> "If the altitude and base are correctly given, the hypotenuse is almost exactly 92 feet [28 m]; if the base and hypotenuse are as stated, the height must be about 34 feet [10.4 m]. There is on the assumption that the slope of the mound is uniform and in a straight line from summit to base; if the surface of the mound be curved, as must naturally be the case, then the assumed height the hypotenuse, if measured on the ground, must be greater than 92 feet [28 m]; or if measurement of 88 feet [27.8 m] be correct the elevation is less than 34 feet [10.4 m]. Accepting, however, the figures as to the altitude and circumference, we find the solid content of a cone having these dimensions is in round numbers 297, 800 cubic feet [8434 m³]; and the content of the segment of a sphere of these measurements, which is larger than a mound exposed the elements could possible be, is about 488,000 cubic feet [13,820 m³]. Thus we see that the mound is certainly less than three-fifths of the asserted size. On the other hand a cubic foot of perfectly dry common loam, which is material composing most of the mounds, weighs about eighty pounds [36.3 kg]; the weight varies somewhat according to the moisture and to the way it is packed, but the above will fall very close to the average when it is allowed settle naturally.

If we admit, for argument, the preposterous intimation that the average distance which this earth is carried is one mile [1.6 km] – though why an Indian or any one else would carry dirt a mile when he could get it within a few rods, is past human understanding – then if we suppose a man to walk, with a load, three miles per hour [4.8 km] he must in a day of ten hours travel thirty miles [48.3 km] and must carry for half that distance a load of 117 pounds [53.1 kg], in order to deposit upon the mound as much as one 'wagon load' of twenty-two cubic feet [0.62 m³] in a day. In order to complete his allotment of ten wagon loads per day, which out author has assigned him he would, if we change only one of the factors in the problem have to walk thirty miles an hour; or carry over 1,170 pounds [530.7 kg] at a load; or work one hundred hours in a day. No evidence has yet been discovered to justify the supposition that any of the Mound-builders possessed such a degree of speed strength, or endurance!" 1901: 83–84).

Using his experience in excavating Ohio mounds, Fowke further noted:

"Observations in a number of mounds indicate that the average load as carried in during the construction, was not far from half a cubic foot [0.01 m³]; if any difference the amount is a little more. Assuming this amount as approximately the load, the weight will be about forty pounds [18.1 kg] for loam and about fifty pounds [22.7 kg] for sand; which is about as much as a man will want to carry for any considerable distance. By carrying thirty loads a day of this size – a reasonable estimate, for such an amount – a laborer would add fifteen cubic feet [0.43 m³] to the pile every day. If we allow 450,000 cubic feet [12,744 m³] for the solidity of the mound in question – which is certainly beyond the actual amount – one hundred men will complete it in 300 working days; that is, within one year. Not a yard of this earth need be carried more than 600 feet [183 m]; for if a circle be laid off with this radius and the earth removed to a uniform depth of a small fraction less than five inches [12.7 cm] (excluding that portion of the area which the mound stands) the amount so obtained will be ample for the construction of the tumulus.

Supposed we put the calculation in a different form. A regular cone twenty feet [6.1 m] high and one hundred feet [30.5 m] in diameter at the base, will contain 1940 cubic yards [54.9 m³]. For one mound that will exceed this size there are a hundred that will fall below it. Taking it as the average, and accepting the usual estimate of 10,000 as correct the entire amount of earth – and stone – in the mounds of the State will be about 19,400,000 cubic yards [549,408 m³].

A regular enclosure 1,000 feet [304.8 m] square or 1,275 feet [388.6 m] in diameter, measuring twenty feet [6.1 m] in breadth at the top, forty feet [12.2 m] at the base and six feet high [1.8 m], with four gateways each twenty-five feet wide [7.6 m], will contain 26,000 cubic yards [736.3 m³]. It is doubtful whether any one, except two or three hill-top forts, is so large. The equivalent of four hundred such will fully equal the contents of all enclosures, making in all about 30,000,000 cubic yards [849,600 m³] for the entire solid contents of aboriginal remains in Ohio. No one familiar with them will dispute the liberality of these figures.

The lenticular masses noticed in so many mounds, each of which represents the amount carried in at a load, vary in volume from a peck to two pecks [8.8–17.6 litres]; if the average load be taken at one-half a cubic foot [0.01 m³], it well represent almost the mean between these figures. It would require 104,760 such loads to complete the mound. Twenty of these loads would be an easy task for one day; with fifty persons continually at work, 1,000 loads would be piled up each day. Consequently one hundred and five working days would see the mound completed.

With the same force working in the same way, an embankment of the size above given could be finished in 1404 days.

But a village which would require an enclosure of such magnitude could furnish a much larger force of workmen; if 200 were steadily engaged, the wall could be easily finished within a year; while with the same number, less than a month would be needed for the mound.

On the estimate of 30,000,000 cubic yards [849,600 m³] for the prehistoric works of the State, one thousand men, each working three hundred days in a year, and carrying one wagon load of earth or stone in a day, could construct all the works in Ohio within a century." (Fowke 1901: 84–8)

In reading *An Archaeological History of Ohio*, we can easily discern that the author is still striving to end speculation about the origin of the mound-builders. We can certainly share his frustration about the speculative nature of many early accounts, particularly a discussion by Frederick Larkin about the construction of the mounds at Cahokia in west-central Illinois:

"one thousand men could not have performed the great labor' of erecting all the Cahokia group in a generation. If one thousand men were employed upon these great works for forty or fifty years it would surely have taken nearly twice that number to have supplied them with food, clothing, fuel and other necessaries during that long period of time, and then again, we must suppose a numerous train composed of women and children and feeble persons ... which had to be fed, clothed and maintained." (Larkin 1880: 143)

Larkin then proposes that the prehistoric labor shortage at Cahokia may have been solved by the use of animal labor.

"My theory that the prehistoric races used, to some extent, the great American elephant or mastodon, I believe is new. ... Finding the form of an elephant engraved upon a copper relic some six inches long and four wide, in a mound on the Red House Creek, in the year 1854, and represented in harness with a sort of breast-collar with tugs reaching past the hips, first led me to adopt that theory. That the great beast was contemporary with the Mound-builders is conceded by all, and also that his bones and those of his master are crumbling together in the ground.

It is a wonder, and has been since the great mounds have been discovered, how such immense works could have been built by human hands. To me it is not difficult to believe that those people tamed the monster of the forest and made him a willing slave to their superior intellectual power. If such was the case, we can imagine that tremendous teams have been driven to and fro in the vicinity of their great works, tearing up trees by the roots, or marching with their armies into the field of battle amidst showers of poisoned arrows." (Larkin 1880: preface and p. 3)

As Moorehead (1902) wrote in the review of his book, Gerard Fowke was overly critical of 19th century writers who did not have access to the vast amount of data generated by the Bureau of Ethnology Mounds Exploration Division. Ironically, many of the observations and interpretations offered by Fowke (1902) have been revised or rejected by more contemporary studies. Like his archaeological contemporaries and many subsequent generations of Ohio archaeologists, Fowke believed that the large mounds and enclosures must have been associated with large villages. These villages, which have never been located, are fundamental assumptions in his pioneering effort at energy and labor analysis associated with Ohio Hopewell ceremonial landscapes.

Thirty years later in his own synthesis of Ohio archaeology, *The Mound-builders*, Henry C. Shetrone relied heavily on Fowke's calculations and logic in estimating the labor invested in building the giant mound at the Seip Earthworks:

> "This expenditure of labor not only has been a matter of wonder and speculation, but has received rather serious consideration, for the most part by those who have recognized, quite properly, the importance of correcting early imaginative theories regarding the mound-building peoples. As an example, is the estimate of a prominent archaeologist, who, by careful mathematical calculations, showed that a conical mound 20 feet [6.1 m] high, 100 feet [30.5 m] in diameter at the base, and containing a trifle less than 2,000 cubic yards [56.6 m³] could be constructed by fifty laborers under primitive conditions in slightly more than 100 days. These calculations assume that the primitive workman would carry an average of one-half a cubic foot [0.01 m³] per load, equivalent to 45 pounds [20.4 kg] in weight, and that the distance traveled to obtain the earth should permit him to contribute at least twenty such loads per day. In the case of larger mounds, particularly as the growing structure increased in height, the individual laborer's daily contribution would be decreased. The writer's observations in connection with mound exploration, checked by careful measurement and weighing of individual loads of earth composing the tumuli, led to the belief that the primitive workman seldom carried loads above 20 or 25 pounds [9.1/11.3 kg] in weight, presumably for the reason that the primitive carrying baskets were not adapted to greater strain.
>
> Computing the time required for construction of earthworks under primitive conditions, however, is much like figuring an extended automobile trip on paper. In practice the estimates usually fall short of actuality. If it could be assumed that each individual worker engaged in erecting a mound was 100 per cent efficient; that he expended the full eight or ten hours each day for the entire period; and that weather and other factors remained constantly favorable, then such calculations would be much more dependable. Assuming, however, that the figures cited are reasonable accurate, and that fifty workmen would construct a mound containing 2,000 cubic yards [56.6 m³] of earth within a period of approximately 100 working days, then we find that the Seip Mound, with a cubic content of 20,000 yards [566.4 m³], should be built by fifty workmen in 1,000 days. By varying the number of workmen, guessing the number of days in each year on which they could or would work, and making allowances for other factors entering into the primitive human equation, some idea of the time required for mound construction may be gained. In a mound 30 feet [9.1 m] in height, like the Seip Mound, the labor naturally would become more arduous as the prospective mound increased in height, and the requisite time would be much longer.
>
> The same authority, computing the cubic contents of all the mounds and earthworks in the state of Ohio to be 30,000,000 cubic yards [849,600 m³], finds that a thousand men working 300 days in the year, each contributing the equivalent of one wagonload of earth daily, would accomplish the task of building them within a century. No small labor this, if the estimate is accepted as reasonable; and when it is applied to the probably 100,000 artificial earthworks of the entire mound area, the aggregate of labor, energy, and industry becomes surprising to contemplate."
> (Shetrone 1930: 41–3)

Any labor analysis of monumental earthen construction is inevitably based on certain assumptions. Fowke based part of his estimate of daily work-load potential on his observation of the volume of individual basket-loads in mound fills. Unfortunately, his estimation of what a person might carry in a day is based on freight haulers of the late 19th century, and did not really have any direct connection to mound construction. This has been partly resolved in a paper by Charles Erasmus who conducted experiments in mound construction with paid laborers in Mexico (Erasmus 1965).

Erasmus noted that availability of building material is a critical element of monument construction world-wide. He also notes that it is almost universally assumed that monument construction is always associated with some form of food production. In an analysis of Mayan swidden agriculture, Morley and Brainerd (1956) estimated that basic subsistence needs could be met in only 48 days of farming per year. The assumption being that a surplus to support public works projects could be easily achieved.

The experiment that Erasmus conducted was at Las Bocas, Sonora, Mexico, where he measured the work accomplishment of paid laborers using simulated prehistoric techniques in excavating earth, carrying it, and depositing it in a pile. The experiment showed that work performance diminished rapidly after 5 hours in a day. Erasmus' workers excavated and carried loads that averaged 28 kg and he measured their rate of achievement carrying those loads 50 m and 100 m before depositing them in a pile. The experiment had one person digging up earth and one carrying it. The team that carried their load 50 m made an average of 206 trips in a 5 hour day, while the team carrying 100 m made an average of 116 trips in the equivalent time. The estimated volume of their two-person workday was respectively 3.62 m^3 and 2.05 m^3.

Wesley Bernardini (2004) used an energy analysis of five tripartite Hopewell monuments in the Scioto River valley of southern Ohio: Seip, Baum, Frankfort, Liberty, and Works East. Each of these is formed by three conjoined geometric enclosures. While they differ in the scale, morphology, and placement of the geometric shapes, they also possess a remarkable similarity. In a region where Hopewell earthworks are noted for their surprising variety of shapes and forms, these five are remarkable for their comparability of size, scale, and form. Their similarity is such that some authors believe there was close interaction between the people who built them (Greber1997: 219). Bernardini reports that the late James Marshall, a well-known surveyor of Ohio Hopewell earthworks, told him that he believed the five sites had been laid out by the same person.

Bernardini used his experience at the Hopeton Earthworks to estimate the size and shape of embankment walls at the five tripartite earthworks, and noted that the major tasks in constructing them would be digging up dirt and carrying it to the desired point of deposit. He also notes that, at Hopeton and other nearby sites, there is evidence that the natural topsoil was removed before the wall was actually built at that position. Using these factors, he uses the labor estimates recorded by Erasmus (1965) and calculates the work effort required to build a series of large monuments in the Scioto drainage. Bernardini estimates that work crews of about 200 people working 20–25 days per year would require ten years to build each of

Fig. 2.21. Mound A, Poverty Point, Louisiana (photo: author).

the tripartite earthworks. He concludes that the population density associated with the dispersed population model that is now widely accepted for Ohio Hopewell people would not be sufficient to construct all of these sites. He proposes that a larger regional-network of people must have contributed labor to the construction of the larger tripartite earthworks.

Labor estimates for the construction of Pinson Mounds (Mainfort 2013) indicate substantial amounts of labor were invested by small-scale societies in building monumental earthen landscape features. Mainfort argues construction of the largest Middle Woodland mound ever constructed, along with about 11 other mounds and numerous earthen embankment features, was likely accomplished with the aid of pilgrims who came to Pinson from across the South-east. Construction of the earthen landscape at Pinson likely was accomplished by numerous generations, perhaps spanning several hundred years.

The construction of Mound A at Poverty Point (Fig. 2.21) represents an earlier (Late Archaic) example of hunter-gatherer societies mobilizing a large labor force for a short period of time to construct an important ceremonial landscape feature (Ortmann and Kidder 2013). Geoarchaeological evidence from Mound A failed to yield evidence of pedogenic activity or erosion in the structure of the mound that might indicate that it had been built over a period of time when it would have been exposed to these natural processes. Geoarchaeological studies also indicate that the mound was not simply built by piling up dirt, but involved substantial planning and selection of materials. Ortmann and Kidder (2013) estimate that the large mound was built by several thousand people in about 30–90 days. This would have required drawing volunteers from a fairly large area, and the authors propose this ritual activity was motivated by situational leadership with a need to integrate a large regional population.

Estimating the energy or labor required to construct monumental earthen landscapes is certainly a worthwhile task and has utility in estimating the network of people who participated in their construction. Most estimates make calculations based upon two tasks: digging earth and putting it in a container, and carrying that earth to a location and depositing it in a specific place. However, ongoing analysis of Ohio Hopewell earthen landscape construction is providing substantial evidence that much more effort and thought went into building monumental earthworks than these two simple tasks. There is also the difficult problem of estimating how many years were required to build individual earthworks. We will consider what evidence exists to support some of these assumptions in more detail in Chapters 3 and 4. There are two issues that are rarely incorporated into models of earthwork labor construction: vegetative clearing and monument maintenance. We will return to these topics in Chapter 6.

Before leaving this consideration of energy analysis, we must return to the debate about the settlement and subsistence practices of the local populations that built and maintained these vast constructed landscapes. Central to understanding how these great earthen monuments were built is the question: Where did Hopewell people live and how were they organized?

As noted in the first chapter, one of the more basic tenets of anthropological theory has been that construction of large community features and monuments coincides with the adoption of food production practices and the creation of a surplus. The monumental character of the Ohio Hopewell earthworks has led most early observers to assume that they were built by at least a moderately large population, and almost certainly a civilized population that was in conflict with the savage people that surrounded them (Silverberg 1968). Elsewhere in our discussion, we noted that the respected early anthropologist Lewis Henry Morgan (1881) believed the High Bank Works was the foundation for pueblo-like apartments where the population of the site must have lived. Whether the large earthworks were cities or villages, early observers consistently assumed that the people who built these great earthen complexes must have lived in towns or villages. Anthropological theory had few examples of monumental community features being built by mobile hunters and foragers.

Most of the early Hopewell archaeologists believed that villages were located in reasonable proximity to the large enclosures. In a few instances, like Fort Ancient, early archaeological investigations (Moorehead 1890) discovered large cemetery areas within or near the enclosure, which was interpreted to mean that people lived there and buried their ancestors in proximity to their homes. Work at the Hopewell site (Moorehead 1922) and Baum (Mills 1906a; 1906b) also yielded evidence that was interpreted to represent village remains in proximity to large enclosures. Later analysis would reveal that in all these cases, the occupation evidence found in or near large enclosures were the refuse and debris of either earlier or later populations.

Sedentary farmers or mobile foragers?

While mounds and earthworks are the most visible aspect of the Ohio Hopewell archeological record, scholars have long assumed that the people who built the great earthen ceremonial landscapes must have lived in or near these important centers. The assumption that Hopewell earthwork centers were built by sedentary villagers is firmly rooted in the writings of early anthropologists (Morgan 1881) who assumed that agriculture and sedentism were necessary to generate enough surplus food and other essentials to permit people to make significant investments in public architecture (Fig. 2.22). The presence of village sites near the large ceremonial centers was implicit in the research of many early Ohio Hopewell scholars. James B. Griffin (1996), one of the most knowledgeable and respected of all Ohio Hopewell experts clung to his belief that there were villages at some of these sites throughout his career. It is worth noting that habitation areas or residential sites are found near Hopewellian mound and earthwork sites in the

Fig. 2.22. Lewis Henry Morgan (1881) proposed that the builders of the High Bank Works created the embankment walls as a foundation for their houses, and the enclosure served as a plaza.

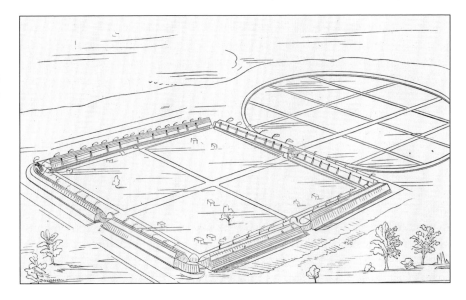

Lower Illinois and Lower Wabash valleys (Ruby *et al.* 2005). Understanding how and where the people who built the Ohio Hopewell ceremonial landscapes lived has yet to be fully resolved.

One of the fundamental problems in answering this question, is that the majority of scholars who voice an opinion on this issue have taken polemical positions on what is almost certainly a complex and highly variable adaptive strategy. While this is not a central element of this discussion about ceremonial landscapes, the question about where people lived and how they lived relates directly to their social organization, and this relates directly to how these monumental landscapes were built.

As we have noted earlier in this discussion, Olaf Prufer (1964) proposed that the great Hopewell centers were actually vacant during most of the year, and were only used by local/regional residents for ceremonies and special events. The vacant ceremonial center model suggested that Ohio Hopewell people lived in small hamlets scattered around the large earthwork centers. Prufer's model was inspired by settlement studies around Mayan ceremonial centers where this pattern was well established. Berle Clay (1991) called this the "bull's-eye" model, where a group of households were scattered around each of the larger mound or ceremonial centers.

A few current researchers are investing substantial energy toward identifying and interpreting Hopewell habitation localities. William Dancey and his students have generated a model that builds upon Prufer's (1964) vacant ceremonial center model (Dancey 1991; 2005; Dancey and Pacheco 1997; Pacheco and Dancey 2006). Dancey developed his ideas during intensive research at the Murphy site near the Newark Earthworks. This model proposes that Ohio Hopewell people lived in dispersed sedentary communities. The primary sites associated with this settlement pattern were dispersed sedentary households comprised of single or extended families occupied over multiple generations. These household sites were clustered around earthworks or mound centers and spaced along major river valleys. The people living around the earthworks and mound centers practised hunting and gathering and cultivation of native, starchy seed plants.

Paul Pacheco, DeeAnne Wymer and Jarrod Burks have conducted several seasons of excavation at sites near the Liberty Works that they believe provide firm evidence of sedentary hamlets in proximity to a large vacant ceremonial center (Pacheco *et al.* 2006; 2009a; 2009b). Their research focused upon two sites, Browns Bottom #1 and Lady's Run, both located north-east of the Liberty Works on low rises in the Scioto River floodplain. Each site has produced evidence of a rectangular to square house with four associated hearths or earth ovens and other features. Macrobotanical data suggests consumption of native cultigens along with wild plant and animal foods. These carefully excavated sites provide some of the best evidence for sedentary hamlets in the Scioto River valley, but until more data become available, it is quite possible that structures of this type were built as part of the ceremonial or ritual landscape.

Bruce Smith (1992) proposed that Hopewell across most of the Eastern United States developed around small farming communities. His model is based on the dramatic increase in native starchy seeds recovered from sites during the Middle Woodland period. Smith has advocated that people living in small, sedentary hamlets grew squash (*Cucurbita pepo*), sunflower (*Helianthus annuus*), chenopodium (*Chenopodium berlandieri*), sumpweed (*Iva annua*), knotweed (*Polygonum erectum*), maygrass (*Phalaris caroliniana*) and little barley (*Hordeum pusillum*) in small fields associated with their settlements. Following the model proposed by Prufer (1964), Smith said the hamlets and farm fields were part of the Hopewell domestic sphere, while the mounds and earthworks were part of the corporate sphere of Hopewell socieites.

Bret Ruby has proposed a much more detailed variation of this model that is strongly based on the ecological diversity of southern Ohio (Ruby *et al.* 2005). This model proposes that people living in the Scioto Valley during the Hopewell era lived in small, sedentary residential groups. Ruby notes that the Scioto Valley region of southern Ohio is a very diverse biotic area, and unlike other models of sedentary Hopewell settlements, he proposes that these small residential units were organized in symbolic communities that transcend or crosscut local residential units. Symbolic communities formed for political, economic, social, and religious purposes and do not necessarily correspond directly to individual mound or earthwork centers. Ruby also notes that in parts of the Scioto Valley ceremonial centers are so tightly spaced that they could not have served as independent ceremonial centers for corresponding domestic populations. He proposes that "multiple local symbolic communities in the Scioto area probably used singular earthwork–mound sites suggests that such sites probably served more than one type of community: not only local symbolic communities, but also a larger sustainable community (Ruby *et al.* 2005, 166).

Not all scholars support the dispersed sedentary community model. Richard Yerkes, who has recently worked on European Neolithic archaeology has argued that Ohio Hopewell were complex but mobile tribal societies (2005; 2006). Yerkes proposes that the Hopewell achieved considerable cultural complexity through organizational flexibility without food surpluses, specialized production, or permanent residences. In his view, the Hopewell relied on a diverse range of subsistence resources including the use of starchy seeds supplemented by other wild foods. Yerkes suggests the construction and use of earthen enclosures served to bind dispersed members of mobile societies.

Frank Cowan (2006) believes that Ohio Hopewell was comprised of mobile populations based on his work at Fort Ancient and the Stubbs Earthwork, plus his experience with lithic technology. Cowan observes that if bladelets are removed from Ohio Hopewell lithic assemblages, what remains are largely the products of bifacial reduction technology, which is commonly found in association with mobile hunting and gathering societies. He notes that while bifaces represent a greater initial effort, they are multi-function tools that effectively serve mobile hunting and gathering groups. Cowan also notes that, among the numerous structures that have been recorded at Fort Ancient and Stubbs, there is considerable variation in structural forms, and very few yielded refuse or storage pits that might be expected with sedentary occupations.

The discussion about the nature and meaning of Ohio Hopewell archeology will likely continue for many years and both sides of this argument may ultimately prove to be correct. Since we have only limited knowledge about the chronological relationship between Ohio Hopewell sites, the character of settlement-subsistence practices very likely changed over the course of the Hopewell era. It is even possible that some Ohio Hopewell people were living in sedentary farming hamlets while others were continuing to live a more mobile foraging life. Distinguishing between these two subsistence strategies is further complicated because many of the scholars cannot agree on the characteristics that would be associated with each settlement type. The variety of different adaptations among the small-scale societies that built and used the great ceremonial landscapes is potentially considerable and might have been variable even during individual generations during the Hopewell era. Answering current and future questions about Ohio Hopewell societies will require new data that can only be collected from future field investigations. Additional remarks about Hopewell settlement and subsistence practices are included in the final chapter of this volume.

Mensuration, geometry and the sky

Until Thomas A. Edison and modern electrical technology turned the dark half of each day into light, humans on every continent were exposed to the diurnal movement of the sun, moon, stars, and planets. There are intellectual leaders in every generation, and some of them were able to decipher the subtle and long-term patterns of the objects in the sky. However, understanding the sky and the seasons was a basic skill for everyone who lived in a nature-driven world. While some ancient societies developed technologies to better cope with the harshness of the natural world (e.g. irrigations, prescribed burning of forests), most people who are the subject of archaeological inquiry in North America had only limited impact on the environment. Successful living in the natural world of 2000 years ago required some understanding and appreciation for the celestial objects that appeared regularly in the night sky.

The relationship between Ohio Hopewell ceremonial landscapes and celestial events is, at best, poorly understood at this point. The great geometric earthen monuments in southern Ohio were built on a scale that is best viewed from high above – from a bird's eye view (Brown 2006). Even the earliest scholars observed that the vast scale of these earthen monuments could not be reasonably viewed from the river valleys where they were built. For non-native immigrants into the Ohio Valley, these factors almost certainly contributed to their mysterious character and the mound-builder mythology.

The search for celestial meaning among North American archaeological sites was triggered with the publication of the popular book Stonehenge Decoded (Hawkins 1965). Hawkins proposed that stone monuments at Stonehenge and Salisbury Plain were calendrical, marking the extreme rising and setting points of the sun and moon as seen on the horizon surrounding Stonehenge. Subsequently, archaeologists discovered solstice or lunar markers associated with Puebloan sites in south-west that are thought to have been used to schedule festivals (McClusky 1977). Archaeologists recognized that more than 100 mounds at the Mississippian center of Cahokia were built on a true north–south alignment, and a circular ring of upright logs in the form of a woodhenge marked the summer solstice sunrise on the largest mound in the Cahokia complex (Wittry 1969). Eddy (1974) was first to recognize that the Big Horn Medicine Wheel in Wyoming and other rock-wheel alignments display alignments with solsticial and lunar positions. Other Plains anthropologists have noted that Skidi Pawnee earth lodges were aligned so the sun would shine through the door of the lodge onto an altar on the equinox sunrise. The role that geometry and celestial alignments played in the lives of American Indians has been noted in many ethnographic reports, and the process of relating these data to the archaeological record has produced substantial discussion. Readers wishing a deeper understanding of the place of archaeoastronomy in the Western Hemisphere might consult Aveni (2008) for a more detailed review of the cosmos among ancient humans world-wide.

Many modern Hopewell scholars have made observations, or offered hypotheses and models about some relationship between individual earthwork sites. The dense concentration of these monuments in the Scioto and Great Miami-Little Miami river valleys make it clear that they were not random constructions. Published discussions have included the proposition that the Hopewell utilized a standard unit of measure, hypotheses that embankment walls within individual enclosures were built to align with other earthworks, and suggestions that embankments were built to align with a range of celestial events. Some of these ideas warrant discussion before we consider the evidence about how, when, and for what purpose the Ohio Hopewell Ceremonial landscapes were built.

Early observations about the regularity of size and shape of Ohio Hopewell earthen enclosures led to the first speculation that the builders may have had a standard unit of measure. Squier and Davis were the first to publish maps of many of the earthworks and associated mounds, and they noted that the circular enclosures at High Bank and Hopeton are of equal diameter. They also observed that some square earthworks have sides 1080 ft (329.2 m) in length, which led them to suggest the mound-builders had some standard unit of measure (Squier and Davis 1848: 48–9). Charles Whittlesey (1884) also surveyed many earthworks in Ohio and based upon uniformity of embankment dimensions, he proposed a basic unit of measure of about 30 in (*ca.* 76 cm).

In 1965, civil engineer James A. Marshall began a detailed study of the extant earthworks in southern Ohio. Over the next 30 years he surveyed more than 50 sites and became convinced that the Ohio Hopewell earthworks were built on a 57 m square grid, which was the same grid system used to lay out the Meso-American center of Teotihuacan (Millon 1967). Marshall believed that the size, orientation and configuration of the geometric enclosure walls demonstrated that the builders of these sites had substantial knowledge of mathematics.

Building upon Marshall's work, William Romain (1991) published an important paper proposing a different Ohio Hopewell standard unit of measure. He says Ohio earthworks reflect repeated use of certain linear units of measure (Romain 1991). He proposes: "the Mound-builders possessed detailed observation knowledge of astronomical phenomena, a method of counting and manipulating fairly large numbers, an accurate means of measuring both angles and distance, and a basic unit of measure" (Romain 1991, 2), which he suggests is equal to 1.053 ft or about 12.6 in (*ca.* 32 cm). Romain suggests the basic unit of measurement may have developed from the use of a human arm (assuming an average height of a Hopewell male estimated at 66.5 in (166.4 cm), and the length of the shoulder joint to distal metacarpals of an average adult Hopewell male was 25.3 in (64 cm) – which is exactly twice the proposed standard unit of measure.

Romain generated this proposed standard unit of measure by studying the floor plans of excavated sub-mound houses at Seip, Mound City, and Liberty (Harness Mound). At Seip perimeter house posts were set 1.053 ft/12.6 in (32 cm) apart. At Mound City posts for Mounds 10 and 13 were placed 2.106 ft/25.3 in apart (64 cm).

At the Harness Mound big house, post-hole distances reflect three different multiples of the proposed basic unit of measure. Romain also notes that at Serpent Mound, one quarter of the Serpent is equal to 31.6 ft (9.60 m) or 30 times the basic unit of measure; the fundamental unit at Serpent Mound is 126.4 ft (38.5 m) which is 120 times the basic unit of 1.053 ft/32 cm. While Romain raises some interesting ideas about Ohio Hopewell construction, it is important to note that post-hole patterns from Ohio Hopewell structures often do not reflect a standard interval between posts, and building shapes are sometime irregular and asymmetric.

Further support for Romain's proposed standard unit of measure may be seen in the research of Ray Hively and Robert Horn at the Newark Earthworks. Hively and Horn (1982; 2006) suggest all aspects of the Newark Octagon could be laid out using only the diameter of the Fairground Observatory Circle (321.3 m), and Romain notes this is 1000 times the proposed basic unit of measure. Further support is seen at Baum and Liberty, where the diagonal of the square enclosures is three times the radius of the Newark Fairgrounds circle. Romain says this is about equal to 1500 times his basic unit of measure. Romain further observes that at High Bank, Hively and Horn report the diameter of the circle is 320.6 m, which equals 1051.6 ft – close to 1000 times the suggested basic Hopewell unit of length (Romain 1991).

Although the origins of the proposed standard unit of measure are unknown, Romain (1991) notes that regularity of embankment length and spacing at Poverty Point may reflect an earlier standard unit of measure. He also notes that some authors have proposed that Poverty Point is aligned upon lunar events – just as are Hopewell earthworks. A standard unit of measure, called the Toltec Module, has been proposed for a series of more recent prehistoric sites in the Lower Mississippi River Valley (Sherrod and Rolingson 1987). There is ample evidence in surveys of the Ohio Hopewell earthworks that the builders of the ancient monuments were aware of fundamental geometric principles and built circles and squares of comparable sizes at many different sites.

As Europeans began to explore and colonize North America, they injected a system of land ownership that was very foreign to Native Americans. The western system of land ownership required boundaries and legal titles, and today these are extremely precise and must be established by licensed surveyors. When the Ohio valley was being explored and settled, land claims were much less precise and frontier surveyors used landmarks like a creek bank or a large tree to describe boundaries to a property claim. Similarly, distances were measured in the number of hours required to walk or ride a horse from point to point. Such imprecision seems unmanageable today, but it was common throughout most of human history.

In our contemporary society, we learn standard units of measurement (inch, foot, yard, meter) at an early age, and by the time we are adults it is hard to image a world that lacked such concepts. However, standard units of measure are relatively new in the overall span of human history, and did not become widespread and important until they were needed by the first hierarchical societies. Rulers to measure feet and inches did not come into widespread use until the 19th century. In trades like cabinet-making and plane-making, there is little evidence of size standardization in furniture or woodworking planes made in the 18th century. Even early railroads were so variable that equipment could not be interchangeably used on different tracks. Standardized units of measure were more important to elites of western society, particularly people with access to information and education. Only with the Industrial Revolution did standard measurements begin to affect ordinary people on a daily basis.

How does this affect the idea that the Hopewell possessed a standard unit of measure? It seems likely in building earthen walls, that Hopewell people had some shared concept of length that could be generally understood among the people who designed the walls and enclosures. This might easily have been a length of rope, or an established number of paces. Some Ohio Hopewell ceremonial landscapes exhibit remarkable mathematical precision in their design and construction, but not all sites are made to a high degree of precision. This has been recognized by scholars for two centuries, but it is unclear what this means. Are the differences related to differences in the time when they were built, in the purposes for which they were intended, or were they built by different groups of people?

In his engineering studies of Ohio Hopewell earthworks, James A. Marshall (1969; 1978; 1980) believed that the builders of these sites used a standard unit of measure, and scale-plans were prepared prior to construction of the earthworks. Early in his research, Marshall felt the survey data he collected demonstrated that "A knowledge of geometry was demonstrated that entailed at least the use of right triangles with precise geometric proportions." He also claimed "There existed among the Hopewell a "school of mathematics" whose musings on geometrical concepts, differed from the Pythagoreans of ancient Greece only in degree (Marshall 1980: 8)."

Later in his career, Marshall (1996) proposed that Ohio Hopewell earthen enclosures could be classified into five categories based upon the geometrical complexity exhibited in the configuration and scale of the enclosure walls. The simplest class is hilltop enclosures, which simply conform to the shape of a natural landform. The simplest forms among the geometric enclosures are circles and squares built in simple multiples of the 57 m grid system that Marshall believed represented a standard unit of measure among many native people of the Western Hemisphere. Marshall suggests that the third class of earthen enclosures is cryptographs:

> "If one locates the center of a geometric earthwork, such as a square, circle, rectangle, octagon, or ellipse, then draws straight lines from it to the centers of nearby geometric earthworks, then passes true north–south and true east–west lines through these centers, the resulting lines on some of these works will form geometric configurations that utilize the 57 m (187 ft) and also form simple right triangles". (Marshall 1996, 213)

The most common are 3–4–5 right-angled triangles, and this is indicative that construction was done with principles of Pythagorean Theorem. Cryptographic earthworks are most common in Ross and Licking Counties, Ohio and the most distant example is Fort Center in Clades Co., Florida. The Mann site in Posey Co., Indiana, also fits this pattern.

Marshall calls the fourth class Cryptographic Overlays, which he says were built:

> "when the plan of one work is placed over another, so that centers of the geometric figures coincide or very closely agree, then straight walls of one work match or are parallel to their counterpart on the other earthwork. The situation where the circle on one earthwork is tangent to the circle on another earthwork is also considered a case of cryptographic overlays". (Marshall 1996: 214)

He suggests these overlays indicate that major Hopewell sites were laid out by people who clearly understood geometry of corresponding earthwork, possibly even the same person. The principles of cryptographic overlay allow enlargement of one earthwork plan at another location using the standard 57 m unit of measure.

Marshall's most complex class of earthworks reflects the concept of Pi. These are earthworks that reflect an understanding of the circumference to the diameter of a circle. He observes that Hopewell enclosures were built to sizes whereby the circle and squares had roughly corresponding areas and this requires an understanding of mathematic principles. In Marshall's view this understanding of geometry was necessary to design the octagons found at High Bank and Newark.

Earthworks built to classes 1 and 2 are widespread in the Eastern United States. Earthworks that exhibit Classes 3–5 level of construction are restricted primarily to southern Ohio:

> "The cryptographic overlays between geometrically related sites such as Seip and Newark, and High Bank and Fort Ancient, for instance, indicates the close relationships

between earthworks within Ohio. The existence of these relationships suggests a mathematical definition to the Ohio Hopewell Core, refined by reference to the mathematical linkage between Liberty Township, Seip, Newark, High Bank, and Baum Works. Together, these works might be considered the True Core of Ohio Hopewell. The cryptographic overlays and projections between and within these earthworks indicates an attempt to develop octagons and polygons with greater number of sides that might yield more precise values of pi. As such it is argued that these works are evidence of the work of a residential school of Pythagoreans similarly preoccupied with mathematics. If there is an ultimate geometric center to the Ohio Hopewell core, it has to be the High Bank Works, with its strongly implied 22 sided figure". (Marshall 1996, 218)

Marshall proposes that these sites were built on grids and likely were planned on some type of drafting table, at least one meter on a side, with actual construction being expanded from that plan to a layout 2000 times the original drawing size.

William Romain (1992, 2000) has also written about the importance of geometry in the design and construction of Ohio Hopewell earthworks. He notes that some enclosures are closer to being idealized geometric shapes than others, but he believes that precision in construction was less important to the builders than the symbolic meaning of the circles, squares, and octagons. Romain observes that Hopewell geometry is based upon multiples of the Hopewell unit of length (Romain and Marshall are not in agreement as what that standard length is), with sites reflecting multiples of this unit in their dimensions. Romain argues that individual components of the sites, circle, and squares, were oriented to reflect astronomical events like solstice and lunar standstills, and each site is oriented so that one side of a square enclosure is parallel to a nearby river, stream or creek (Romain 1992: 40). He also explains how many of these geometric forms might have been laid out with the use of a rope or cord, and did not require complex survey instruments.

Most Ohio Hopewell scholars will likely agree that the recurrent use of geometric figures to form geometric enclosures reflects symbolic values of the people who built these sites. Charles Faulkner (1977) was among the first to draw attention to the Southeastern Indian practice of building circular winter lodges and rectangular (ramada) summer lodges. The importance of the circle to the Algonkian-speaking Cheyenne is documented in their circular lodges and the circular pattern in which the lodges were assembled even after they had moved from woodlands onto the plains. Romain (2000) proposes that large square enclosures represent the sky and large circles represent the earth. He also suggests that tripartite earthworks may represent the three components of the cosmos, upper world (sky), earth, and underworld.

Geometric earthworks are a central component of the Ohio Hopewell archaeological record. From simple circles and squares to complex combinations of forms, these vast constructed landscapes have raised questions and stirred the imagination. As Marshall (1996) has observed, the simplest of these forms is found across much of Eastern North America, but the more complex forms are concentrated in the River Valleys of southern Ohio. Marshall's data about the size and complexity of earthwork construction combined with data about mortuary and ceremonial complexity, and the sheer number of large Hopewell centers makes it clear that Ohio was the center of the Hopewell world.

Interpretations about the design and construction of these sites tend to assume that individual sites were designed and then built to a specific plan. Byers (2004) has argued that earthworks and mounds were built and then managed by a "sacred earth principle", which prohibited disturbance or displacement of soils that had been used to build a sacred monument. This may be a valid concept, but we have very little empirical evidence to support these assumptions. In fact, in one of the few earthworks that have been thoroughly investigated, Robert Riordan (2006) has documented that the embankment walls at the Pollock Works were built, remodeled and rebuilt a number of times. Do the geometric earthworks of southern Ohio reflect the design that was envisioned nearly 2000 years ago, or do they represent the final remodeling by succeeding generations?

Alignments and reading the heavens

Some of the earliest maps of Ohio Hopewell earthworks depict long parallel walls in association with circular and square enclosures. Squier and Davis (1948) in their landmark study described these avenues flanked by parallel walls as graded ways. David Brose (1976) proposed that the long parallel walls at the Hopeton Earthworks are aligned with summer solstice sunset. Recent research by Bradley Lepper (1995; 2006) suggests that a ceremonial road of this type may have been built to connect the great Newark Earthworks with the vast network of earthworks around Chillicothe. Whether these parallel walls or graded ways were designed as ceremonial passages is uncertain, but they have served to encourage speculation about possible connections between individual earthworks.

Stephen Peet (1903) over 100 years ago suggested that Mound City and Hopeton were built to align with one another. James Marshall in his survey of the Hopeton Earthworks and Mound City noted that a line drawn westward along the south wall of the square enclosure at the Hopeton Earthworks intersects with Mound City (Marshall 1996). Many other writers have cited this alignment as evidence that Hopeton and Mound City are paired, and their three larger enclosures represent a triad in the terminology of Byers (2004) and DeBoer (2010). This may be a useful analytical and interpretive unit, but current radiocarbon evidence indicates a much greater span of use at Mound City. Radiocarbon evidence also suggests the enclosure walls at Hopeton were completed two centuries before the Mound City enclosure wall and borrow pits were built. This does not negate their being built as part of a larger landscape, but it does raise the issues of evolving plans, design continuity, and social stability.

The practice of discovering alignments between sites in the Scioto Valley continues and reaches high levels of sophistication among contemporary authors. Warren DeBoer (2010) examined 19 inter-site alignments in the Scioto drainage and observed that some of these alignments spanned many kilometers and six of the 19 crosscut river drainages. The implication of his study is that these sites are connected by something more than just sightlines. His argument also notes that some sightline connections likely extend through time to connect different generations of enclosure builders, a pattern that has also been observed among

Chacoan sites in the south-west. DeBoer also adopts the site seriation proposed by Martin Byers (2004), for which there are very few reliable radiocarbon or other dates to support or substantiate their proposed sequence. Like so many aspects of Ohio Hopewell archaeology, interpretive models are often difficult to evaluate because there is so little hard evidence to support the models or the assumptions upon which they are built.

The possibility that some of the great Ohio Hopewell earthworks were built to mark celestial events became a point of discussion through the work of Ray Hively and Robert Horn (1982; 1984). Their preliminary studies at the Newark circle and Octagon and High Bank circle and octagon provide documentation that alignment of some of the earthen walls marked the extreme rise and setting points of the moon. While the possibility that these earthworks had been built, in part, as celestial observatories was a dramatic revelation, the authors noted that additional work would be needed to confirm that alignments were intentional.

Fig. 2.23. Lunar rise at Newark (image courtesy of the University of Cincinnati/CERHAS: www. ancientohiotrail.org).

In subsequent studies at the Newark Earthworks, Hively and Horn (2006; 2010) conducted additional surveys and subjected their data to rigorous statistical analysis. Their study of the octagon identified five alignments that mark lunar standstills, which are points on the horizon marking the maximum and minimum north and south extremes of lunar rising and setting points every 18.6 years (Fig. 2.23). Four of the alignments are along the Octagon walls, and one is along the avenue axes that connect the Octagon with the adjoining circle. The scale of the enclosures is so large that they cannot be clearly viewed from the ground.

Hively and Horn showed that the builders of the Newark Octagon possessed skills in both geometry and astronomy. They also noted:

> "this dual geometrical and astronomical significance is only possible in a very narrow range of latitude, which includes the Newark site. This combination of astronomical and geometrical regularity is only possible at Newark because of two facts: (1) the difference between azimuths of the maximum northern and southern moonrises (78.0 degrees) is closely equal to half of the major vertex angle associated with the plan in Figure 2 (77 degrees .9); (2) the difference between the azimuths of the southern minimum moonset and the southern maximum moonrise (115 degrees.2) is approximately equal to the smaller of the vertex angles for the octagon plan in Figure 2 (114 degrees .3). The sum of the angular deviations for these two near equalities is 1 degree .0. It is of some interest to establish the range of latitudes for which the sum of these two angular deviations would be 1 degree or smaller." (Hively and Horn 2006: 306)

Through their careful studies, Hively and Horn (2010) have shown that the Newark Earthworks exhibit 17 possible alignments to local horizon rising and setting extremes of the moon over its 18.6-year cycle. One of the five possible lunar alignments along the Octagon was less precise than the other four and led

Hively and Horn to consider whether rise and set points were observed from places un-obscured by local terrain:

> "The most logical place to make and record repeatable observations of lunar rise/ set points would indeed be from high places with unobstructed views of distant horizons. Such high places could be dedicated to long-term observations, as they would not have been prime areas for other activities." (2010: 133)

They propose that any high point that may have been used for long-term lunar observations, must have served as a back-sight for a zero-altitude horizon view of a lunar extreme over the full length of the octagon wall. They also propose that this topographic high point would be prominent among the surrounding hills and display evidence of Hopewell activity. They propose that Hill H1, south-west of the earthworks, fits all criteria and even had a small enclosure reported by an antiquarian at this locality in 1890. Coffman's Knob, another prominent local topographic feature, is a possible vantage point for the alignment of earthwork features focused upon maximum north and minimum north moonset.

The octagonal and circle earthworks at Newark and High Bank are truly unique among all the earthen monuments in southern Ohio, and both exhibit alignments that mark lunar extremes. High Bank Octagon is:

> "optimum shape for aligning with a combination of solar and lunar extremes rise and set points at its latitude; yet compared with the Circle-Octagon at Newark, it fails to encode that astronomical design on the most prominent feature, its long axis". (Hively and Horn 2010: 139)

Ray Hively and Robert Horn have also noted that earthworks in the Scioto River valley tend to be sited to align with prominent local topographic features and are aligned with other earthworks over considerable distances. Their studies indicate that High Bank Works and some other Chillicothe earthworks mark lunar extremes and also align with local topography as part of what may have been a grand regional plan linking many of the major earthen monuments (Hively and Horn 2010). For example, at Mound City the monthly minimum extremes of moon rise every 8.6 years are marked by Sugarloaf and Mt. Logan as viewed from Mound 7. Mound 7 is the largest of mound at Mound City and excavations by Squier and Davis (1848) and Mills (1922a; 1922b) exposed a deposit of crescent-shaped mica cut-outs. In a brief analysis of the Shriver Circle, less than a kilometer south of Mound City, Hively and Horn (2010) observe that from the mound near the center of the circular embankment, gates in the embankment wall align with Mound City, Hopeton, Mount Logan, and Works East. One of the gates aligns with the winter solstice set and two gateways mark northward maximum moonrise and south maximum moonrise from the mound. They acknowledge that these observations are imprecise due to their dependency on the Squier and Davis (1848) map. They also propose that geophysical survey data may provide a more accurate map to evaluate any potential alignments at Shriver.

Hively and Horn (2010) have generated considerable new food for thought with their on-going studies at Newark and some preliminary studies of the major earthworks in the Scioto River valley. In their first consideration of the "zero-altitude hypothesis" for Scioto-Paint Creek area, they note that Mount Prospect, where Worthington Estate was built, provides a commanding view of several major enclosures. From Mount Prospect, north maximum moonrise (52.1°) aligns with the center of the Shriver circle and south-west corner of Hopeton. From the same point on Mount Prospect, the southernmost moonrise (129.3°) passes through the center of the large circular enclosure at Works East, and also the southern Extension of High Bank and north-east corner of Liberty square. South maximum moonset (230.7°) passes through the south-east corner of Seip square, and north minimum moonset (293.7°) passes within 10 m of the north-east corner and Anderson Square and comes within 100 m of Frankfort Square. Hively and Horn observe that the Mount Prospect location provides a vantage point to seven major enclosures, but does not provide views of others. This prominent ridge may have served as a back-sight for placement of some central Scioto earthworks.

Hively and Horn (2010) note many of the same long-distance alignments of Scioto River valley enclosures proposed by DeBoer (2010), and they present evidence that many of the enclosures may have been integrated into a regional plan. For example, north maximum moonrise connects Seip with Shriver and Hopeton and passes over Prospect Point, while north minimum moonrise is an alignment between Seip, Mount Prospect, and Works East. Hively and Horn present possible mechanisms by which many of large enclosures may have been built on lunar and sighting alignments separated by as much as 27 km (16.7 miles). They fully acknowledge the difficulty of this task, and also note that generating these long-distance alignments is based upon Mount Prospect (Prospect Point) serving as a back sight, and there has never been any evidence of Hopewell presence reported from this location.

Individual components of the potential regional plan are fairly well documented:

> "1. Alignments to two lunar and two solar extremes seen from Mound City over prominent points on the Logan Range.
>
> 2. Alignments to four solar and eight lunar extremes on the Circle-Octagon at High Bank.
>
> 3. Three sites (Works East-Liberty-High Bank) aligned on the 143.4 bearing of the Teays Valley, orthogonal to the minor axis of the High Bank Octagon and to the 53.4 degree azimuth of the north maximum moonrise.
>
> 4. Alignments from a single point at Seip to Shriver and Hopeton on the north maximum moonrise, and to Baum and Works East on the north minimum moonrise.
>
> 5. Eight Paint Creek valley sites (Baum-Spruce Hill-Mound City-Cedar Bank, Seip-Bournville-Anderson-Dunlap) aligned along opposite sides of the valley on 44.3 degrees." (Hively and Horn 2010: 157)

Not all of the potential alignments in the Chillicothe area involve Mount Propect. However, if the Hopewell earthwork builders did utilize Mount Prospect as a regional focus, Hively and Horn (2010: 158) note that:

> "1. Eight of the sites which fall on the above more secure alignments also fall on five lunar extremes as viewed from Prospect Point (Shriver-Hopeton, Works East, High Bank-Liberty, Seip, Anderson-Frankfort).

2. Liberty and Works East are located at the intersection of lunar rise extremes, as viewed from Prospect Point, with the Teays Valley 143.4 degrees axis.

3. Seip is located at the intersection of two lunar set extremes as viewed from Prospect Point and from Works East, and the 44.3 degree line which passes through Bournville, Anderson, and Dunlap.

4. Baum is located on the intersection of a lunar rise extreme as viewed from Seip and the 44.3 degree line which passes through Spruce Hill, Mound City and Cedar Bank.

If we assume that Mount Prospect played a central role in Hopewell planning at Chillicothe, the suggested scenario accounts for these phenomena:

1. The location of the Shriver-Mound City-Hopeton complex, in terms of its broadly economic suitability and in terms of its situation relative to the Logan range and the visible extremes of the rising sun and moon.

2. The locations of Liberty and Works East along the Teays Valley, by their relation to the long axis of High Bank and their position on lunar extremes as viewed from Prospect Point.

3. The location of Seip relative to lunar extremes from Works East and Prospect Point.

4. The location of Baum relative to lunar extremes and the old Paint Creek valley topography (44.3degrees parallels).

5. The locations of Anderson and Frankfort on a lunar extreme as seen from Mount Prospect."

Celestial alignments have been proposed at a number of other earthworks by a variety of Hopewell scholars (Brose 1976; Romain 2000). While some of these alignments may have been intended to mark celestial events, none of those in the Chillicothe area appear to have been constructed to the degree of precision as were the enclosures at Newark. Many of the alignments proposed by scholars other than Hively and Horn, are documented by noting key azimuths of celestial events and then searching aerial photographs and maps for potential matches among Hopewell earthworks. While these observations have made Hopewell scholars aware of the strong possibility that some embankment walls were built to align with celestial events, other than the careful work of Hively and Horn, they have not conducted the rigorous analyses needed to demonstrate the possible alignments were in fact intended alignments.

Like most significant contributions to Ohio Hopewell studies, thoughtful and long-term research by Ray Hively and Robert Horn has generated an impressive array of systematic and carefully analyzed data that has huge implications for the understanding of Ohio Hopewell ceremonial landscapes. Although their research is on-going, they have produced sufficient evidence to convince even the strongest skeptics that some of the earthen monuments were built to mark celestial events. In combination with the work of Warren DeBoer (2010) they have provided tantalizing evidence that many of the large earthworks in the Scioto River Valley may have been built to align with one another, or to important local topographic vantage points. Based upon the data presented by these authors, it seems likely that at least some of the locations of the major geometric enclosures were selected to mark and view celestial events, and major topographic features may have served as the vantage points from which these alignments were measured and sited.

If all, or even many, of the large earthen enclosures in the Scioto River Valley are integrated and aligned as part of a regional plan as Hively and Horn (2010) and DeBoer (2010) have hypothesized, this will require significant reconsideration of existing models about chronology, social organization, social continuity, labor, and the scope and scale of participation in ceremonial landscape creation, and the role of individuals with the knowledge and power to lead people in building ceremonial landscapes on such a massive scale.

Most readers will agree that there are far too many potential alignments with celestial events, natural topographic features, and between individual earthwork sites for these to all be accidental. Unfortunately, better evaluation of the many proposed alignments is handicapped by our inability to understand the internal chronology of Ohio Hopewell ceremonial landscapes. Were all of the large earthworks in the Scioto River valley located and built as part of a massive plan, or were a large number of smaller ceremonial sites selected through time to be enlarged and modified into the forms observed in historic times? Our inability to order the construction events associated with these ceremonial landscapes continues to limit our ability to make meaningful interpretation about the people and societies that built them. This theme will be recurring throughout this discussion of Ohio Hopewell ceremonial landscapes.

The Great Hopewell Road

Bradley Lepper (1995; 1996; 2006) has offered one of the truly new and testable hypotheses regarding the Ohio Hopewell archaeological record. He has found a number of historic records and some aerial images that suggest the parallel walls that begin at the Newark Earthworks stretch for at least 60 miles (96.5 km) to the south-west, and likely connected Newark with the great ceremonial centers of the Scioto River valley near Chillicothe (Fig. 2.24).

In presenting his case for the Great Hopewell Road, Lepper points out that other prehistoric societies in the Americas (Mayans, Chaco Canyon) built elaborate road networks. He draws upon the observations of James and Charles Salisbury in 1862, who followed the parallel walls that originate at Newark for 6 miles (9.7 km), and although the road continued they stopped, while assuming it continued on to Circleville or Chillicothe. Lepper also cites an account of local historian Samuel Park, who recorded in 1870 the presence of a graded road visible in the timber on the land claim of Jesse Thompson near Walnut Creek in Fairfield County. Lepper also reports that in 1930 Newark businessman Warren Weiant Jr used an airplane to follow parallel walls from the Newark Octagon south-west in a straight line to Millersport, Ohio.

The possible existence of some transportation corridor, whether it was a ceremonial road or a trail, between Newark and Chillicothe is certainly not hard to imagine. The striking similarity between the Newark Octagon and its attached Circle and an earthwork configuration at the High Bank site has been

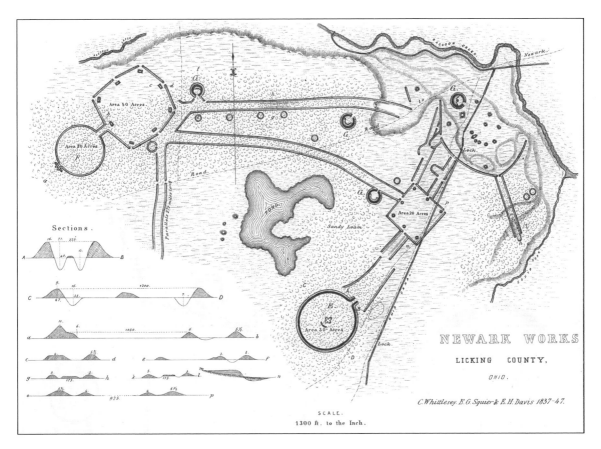

Fig. 2.24. Map of the Newark Earthworks showing several long parallel walls. Were these passageways built to guide people into the enclosures for ceremonies? Bradley Lepper has suggested that a ceremonial roadway of this type may have connected Newark with the great concentration of Hopewell earthworks around Chillicothe, more than 50 miles (80.5 km) to the south. This Great Hopewell Road may have guided pilgrims to the Newark Earthworks to aid in construction and to participate in ceremonies (Squier and Davis 1848. pl. xxv).

a topic of discussion for archaeologists since the days of Squier and Davis. The fact that Newark and High Bank were the only octagonal enclosures built by Ohio Hopewell people seems intuitively to be important. It is also important to note that the main axes of these two enclosure groups are precisely orthogonal to one another. Whether the relationship between the sites was one of temporal equals, or whether one was ancestral to the other is not supported by any evidence at this point. Future archaeological work will certainly sort out this connection, and may provide additional evidence to support Brad Lepper's hypothesis of a ceremonial road connecting two important ceremonial centers.

One other element of Lepper's Great Hopewell Road model deserves elaboration. He also proposes that the ceremonial road served as an important conduit to guide pilgrims to the Newark ceremonial center. Lepper proposes that the Ohio Ceremonial centers were also pilgrimage centers. During the Hopewell era, people from across the Ohio River valley, and possibly across much of Eastern North America came to the region with offerings of rare and precious items that became part of the massive ceremonial artifact hoards that were buried under many of the major Hopewell mounds in this region. Pilgrims coming to Ohio might contribute labor in building the large ceremonial landscapes in exchange for the healing of an illness, spiritual teaching, or the opportunity to learn about ceremonial practices that might enhance the lives of people in their homeland.

Katherine Spielmann (2002; 2009), building on the work of Mary Helm (1988; 1993), has noted that individuals from many societies participated in quests, where their travels might take them to strange and distant lands. They would obtain important knowledge on these journeys and return with items that symbolize the places they may have visited. These two processes, pilgrimage and quests, seem to help explain the presence of so many wonderful and rare objects and works of art among the ceremonial and mortuary remains of the Ohio Hopewell people. One can easily imagine young people from southern Ohio traveling to the Gulf of Mexico, or the Rocky Mountains, or the Northern Great Lakes and spreading the word about Ohio Hopewell belief systems and landscape construction. The people on these power quests might stimulate pilgrims from societies along their routes to come to Ohio and participate in the ceremonial activities. These contacts would build and maintain societal networks, and create opportunities for shared ceremonies, trade, marriage arrangements, and information exchange.

The hypothesis offered by Brad Lepper regarding a formally constructed ceremonial road connecting Newark and Chillicothe has been met with skepticism among some scholars. Although there is insufficient evidence to conclude that there was indeed a formal ceremonial road crossing this region, it is a testable hypothesis and it should be possible to conduct a more systematic investigation to determine if remnants of the road still exist. Long parallel walls are associated with a number of different Ohio Hopewell earthwork complexes, but the one at Newark is by far the longest that has been documented thus far. Whether there is a formal road connecting these two great ceremonial precincts, at Newark and the Scioto River-Paint Creek region, is less important than the pilgrimage and quest model that helps explain how local Ohio Hopewell societies accomplished so much earth moving with relatively low permanent populations in that region.

Were ceremonial landscapes planned designs? Models and hypotheses

A colleague once remarked that Hopewell archaeologists generally fall into two categories: dirt diggers and big thinkers. Although this is just a humorous dichotomy, it does have some basis in reality, particularly in regard to the interpretation of Hopewell ceremonial landscapes. Scholars have been offering ideas about the purpose or meaning of the great earthen monuments since the Europeans entered the region in the 18th century. Most of the early writers clearly favored the idea that these sites were built as defensive fortifications, which kept the builders safe from the resident savages (Silverberg 1968). Until Squier and Davis (1848) began systematic excavations into the mounds, the ideas that were offered about these sites were based largely on speculation, and many of the writers lived at a great distance from the Ohio River valley and likely never actually visited the sites.

More than a century and a half of archaeological research has produced a fairly substantial body of data, primarily about the character of the mounds and their contents. Modern scholars consequently have much more information on which to build their models and hypotheses than did the writers of the 19th century. Particularly noteworthy is the work of A. Martin Byers (2004). Byers' massive book is a comprehensive model about the interpretation of Ohio Hopewell earthen enclosure sites. Byers (2004; 2011) subsequently added several addenda and clarifications, and he has offered so many hypotheses and ideas that it would take several volumes to address his published ideas adequately. An overview of his perspective certainly has merit in the discussion of ceremonial landscapes.

Although Byers is trained in archaeology, the basis for his interpretive model of the Ohio Hopewell world is derived largely from structuralist theory and Native American ethnographic data. At the heart of his model is his belief that Native Americans viewed the world as eminently sacred and as human societies developed they increasingly polluted the sacred world with their actions, which required that societies must regularly perform world renewal ceremonies to mitigate the polluting actions of human societies, particularly clearing land for cultivation. He argues that since the world is sacred, it cannot be divided or owned and land rights were inclusive among all people. He further argues that although people lived in kin-based small communities, Ohio Hopewell monumental earthwork sites were built by companion-based groups or sodalities that served to integrate local kin groups into larger, regional groups capable of collective action. Byers calls this the "Dual Clan-Cult Sodality Model."

The Dual Clan-Cult Sodality Model emphasizes that groups maintained autonomy within and between the various clans and sodalities. The variability that is observed between individual Ohio Hopewell earthwork sites is explained by this model, and each of these monumental sites was constructed to perform world renewal rituals. Through the autonomy of these different societies:

> "each mutualistic cult sodality heterarchy responsible for a given monumental earthwork locale would determine what would count as an appropriate earthwork form by which the renewal ritual was most effectively performed and each would determine what mutualistic alliances with other cult sodality heterarchies they might make in order to enhance this capacity." (Byers 2011)

Byers argues that variation in earthwork forms is due to differing alternative beliefs between the autonomous cult sodality heterarchies within a particular region. He also argues that earthen enclosures that share the same forms or at least major formal principles tend to reflect shared ideological beliefs.

The basic principle by which Byers measures the similarity or difference between Ohio Hopewell earthwork sites is the morphology of the enclosures. He has proposed an elaborate classification that labels the enclosures according to their morphological shape. For example, he notes that the large earthen wall and ditch that surround the Hopewell site are generally circular, and he classifies this as a C-form embankment type. He notes that C-form embankments are most common in south-west Ohio, what he calls the Miami Fort Tradition (Byers 2004). Byers also observed that the major form of earthwork in the Scioto River valley involves the combination of circular and a rectilinear forms, which he calls the C-R pattern. Byers argues that the Hopewell Mound Group was originally built as a C-pattern enclosure, but the builders later added a small rectilinear shape to the east end of the circular enclosure to accommodate and recognize the nearby C-R cult sodality construction sites of Seip and Liberty (Byers 2010). Byers uses his analysis of earthwork form to propose a seriation of the major Ohio earthen enclosures.

Byers' morphological classification is a useful, although unnecessarily verbose, explanation of the variety of embankment shapes found at Ohio Hopewell ceremonial landscapes. He also proposes that the construction of circular and rectilinear enclosures had a temporal sequence, for which there is little empirical evidence. He argues that the circular forms were derived from the earlier Adena sacred circles and therefore pre-date the rectilinear forms. While there may be some logic to this hypothesis, there is little or no chronological data to support the idea at any major Ohio Hopewell site. To be fair to Byers, he clearly understands that the ideas he presents are models and hypotheses, not factually based interpretations of the archaeological record. However, sometimes it is difficult to separate among the writings of Hopewell scholars what is fact and what is hypothesis.

Another important element of the model proposed by Byers is what he calls the Sacred Earth Principle. He argues that, since the construction of earthen enclosures was essentially a process of building a sacred space, the earth used to build the embankments was therefore sacred and once set in place could not be disturbed. It is likely that most, if not all, Hopewell scholars agree that the creation of ceremonial landscapes was a process of creating a sacred area separate from the profane space of everyday life. However, as we will discuss in this volume, there is archaeological evidence that embankment walls were modified, likely to accommodate changing needs of the people who built them. It should also be noted that at Mound City in Ross County, Ohio, human remains were found buried in the embankment wall and borrow pit areas. These burials were made by digging a burial pit into these previously constructed earthen features. As we will show throughout this book, the construction of Ohio Hopewell ceremonial landscapes involved the movement of massive amounts of soil and rock. It is also likely that these landscapes were altered or expanded during and possibly after the Hopewell era.

In an important paper about the shape of Woodland houses, Charles Faulkner (1977) noted that two different types of domestic structures are common. A circular house is used during the winter seasons and a rectangular house in the summer months. Warren DeBoer (1997) has noted that this pattern is consistent with ethnographic patterns recorded in the south-east, and reflects sub-mound house shapes found at Ohio Hopewell ceremonial centers. DeBoer argues that Hopewell ceremonial centers were more than mortuary places but served a variety of functions, including gathering places for the negotiation of marital alliances.

DeBoer sees the large circles and squares in Hopewell earthwork complexes as one of many dualities in the Hopewell world. He agrees with Byers' seriation model and bases his own interpretations on the assumption that large circles preceded large squares/rectilinear forms in the construction of complex enclosure sites. He proposes that these two forms represent symbolic struggle for power among

Hopewell societies, the "foreign" squares versus the native circles. While this does offer a potential explanation for the variation in embankment form, the empirical evidence to support it has yet to be uncovered.

DeBoer (2010) has also offered an interesting model that proposes that most of the larger earthen ceremonial centers in the Scioto River drainage were built along specific sightlines. This model implies that over time some centralized design for the placement and possible orientation of these large constructions developed. The model offers only a general sequence of the construction of these sites. It does, however, offer considerable food for thought about how these site locations were chosen and whether all of these sites are somehow connected through some grand plan that was implemented over four to five centuries.

The most detailed and complex interpretive model of Ohio Hopewell lifeways has been proposed by Christopher Carr (2005a; 2005b). In two volumes covering a vast array of Hopewell topics, Carr and his co-editor Troy Case and a host of collaborators offer extensive reviews and interpretive models of the Ohio Hopewell archaeological record (Carr and Case 2005; Case and Carr 2008). The breadth and diversity of these papers are beyond the scope of this discussion, although it is necessary to review Carr's interpretation of the ceremonial centers.

Carr's (2005a; 2005b) interpretation of the Hopewell ceremonial centers focuses on only those sites in the Scioto–Paint Creek area. He recognizes four types of centers: lowland enclosures with burial mounds, lowland enclosures with flat-topped mounds, lowland enclosures with mainly open space, and hilltop enclosures. All four of these are present in the Scioto–Paint Creek region, but Spruce Hill is the only hilltop enclosure in that area. This region has long been recognized as having the highest density of large Hopewell enclosures and Carr believes this is evidence that local symbolic communities in the region used multiple earthworks because these ceremonial centers are "too close to each other to have each served as the focus of its own local symbolic community" (Carr 2005a, 92; see also Ruby *et al.* 2005).

Carr (2005a) also proposes that ceremonial centers in the Scioto–Paint Creek area were built to align with the cardinal directions. He points to Mound City and Hopeton, which he argues were paired based upon their proximity and differences in their morphological forms. He believes Mound City and Hopeton were among the earliest ceremonial centers to be built in the Scioto–Paint Creek region, and that the:

> "ancestral orientation established with Mound City and Hopeton, and perhaps Anderson, was continued later in time during a middle era when the two-part Hopewell earthwork was built, and yet later in time when the three part Seip earthwork was constructed." (Carr 2005a: 87)

Carr argues that many of the Scioto–Paint Creek ceremonial centers were paired, and proposes that shared labor pools were from "recognized, local symbolic communities." He hypothesizes that Seip and Baum were paired in the Paint Creek area, Works East, and Liberty were paired in the Scioto area, with Frankfort and Hopewell paired in the North Paint Creek area.

Although Carr describes his evidence for the pairing of sites and the contemporaneity of paired sites with terms like "rigorous case" and "robust data", and while we must respect the intensive research he has conducted on archives and museum collections from these sites, much of the data he has available was collected with fairly crude excavation methods, and the field records from these excavations are not comprehensive. Certainly Carr's research has been rigorous and significant, but many of his interpretations must be treated as hypotheses due to the paucity of key supporting empirical evidence. For example, many scholars assume that the five tripartite enclosures were among the final earthworks built in the Scioto–Paint Creek region, and while this may ultimately be demonstrated to be true, there is not a single radiocarbon date to document the age of these earthen constructions. The absence of chronological control in regard to earthen constructions at most sites is one of the biggest obstacles to understanding fully the construction history and use of these ceremonial centers. Part of the evidence that Carr documents in support of the pairing of sites is drawn from sub-mound structures and mortuary deposits at the sites. Yet we don't know if the mounds were built at the same time as the earthen enclosure walls, or as in the case of Mound City, perhaps the embankments were the final landscape construction elements at these sites. We will return to this topic later in the volume and consider what evidence actually exists for contemporaneity and the pairing of sites.

In reviewing the literature on Ohio Hopewell ceremonial landscapes, we cannot avoid the question as to what is the empirical basis in support of the models and hypotheses that have been offered regarding Ohio Hopewell ceremonial landscapes. The discovery of a giant post circle at the Stubbs earthwork (Cowan and Genheimer 2010) made a whole generation of people working on Hopewell earthwork sites wonder if this was an anomaly or whether we should be looking for similar features elsewhere.

Between 1998 and 2004 the Cincinnati Museum Center conducted investigations at the Stubbs Earthworks, Warren County, in south-west Ohio. Charles Whittlesey published the first map of the site in 1851 and although the earthen features had already been degraded by agriculture, one of the features Whittlesey recorded was an open circle immediately south of the main enclosure. The open circle embankment was no longer visible in 1998 when Cowan and his colleagues from the Museum Center began excavations at the site. With plans for a new school likely to impact this area, Cowan and his associates stripped an area where they believed the open circle embankment might be located. They encountered an arc of post-holes, and when they followed this to its full extent, it revealed a Great Circle, 73 m in diameter. There were 172 post-holes forming the circle, ranging from 68–130 cm deep and averaging about 33 cm in width. Limestone and shale slabs were found in some post-holes, apparently for bracing the upright posts. It appears that, prior to the construction of the open circle embankment, all the posts were pulled out and the holes were filled with midden soil. This combination of a circle of posts that were eventually covered by a circular embankment has some similarities to a smaller feature that has never been adequately published near Fort Hill. It also raises the possibility that many wooden architectural features were important parts of larger ceremonial landscapes seen at Hopewell sites across southern Ohio.

The Stubbs Great Post Circle discovery raises a number of questions about the planning and chronology of constructing these large ceremonial landscapes. Warren DeBoer (2010) has suggested that the construction of the Great Post Circle was the active phase of ceremonial activity, while the construction of the earthen embankment marked a shift to a more passive phase. Like many other interpretive statements about the ceremonial landscapes, embankments, and related features, this is a reasonable hypothesis. Unfortunately, the literature on Ohio Hopewell ceremonial landscapes is dominated by hypotheses and suffers from a paucity of data. The presence of large post circles along with large wooden buildings, often called Great Houses, may have preceded the construction of embankment walls and mounds at many sites, but more documented examples of these features are needed.

There are only a few places in Ohio where we can go today and witness the size and scope of the earthen constructions that formed the Ohio Hopewell ceremonial landscapes. Years of cultivation and urban development have flattened most and impacted all of these great earthen monuments. Unfortunately, most of these sites received little additional attention after the sites were mapped by Squier and Davis and their contemporaries. Consequently, modern interpretations about these sites still rely heavily on 19th century maps, many of which were even critiqued only a few decades after they were published (Thomas 1889a). Rapidly developing geophysical, geoarchaeological, and remote sensing techniques such as LiDAR offer archaeology the opportunity to map earthen features that are no longer clearly visible on the surface. The combination of a variety of techniques overlain through digital formats have helped generate maps that are more accurate than those published in the 19th century (Burks 2014; Burks and Cook 2011; Weymouth *et al.* 2009). Although we must still find ways to address hypotheses about contemporaneity and construction sequences, these new technological applications have the potential to convert hypotheses about alignments into factual data. This is an extremely exciting time to be involved in Hopewell archaeology.

3

The Hopeton Earthworks Project

The small community of Hopetown was about 4 miles (6.4 km) north of the city of Chillicothe in the mid-19th century. The Hopeton Earthworks is west of Hopetown on a large alluvial terrace inside a horse-shoe bend of the Scioto River (Fig. 3.1). The site lies on the east side of the river opposite the well-known Ohio Hopewell site of Mound City (Squier and Davis 1848; Mills 1922a; 1922b). The first published map of Hopeton, submitted by an author identified only by the initials J. C. (Fig. 3.1) appeared in the *Portfolio* in 1809. Several other versions of this map have been found in unpublished form in archives with papers from the period.

Squier and Davis (1848: 50–2) published a more accurate map of the site (Fig. 3.2) along with the first detailed description of the embankment walls:

> "They consist of a rectangle, with an attached circle, the latter extending into the former, instead of being connected with it in the usual manner. The rectangle measures nine hundred and fifty by nine hundred feet [*ca.* 290 × *ca.* 274 m] and the circle is ten hundred and fifty feet [425 m] in diameter. The centre of the circle is somewhat to the right of a line drawn through the centre of the rectangle, parallel to its longest sides. The exterior gateways are twelve in number, and have an average width of about twenty-five feet [7.6 m]. The chord of that part of the circle interior to the rectangle is five hundred and thirty feet [161.5 m]. On the east side are two circles, measuring two hundred, and two hundred and fifty feet in diameter respectively [*ca.* 61 and *ca.* 76 m]; one covering a gateway, the other extending into, and opening within, the work. About two hundred paces north of the great circle is another smaller one, two hundred and fifty feet [*ca.* 76 m] in diameter.
>
> The walls of the rectangular work are composed of a clayey loam, twelve feet high by fifty feet base [3.66 × 15.2 m], and are destitute of a ditch on either side. They resemble the heavy grading of a railway, and are broad enough, on the top, to admit the passage of a coach. The wall of the great circle was never as high as that of the rectangle; yet, although it has been much reduced of late years by the plough, it is still about five feet [1.5 m] in average height. It is also destitute of a ditch. It is built of clay, which differs strikingly in respect of color from the surrounding soil. The walls of the smaller circles are about three feet [0.9 m] in height, with interior ditches of corresponding depth.
>
> Parallel walls extend from the north-western corner of the rectangle, towards the river to the south-west. They are twenty-four hundred feet [*ca.* 730 m], or nearly half a mile [0.8 km] long, and are placed one hundred and fifty feet [45.7 m] apart. They terminate at the edge of the terrace, at the foot of which, it is evident, the river once had its course; but between which the present body of the stream, a

broad and fertile 'bottom' now intervenes. They are carried in a straight line, and although very slight, (nowhere exceeding two and a half feet [0.76 m] in height,) are uninterrupted throughout. They do not connect directly with the main work; at least, they are not traceable near it." (Squier and Davis 1848: 51–2)

In their description of the site, Squier and Davis (1848) raised the question about the source of the material used to build the earthen embankment walls. They note that although there are several large pits to the east and south-east of the enclosures these are not sufficient in size or number to account for the massive amount of soil that was used to make the walls. It is worth noting that the earlier map of Hopeton published in *Portfolio* in 1809 shows a different location for the long parallel walls and it illustrated a circle at the south-west end of those walls.

Cyrus Thomas of the Bureau of Ethnology (1889) challenged the accuracy of the map prepared by Squier and Davis in a paper titled "The Circular, Square and Octagonal Earthworks of Ohio." Thomas sent Col. Charles Middleton to resurvey many of the mounds and earthworks described by Squier and Davis nearly 40 years earlier. In addition to pointing out the inaccuracies in the Squier and Davis map of Hopeton, Thomas notes that the "only parts of this group we notice here are the large circle and the connected square (1889b: 23)." The damage to the embankment walls from agricultural activities in the intervening 40 years is further documented in the reduced height of the walls reported by Thomas who observed that the:

"lowest point of the square is yet 5 feet [1.5 m] high. The circle is more worn, the western half averaging about 2 feet [0.6 m] high, while the eastern half is lower, fading out for short distance near the northeast corner of the square." (1889b: 23)

This information suggests that both of the larger geometric enclosures at Hopeton were reduced in height by 50% or more, and many of the smaller embankment features became hard to recognize between 1848 and 1889.

Archaeological interest in Hopeton seems to have declined after the Bureau of Ethnology mapped the two large enclosures. Although there are collections in the Ohio Historical Society from one or more visits to the site by Warren K. Moorehead, it appears that sustained interest in the site waned until efforts were made to declare it a National Historical Landmark in the 1960s (Cockrell 1999). Degradation of the earthworks from agricultural activities continued throughout the first half of the 20th century and accelerated with the introduction of larger and more powerful tractors in the 1950s (Blank 1985). Annual cultivation of the embankment walls was finally terminated when the site was purchased by the National Park Service in 1990.

National Park Service archaeological study of the Hopeton Earthworks was initiated in 1994. The first test excavations were designed to investigate an area called the Triangle site, located along the terrace edge where artifact collectors had found considerable lithic debris and fire-cracked rock. Since this is also the location of the western terminus of the long parallel embankment walls, it was anticipated that the area might produce evidence of Hopewell habitation near the earthworks. Although numerous features were exposed and excavated, no evidence of occupation associated with the Ohio Hopewell period was discovered (Lynott 2009a).

Bret J. Ruby conducted the first study of the embankment walls at Hopeton in

1996. Ruby's field team excavated a trench across a segment of wall on the north-west side of the rectangular enclosure (Ruby 1997a; 1997b). The 1 m wide trench produced evidence about the material used to construct the wall and exposed features near the base of the wall. Two radiocarbon dates were obtained from the excavated features, which were the first dates that directly identified episodes of embankment wall construction at Hopeton.

In 2001, the Midwest Archeological Center, National Park Service, initiated a multi-year study of the geometric earthen enclosures at Hopeton (Lynott 2001; 2002; Lynott and Weymouth 2002). One of the main motivating factors of this study was to test the understanding that many of the interpretations about Ohio Hopewell are based on assumptions about the chronological placement of individual sites and their relative chronological relationship to one another. A wide range of models has been proposed to explain the Ohio Hopewell archaeological record, ranging from settlement systems (Dancey and Pacheco 1997; Pacheco and Dancey 2006; Prufer 1965; Yerkes 2005) and the role of geometric enclosures in Hopewell society (Byers 1987; 2004), to the use of enclosures as astronomical observatories (Romain 2000; Hively and Horn 1982; 2010). All of these interpretive models make some assumptions about the chronology of Ohio Hopewell sites.

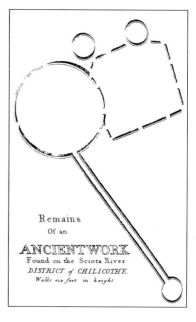

Fig. 3.1. Early map of the Hopeton Earthworks published in *The Portfolio* in 1809. The map brief accompanying the description is anonymous, but the initials J. C. on the map have been suggested to identify John Poague Campbell. Different versions of this map occur in the Wisconsin State Historical Society in Madison, WI, and the Ross County Historical Society, Chillicothe, OH.

Unfortunately, at the onset of the study at Hopeton, we were able to answer the most basic questions about embankment wall construction at only one site in all of southern Ohio. Robert Riordan's (1996) multi-year effort to unravel and date the construction sequence at the Pollock Works near Dayton, Ohio, had documented that the embankment walls at that hilltop enclosure were built to include a palisade. Riordan's systematic work over many years demonstrates that the Pollock Works were built, augmented, altered, and remodeled during the period AD 1–300 (Riordan 2006). The work of Robert Connnolly (Connolly and Lepper 2004), building on the efforts of the late Patricia Essenpreis and Richard Morgan at Fort Ancient, has also demonstrated that embankment wall construction was conducted in stages and occurred over several centuries. The dating of the construction sequence at Fort Ancient is not nearly as precise as has been achieved for the Pollock Works.

At the start of the Hopeton Earthworks Project, it was unclear how much time was involved in the construction of any single geometric earthen enclosure in the Scioto River Valley. Whether a large embankment complex was built by a single generation, or by the combined efforts of multiple generations, clearly has profound effects on our interpretation of the Ohio Hopewell archaeological record. The dense concentration of these earthen monuments in the area around Chillicothe, Ohio also raised the question whether or not they were built and used at the same time, or if there was a sequence to their construction and use. One of the primary goals of the study at Hopeton was to understand when the earthen walls were built, and how much time was spent in their construction and use. Fortunately, the people who built the earthen walls at Hopeton made frequent use of small fires as part of the construction process, providing suitable material to directly radiocarbon date wall fill depositional episodes.

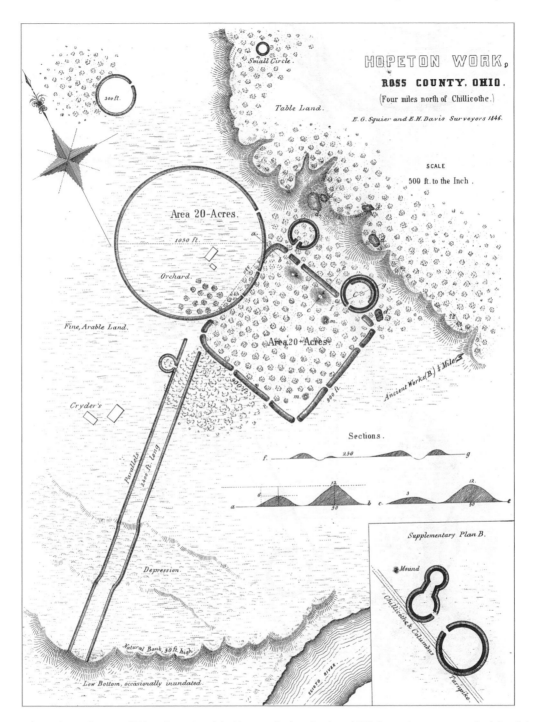

Fig. 3.2. When Ephraim Squier and Edwin Davis visited the Hopeton Earthworks about 1846, the earthen monument had already been subjected to a half century of agricultural degradation. Squier and Davis provided a fairly detailed description of the major earthen features. Their map, although it exaggerates the regularity of the geometric features of the enclosures, has become the standard for use by many contemporary archaeologists (Squier and Davis 1848, pl. xvii).

Geophysical survey and trench excavations

Throughout the majority of our research at the Hopeton Earthworks, decisions about all aspects of geophysical survey were guided by the experience and wisdom of the late John W. Weymouth. His experience with geophysical prospection and knowledge of geophysical theory guided the project from inception until we shifted our research to Mound City in 2009. In our work at the nearby Triangle site (Lynott 2009a; 2009b) from 1994 to 1998, we concluded that geophysical surveys can be effectively used to locate large and mid-sized subsurface features at Hopeton. Surveys with a G-858 gradiometer, FM-36 gradiometer, and RM-15 resistance meter were all effective in identifying subsurface anomalies. After analysis of the quality of the geophysical data combined with the labor costs associated with each instrument, we elected to use the G-858 gradiometer for survey of embankment walls and enclosures. The G-858 was selected for its combination of speed, high sensitivity and negligible drift.

The G-858 gradiometer was configured in the vertical mode with the lower sensor 30 cm above the surface and the upper sensor 100 cm above the lower sensor. The unit was operated with a two-person crew, with one surveyor holding the staff and the other holding the electronic pack and batteries. The team gathered data in

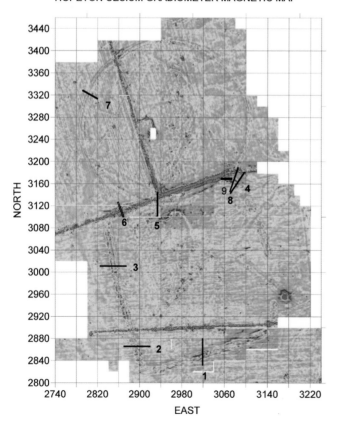

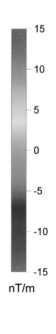

Fig. 3.3. Nearly a decade of research at the Hopeton Earthworks has shown that geophysical surveys can produce highly accurate maps of earthen walls and ditches which have been gradually leveled through years of agriculture. Although these features may still be detected through topographic analysis, small walls and ditches have been leveled and larger walls have been lowered and spread. This magnetic map shows accurately the major enclosure walls as they were built (image courtesy of Midwest Archeological Center, Lincoln, Nebraska).

continuous or walking mode at 0.2 sec cycle time, which generated measurements at 20 cm intervals. Survey blocks were 20 × 20 m in size, with traverses spaced at 1 m intervals across each block. With a cycle time of 0.2 seconds, the G-858 specifications indicate that the sensitivity of each sensor is 0.03 nT.

Raw data was initially processed with MagMap software by Geometrics. Subsequent processing was accomplished with the Golden Software program Surfer. The data were not de-spiked, and the occasional metal anomalies were left where they occurred. Since data collection was unidirectional, it was not necessary to de-stripe the data. The data were gridded with Surfer's Kriging algorithm at an interval of 0.25 × 0.25 m and individual grid blocks were combined into mosaics for final mapping.

Magnetic survey was initiated in 2001 across the wall segments that form the south embankment wall of the square enclosure. The 2001 survey consisted of 37 (20 × 20 m) blocks. The survey was continued annually through 2005, collecting 686 survey blocks of data. The 27.44 hectare area that was mapped is shown in Figure 3.3.

The embankment walls of the two large enclosures are clearly visible in the magnetic data. The two smaller "sacred circles" (Squier and Davis 1848) are also visible in the data, but they are not as clearly visible as the larger enclosure walls, particularly at the resolution needed to produce this total site map. Careful analysis of the data surrounding the smaller circles also produced evidence of a third and even smaller circle along the east side of the square enclosure (Weymouth 2002).

The magnetic data depicts the embankment walls as essentially the same size and form as is shown in Squier and Davis' (1848: xvii) map. Upon closer examination, however, it should be noted that there are significant differences between the two maps (Fig. 3.4; Lynott 2007). In the magnetic survey data, none of

Fig. 3.4. Many scholars use the maps published by Squier and Davis to interpret the size, orientation, and geometry of Ohio Hopewell earthworks. This comparison between the Squier and Davis map of the two main enclosures at Hopeton and the magnetic data collected in 2001–2005 illustrates that the symmetry between the two enclosures is exaggerated in the 1846 map. It also shows that neither the circular or rectangular enclosures are as geometrically perfect as depicted in *Ancient Monuments of the Mississippi Valley*.

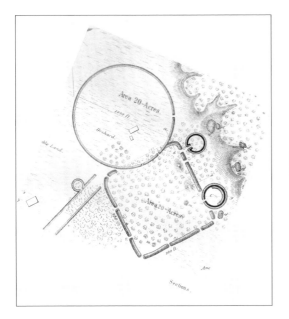

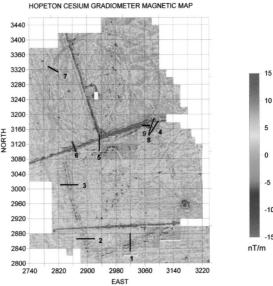

the wall segments forming the square enclosure are straight, which contrasts with the relatively straight wall segments presented by Squier and Davis. While Squier and Davis depict the large circular enclosure as a near perfect circle (1848: xvii), the magnetic data shows that it is somewhat more oval. Squier and Davis (1848: 51) note that the "centre of the circle is somewhat to the right of a line drawn through the centre of the rectangle, parallel to its longest sides." A comparison of the magnetic data with their map indicates that this is clearly understated. Later scholars have interpreted the asymmetry between the large enclosures as being due to the sequence of construction (Byers 2004; DeBoer 2010). Problems with the map of Hopeton and other major sites is likely due to the blistering pace set by Squier and Davis in their efforts to record Ohio earthworks. Squier (1847) notes that he and Davis examined over 100 enclosures and excavated nearly 200 mounds during their relatively brief 2-year partnership.

Although remnants of the earthen embankment walls are visible at many points at Hopeton, two centuries of cultivation have flattened them sufficiently as to obscure all but the general shape, size and orientation (Figs 3.5 and 3.6). The magnetic survey data illustrates that resurvey of many of the large Ohio Hopewell enclosures may yield productive information that may be more accurate than the maps published by Squier and Davis and other early scholars. Recent work by Jarrod Burks has refined and confirmed the effectiveness of this approach at a number of other Ohio Hopewell sites (Burks 2014; Burks and Cook 2011).

The clarity of the wall edges in the magnetic survey data was used in planning a series of trenches across the embankment walls. These trenches were intended to collect information to address two primary research questions: when were the walls built and how were they constructed? We also planned to use the excavation trenches to collect subsurface geophysical data to better determine the relationship between the surface magnetic data and the truncated earthen walls.

Between 2001 and 2009, nine trenches were excavated to traverse wall segments forming the large circular and large rectangular enclosures at the Hopeton Earthworks (Fig. 3.3). Two of these trenches exposed portions of the wall forming the Great Circle, six trenches exposed segments of the square enclosure, and one trench exposed the common wall section forming the intersection between these two large enclosures. In addition to the nine trenches across the major enclosure walls, two were excavated to examine the wall and ditch combination that form the two "sacred circles" on the east side of the square enclosure (Bernardini 2004).

The nine trenches through the large enclosure walls were excavated with a backhoe. Each trench was then carefully excavated while being monitored by two or more archaeologists. This approach was adopted following Ruby's (1996) hand excavated trench, which indicated the walls were constructed of geological materials that are mainly culturally sterile. When a change in soil color, texture, or evidence of a feature was exposed by the backhoe, work was stopped and the area was examined by archaeologists. In those instances where a potential feature was present, the backhoe operator moved forward in the trench and the feature was left as a pedestal for hand excavation. This approach worked very well, and multiple features were recorded and excavated in each of the nine trenches.

The trenches we excavated across the walls of the two large enclosures ranged in

Fig. 3.5. An undated photograph from the early 20th century shows the wall segments that form the north-west corner of the rectangular enclosure. The walls are seen from inside the enclosure looking to the north-west. A wooden fence, which was later replaced by a wire fence, may have served to reduce cultivation on this segment of wall for much of the 20th century.

Fig. 3.6. An undated photograph from the early 20th century showing the south-west corner of the rectangular enclosure at the Hopeton Earthworks.

length from 21 m to 50 m. The first seven trenches that were excavated (Trenches 1–7) were 1.5 m wide, while the remaining trenches (#8, 9) were 2 m wide. The slightly wider trench format was adopted to provide better visibility of the walls for geoarchaeological study, mapping, and photography.

In addition to the nine trenches across the larger enclosure walls, two hand-excavated trenches were laid out to examine the sacred circles on the east side of the square enclosure and were 1 m wide and 7.5 m long (Bernardini 2004). Although the location of the embankment wall and/or interior ditch forming these two circular enclosures is visible in the magnetic surface survey data, neither the wall nor the ditch could be visually identified in the trenches that cross-sectioned them. Magnetic susceptibility study of the excavated wall profiles confirmed the presence of the North Sacred Circle and demonstrates the importance of integrating geophysical data collection and analysis into earthwork excavations (Dalan 2007).

Embankment wall features

One of the central goals of the project has been to develop a better understanding of when the earthen walls were built, and how much time elapsed during the construction of the enclosure complex. Fortunately, features associated with earthen wall construction were encountered in all nine trenches. Some features were found outside the margins of the embankment walls, and were not related to the period of their construction. Most of the 28 recorded features were found under or within the fill of the embankment walls and were formed by activities associated with wall construction. These included post-holes, burned logs or large pieces of burned wood, and a diverse range of small features reflecting the use of fire.

Three post-holes were identified in association with earthen walls during the excavation of the trenches. They ranged in size from 20 cm to 25 cm in diameter, and 10–32 cm deep. One post-hole was found under the wall fill, penetrating into the subsoil, and may pre-date wall construction activities or may be related to the planning and laying out of the embankment walls. Several additional post-holes were found penetrating the subsoil, but these were outside the margins of the embankment wall. There was no obvious pattern to the post-holes, so any relationship between them and the embankment walls is speculative at best. Three post-holes were found in the wall fill, and their purpose is unknown. In all three instances, the posts appear to have been pulled from these holes and the post-holes were backfilled with soil of a contrasting color. Some small amounts of charcoal were found in the fill of these post-holes, but since the source of this material is unclear, they were not given a high priority for radiocarbon dating. The isolated character of these post-holes and the nature of our excavations make it impossible to determine if they were part of a larger pattern or what function they might have served. Certainly some marker posts were used to lay out the design of the enclosures on the ground, and in several instances, archaeologists have documented that post structures preceded these earthen enclosures (Chapter 4). There simply is not enough information at this time from Hopeton to determine what role these isolated posts played in the building or use of the enclosures.

Twenty features found at the base of the embankment walls or within the wall

Below left: **Fig. 3.7.** Feature 17 was exposed at the bottom of Trench 3 that transects one of the northern segments forming the west wall of the rectangular enclosure. This small feature appears to be the remains of a brief fire made on the surface of the truncated B horizon immediately before wall fill was placed at this location. An AMS date from the burned wood in the small feature yielded a date of 1910±40 BP (Beta-176580) with a calibrated date at 2 sigma of AD 20–220 (photo: author).

Below right: **Fig. 3.8.** Feature 11 was exposed at the bottom of Trench 2. Trench 2 transects a segment of the west wall of the rectangular enclosure. The small area of burning was found on the surface of the truncated B horizon and it was covered by baskets of wall fill. The intact edges and materials in the feature indicate that the burned area must have been covered fairly quickly since little of these materials became scattered by human or natural elements. An AMS date from wood in the feature produced a date of 1710±80 BP (Beta-176577) with a corrected age at 2 sigma of AD 130–530 (photo: author).

Fig. 3.9. Burned area designated Feature 04-04 from Trench 6. This trench transects a wall segment in the north-west corner of the rectangular enclosure that was protected from cultivation by a fence throughout most of the 20th century. It is the best preserved wall segment at Hopeton. Two radiocarbon dates from this feature were reported by Bret Ruby from his 1996 trench (see Table 1) (photo: author).

fill resulted from brief burning activities associated with wall construction. All of these were situated either on top of the truncated subsoil or on the top of a soil layer used in wall construction. Finding features at the interface of two different types of soil is relatively common in the walls at the Hopeton Earthworks. No features were found within a large homogeneous soil layer in the wall fill. Even though much of the wall excavations were done by backhoe, the process was undertaken with sufficient care and observation to make us confident that most of the features in these trenches were observed and recorded. Features exposed in the excavation of the nine trenches at Hopeton are briefly described in Table 1.

The most common type of feature encountered in the trench excavations was lenses or pockets of burned soil and charred wood (Figs 3.7–3.9). Twenty of these features were recorded, with at least one found in each trench. All contained charred wood, and burned soil was observed in all but three. Most (n=16) were less than 0.5 sq. m. in horizontal extent and all were 10 cm or less in thickness. The sharp boundaries of these compact features suggest they were buried fairly promptly after burning, perhaps within hours. Four larger burned features with less distinct boundaries were encountered, and the scattered nature of the charcoal and burned soil suggests these may have been left exposed for a longer period of time before they were covered with wall fill.

Fig. 3.10. Excavation of Trench 9 revealed the presence of a large burned log at the base of the wall resting on the truncated B horizon. The log is still largely intact and must have been covered with wall fill, perhaps while it was still warm (photo: author).

Fig. 3.11. Excavation of Trench 4 across the curved wall segment that forms the north-east corner of the rectangular enclosure. At the base of the wall excavators uncovered two areas of burned calcite resting on the truncated B horizon surface and covered with wall fill which produced a radiocarbon determination of 1000±40 BP (Beta-182629), with a calibrated date of AD 980–1055. A very comparable date was obtained from another burned feature in the same trench and suggests that this portion of the enclosure wall was either rebuilt or repaired perhaps eight centuries after the original large enclosures (photo: author).

Trench	Feature	Year	Description
1	5	2001	Post-hole
1	6	2001	Burned log
1	7	2001	Post-hole
2	11	2002	Lens of burned soil & charcoal
3	14	2002	Lens of burned soil & charcoal
3	17	2002	Lens of burned soil & charcoal
3	22	2002	Small pit in subsoil
4	100	2003	Charcoal & white mineral resting on subsoil
4	101	2003	Small lens of charred wood
4	103	2003	Small lens of charcoal & burned soil
5	105	2003	Small lens of charcoal & burned soil
5	106	2003	Post-hole
4	107	2003	Large block of burned wood
4	108	2003	Linear band of charred soil & white mineral resting on subsoil
7	04-1	2004	Burned soil & charcoal
6	04-2	2004	Burned soil & charcoal
6	04-4	2004	Burned soil & charcoal
8	5-1	2005	Lens of burned soil & charcoal
8	5-2	2005	Burned soil & charcoal
8	5-3	2005	Layer of burned soil & charcoal
8	5-8	2005	Lens of burned soil & charcoal
8	5-9	2005	Lens of burned soil & charcoal
8	5-10	2005	Lens of burned soil & charcoal
9	801	2008	Scatter of charcoal & burned soil
9	802	2008	Small area of burned soil, charcoal
9	803	2008	Dense concentration of charred & partially burned wood
9	804	2008	Large burned hickory log
9	805	2008	Small pit containing charcoal, burned earth & ashy material

Table 1: Hopeton Earthworks: features exposed within embankment walls.

In addition to charred wood, these features resulting from brief episodes of burning sometimes included small quantities of fire-cracked rocks, lithic debris, flecks of mica, and burned bone. Only a few objects were found with any individual feature. These small burned features were generally found at the base of the embankment wall, resting on the truncated subsoil. There were a few instances where the burned feature rested on a layer of fill that had been deposited as part of the wall construction. In those instances, the burned feature was covered by a different type of wall fill.

Two large pieces of a burned log were found in Trench 1 during the 2001 excavations. These were found resting horizontally on the truncated subsoil and covered by wall fill. There was no evidence of burned soil in contact with the log fragments, so it is likely the log was burned elsewhere. The log was discovered resting on yellow-brown subsoil and had been covered by similar material to form the interior part of the wall at this point of the rectangular enclosure. DeBoer (2010) has suggested that this burned log was part of a "post fence or similar structure [which] was dismantled and then subsequently covered by an earthen wall" (2010: 176). While this and another burned log exposed in Trench 9 may have been part of a larger partition or wooden feature that pre-dates the embankment wall, current data are far too scant to confirm this hypothesis.

A much larger piece of a burned hickory log was uncovered under the embankment wall in Trench 9 (Fig. 3.10). The log was at least 70 cm in diameter and rested on the truncated subsoil surface. Burned soil, fire-cracked rock, lithic debris and a projectile point fragment were found in association with the log. The intact nature of the log and oxidation of the soil adjacent to it suggests the log was probably covered with soil before it had fully burned. A short distance to the east in Trench 9, a second large piece of burned wood was uncovered. The partially charred wood and burned soil were also in an excellent state of preservation, and it is likely the wood was covered with soil while it was still hot.

Small shallow pits were found excavated into the subsoil near the center of the wall segments in Trenches 3 and 9. The dark fill of the pits contained burned soil, fire-cracked rock, and non-diagnostic lithic debris. Both of these pits were covered by wall fill.

Two very unusual features with concentrations of crushed calcite were found resting on the subsoil at the base of the wall in Trench 4 and covered with wall fill. These features were near the center of the wall segment and exhibited no evidence that they had been disturbed by later intrusive activities. The presence of white powdery calcite is the only instance where this material has been found at Hopeton, and a radiocarbon date from one of these features and a block of burned wood in the same trench suggests they date as much as 800 years later than other embankment wall features (Fig. 3.11).

In addition to the features described above, excavations revealed the presence of a series of discrete soil layers deposited as part of wall construction. These small layers and lenses initially looked like features, but were determined to have been basket-loads of different soils. Lenses of gravel, sand, clay, and other material were visible in Trenches 4, 8, and 9 (Fig. 3.12). In all the other trenches, wall fill was sufficiently homogeneous that individual basket-loads could not be visually identified. The complex nature of these wall fills and their source material was the subject of geoarchaeological study.

Geoarchaeology

Field and laboratory geoarchaeological study of the embankment walls has been a central component of the Hopeton Earthworks project (Lynott 2004; Lynott and Mandel 2006; 2009). Geoarchaeological study has been integrated into the project to better understand earthen wall construction methods, to discover the source of the materials used in building the walls, and to look for evidence of weathering, erosion, or soil formation that might offer a geochronological assessment of the various wall segments. The majority of the geoarchaeological study at Hopeton focused upon the trenches across the embankment walls, and cores excavated across much of the landform on which the embankment walls were built.

Based upon the large amount of soil stripping that is evident at Hopeton, the builders of this site must have used some system to mark out the enclosure plans

Fig. 3.12. Most of the wall segments that were examined at Hopeton revealed that, while the walls were constructed in stages using two or more types of earth, selection of wall fill material emphasized the use and placement of homogeneous soil material. Visible basket-loads were only seen in Trenches 4, 8, and 9 which were excavated into the walls in the north-east corner of the rectangular enclosure (photo: author).

on the ground prior to the start of construction. Geoarchaeological study of the backhoe trenches produced substantial information about how the walls were built. This study has shown that the first step in wall construction was removal of the A horizon and upper B horizon across the area to be built upon. It is uncertain if topsoil was initially removed from the area comprising both large enclosures, or if the stripping and wall building was accomplished in stages. Some support for the latter model is derived from the diverse range of radiocarbon results obtained from different wall segments. The segment-like character of the rectangular enclosure may be evidence for the latter scenario. There is clear evidence that the embankment walls were built on a truncated B horizon, a situation that was recorded in each of the trenches that cross-cut the major embankment walls. The small burning episodes that produced the hearth features, discussed above, were conducted on the surface of the truncated soil profile. As noted previously, the intact nature of the small hearths can be explained because these small fires were immediately covered by a layer of wall fill, possibly while they were still burning.

For the majority of the large enclosure walls, homogeneous soil material was used to build the basal components of the walls (Figs 3.13 and 3.14). In most of the wall segments that were examined, two or three different soil materials were used, but these were carefully sorted and placed so that there was minimal mixing, and the boundaries between the different soils were sharp and distinct. There is a strong

Left: Fig. 3.13. Trench 1. Most trenches revealed that the walls of the large Circle and Rectangular Enclosure were built with two or more types of soil. Selection and placement of wall fill material emphasized homogeneity of the material in each layer and the margins between two different soil types remains clear and sharp even after two millennia (photo: author).

Right: Fig. 3.14. Trench 6 exposes the highest wall segment remaining at Hopeton. This wall segment was built with multiple layers of soil, but each layer is highly homogeneous (photo: author).

Fig. 3.15. After the earthen walls at Hopeton were built, they became exposed to the same natural forces that affect all soils in this region of Ohio. Soil development included the formation of an A horizon on the surface of the earthen wall. When the walls were subjected to cultivation, the upper wall fills were pulled and washed down the sides and outward from the core of the wall. This process buried the A horizon that formed along the lower margins of the embankment. This surface is visible in Trench 2 as a dark layer that rises gently upward in the trench wall. This A horizon has been truncated toward the center of the wall by two centuries of plowing (photo: author).

tendency for soils with a reddish color to be placed on the exterior side of the enclosure wall, while soils with a more yellow color were placed on the interior side of the wall. Although soil colors exposed within individual trenches were fairly homogeneous, there is considerable variation between the colors used in the different embankment wall segments. Stages of construction, as represented by different soil layers, seem to be a common attribute of Ohio Hopewell earthen features.

It is important to note that the process of earthen wall construction involved both selection of homogeneous soil material to form the wall, and careful placement of those soils to insure that the different types of soils used to build the wall were not mixed. As we discuss later, there are places where individual basket-loads of soil can be identified as lenses when viewed in an excavation profile. However, for most of the trenches that were excavated, individual basket-loads were not visible to excavators. The large amounts of homogeneous fills used in wall construction required that large surface areas had to have been stripped of topsoil and exposed for quarrying of soil. There would not have been enough homogeneous soils exposed if soil stripping had been limited solely to the area under the walls. Additional evidence for widespread soil stripping is presented with soil core data later in this chapter.

Examination of the wall fill layers in the trenches indicated no evidence for a significant time lapse during construction of individual wall segments. No evidence of weathering, erosion, or soil formation was observed within the wall fill (Mandel *et al.* 2003; 2010). After the embankment wall was completed, a soil formed on the surface of the wall. This soil is preserved along the sloping margins at the base of the walls, and has been covered by wall spill that was plowed and eroded off the upper portions of the embankment wall by historic agriculture (Fig. 3.15). The basal components of the embankment walls are preserved under this eroded wall spill, and the wall edges are detectable through surface magnetic survey.

In the majority of wall segments, the soils used to build the walls consisted of large and homogenous layers that were carefully deposited on the wall with

Fig. 3.16. Trench 9 exposed a layer of sheetwash resting on the surface of the truncated B horizon at the base of the embankment wall. Trench 9 is located at the intersection of the two enclosures. Diverse materials were used in the wall construction at this locality and individual basket-loads of fill may be seen in the wall (photo: author).

no visual evidence of basket-loading. The one area where the wall fill was less homogeneous and basket-loading was visually detectable was in the north-east "corner" of the rectangular enclosure (Trenches 4, 8, and 9). This is the only curved wall segment forming the rectangular enclosure, and the only "corner" that is not open. The heterogeneous character of soils in different basket-loads and the liberal use of lenses and layers of gravel are unique in the construction of this segment of the enclosure (Fig. 3.12).

Another unique element in the curved wall segment forming the north-east corner of the square enclosure is a laminated sheet wash that was exposed in Trenches 8 and 9. This is the only area of the site where the two large enclosure walls are believed to intersect. This 1–5 cm thick layer comprised numerous thin layers of silt that were deposited on top of the truncated B horizon in this area. The area was left open long enough for numerous large rains to deposit sheet wash from the hillside to the east on top of the truncated soil surface. Micromorphological analysis (Mandel *et al.* 2010) of the sheet wash layer indicates it lacked internal bedding of fine-grained laminae, and is characterized by movement of a large volume of sediment and low volume of water. These sediments reflect redeposited C-horizon material that is probably derived from a steep scarp to the east, which rises to an old loess-mantled terrace. The sheet wash contained charred wood and a few artifacts and has been radiocarbon dated to 30 cal BC–cal AD 130 (Beta-249009; see Table 2). The laminated character of this sheet wash layer implies that the truncated B horizon under this area of the enclosure remained open to these fine depositional events for at least a brief interval (Fig. 3.16). It also suggests that areas uphill and to the east of this point in the Hopeton earthwork had been stripped of the upper soil horizon which thus exposed the C-horizon material to erosion and downhill transportation during rains. Different layers of wall fill material were placed on top of the sheet wash when this segment of the embankment wall was constructed.

A Giddings coring rig was used to extract soil cores from locations in and around the Hopeton Earthworks (Fig. 3.17). The cores were initially intended to discover the quarry source for the soil material used to build the embankment walls, but cores were also subsequently used to examine aspects of embankment wall construction (Dempsey 2008). The soil coring program produced substantial evidence that once the A horizon within the large earthen enclosures was stripped off the exposed B horizon was quarried for soils to build the embankment walls. The cores showed that in many areas, as much as 0.5 m of B horizon had been removed from inside the enclosures (Fig. 3.18). Deeper quarry pits into the B and C horizons may be visible in the magnetic survey data, but this can only be confirmed by additional excavation. Quarrying soil from inside the enclosures served to make the embankment walls taller from that perspective. This would produce a similar visual effect to the large interior ditch at the Fairgrounds Circle at the Newark Earthworks, making the walls appear larger from the inside of the enclosure.

Removal of the A horizon across about 15 ha that form the location of the two larger geometric enclosures produced a substantial amount of fill. It is unclear how this A horizon fill was used, but it may have been used to build the long parallel walls. There is no conclusive evidence to support this interpretation at this time, but the inability to detect

Table 2: Chart of weighted averages for radiocarbon dates from features in trenches (CalPal-2007 online; see also Appendix 1).

	No. dates	Calibrated age (1σ)
Trench 1	4	AD 117 ± 44
Trench 2	1	AD 320 ± 90
Trench 3	2	AD 91 ± 18
Trench 5	2	AD 259 ± 48
Trench 6	4	AD 121 ± 34
Trench 7	1	AD 169 ± 47
Trench 8	2	AD 172 ± 38
Trench 9	3	AD 153 ± 53

Fig. 3.17. Rolfe Mandel used a Giddings coring rig to examine the soil profiles across much of the landform on which the Hopeton Earthworks was constructed (photo: author).

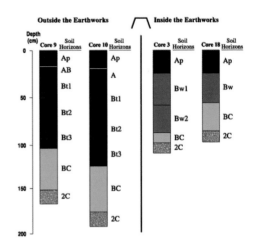

Fig. 3.18. Rolfe Mandel discovered that the area under the embankment walls and inside the large enclosures had been stripped of topsoil as the first step in building of the Hopeton landscape. Subsoil was then quarried from the interior of the enclosures to build the different wall segments. This schematic comparison of soils inside and outside enclosure shows the extent of stripping and quarrying within the enclosure (image courtesy of Rolfe Mandel).

the parallel walls in geophysical survey data anywhere other than adjacent to the two large enclosures suggests the material used to build the walls did not contrast greatly with the material forming the current plowzone (Ap). The original height of the parallel walls is unknown, but they are clearly visible on aerial photographs dating as late as 1951. We must also consider the possibility that the A horizon was simply spread across the landscape, which would seriously affect the redistribution of artifacts and any interpretation of these materials. Considering the amount of earthmoving that is apparent at Hopeton, we urge caution in relying heavily only upon the surface distribution of artifacts to interpret these large complex sites (i.e. Seig and Burks 2010).

Geoarchaeological study has provided some general data about the chronological factors relating to earthen wall construction at Hopeton Earthworks. First, it is important to note that the rectangular enclosure is actually formed by eleven separate wall segments, with a large circle extending into the north-west side of the rectangle. One of the two smaller circles intrudes into the rectangular enclosure, and also forms part of the eastern wall. Although somewhat different construction methods and materials were used in all sections of the embankment walls that have been examined to date, there is no indication that any of the different soil layers within the walls were exposed to erosion or weathering. There is evidence that the truncated B horizon under the intersecting point of the large circle and the rectangle was left exposed long enough to be covered by multiple layers of fine sheet wash. In every other locality, it would seem that a section of wall was started and completed promptly. Radiocarbon dates derived from features associated with wall construction provide greater clarity about the temporal context of these events.

Squier and Davis identified two topographic features inside the east wall of the rectangular enclosure as mounds. Geoarchaeological analysis of cores extracted from those features indicates that they are more likely natural colluvial remnants because the sediments in the raised features were well-sorted and there was no stratigraphic break between the sediments forming the raised features and the subsoil below. Mound excavations at other sites have shown that Hopewell mounds were consistently built over the remains of a structure, prepared floor, or some other cultural feature. The absence of any similar features in these landforms also indicates these are colluvial remnants rather than Hopewell mounds.

Radiocarbon results

Radiocarbon samples have been collected from numerous features both within and near the embankment walls at the Hopeton Earthworks. Samples that have been submitted for dating were selected after a careful consideration of the nature of the sample and the context in which it was found. Since one goal of this study is to identify the time period during which the enclosures walls were built, we have strived to select samples with the potential for providing the highest chronological resolution possible. This could best be accomplished by selecting samples from features that exhibit evidence of *in situ* burning. Wall building at Hopeton was accomplished by people who quarried, carried, and carefully placed massive amounts of sediments. Although the wall material we have observed is predominantly geological in nature, selecting samples with evidence of *in situ* burning reduces the possibility of dating redeposited charred botanical remains. We are fortunate that many of the features at Hopeton reflect *in situ* burning episodes, and all of these appear to be brief episodes. Most of the features that were dated exhibited oxidized soil with a sharply defined concentration of charred botanical remains, which reflects that these features were promptly buried under wall fill. These hearth-like features are fairly common under the fills used in wall construction, and because of their brief use and lack of associated habitation debris, they appear to be ritual or ceremonial in character. Botanical identification of the samples was undertaken prior to dating. Although ideally it would have been better to date short-lived specimens like nut hulls or twigs, the vast majority of carbonized material at Hopeton appears to be small pieces from hardwood species like oak and hickory. With the exception of two large burned logs, all of the features discussed in this section seem to represent small, brief fires.

Twenty-two radiocarbon dates have been obtained from samples associated with embankment wall construction at Hopeton (see Table 3), and most of the dates (n=15) have standard deviations of 40 years. Twenty of the samples yielded dates consistent with a Middle Woodland age, with two samples falling into a later prehistoric context.

Geoarchaeological examination of wall fill material exposed in the nine trenches produced no evidence that any of the wall sections examined were left exposed long enough for erosion or weathering of wall fill to occur. No evidence of soil formation was observed in any of the exposed wall fills, except those sloping soil layers that formed on the surface of the embankment walls. However, we must also remember that the upper two-thirds of most segments of embankment wall have been eroded away by more than two centuries of cultivation, and it is possible that evidence for temporal lapses in the construction of the walls has been destroyed. The sharp boundaries between different types of materials used in wall construction also suggest that wall fill was not left exposed for any substantial

Table 3: Hopeton Embankment Wall radiocarbon dates. Calibrations were calculated using the University of Washington Quaternary Isotope Lab Radiocarbon Calibration Program Rev. 4.3, based on Stuiver and Reimer (1993) and Stuiver *et al.* (1998).

Sample no.	Determination BP	Standard error	$\delta^{13}C/^{12}C$ ratio	Calibrated date 2σ (95.4%)	Context
Beta-177506	2040	80	-25.0	BC 350–AD 120	F. 6, Trench 1
Beta-176576	1990	130	-25.0	BC 370–AD 330	F. 6, Trench 1
Beta-177507	1990	70	-25.0	BC 170–AD 140	F, 6, Trench 1
Beta-159033	1740	50	-25.0	AD 150–410	F.6, Trench 1
Beta-176577	1710	80	-25.0	AD 130–530	F.11, Trench 2
Beta-176579	1910	40	-24.5	AD 20–220	F. 14, Trench 3
Beta-176580	1910	40	-23.7	AD 20–220	F. 17, Trench 3
Beta-233776	1870	40	-23.6	AD 60–240	F. 105, Trench 5
Beta-182632	1680	40	-23.6	AD 255–435	F. 105, Trench 5
Beta-233777	1900	40	-25.0	AD 20–220	F.04-2, Trench 6
Beta-198332	1860	40	-25.7	AD 70–240	F.04-2, Trench 6
Beta-96598	1930	60	-25.0	BC 40–AD 235	Trench 6, Ruby
Beta-109962	1840	50	-25.0	AD 75–330	Trench 6, Ruby
Beta-198331	1840	40	-26.6	AD 80–250	Trench 7, F. 04-1
Beta-233775	1890	40	-24.8	AD 30–230	Trench 8, F.05-2
Beta-213026	1790	40	-26.7	AD 130-350	Trench 8, F. 05-4
Beta-249012	2130	40	-26.7	BC 350–50	F. 805, Trench 9
Beta-249009	1940	40	-25.4	BC 30–AD 130	F. 801, Trench 9
Beta-249011	1830	40	-24.6	AD 80–310	F. 804, Trench 9
Beta-249010	1820	40	-23.6	AD 90–320	F. 803, Trench 9
Beta-182630	1010	40	-24.1	AD 980–1050	F. 107, Trench 4
Beta-182629	1000	40	-24.0	AD 980–1055	F. 100. Trench 4

period of time. This evidence suggests that features within individual trenches are roughly contemporaneous, at least in terms of radiocarbon years. Due to the different wall segments that form the enclosures at Hopeton, we cannot make a similar assumption about the features and dates between different wall segments.

In an effort to determine the period of wall construction, two different methods of analysis were applied to these radiocarbon results. Weighted averages were calculated for eight of the nine trenches using calibrated radiocarbon ages and the methods recommended by Long and Ripeteau (1974). Trenches 1–3 and 5–9 produced weighted averages that clearly reflect construction during the Middle Woodland, but the two dates from Trench 4 reflect activities that occurred many centuries later. Overall, the radiocarbon evidence from the embankment walls reflects two different periods of activity. The first is clearly associated with the Hopewell or Middle Woodland period in southern Ohio, and the Trench 4 dates provide evidence of later modification or repair of the original embankment wall. Further discussion about the later dates and wall construction activities will follow after some observations about the chronological data associated with the Hopewell era.

The eight Middle Woodland weighted averages reflect a time span of 211 years (Table 2). Closer examination of the weighted averages shows that the most recent weighted average is from Trench 2, and is based on a single radiocarbon date. While we cannot be certain that this date is a less accurate estimate than any of the others, the standard deviation for this date (±90) is one of the largest of any of the dates obtained for the Hopeton Earthworks. If this date is eliminated from consideration, the range of weighted averages falls to 168 years, cal AD 91–259, with standard deviation ranging from 18 to 48 years. It is noteworthy that the single date from Trench 2 overlaps the modified range of weighted averages at one standard deviation, and it seems likely that if further radiocarbon assays could be obtained from contexts that are contemporary with the feature in Trench 2, the weighted average of these dates would be consistent with the other Middle Woodland ages for the embankment walls.

One of the key goals of the Hopeton Earthworks Project has been to determine when the embankment walls were built. Recognizing that interpretation of the Hopeton radiocarbon dates is extremely important to the understanding of embankment construction, I asked my colleague Timothy Schilling to conduct an independent analysis of the dates using Bayesian probability analysis. Although he has not worked directly on Ohio Hopewell sites, he has dealt with complex combinations of features and radiocarbon dates at other sites, most notably Monks Mound at Cahokia near East St Louis, Illinois (Schilling 2013). His analysis of the radiocarbon results from features under the Hopeton embankment walls is included here as Appendix 1.

Several issues must be kept in mind when considering these radiocarbon results. First, all of the Middle Woodland dates were collected from features resting on truncated subsoil and covered by fills that formed the base of the earthen walls. Consequently, the features being dated actually pre-date the start of wall construction. Secondly, the small size, sharp margins, and intact nature of these features suggest they were covered with wall fill shortly after being extinguished, or possibly even while still burning. The materials that were dated were hardwood species, making it possible that the older growth rings might skew the results to a slightly earlier age. However, with the exception of the two large logs that were dated, the small size of the features and the small quantity of charred material found in the features makes it unlikely that large pieces of old wood may have been burned.

Despite the possibility that "old wood" was included in the burned features under the embankment walls, the wide disparity in radiocarbon dates provide fairly strong evidence that the geometric enclosures were built over multiple generations. Due to the character of radiocarbon dating it is not possible to precisely determine the length of time that elapsed during the construction of the embankment walls, but a minimum of a century is a reasonable minimum estimate. A more general estimate that the walls were built over four to six generations has significant implications relating to social organization, social continuity, and the effective labor pool that contributed to this monumental construction. Most of this activity appears to have been conducted in the second century, but as Schilling notes in Appendix 1, the dates may represent a much longer construction episode.

Geoarchaeology

Geoarchaeology is the study of the processes leading to changes in the physical landscape which both effect and affect ancient communities and the survival of their cultural remains. Human populations inhabit inherited landscapes that have been altered and reshaped mainly by natural processes but which may also include deposits such as alluvium and colluvium (hillwash). These deposits may have been initiated, accentuated or accelerated by human action, and may themselves erode, transform and bury archaeological evidence and sites.

The study of soils can be an important element in archaeological research . Their development and the evidence they contain may be affected by human activity such as vegetation removal, plowing, trampling, and occupation. The recognition of transported soils, their former character and history, and the distinction between soils and sediments is important in understanding the cultural history of a site under investigation.

At the Hopewell sites, particularly at Hopeton, geoarchaeological investigation is a relatively new addition to the suite of scientific techniques archaeologists are applying to the study of these complex earthworks. It has so far been largely restricted to analysis of deposits to determine if they were soils or sediments, their origin and nature, and how they were manipulated and utilized in the construction of the enclosures.

What is a soil? And what is a sediment

Archaeologists often just call the dirt we dig "soil", but much of the dirt on an archaeological site is actually sediment. "Soil" is a very specific term describing the biotic weathered and altered parent material or "natural" (at Hopeton: the terrace gravels and sands). The soil is a matrix in which plants grow and die and small soil fauna live and expire , thus enriching the upper part with organic matter (A horizon). The main constituent part of a soil, however, is the weathered natural mineralogenic elements (the B horizon). Soils grow downwards by weathering the natural parent material (C horizon), breaking it down, mixing it with material from above, and transforming it. During soil formation (pedogenesis) complex water, chemical, and mineral transactions and movements occur, resulting in a transformation and *in situ* development of horizons (see below). These horizons are zones with distinct mineral, organic and structural (ped) components, formed *in situ* but, unlike archaeological (and geological) contexts, they are not chronologically successive. The soil and all of its horizons constitute a single "living" entity, mantling the geology and providing a matrix for plant growth.

Sediments are largely minerogenic deposits that have been transported, and deposited, by wind, water, gravity, or man. The process of transportation may alter and select specific size (or specific gravity) of elements from the original material, sorting them into fine-grained material (silt and clay) or larger-grained sands, or rocks and boulders, as in alluvial and flood deposits. Colluviation and mass movement may result in unsorted (jumbled and mixed) deposits. The character of the sediment is dependant on the nature of the eroded source material – soil, and/or natural geology – and may incorporate both these elements from along the entire erosion and transportation path.

Two common sediments are colluvium and alluvium. Alluvium is material transported by rivers and deposited as overbank floodplain alluvium, flood deposits and channel fills. These vary from fine grained silts and clay to rocks and boulders depending on the energy of the river. Colluvium is a terrestrial deposit resulting from the erosion and deposition largely of soil material moved downslope by gravity. It can be accelerated and accentuated by rain and water, and by human activities such as deforestation, vegetation clearance, soil disturbance and plowing. Of course, man-made accumulations (i.e. archaeological deposits) are anthropogenic sediments.

Soil horizons

As soils form they weather the parent material or natural. This is the C horizon, or R (regolith) if soft geology. The main weathered and altered natural geology is minerogenic (the B horizon) – the source of minerals for plant growth. As plants grow, and soil fauna (worms and insects) live and die in this medium they introduce organic material transforming it into an A horizon (sometimes called topsoil). The upper part of the A horizon receiving dead plants and containing the herbaceous root mat is the Ah (A humic) horizon, and the lower part is that which is heavily biotically mixed by roots and soil animals (A). When the topsoil is plowed these two layers are mixed, sometimes incorporating part of the upper portion of the B horizon, to form an Ap (A plowed) horizon.

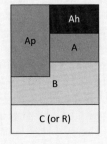

Ah	The upper topsoil rich in dead & decaying plant matter & herbaceous roots
Ap / A	Topsoil with high organic matter from rotted down vegetation, decayed soil fauna & faecal matter
B	Weathered parent material or natural geology – the minerogenic horizon in which minerals may have been leached or redeposited
C (or R)	Parent material, natural geology. C = rock; R is soft weathered geology

There is a low probability that the Hopeton enclosure walls were built during a single generation or less.

We further note that groups of radiocarbon dates from de-commissioned structures located at Hopeton and at a site immediately north of Mound City (Brady and Pederson Weinberger 2010) are internally consistent and statistically reflect use by a single generation. We know that radiocarbon cannot consistently achieve these levels of internal consistency, but we believe the number of dates and the temporal span they represent from the Hopeton Earthworks reflects at least one century of construction activity. Further evidence for construction spanning multiple generations might be seen in the wall segments that form the large circular and square enclosures at Hopeton. Some might argue that these segments and gateways were associated with celestial events (Romain 2000), but they could also reflect separate episodes of construction. Builders of Hopewell enclosures at other locations have demonstrated their ability to design and build geometric enclosures depicting true circles and straight rectangular walls. This is not the situation at Hopeton, as can be seen in the magnetic survey data reported in this paper. The asymmetric character of these enclosures might be due to their being constructed by multiple generations.

Geoarchaeological evidence also contributes to our argument that embankment wall construction occurred over several generations. In Trench 9, a series of laminated sheet wash deposits was recorded resting on top of the truncated B horizon and subsequently covered by wall fill. These laminated silt layers reflect a series of significant rainfall events that deposited these fine sediments after the B horizon was truncated and before the wall segment was built. While there is no evidence as to the length of time that elapsed while these laminated layers were being deposited, their presence suggests that this area of the enclosure was likely constructed after other wall segments were completed.

In considering the evidence for wall construction at Hopeton, readers must keep in mind that the two large enclosures were formed by 14 segments of earthen wall. Three wall segments form the Great Circle and 11 wall segments form the rectangular enclosure (Squier and Davis 1848). We must also emphasize that the evidence that remains for us to study of these wall segments is only the basal portions of the earthen walls. The roughly upper two-thirds of the walls have been removed by cultivation. While even the basal wall remnants available for study provide evidence that walls were built in stages, without any evident pause in construction activities, we do not know if the fill material in the upper portions of the wall segments would have reflected this same evidence.

It was noted earlier that the radiocarbon dates from features associated with wall construction in Trench 4 are significantly different from the Middle Woodland ages obtained in the other trenches. Trench 4 was excavated in 2003 and was oriented south-west to north-east across the curving wall segment that forms the north-east corner of the rectangular enclosure. It was 1.5 m wide and 41 m long. Due to the relationship of this wall segment to the Great Circle, it seems likely that this was either the first or last segment of the rectangular enclosure to be constructed. This is the only curved segment of wall associated with the rectangular enclosure, and the only segment of that which was in direct contact with the Great Circle. As noted in all other trenches, construction of this wall segment was initiated by removal of topsoil and the top of the B horizon from the area where the wall segment was placed. The reddish color of the subsoil in this area of the site is visually distinct from the yellow-brown subsoil exposed under the other wall segments. Once the topsoil was removed, a dark gray loam with lenses of fine gravel was laid down that covered the red subsoil under the wall segment and merged with the dark gray topsoil that was not removed from the north side of the wall. The remains of this wall segment are comprised of three large and fairly homogeneous soil deposits and dozens of smaller ones.

Excavations (Trenches 4, 8, and 9) in the north-east corner of the rectangular enclosure have revealed a complex series of loaded fills comprised of diverse sediments. In all other embankment wall segments that have been examined, the walls were built with large quantities of fairly homogeneous subsoil. Although these wall segments were almost certainly built by depositing basket-loads of a carefully selected homogeneous matrix, individual basket-loads are rarely visible in the exposed wall profile. In Trench 4, the situation was quite different (Lynott 2007). While the core and south side of this segment of embankment wall appears to have been built with large amounts of fairly homogeneous soil, the north side of the embankment wall is different. The two largest fill layers on the north side of the wall are gray loam and gray-brown loam. The contact between the gray and the gray-brown loam is marked by numerous lenses of gray loam, gray-brown loam, red sandy-loam, and gravel (Fig. 3.12). These lenses appear to be from individual basket-loads of a fill that was less homogeneous than we have observed elsewhere at the site. Visual evidence of basket-loading is fairly unique at the Hopeton Earthworks, and is only known to occur in this area of the earthworks (Trenches 4, 8, 9).

The less homogeneous basket-loads seen in these three trenches likely reflect their close proximity to the edge of the higher terrace immediately to the east. It may also mean that more homogeneous soils found inside the two large enclosures had already been used in building other wall segments. Further geoarchaeological analysis may eventually shed additional light on the meaning behind the variability in embankment wall fill.

Several features were exposed in Trench 4. Two unusual linear features comprised of burned wood and crushed calcite (Shearer 2009) and were found resting on top of the truncated subsoil at the base of this wall segment, clearly placed at this location as part of wall construction (Fig. 3.12) It is unclear what these features represent. Within the wall fill, three different small features comprised of burned wood and burned soil were identified. These were similar in size and form to the features recorded from other wall segments.

We noted that the construction of the wall segment exposed by Trench 4 was significantly different from the other wall segments at the rectangular enclosure (Lynott 2007). The majority of radiocarbon dates from the Hopeton embankment walls fall within the Middle Woodland period. The two radiocarbon dates obtained from features in Trench 4 are both at least 800 years more recent than those obtained from the other trenches. Since one of the samples was taken from a feature at the very base of the wall segment, it seems highly unlikely that these represent intrusive episodes that post-date actual construction. When these later dates are considered in association with the construction methods recorded in Trench 4, it seems likely that this wall segment was either built many centuries after the other wall segments or, more likely, modified or repaired at this later time. This revelation has serious implications for any interpretive model that assumes all the earthen features associated with sites we have labeled Ohio Hopewell were built solely during the Middle Woodland period and remained unmodified.

Non-embankment wall features

One of the first projects undertaken at the Hopeton Earthworks was a study at the Triangle site to attempt to locate evidence of Middle Woodland era habitation sites and features in close proximity to the earthworks themselves. The Triangle site was selected because several surface collectors, who had seen the site in regular cultivation over many years, reported that the area along the terrace edge (Triangle site) had the highest density of artifacts and, particularly, fire-cracked rock of any place they had collected on the terrace. In 1994–95 we excavated a series of 1 × 1 m test units to evaluate the content and character of the archaeological deposit. Since the site was covered by grass, we selected test locations that were scattered across the site area, but there was no relationship between test localities and known archaeological resources. The test units did give us some sense of the depth and character of the deposit, and we were also lucky enough to expose a large earth oven. Unfortunately, the earth oven lacked any temporally diagnostic artifacts and the sample submitted for radiocarbon dating yielded a Late Archaic date (Table 3).

When we returned to work at the Triangle site in 1997–98, we were determined to test the utility of geophysical survey as a means to locating subsurface features in the terrace soils on which the Hopeton Earthworks and associated sites were built. Under the direction of John Weymouth, we surveyed an area of 8800 sq. m in the fall of 1997. The survey utilized a G858 cesium gradiometer, an FM36 fluxgate gradiometer, and an RM15 resistance meter. Although there is no longer any visible evidence for the parallel walls crossing the Triangle site, aerial photographs from the 1950s and earlier show the low embankment walls fairly clearly crossing this tract of land and ending at the terrace edge. Our study area was selected to transect at least one and possibly both of the parallel walls. Unfortunately, the geophysical survey data and subsequent testing failed to reveal any evidence of these long linear earthen features. Recent survey by Jarrod Burks (2013a) may have identified a remnant of these walls closer to the two large enclosures, but the majority of these two long and low

Fig. 3.19. Excavation of a large block at the Triangle site exposed a variety of features, but no evidence of people using the area for settlements during the Middle Woodland period (photo: author).

earthen walls appear to have been flattened beyond recognition for most of their length. The geophysical survey did, however, produce evidence of a number of anomalies that were the size and had the magnetic/resistance intensity consistent with potential prehistoric features.

Since the study we were conducting was designed to guide long-term research at the Hopeton Earthworks, we planned to evaluate the data generated by the geophysical surveys to determine whether the instruments could successfully locate subsurface prehistoric features. Based upon our experience with geophysical survey at numerous other locations in the Midwest, we were fairly confident that the geophysical instruments could locate subsurface features. What we also wanted to know was what possible size and types of features might not be detected by the instrument and methods we selected.

Details about the research at the Triangle site have been published elsewhere (Lynott 2009a), but the 1998 excavation involved stripping the plowzone from two large blocks of ground (Fig. 3.20) and digging five test units (2 × 2 m) over promising magnetic anomalies. Test excavations were placed over 11 different magnetic anomalies that varied from 5.3 to 20 nT/m. Archaeological

Top: **Fig. 3.20.** Structure 1 was uncovered just to the west of the large rectangular enclosure. This photo shows the post-holes forming the east and south walls of the building (photo: author).

Bottom: **Fig. 3.21.** Post-holes forming the south and east walls of Structure 1. The trench at the top of the photo transects the building and was designed to examine a thermal feature near the center of the structure. Unfortunately, the thermal feature had been disturbed by years of cultivation (photo: author).

features were identified in association with seven of these anomalies. Although no feature was identified in Test Unit 8, a substantial amount of fire-cracked rock (FCR) was collected from the plowzone, suggesting that a feature was formerly present in this area but had been disturbed by cultivation. Of the total number of features recognized in excavation units, seven were easily identified in the magnetic survey data. Features were classified into small, medium, and large based upon total volume, and the data was analyzed in terms of magnetic strength and physical volume.

These data suggest that the magnetic survey data was very successful in identifying large features, particularly those over 100,000 cu cm. Of the seven large features that were identified, five of these were clearly visible in the magnetic data. Only one medium sized feature was excavated, and it was not noticed in the magnetic survey data. Magnetic survey was only successful in identifying two of the 23 small features that were exposed by testing.

We were clearly able to identify more anomalies in the geophysical survey data than we did prior to our use of that technology in 1997–98. The Triangle site research was successful because it demonstrated that we are able to identify magnetic anomalies that represent prehistoric features. The anomalies we focused on in 1998 turned out to be large and small pits. The geophysical survey was successful in identifying Feature 64, a large Hopewell pit, and four other large pits from the Late Archaic occupation of the area. The magnetic survey was less successful in distinguishing smaller features. We were convinced at the time that reducing the interval between geophysical survey transects would produce more data and make smaller features easier to identify, but we also recognized that it would increase the cost and time required for survey. Subsequent refinements in survey methods and improvements in equipment and software for geophysical surveys have led to standardizing survey intervals at 0.5 m. However, the biggest question still facing geophysical practitioners is not whether they can locate subsurface features, but what possible subsurface features are their methods and equipment failing to locate.

In 2001, we initiated a geophysical survey to map the two large enclosures at Hopeton. In addition to looking for evidence of the large embankment features, we were interested in recording anomalies located inside the enclosures in areas outside and adjacent to the enclosures. Since one key component of the research plan at Hopeton was to learn how the enclosures had been used, we believed that identifying and examining features inside and adjacent to the enclosures would provide clues about the activities conducted in these areas. We also thought geophysical survey of these areas might produce evidence pertaining to the construction of the large earthen features. Consequently, magnetic anomalies were examined through test excavations conducted during the field seasons of 2001–05, and 2007 and 2008.

During the first few years of this century, archaeologists at Hopewell Culture National Historical Park were engaged in a study to record the surface distribution of artifacts in and around the Hopeton Earthworks (Ruby and Lynott 2009; Ruby and Troy 1996; Burks and Seig 2010; Burks and Pederson 2006). This research included some interval shovel testing (Ruby and Troy 1997), along with carefully controlled, piece-plotted surface data that indicates that very few artifacts were deposited inside the two large enclosures, while quite a few artifacts are present immediately outside the enclosure walls and along the edges of the terrace on which the earthworks were built. Some caution must be exercised in the use of the surface artifact data from Hopeton, because geoarchaeological study has shown that a great quantity of material from the upper soil profile was removed from inside the enclosures as part of the process of building this ceremonial landscape. Despite this fact, the paucity of surface artifacts and significant magnetic anomalies inside the large enclosures is more likely a reflection of their use by the Hopewell builders than it is a product of earthwork construction.

Through this combination of surface survey, shovel testing of specific locations, and geophysical survey, we have developed a reasonable understanding of the archaeological record inside and around the Hopeton Earthworks. The paucity of surface artifacts and magnetic anomalies inside the large enclosures is fairly striking in both data sets. However, it should be noted that the density of artifacts and features at Hopeton is in general fairly low when compared to more intensive permanent village settlements associated with the Mississippian period in the Midwest. While this impression is hardly quantifiable, it does provide support to the widely held belief that Hopewell ceremonial landscapes were vacant ceremonial centers.

Most of the subsurface features encountered inside and adjacent to the large earthen enclosures have been small pits and apparently isolated post-holes. The presence of fire-cracked rock in the fill of these small features, generally less than 25 cm in diameter, is the most likely reason they were detectable through magnetic survey. Most of these small pits and post-holes lacked diagnostic artifacts, but it was not uncommon for excavators to find a few flakes with some fire-cracked rock in the feature's fill. None of these features contained any significant remnants of food remains. In point of fact, animal bones were extremely scarce and only occurred in very fragmentary form in features associated with the large enclosures. Of all the charred plant remains collected during the excavations near the earthen walls, 98% of these are fragments of burned wood (Wymer 2006), with charred nuthulls, seeds, and other potential food remains being less common.

A test unit (2002) was placed in the area immediately west of the rectangular enclosure to examine a magnetic anomaly detected during analysis of the geophysical data. Once the excavators removed the plowzone from the test unit, they identified a line of four post-holes running in a north-west to south-east direction across the floor of the unit. Excavation of the post-holes revealed that while they did contain some charcoal, chipped stone, and small fire-cracked rocks, the magnetic susceptibility of the post-holes was insufficient to have generated the anomaly that led to the selection of this location for testing. Excavation of two additional adjacent but staggered test units in 2002 exposed more post-holes and confirmed that a wall of a prehistoric structure had been discovered (Structure 1; Fig 3.20).

Additional excavations in 2003, 2004, and 2005 were aimed at exposing enough of the perimeter of the building to identify the shape and size of the structure (Fig. 3.21). Excavations were also conducted inside the structure to examine two anomalies and attempt to determine whether any of the original floor of the structure remained intact. Excavations in 2003 under the direction of Katherine Spielmann exposed the two internal features, one of which was determined to be a disturbed thermal feature and the other a small pit or pair of post-holes (Spielmann 2003). The thermal feature is located in a central part of the building, but plowing had disturbed the entire feature and scattered small fragments of burned soil, charcoal, and calcined bone through the plowzone. A small area of oxidized soil was all that could be found intact after removal of the plowzone.

During the four seasons of excavation at Structure 1, excavators often found it difficult to identify individual post-holes, even when they were following an obvious line of these features. There are several possible reasons for this problem. First, and most clearly, all of the timber posts that were formerly in these holes had been pulled out when the building had been decommissioned and the location abandoned. It is also likely that this building was only used for a short period of time and for special activities that did not produce large quantities of refuse. The relatively small quantity of artifacts and the comparatively small size of the artifacts that were found are indicative that the area was kept clean or was cleaned as part of the act of decommissioning the building. Due to the lack of organic refuse, the fill of the post-holes was difficult to identify unless artifacts had been placed or swept into the abandoned post-hole.

The post-holes that were most easily identified had been deliberately filled and often contained fire-cracked rocks or other large artifacts. This was most frequently the case with those forming the west, south, and north walls of the structure. These walls were formed by a single row of posts, and post-holes were often visible as a halo of fine charcoal flecks and slightly darker soil. The east wall of the structure was a perplexing array of post-holes. The reason for this is uncertain, and the post-holes forming the east wall tended to be slightly smaller in diameter than those forming the other walls.

Charred wood was present in the fill of many of the post-holes and four samples were submitted for radiocarbon dating. One of these samples yielded a date that was essentially modern, but that sample had been collected from a post-hole that contained substantial amounts of bark, and it is quite possible that the post dated to the historic farming era at this site. The other three samples yielded calibrated dates of cal AD 30–120 for Feature 33 (Beta-197242); cal AD 30–220 for Feature 23 (Beta-176581); and cal AD 70–250 for Feature 34 (Beta-197241) (Table 3). The calibrated average for these three dates at 2 sigma is cal AD 30–250. Since the charcoal that was dated did not likely originate in the post-holes, the context for these dates leaves questions about the origin of the charred wood that was dated. Considering the close concurrence of the sample results, it would seem likely that all the dated samples came from the same original burned context. Since many post-holes from Structure 1 were capped by one or more rocks, it is unlikely that the wood in the holes is from the original posts, but this cannot be totally ruled out. Additional dates could certainly refine the dating of Structure 1, but for now an estimated age of the 2nd century AD seems reasonable.

The building measures roughly 9.2 m north-west to south-east, and 7.2 m north-east to south-west. A layer of coarse sand and fine gravel was deposited against the inside south-west wall of the building (Fig. 3.22). It is unclear if this is a remnant of the floor of the building, or material used in the construction and stabilization of the wall. The sand/gravel deposit was 5–10 cm in thickness and about 25 cm wide. Artifacts found in the excavations around Structure 1 included lithic debris, bladelets, ground stone, a few ceramics, mica, and tiny fragments of calcined bone and charred wood. The low density of artifacts and the manner in which the building was dismantled suggest it was used for some special purpose associated with the earthen enclosures. It does not seem to have been used for domestic activities. The unusual form of the east wall is not surprising when compared to the diverse range of buildings that were recorded under mounds at the nearby Mound City site. Like most architectural features and many artifacts found at Ohio Hopewell sites, buildings display an incredible diversity of size and forms.

The reader will recall that the discovery of Structure 1 was made in 2002 while we were attempting to examine a magnetic anomaly. While the post-holes themselves did not produce the anomaly at this location, we did observe some red, oxidized soil a few centimeters below one of the post-holes. Since excavation of the Structure 1 occupied significant amounts of time during the 2002–2005 field seasons, the question as to what had generated the magnetic anomaly that led to the accidental discovery of the building went unanswered for a number of years.

In June 2013, I returned to the original 2 × 2 m test unit that led to the discovery

Fig. 3.22. Structure 1 was
excavated from 2002 to
2005. This composite map
shows the post-holes that
formed the walls. All posts
had been removed. Many
were filled with fire cracked
rock (FCR) or dark soil
containing small artifacts
(image courtesy of the
National Park Service).

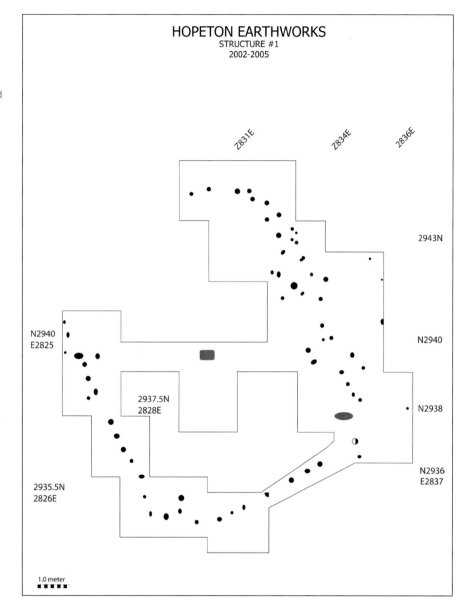

Fig. 3.22. Structure 1 was excavated from 2002 to 2005. This composite map shows the post-holes that formed the walls. All posts had been removed. Many were filled with fire cracked rock (FCR) or dark soil containing small artifacts (image courtesy of the National Park Service).

of Structure 1 with the goal of excavating through the post-holes and discovering if the reddened soil could have produced the magnetic anomaly. The excavated post-holes had been covered by plastic so it was easy to remove backfill and begin excavating into what appeared to be the intact yellow-brown Bt horizon. The fill surrounding the post-holes was gradually removed and, when only the very bottoms of them were still visible in the excavation unit, patches of hardened red soil began to appear across most of the central portion of the test unit. Further excavation revealed that these patches of red soil were very clay-rich and they were associated with pockets of darkened soil and charred organic material

(Fig. 3.23). Analysis of flotation samples from the feature beneath the structure indicates that while there are traces of wood charcoal in the soil, the majority of macrobotanical material is charred walnut meats (Leone 2014). Few food remains have been collected at the Hopeton Earthworks and when they are present it is usually in the form of charred seeds or nut hulls. Consequently, it seems likely these walnut meats are remains from a ceremonial or ritual activity.

Analysis of this feature is on-going, but it is clear that however this red and black feature material came to be deposited at this location, it was carefully covered with a yellow-brown soil that is macroscopically indistinguishable from the Bt horizon in this area. Since no evidence of a pit was seen in the test unit that exposed the reddened soil, we must assume that this feature is either part of a pit that is larger than the 2 × 2m test unit, or it has been covered by a soil mantle or low mound of soil. We cannot be certain if the construction of Structure 1 above this feature was intentional or not, but the association of these two stratified features is a very strong inducement to include geophysical studies with all excavations at Ohio Hopewell sites. It is also a strong reminder that Ohio Hopewell landscape construction sometimes involved careful selection and placement of soils. These are very complex sites that reflect substantial effort and planning.

Soon after we finished our fieldwork in 2001, Katherine Spielmann contacted me to discuss her interests in studying whether there was evidence of craft specialists in the Hopewell archaeological record. Her communication was timely because one of the features we had exposed in 2001 was a large pit located immediately outside the south wall of the rectangular enclosure. The pit was identified as a magnetic anomaly and the 2001 excavations had to remove 50 cm of disturbed and redeposited soil material that had been plowed and eroded off the adjacent earthen embankment wall. In 2001 we were only able to remove the upper 10 cm of the pit fill, but it was more than enough to demonstrate that it was not an ordinary refuse pit.

The pit was roughly oval in plan and the exterior margins were very difficult to identify. This is fairly common with Hopewell features in general, and particularly common among those at the Hopeton Earthworks. In this particular pit, Feature 6, we were able to find the outer edges of the upper pit because potsherds had been laid in a vertical position pressed against the outer pit walls. These sherds were not continuous and they were often in bundles of up to five sherds. Some of the bundles had sheets of mica placed between the sherds in the manner of a multi-layered sandwich. The pit fill also contained bladelets, lithic debris, fire-cracked rock, and a badly battered and broken ground stone celt (axe). This unusual pattern of refuse deposition strongly suggested that the pit contained materials that had been significant and likely had been used in ceremonial activities. Since we were unable to do more than examine the upper portion of the pit fill, the materials were returned to the laboratory at the Midwest Archeological Center for study.

Katherine Spielmann came to Lincoln to examine the collection from Feature 6 and at our invitation she joined the 2002 research team and took responsibility for its continued excavation (Spielmann 2003). Her careful excavation in 2002 produced valuable information about the structure and fill of the large pit (Fig. 3.24). Near the surface the pit was roughly oval shaped and 2.0 × 1.4 m in size. The sides were fairly steep and the bottom was reached at a depth of slightly more than 1 m below the surface. What made the pit of great interest was the types of artifacts that were discarded and the uneven and obviously careful deposition of them in different fill layers inside the pit (Fig. 3.25).

Deposition of sediments and artifacts was sporadic and uneven during the time this pit was in use. More than ten different fill layers were recorded. Within these fill layers, the quantity and types of artifacts placed in the pit varied too. Considering the large volume of this pit, the number of artifacts placed inside it is not great. These included pebbles, lithics, ceramics, and mica. Chipped stone was found throughout the fill but was not very abundant. A quantity of Wyandotte chert bladelets (from Harrison County, Indiana) was in the upper fill layers of the pit, and other notable stone artifacts included a chert drill and the previously mentioned ground stone celt. During her excavations, Spielmann observed that the chert objects in the upper fill layers tended to be gray colored Wyandotte chert, but the chert objects in the deeper fills of the pit were different colors and likely represent Upper Mercer (east-central Ohio) and, possibly Flint Ridge (Licking-Coshocton Counties, central Ohio), cherts (Spielmann 2003).

Although ceramics were found throughout the fill of the pit, they were particularly concentrated in the north-west quarter of the feature, especially along the northern edge. In numerous instances, ceramic sherds were found with mica adhering to the inner or outer surface. Several different vessels were likely deliberately broken and placed in this feature, including at least one with tetrapodal feet (Fig. 3.26). Surface treatment of the ceramics was generally cordmarked or plain, with only a few sherds displaying any additional decorative treatment.

Spielmann excavated Feature 6 in part, due to her interest in discovering whether evidence for craft specialization is present during the Ohio Hopewell era. Her examination of the mica fragments (Fig. 3.27) during excavation is particularly insightful. She notes that the wet, clayey sediment in the pit impeded recovery and made it difficult to determine whether the mica fragments represented waste from cutout production or disintegrated cutouts. She observed that:

> "we recovered primarily finished pieces rather than workshop debris. The deposits appear to reflect ceremonial discard after an event had been performed that involved fire (burned SS, FCR), ceramics, and mica cutouts." (Spielmann 2003: 14)

Further analysis is certainly needed on this subject, but the evidence from Feature 6 suggests that ceramics and mica were linked in some ceremonial context and the careful manner of their disposal in the large pit reflects their symbolic importance in the performance of one or more ceremonies. Subsequent examination of the artifacts from Feature 6 indicates that several ceramic vessels were deposited in the pit, but none of these is even close to being a complete vessel. Based on what has been learned about ceramic disposal at other Hopewell sites, it is likely that the vessels in Feature 6 were deliberately broken and quite likely divided for disposal in two or more locations. A small quantity of charred wood associated with one of the small concentrations of artifacts was submitted for radiocarbon dating and yielded a date calibrated at 2 sigma age of cal AD 40–235 (Beta-96598; Table 3).

Fig. 3.23. Analysis of this deeply buried feature found under the west wall of Structure 1 is still underway. The dark red soil has a high clay content and is strongly magnetic. We are attempting to determine if this soil was burned and if so, was it burned in place or burned at another location and transported here. The feature was detected in magnetic survey and is 10–15 vertical cm below the bottoms of the post-holes of Structure 1 (photo: author).

Fig. 3.25. Potsherds and mica were carefully packed into pockets of sterile soil in Feature 9 (photo: author).

Fig. 3.24. Feature 9 was located in the magnetic data just outside the south wall of the Rectangular Enclosure. Excavation in 2001 and 2002 revealed a large pit with considerable amounts of broken pottery, mica, bladelets, and other non-residential refuse (photo: author).

Fig. 3.26. Several tetrapodal feet from one or more ceramic vessels were found in the pit fill. These ceramic vessels, which are squarish in shape, are found in ritually charged deposits under Ohio Hopewell mounds. The photograph is of a plaster cast of a highly decorated example from Mound 12 and Mound City featuring an incised, abstract bird design, possibly a duck, on each of its four sides with many punctuate indentations on the upper rim, body and feet (photo courtesy of the Ohio History Connection and Hopewell Culture National Historical Park).

Fig. 3.27. A photograph made through a microscope shows two cut edges of a mica fragment from Feature 9 (photo: courtesy of the National Park Service).

Fig. 3.28. Excavations in 2001 exposed a prepared clay basin that had been baked to the hardness of soft bricks by high temperatures. The basin contained burned wood, ash, and burned soil. Radiocarbon dates from wood charcoal in Feature 1 produced dates that reflect use during the protohistoric period, probably in the 17th century (photo: author).

HOPETON TRIANGLE 98
BLOCK B
FEATURE 104

7-23-98

Fig. 3.29. Excavation at the Triangle site near the long parallel walls exposed this small circular clay basin that has been hardened by fire (photo: author).

The data collected from Feature 6 provide important insights into activities conducted at the Hopeton Earthworks, but pits containing ritual refuse are not rare at Ohio Hopewell ceremonial centers. A similar pit, although it contained far fewer artifacts, was found at the Triangle site near the western end of the long parallel walls. We will also discuss, in Chapter 5, two similar features that were found at the Riverbank site, adjacent to the Hopewell Mound Group.

Another class of important features at the Hopeton Earthworks is ritual fire basins. These features vary greatly in size and amount of preparation. They also vary in regard to the temporal period when they were built and used. We have already described some of the many small burned features found under the earthen wall. The discussion here will focus solely on burned features found near the different embankment walls.

The most impressive burned feature at Hopeton is a large clay basin that was carefully prepared and heavily used. This basin was built on the outside edge of one of the gateways in the south wall of the large rectangular enclosure (Fig. 3.28). Only the western portion of the basin was excavated in 2001, so the length of the feature cannot be determined. Although this feature was not fully excavated, it is apparently a rectangular basin (estimated at 2 × 1 m) that was built to have an obvious ridge around the perimeter of the large clay platform. The basin contained charred wood, ash, and a little burned soil. It had likely been used repeatedly, because the clay that was used to form the basin has been hardened to a level comparable to a soft brick. Based on the contents of the feature and its location at a gateway to the rectangular enclosure, it seems apparent that this was not used for basic domestic functions. However, interpretation of the large basin is complicated by the results generated by radiocarbon dating samples of the burned wood from the basin.

Two additional prepared clay fire basins have been found during the research at the Hopeton Earthworks. Just to the west of the wall of the rectangular enclosure, not far from Structure 1, a test excavation revealed another large prepared clay slab that had been baked hard by repeated heating. Unfortunately, this feature has been heavily damaged by cultivation and only a small section of it remained intact. Although charcoal was present in the soil around this feature, the extensive disturbance to the feature made it difficult to determine if the charcoal was associated with the clay platform and no radiocarbon samples were submitted for dating.

The third example of a prepared clay basin was found at the western end of the parallel walls during the work at the Triangle site (Lynott 2009a). It was circular in plan form and about 60 cm in diameter (Fig. 3.29). When viewed in cross section, the outer edges of the basin were about 3–5 cm higher than the slightly depressed basin center. The basin was formed of hard, mottled red and yellow clay about 6 cm thick. No datable materials were found in direct association with this feature, but it does seem to be similar to other "clay altars" reported from excavations at Hopewell sites in Ross County, Ohio.

One additional smaller burned feature should be mentioned in this discussion. In this case, the feature was a small hearth resting at the base of the exterior wall forming the rounded north-east corner of the rectangular enclosure. It was buried by redeposited soil from the embankment wall and built on top of a buried A horizon that formed after the embankment wall had been constructed. This small lens of red and orange soil with some wood charcoal was only about 35 cm in diameter. This feature is similar in size to those we frequently found buried under the embankment walls, but as noted earlier, this burned feature was on top of the soil horizon that formed *after* the embankment wall was built. A radiocarbon date on the wood charcoal from the feature yielded calibrated ages of cal AD 1530–1545 and cal AD 1635–1680 (Beta-182631; Table 3).

More than a decade of research at the Hopeton Earthworks has produced significant new information about when the great ceremonial landscape was constructed, how the landscape was built, and how this site might have been used. Before reviewing what we have learned from this research, it is critical that we remind the readers that despite the extensive efforts that have been invested at the Hopeton Earthworks by teams of archaeologists and students, far less than 1% of the site area has been fully investigated. A great deal has been learned about the Hopeton Earthworks, and Hopeton is one of a small number of sites that have received substantial archaeological attention, but there are still many questions to be answered about the Hopeton Earthworks itself and its relationship with other sites in the Scioto-Paint Creek Region.

Near the earthworks: Triangle, Red Wing, Overly, and Cryder sites

In addition to the features that have been found mainly around the outer periphery of the larger enclosure walls, there are several additional important archaeological sites located on the same alluvial terrace as the Hopeton Earthworks. Most of these sites have been given separate site designations to assist with the spatial and geographic organization of these archaeological remains by the National Park Service, who owns much of the property. All of the sites have yielded information about activities conducted in and around the Hopeton Earthworks.

The Triangle site is located along the south-west edge of the large alluvial terrace where the Hopeton Earthworks were built. The western end of the parallel walls, which originate between the large circular and rectangular enclosures, cross through the Triangle site and end at the edge of the alluvial terrace. The Midwest Archaeological Center conducted limited testing, geophysical survey and strategic testing at the Triangle site from 1994 through 1998 (Lynott 2009a). When this area of the Hopeton Earthworks was still in private ownership, it was cultivated annually and collectors searched the fields for artifacts. Several people who had seen the site many times indicated that the Triangle site had some of the largest concentrations of fire-cracked rock in the area. The Midwest Archaeological

Center's studies were aimed at trying to discover if there was evidence of Hopewell settlement sites in the area, and what if any physical evidence of the parallel walls still remained at this location.

Goodman (1973) reports that a Hopewell burial was exposed by cultivation in this area. Excavation by Alva McGraw (a knowledgeable and self-trained archaeologist) and Richard Faust of Mound City National Monument revealed the bones of an adult female, with a round mica mirror and a bone needle resting on the chest. A conch shell was found near one ankle, a ball of red ochre was in the palm of the left hand, and a plain potsherd and a pipe fragment were found nearby. Fragments of a second body were found about 8 m to the north, along with some mica flakes, a bone knife and a flint flake. The author suggests the remainder of the body was excavated by an unknown individual who used an Ohio license plate as a shovel, which was also found near this fragmentary burial. While several other instances of human remains have been reported by artifact collectors (Brose 1976), it appears that burial of human remains was not a major function of the Hopeton Earthworks.

National Park Service research at the Triangle site from 1994 through 1998 was introduced earlier in this chapter, and suggests that evidence for a wide variety of prehistoric and historic use of this terrace edge is present. Test units and larger block excavations revealed a wide range of features, most of which lacked temporally diagnostic artifacts. Radiocarbon dates from larger pits filled with FCR appear to be from Later Archaic use of the landform, while a single pit filled with food refuse indicative of later winter use and dating to the Late Woodland period was also recorded.

The vast majority of features recorded at the Triangle site are pits and post-holes. The 34 pits can be grouped into three categories based on volume. There are 24 small pits and post-holes, which are 20,000 cu cm. or less in volume. Medium pits are greater than 20,000 cu cm. but less than 100,000 cu cm in volume, and large pits are greater than 100,000 cu cm in volume. Only six large and one medium pits have been recorded and excavated.

In addition to pits, four hearths were also recorded and excavated at the Triangle site in 1998. All three appeared to be the product of intense heat. Features 20 and 157 were circular to oval areas of red-yellow soil about 60 cm in diameter. Both comprised thin (4–5 cm) lenses of heat-altered soil and charcoal that appeared to have formed without intentional preparation. Feature 72 was a circular lens of fire-cracked rock. The fire-cracked rock lens was 25 cm in diameter and only 4 cm thick, suggesting a relatively short period of use. Feature 104, described above, was a prepared clay basin that had been subjected to intense heat (Fig. 3.29). No artifacts, with the exception of charred wood, were found in direct association with any of the hearth features, but the prepared nature of Feature 104 is reminiscent of Hopewell fire basins at other sites in Ohio.

Prior to the 1998 excavations we assumed that, due to the proximity to the parallel walls, it was likely that most of the Triangle site features were associated with the Hopewell occupation of the area. Since most did not contain temporally diagnostic artifacts, the field investigations produced little obvious evidence to change that assumption. However, when we began to conduct more detailed analysis of the artifacts and received radiocarbon and AMS dates from samples collected from those features, it became obvious that the Triangle site was utilized over thousands of years.

Eight radiocarbon samples were submitted to Beta Analytic for either radiometric or AMS dating (Table 3). Five of the eight dates from the Triangle site document Late Archaic use of this landform. Charred hickory wood from Feature 17 yielded a date calibrated to 2 sigma of 1520–1390 cal BC (Beta 147183). A sample of charred walnut hulls from Feature 1, another large pit filled with fire-cracked rock, yielded a date of 1620–1440 cal BC (Beta-147190). A sample of charred True Hickory wood from Feature 149 yielded a date of 2010–1690 cal BC (Beta-147189). Another sample of charred True Hickory wood from Feature 143 was dated by AMS to 2200–1890 cal BC (Beta-147186). The final Late Archaic date, obtained from unidentifiable wood charcoal collected from a post-hole (Feature 50), was 3780–3510 cal BC (Beta-147187). With the exception of Feature 50, which was a post-hole, the other features that have produced Late Archaic radiocarbon dates are all relatively large pits.

Features that may be definitely associated with the Hopewellian occupation of the site are more limited. Unfortunately, no datable material was collected from the previously described circular basin (Feature 104) that was lined with clay and hardened by heat. Feature 64 was also clearly associated with Hopewell activities at the site. The feature was a large and generally amorphic pit identified through magnetic survey and exposed in a 2 × 2 m test unit. The fill of the pit was mottled and dark brown near the surface but became more yellow-brown with depth until it was distinguishable from the subsoil only by the reduced quantity of fine gravel present. The fill included charcoal, fire-cracked rock, lithic debris, a chert bladelet, the tip of a projectile point blade, pottery, a large piece of cut mica, and a small quantity of calcined bone. A sample of charred True Hickory was submitted for AMS dating and yielded a date of 50 cal BC–cal AD 130 (Beta-147184; Table 3). Although this pit contained fewer artifacts than Feature 6 (described above in association with the rectangular enclosure), the types of materials and large size of the pit suggest it was not constructed to dispose of domestic refuse.

Late Woodland occupation of the Triangle Tract is best documented at Feature 88 (Fig. 3.24). This pit was dark and circular in plan-form, with sloping sides and a round bottom. Unlike most features at the site, this one was loaded with fire-cracked rock, charred macrobotanical remains, faunal remains, lithic debris, chipped stone tools, and grit-tempered pottery. The pottery is cord-marked with diagonal cord-wrapped stick impressions on the lip. The presence of substantial amounts of faunal remains makes this pit unique among features examined at the Triangle Tract. Turtle, raccoon, and elk are present in association with large quantities of deer. Examination of seven deer antler burrs from the pit show that four are still attached to the skull and three have been shed. Assuming that the fill of this pit was from a single year, the pattern of antler shedding and growth would indicate late winter occupation (Bozell 2000). A sample of charred basswood from the feature yielded a radiometric date of cal AD 770–1160 (Beta-147188; Table 3). The quantity of artifacts found in this pit is in marked contrast to the relatively impoverished contents of other features at this site, and seems to reflect a differing use of the site in Late Woodland times. It is worth noting that the radiocarbon results for this small pit are consistent with the two dates obtained from Trench 4 in the earthworks.

While only a very small portion of the Triangle site has been examined, the available data indicate that this edge of the landform was used by Late Archaic people as temporary camps or base camps, before construction of the Hopeton Earthworks, and then by Late Woodland people after the major landscape construction had been completed. It is very likely that additional evidence of Hopewell activities is present at the Triangle site, but it seems unlikely that this edge of the alluvial terrace was used for habitation activities. The few features that were located with likely connections to Hopewell activities look very similar to the types of features found closer to the large enclosures.

Just to the south-west of the large rectangular enclosure, Bret Ruby encountered an area with a dense surface scatter of lithic debris. This concentration of Middle Woodland period diagnostic artifacts was designated the Red Wing Site (Ruby and Lynott 2009) and became the focus of additional investigations in 1997. Within a 60 × 100 m area encompassing the greatest density of Middle Woodland period surface artifacts, National Park Service archaeologists excavated a series of 32 1 × 1 m units spaced at 10–20 m intervals. A resistivity survey was conducted within four 20 × 20 m blocks in an effort to identify potential subsurface features. Forty-five additional excavation units were opened to investigate any anomalies encountered during the initial excavations and remote sensing.

The only subsurface feature that was identified was a midden extending not more than 20 cm below the base of the plowzone. Artifact density was low and the feature was usually detectable only in profile as a faint organic stain. Based upon the test units, it was estimated that the midden covered an area of at least 12 × 12 m, but less than 20 × 20 m. Four possible post-holes were identified in a 2 × 2 m area on the western edge of the midden, but they extended no more than 4 cm below the plowzone and formed no clear pattern.

Two conventional radiometric age determinations were run on wood charcoal recovered from the midden (Beta-109963 and Beta-109964). The first, with calibrated intercepts close to AD 100, fits comfortably within the range expected for the construction and use of Hopewellian earthworks in the Scioto region. The second, with a calibrated intercept at around AD 892, more clearly pertains to the local Late Woodland period and the small trash pit found at the Triangle site, and perhaps the dates from Trench 4 of the earthworks.

The Redwing artifact assemblage is dominated by chert artifacts, but also included one pitted stone in association from the midden and two celts from surface contexts. A single deer tooth and four fragments of mussel shell were collected from plowzone contexts. A limited number (41) of small grit tempered plain and cordmarked body sherds were collected from test units.

Analysis of the lithic assemblage indicated that it was dominated by lithic debris and simple retouched pieces. While other types of chipped stone tools are present, along with fire-cracked rock, these occur in small numbers. Ruby concluded that Red Wing represents a special-purpose ceremonial occupation where the tool assemblage is dominated by lamellar blades. The Red Wing assemblage is also notable for the paucity of blade cores, as might be expected of a manufacturing locality, and the presence of such exotics as obsidian (from Wyoming), Knife River Flint (from North Dakota), and quartz crystal. The location of the Red Wing site adjacent to the large rectangular enclosure, rather than adjacent to the natural resources of the terrace edge or floodplain, also suggest the site was associated with Hopewell activities in and around the enclosures.

In 1996 and 1997, William Dancey (2009) led a team of Ohio State University students in excavations at the Overly site located to the north-west of the large enclosures at Hopeton on the edge of a high terrace overlooking the Scioto River. Surface collections in the area indicated that, much like the Triangle site, Overly had the potential to produce evidence of Hopewell habitations associated with Hopeton. Due to plans by the landowners to strip the site and surrounding areas for topsoil, Dancey was forced to approach the study as a salvage situation. Although the research design had planned to strip substantial areas where surface data revealed potential habitation remains, limitations on time and money forced them to focus on a single area during the 1996 field school and opportunistically address other areas as time permitted over the remaining year before the site was destroyed (Fig. 3.30).

Mechanical soil stripping of an area 25 × 20 m at Cluster A, which was the area closest to the terrace edge and the Scioto River, revealed the presence of 25 features. Most of these were pits of varying sizes and configurations. Dancey sorted the pits into seven classes based on their shape, the slope of their sides, and the configuration of the base. Most contained fire-cracked rock and charcoal, but some also contained potsherds, chipped stone debris, and tool fragments, bladelets, burned bone, ash, clay lumps, mica, and shell. Dancey (2009: table 6-5) reports radiocarbon dates from six of these features. The earliest date of 3510±60 BP likely represents use during the Late Archaic period. Four of the dates fall squarely within the Middle Woodland era and are highly consistent with the dates reported earlier in this chapter for the earthen walls and adjacent features at Hopeton. The sixth and final date of 1450±50 BP is somewhat late for the Middle Woodland

Fig. 3.30. The Ohio State University conducted salvage excavations at the Overly site and found number of features reflecting residential activities during the Late Archaic and Woodland periods (photo courtesy of Ohio State University).

activities around Hopeton, and is significantly more recent than the other Middle Woodland dates from Overly.

Cryder Farm is an important landmark located immediately west of the large enclosures and north of the parallel walls at the Hopeton Earthworks. The site has historic importance because Squier and Davis included it on their published map of Hopeton and the surrounding earthworks (Squier and Davis 1848: pl. xxxvii). Kathleen Brady has done a masterful job of researching the early history of the land encompassing the Hopeton Earthworks, and she reports that during the early 19th century the site was owned by Michael Cryder (Brady and Pederson Weinberger 2006). Cryder was born in Pennsylvannia in 1742 and moved his family to the Chillicothe area in 1796. He purchased 1200 acres (*ca.* 486 ha) just west of Hopeton and built a cabin and later a two storey hewn-log house on the property before dying in 1817. Some of the structures shown on the 1848 Squier and Davis map at the Cryder farm were still present at the beginning of the 21st century, but degradation of the structures and regular vandalism led the National Park Service to remove the wooden parts of the buildings and leave in place the dry-laid stone foundations.

As part of the compliance before the structural demolition was undertaken, archaeologists from Hopewell Culture National Historical Park conducted magnetic survey and excavated test units to evaluate the nature and significance of the archaeological remains around the buildings (Brady and Pederson Weinberger 2006). Most of the artifacts and all of the features that were encountered in testing were from the historic period. In and amongst the historic artifacts the archaeologists also found a light scatter of lithic debris including bladelets. The lithic debris and bladelets do not imply an area of intensive prehistoric activity. However, based upon the surface data and testing at nearby sites, they provide an indication of the overall low density of prehistoric artifacts that occur in relative close proximity to the earthworks. There are areas at Hopeton with a moderately high density of artifacts, but in most instances these are found along the edges of the alluvial terrace. Areas closer to the earthen enclosures tend to exhibit a low to moderate density of artifacts and geophysical anomalies.

Much of the areas to the west and north-west of the Hopeton Earthworks and the Cryder Farm site have been devastated by gravel quarrying activities. In 1990, the National Park Service provided limited funds to support the Cleveland Museum of Natural History in its effort to record features and artifacts as they were being scraped away by earthmoving equipment (Brose 1991). Several features, similar to the ones found at the Triangle site to the south, were observed while large earth-moving equipment stripped away the surface soils to expose the underlying gravel. Unfortunately, the unpredictability of gravel quarry operations made it implausible to continue any long-term monitoring of the site degradation.

Little is known about the floodplains that surround the large terrace on which the Hopeton Earthworks was built. The area represents a series of old point bars and alluvial deposits associated with former channels of the Scioto River. When Squier and Davis mapped the site, the Scioto channel was fairly close to the south edge of the Hopeton terrace. A major flood in 1913 caused great damage to the town of Chillicothe and shifted the river channel farther south away from the Hopeton

Earthworks to its current location. David Brose (1976) reported clusters of artifacts on the floodplain surface, and Bret Ruby (1997) encountered a deeply buried Early Woodland occupation in a test unit to the west of the Overly site. The active character of the floodplain around Hopeton has likely buried other archaeological deposits in the alluvium to the west and south-west of the earthworks.

Although Dancey and his Ohio State University team were unable to accomplish as much work as they had hoped before the Overly site was destroyed by soil and gravel quarrying the data they did collect provide a window into the archaeological record for this important part of the Hopeton Earthworks. Dancey believes the artifacts and features from what he called Cluster A at Overly are "the patterned remains of a settled domestic household engaged in food production for a significant portion of its diet" (Dancey 2009, 85). While this certainly represents the best evidence uncovered thus far for human habitation in the vicinity of the Hopeton Earthworks, the evidence for year-round, permanent occupation at this site is not completely convincing. The radiocarbon evidence could easily support an interpretation that the Overly area was a base camp, or similar activity area that was reused at intervals over a century or two in association with the building and use of the Hopeton Earthworks. Unfortunately, due to the extensive quarrying activities at this site, there is nothing *in situ* remaining to study, so the nature of the Middle Woodland use of this locality is unresolved.

The majority of artifacts, features and sites that are known to exist in the vicinity of the Hopeton Earthworks are located around the periphery of the terrace edges adjacent to where the ceremonial landscape was constructed. None of the sites that have been discovered has exhibited any significant evidence of intensive Hopewell occupation. This is readily seen when compared to later features, like Feature 88 at the Triangle site. More burned and discarded food remains were found in that small pit than have been found in all the other features in and immediately surrounding the large earthen enclosures combined. Through the efforts of several competent archaeologists and other scientists, there is more systematically collected data from the Hopeton Earthworks than almost any other site in the Scioto–Paint Creek region.

What have we learned about the Hopeton Earthworks?

One important contribution of the Hopeton Earthworks Project is that it has demonstrated that a combination of geophysical, geoarchaeological, and archaeological methods can be effectively used to answer important questions about the construction of large Hopewell ceremonial landscapes. As will be discussed in Chapter 4, considerable excellent research has been conducted at other constructed landscapes in southern Ohio. However, the approach used at Hopeton serves as a model for planning future studies of large-scale and complex ceremonial landscapes.

When the project was initiated in 2001, there were many models and hypotheses being generated to explain the relationship between the numerous large geometric earthen enclosure sites in the Scioto–Paint Creek region of Ohio. It was my belief that until it was possible to better estimate the age and duration of construction and use for at least one of the large sites in this region, all the discussion about alignments between sites and pairing of sites was only educated speculation. The study at Hopeton was designed to provide data about three basic questions – which can be abbreviated into "when, how and why?"

When were the walls built, and how long was the site used? The excavations at the Hopeton Earthworks during the past decade have focused on the earthen walls and the areas within the enclosures and immediately outside the enclosures. With the aid of geophysical data, numerous subsurface features have been investigated and samples from these features have been radiocarbon dated (Table 3). The distribution of radiocarbon dates from the Hopeton Earthworks through time is discontinuous, but clusters in subsets that reflect human activity in the Late Archaic, Early–Middle Woodland, Late Woodland, and Proto-Historic/Historic periods. Radiocarbon dates on features associated with earthen wall construction fall mainly in the Middle Woodland, but include two dated features from the Late Woodland (*ca.* AD 1000). One of the goals of our work at Hopeton has been to generate a sample of radiocarbon dates that is sufficiently large to reflect the chronology of construction and use at the site. The only other site in the Scioto River drainage in this area of Ohio with a comparable radiocarbon sample is the Hopewell Mound Group.

As discussed earlier in this chapter, there are 22 radiocarbon dates associated with features reflecting wall construction activities at the Hopeton Earthworks and these dates indicate that wall construction activities occurred over at least a century and possibly longer. I have suggested here that although future research may certainly refine my estimates, the construction of the Hopeton ceremonial landscape required at least four to six generations. It is likely this work began toward the end of the 1st century AD, and was likely completed during the first half of the 3rd century. Many of the features found outside the walls at Hopeton have dated either before or after the Middle Woodland period, but the Middle Woodland features that have been dated (pits, Structure 1) are fairly consistent with the estimated age of the embankment construction. Since all of the radiocarbon dates that have been processed for the Hopeton Earthworks have come from relatively recent excavations and carefully selected contexts, these dates exhibit more internal consistency than many of the dates obtained from legacy collections at other Hopewell sites. We emphasize that every effort was made in submitting samples for radiocarbon dating to weigh the context of the sample, as well as the materials being dated, and only submit samples that we were confident were burned at or near the point of sample collection. The samples chosen for dating Structure 1 represent the only significant exception to this procedure, but the overall consistency of the dates from Structure 1 suggest the charcoal collected from the post-holes likely originated on or near the structure floor. Concern about the temporal placement of sites and features will continue to be a major discussion about Hopewell archaeology until new data are obtained to better clarify the chronological sequence within and between these sites.

The great earthen walls that clearly mark the work of people at this location during the Middle Woodland period are so impressive that it has led generations of archaeologists to assume that the archaeological record associated with the earthworks would also date to the Middle Woodland period. The work at Hopeton has provided substantial evidence that the terrace on which the earthworks was built was occupied prior to and after the Hopewell era in this region. Only one other site in the Scioto–Paint Creek region has yielded a similar sample of radiocarbon dates, and a comparison of those data is instructive.

The Hopewell Mound Group is located on North Paint Creek, 11–12 km to the west of Hopeton. The site was described and mapped by Caleb Atwater in 1820. Squier and Davis (1848) excavated several mounds, and their discoveries led Warren K. Moorehead to conduct excavations in 1891–92 for the 1893 World's Columbian Exposition (Moorehead 1922). The spectacular mortuary remains uncovered by Moorehead encouraged further substantial excavations by the Ohio Archaeological and Historical Society (Shetrone 1926). This sequence of major excavations revealed mounds with complex construction histories. Unfortunately, all of these excavations were prior to the advent of radiocarbon dating. Griffin (1958) recognized the importance of radiocarbon for refining the chronology of Ohio Hopewell and dated charcoal samples from Mound 25 of the Hopewell Mound Group. These early radiocarbon dates provided confirmation of the prehistoric placement of the Hopewell Mound Group and formed the basis for building a more refined radiocarbon chronology.

In subsequent years, new excavations and radiocarbon dating of samples from the museum collections (Greber 2003) from earlier excavations have built a data set of at least 32 radiocarbon dates. This is certainly one of the largest sets of radiocarbon dates from the Scioto River drainage, but it is also derived from one of the largest and likely the most complex Ohio Hopewell sites in this region. Unfortunately, none of the radiocarbon dates from the Hopewell Mound Group is known to directly date an event associated with embankment wall or mound construction. A gross comparison of the radiocarbon dating results from Hopeton and Hopewell is enlightening. A plot of the central tendency of all radiocarbon ages from the two sites shows that both sites were in use at roughly the same times during the Late Archaic/Early Woodland, Middle Woodland, Late Woodland, and Proto-historic periods (Fig. 3.31). It is particularly interesting to note that both sites were either abandoned or less utilized during approximately the same times as well (Lynott 2008). The Middle Woodland radiocarbon ages from the Hopewell Mound Group reflect a longer span of time than do those from the Hopeton Earthworks, and is likely that this is because the Hopewell Mound Group was used for a longer period of time. Although this is only a very coarse comparison, the comparability of radiocarbon dates from these two sites seems to be more than coincidence.

The comparison is complicated, in part, by the confidence in the context of the samples that are dated. While all of the samples that have been dated from Hopeton were collected as radiocarbon samples from excavations since 1994, many of the samples from Hopewell were taken from museum collections from excavations conducted between roughly 90 and 120 years ago. We certainly have less confidence in the context, and subsequent treatment of the samples, from these older excavations than we have from samples collected in the last 20 years. Despite these issues, the comparability of the radiocarbon dates from Hopeton

Fig. 3.31. A simple plot of uncorrected radiocarbon dates from the Hopeton Earthworks and Hopewell Mound Group indicates that both sites were in use about the same times and largely abandoned at the same times throughout prehistory (image courtesy of the National Park Service).

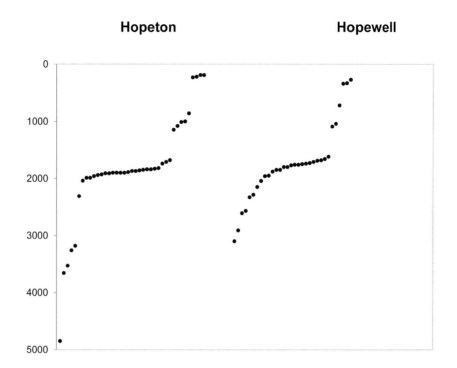

and Hopewell strongly suggests the potential for a similar temporal pattern of construction and use for these two sites. However, it would also appear that the Middle Woodland or Ohio Hopewell use of the Hopewell Mound Group occurred over a longer period than we have estimated for the Hopeton Earthworks. How other sites in the Scioto River drainage fit into this pattern will only become apparent as excavations produce more samples for dating.

How were the walls built? When we began this study, the amount of landscape construction conducted by the Hopewell people was grossly underestimated. Like most other scholars, we did not anticipate the evidence that would be found to show that many acres of topsoil were removed to prepare the site for embankment construction. Research at mounds and in small-scale studies of earthen enclosures may have provided hints about this element of monument building, but until the research at Hopeton, the great scale of soil stripping activities was unanticipated.

The soil volume comprising the original un-eroded embankment walls of the two large enclosures has been estimated at about 32,000 cu m. While this alone represents a considerable amount of labor, it does not take into consideration that before the walls were built the area under the walls and inside the enclosures was stripped of the A horizon and upper B horizon. If we assume that only 15 cm were stripped off the area comprising both enclosures, that would represent another 66,000 cu m of soil that was moved and re-deposited at some other location. The topsoil may have been used to build the upper parts of the embankment walls, but this would have required that it be stockpiled at some locality for later reuse. Without considering the labor needed to build the two sacred circles along the eastern wall of the rectangular enclosure and the long parallel walls that run to the south-west, the soil stripping and the wall building would entail moving 98,000 cu m of soil. Based upon the experiments in earthwork building in Sonora, Mexico, reported by Erasmus, two workers could move roughly 2.05 to 3.65 cu m of material during a 6-hour work day. The lesser estimate was calculated from teams carrying soil 100 m per trip, while the higher estimate is based upon carrying the load 50 m. Using an estimate of 1 cu m per person per day, a rough and very conservative estimate of the labor/energy required for the construction of the two large enclosures at the Hopeton Earthworks would be about 98,000 person days. This assumes movement of 1.0 cu m of soil a distance of 100 m for each person day. It is worth noting that the size of the site would likely require carrying soil for distances greater than 100 m quite often, and the reuse of topsoil stockpiled from initial stripping to prepare the site would add more labor requirements.

We have provided descriptions of the coring and trenches that led to the conclusion that the area under and within the two large enclosures had been stripped of topsoil, but one question that is frequently asked is – what did the builders do with all that soil? There is no data to answer that question at this time, but one hypothesis that may be offered is that some of it was used to build the long parallel walls that run from the large enclosures south-west to the edge of the terrace and what had once been the location of the Scioto River. The parallel walls were still visible on early aerial photographs, but they seem to have become visually indistinguishable from the adjacent terrain sometime in the 1960s. Although we have not made concerted efforts to relocate those two long low earthen walls with geophysics, transects across their known locations at the terrace edge (Lynott 2009a) and near the two large enclosures (Clay 2006) have failed to produce evidence anywhere nearly as convincing as has been seen with the other features at Hopeton that are no longer visible in surface topography. Jarrod Burks (2013a) in a recent magnetic survey west of the large rectangular enclosure has recorded some large anomalies that may be remnants of these long parallel walls, but further magnetic survey and test excavations are needed to confirm that interpretation.

I propose that the parallel walls were built with the topsoil quarried from the area that would become the large circular and large rectangular enclosure. This topsoil was piled on top of existing topsoil and through the historic era at Hopeton the effects of annual cultivation over the parallel walls widened and lowered the embankments. Since the walls were built of the same materials as the soil they were constructed upon, there is very little potential to detect any remnants of these features with geophysical techniques. Certainly more intensive research with a variety of different geophysical instruments is needed before we can conclude that the parallel walls are no longer detectable. Geophysics has been successful in relocating the ditches associated with the sacred circles on the east side of the large rectangular enclosure at Hopeton, and has discovered or relocated similar features at the Hopewell Mound Group (Pederson Weinberger 2007) and the Junction Works (Burks and Cook 2011).

Two additional aspects of landscape construction at Hopeton are worthy of further discussion. Squier and Davis (1848) described a number of small circular enclosures and mounds during their landmark study at Hopeton. Since our efforts

Fig. 3.32. Although the two small Sacred Circles that were part of the east wall of the rectangular enclosure at Hopeton are no longer visible, the interior ditches are detectable in magnetic survey data. The North Sacred Circle is easily seen in this magnetic map, and a smaller and more subtle magnetic feature (potential enclosure ditch) is seen adjacent to it on the west (image courtesy of the National Park Service).

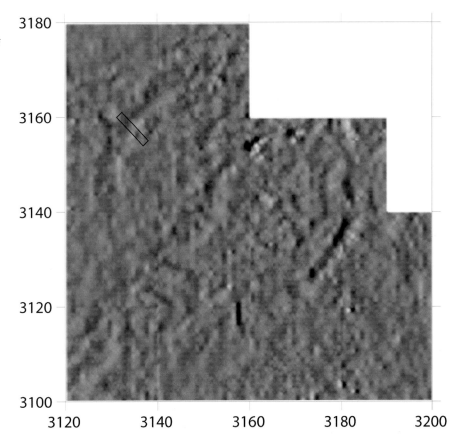

have focused on the two larger enclosures and adjacent areas, no effort has been made to relocate such features that were reported to be peripheral to the large enclosures. During the course of geophysical survey along the outer side of the north-east corner of the rectangular enclosure, John Weymouth (2002) located what appears to be a previously unknown small circular enclosure (Fig. 3.32). The magnetic data suggests this feature is only 10 m in diameter. No subsurface excavations have been conducted to better examine this circular anomaly.

Squier and Davis (1848) included three small mounds on their map of the Hopeton rectangular enclosure. Two of these were inside the eastern wall of the enclosure and the other was inside its south-west corner. Two low topographic rises along the eastern wall of the enclosure are still present and both have been subjected to geophysical survey and geoarchaeological coring. Although geophysical survey has been successful in relocating some mounds that have been reduced by cultivation there is no evidence in the Hopeton data that mounds were present at these locations. The geoarchaeological cores in these features revealed naturally sorted sediments that are more consistent with colluvial deposition than mound fill. David Brose (1976) did record that local amateur archaeologists found human remains and associated grave goods at these locations when they were bulldozed to provide fill for nearby railroad bed construction. This may represent

Middle Woodland burials that were placed in natural topographic features. The presence of human graves at various points around the Hopeton Earthworks is documented (Brose 1976; Goodman 1973), but unlike many Ohio Hopewell sites, there is little evidence to suggest mortuary activites were a significant function at Hopeton.

It is worth noting that we have not answered all of our questions about the construction methods and age of the Hopeton Earthworks. We have quite a lot of data to indicate that the upper soil profile in the area of the two large enclosures was stripped away as part of the construction process. What we do not know is whether this was done in segments, like the construction of the embankment walls, or was most of the area stripped before wall building began? Arguments can be made for either scenario and this question cannot be fully answered without further research. The other question revolves around the removal of native vegetation. Was this done in increments, or was a large area cleared before the earthworks were laid out on the ground? While we know that small prairie areas were found in this region during historic contact times, it seems likely that most fertile valley bottoms (like those at Hopeton) would have been covered with bottomland hardwood forest. Hopeton was built on a large landform and forest clearing would have added time to the process of building the ceremonial landscape.

How was the enclosure used? The Hopeton Earthworks Project has produced substantial information about when the earthworks were built and how the ceremonial landscape was constructed. Less information is available on how the landscape was used by Hopewell people. Bernardini (2004) has suggested that the effort of building this landscape was its primary purpose, and that certainly seems to be a strong possibility. The amount of labor and time required to build Hopeton would have required substantial cooperation, commitment and social stability among the people who participated. If our estimate of the time spent in building the site is correct, the people who initially planned the landscape and its features would not have been alive when the work was completed.

There is very little in the archaeological record investigated to date that would indicate use of Hopeton as a habitation. The low density of artifacts, the specialized character of the artifacts and features all strongly point to ceremonial activities. We cannot rule out the possibility that a small group of people may have lived nearby and served as caretakers, but the absence of any Middle Woodland features that remotely look like vernacular refuse or storage pits, or cooking hearths, is fairly glaring. At the Triangle site, we excavated a Late Woodland trash pit that was filled with charcoal, deer bone, broken ceramics, and other refuse. The soil in the pit was dark gray and that is in great contrast to the Middle Woodland features at Hopeton that are often very similar in color to the natural subsoil. This absence of general Middle Woodland domestic refuse is the strongest argument that exists for the special nature and ceremonial character of the Hopeton Earthworks.

At this point, it is not possible to identify with any certainty the types of activities that were being conducted at Hopeton beyond the construction of the landscape. Buildings like Structure 1 have been identified in association with enclosures at other Ohio Hopewell sites, but the function of those structures are not well established either. Hypotheses about shelters for craft specialists or visiting pilgrims, and preparation for rituals all have intuitive appeal, but evidence to confirm any such suggestions remains to be identified. It seems likely that these large constructed landscapes were used for a variety of periodic or cyclical activities and they must have been awe-inspiring when contrasted within the natural forestlands that abounded in southern Ohio. One thing that Hopeton does not seem to represent is a cemetery. Enclosure sites like Hopeton and High Bank differ from most of the other large enclosures in the Scioto–Paint Creek region because of the paucity of mounds and mortuary activities.

In closing this particular discussion, readers are urged to remember that in most instances, Ohio Hopewell earthen enclosures are huge and complex sites. Archaeological research has focused largely on mounds associated with the enclosures and the few areas other than mounds that have received attention are only a small fraction of the overall site areas. Far less than 1% of the Hopeton Earthworks has received intensive archaeological investigation. Although geophysical surveys are highly useful tools and we have learned what they are capable of detecting, the fundamental question remains as to what geophysical surveys are *not* detecting. It is likely that identification of the different activities conducted at the Hopewell ceremonial landscape sites will become clearer with additional geophysical survey, geoarchaeological, and archaeological study.

4

Studies of Ohio Hopewell
ceremonial landscapes

Substantial surveys and excavations have documented that prehistoric ceremonial landscapes are scattered across the entire State of Ohio. Mounds are by far the most common form of earthen monument, and they were built in an amazing range of shapes and sizes. Enclosures formed by earthen walls are also common and occur in a substantial range of locations, shapes and sizes. Although we believe the vast number of earthen enclosures was built during the Hopewell era, there are known examples of enclosures that were built by earlier and later residents of the Ohio country. There is also some evidence that Hopewell enclosures were re-used by later prehistoric people and perhaps even modified or repaired by those later groups. The earliest enclosures are individual circles and many of these were built by the Early Woodland societies who lived in southern Ohio and northern Kentucky. Hilltop enclosures are well documented in the Middle Woodland period, but hilltop enclosure walls were also built during the Late Woodland period. Jarrod Burks (2013b) has estimated that there were originally more than 600 earthen enclosures in Ohio, and many of these were likely built during the Hopewell era.

The vast majority of Ohio Hopewell sites are located in southern Ohio, but mounds, habitation, and ceremonial sites occur throughout the State. Concentrations of sites and constructed landscapes are found in south-east, south-central and south-west Ohio. These areas correspond in general to the Licking/Muskingum drainage, Scioto drainage, and Great Miami and Little Miami drainages. It is uncertain why people living in these areas approximately 2000 years ago began building these monumental earthen landscapes, but it is clear that the construction of large ceremonial landscapes in Ohio was non-random.

The landscape of southern Ohio was formed by southward flowing streams that originated in the glacial topography of northern and central Ohio. These streams flow out of the glaciated areas of northern and central Ohio and pass through the rocky Appalachian topography of southern Ohio before emptying into the Ohio River along the State's southern border. Ohio Hopewell constructed landscapes are particularly numerous along the southern edge of the glacial terrain, in the primary valleys and at the mouths of major rivers.

Although they were recognized, reported, and mapped by Europeans entering the Ohio country, major earthen monuments at Marietta and Portsmouth have since been largely leveled by urban growth with only minimal scientific study. The wealth of prehistoric earthen monuments that was once present in southern Ohio has been gradually degraded by agriculture, urban development, and other historic land-uses. As we review what has been learned about the landscapes built by Ohio Hopewell people, it is important to remember that a great many important ceremonial landscapes have been lost without any significant study. Very few of the sites reported by Squier and Davis and their contemporaries in the early and mid-19th century have survived without major damage or degradation.

One of the most interesting aspects about these landscapes is the great diversity of shapes and configurations. While authors beginning with Squier and Davis (1848) and continuing through William Romain (1991; 2000) have made a strong case for the use of some standard unit of measure in the construction of geometric enclosures, the variety seen in these sites must indicate that Ohio Hopewell people put great value in the uniqueness of their construction. Measuring this variability is made very complex by our inability to identify the time frames in which individual sites were built and used. The problems associated with our inability to understand the internal chronology of Ohio Hopewell have been effectively summarized by N'omi Greber (2003), and the chronology issue impacts every attempt to interpret the construction and use of Ohio Hopewell ceremonial landscapes.

In the following survey of the evidence relating to Ohio Hopewell landscape construction, we must consider what the uneven distribution of these sites means in the interpretation of the Ohio Hopewell archaeological record (see Figs 1.1 and 2.1). The great concentration of geometric earthworks in Ross County in the Scioto drainage has been attributed to its position on the ecotone between glaciated and unglaciated terrain (Fig. 4.1). The large number of hilltop enclosures in south-west Ohio is certainly due in part to the broken terrain and numerous hilltops adjacent to streams, and the proximity of the largest of all Hopewell earthwork complexes at Newark might in some way be related to its proximity to Flint Ridge. However, if we are to understand fully the significance and diversity of the monumental landscapes, we must learn if the variety that has been observed is due to their construction by different people, construction at different times in the Hopewell era, or construction for widely different purposes.

South-eastern Ohio

The headwaters of the Muskingum River are located in the flint-rich areas of central Ohio, where mounds, enclosures, and important flint quarries occur in significant numbers. The Licking River valley contains a large number of these sites, including the largest of all Ohio Hopewell ceremonial landscapes – the Newark Earthworks. The Licking merges into the Muskingum at Zanesville, and flows generally south where the Muskingum joins the Ohio at Marietta. There are quite a few mound and small enclosure sites between Newark and Marietta, but very little research has been reported from any of these.

One site that is certainly noteworthy in this region is Glenford Fort. Caleb Atwater published the first map of this hilltop enclosure, although this is really

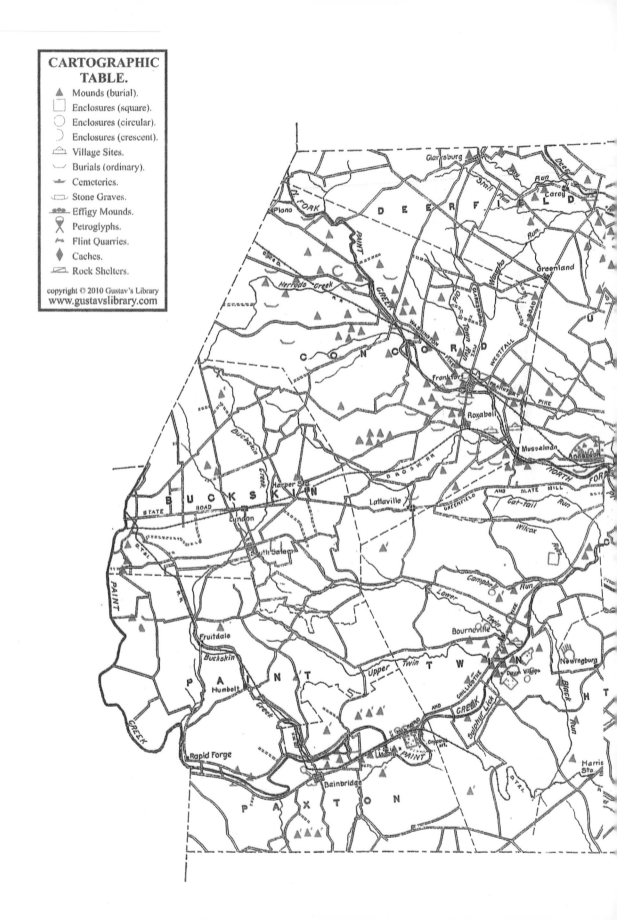

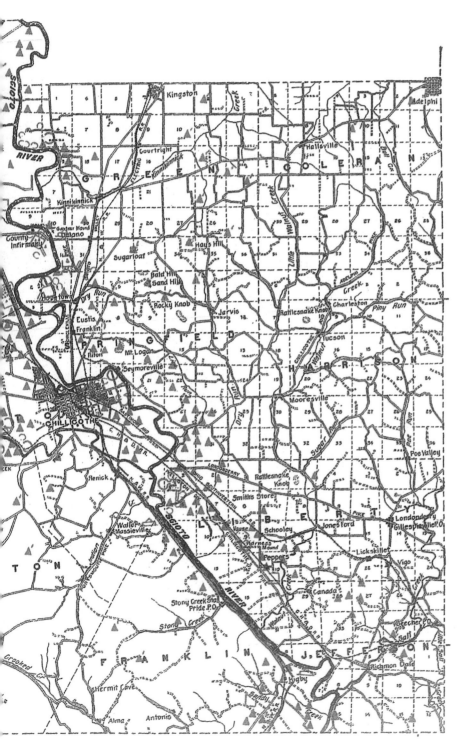

Fig. 4.1. Map of mounds and enclosures in Ross County by Mills (1914). The map is multi-period and serves to demonstrate the density of prehistoric sites in this small region and their strong focus upon the river drainages.

little more than a rough sketch of the hilltop features (Atwater 1820: pl. iii). Charles Whittlesey (1851) made and published a more detailed and accurate map several decades later. Neither Atwater nor Whittlesey were as impressed by the stone wall that forms the embankment. Whittlesey and Atwater both indicate that most of the stone walls that encircle the hilltop, where present, are little more than a collection of stones that have been piled into a low wall. Whittlesey described the wall as "very slight, not, on an average, as large as the stone fence of the New England farmer. The stones may have been heaped together with more regularity than they now present, but were not dressed" (Whittlesey 1851: 13).

A later description by Randall (1908) presents the hilltop construction in more detail and in positive terms. Located in northern Perry County, the site was built on a high, flat hill about 100 m above the Jonathan Creek valley. This area of Perry County is marked by unglaciated hills with flat tops and steep sides. Glenford Fort was built on a hilltop with sandstone caprock that is connected to another section of uplands by a narrow isthmus and surrounded by steep cliffs. The embankment walls were built with blocks of sandstone and fully encircle the caprock edge of the hilltop. Randall estimated that the wall was on average 10–12 ft (3 × 3.6 m) wide at the base and 6–8 ft (1.8–2.4 m) high, with a total length of 6610 ft (1983 m).

There is a single gateway on the south-east side of the enclosure connecting to the isthmus that is linked to other caprock hilltops. The wall is estimated to enclose about 26 acres (10.5 ha), with a single stone slab mound located in the central area of the enclosure. The mound was built with rocks and is about 100 ft (30 m) in diameter and 20 ft (6 m) high. There are other hilltop mounds nearby on the flanks of Jonathan Creek.

The two most recognized enclosure sites in south-east Ohio are Newark and Marietta. In spite of their well deserved reputations among the literature on Ohio Hopewell archaeology, very little recent scientific information has been gathered at either of these sites. Both sites are important geometric enclosures with other earth and stone features that were clearly designed to be specially constructed cultural landscapes. A review of what it known about the sites is important to developing a broader understanding of Ohio Hopewell ceremonial landscapes.

Newark Earthworks

Early in the 19th century, published accounts began to appear about the incredible earthworks between Raccoon Creek and the south fork of the Licking River in central Ohio (Lepper 1998). Caleb Atwater visited the site in 1836, prepared the first detailed map of the large and complex group of earthworks and mounds, and said the earthworks "are quite as remarkable as any others in North America, or, perhaps in any part of the world" (Atwater 1820). No one has accused Atwater of overstating the importance of this amazing site. Newark is the largest of all Ohio Hopewell ceremonial landscapes covering approximately 4 sq miles (10 sq km) with earthworks incorporating 7 million cu ft (198,100 cu m) of soil material (Lepper 2004).

The most incredible feature on the Atwater map is an Octagonal enclosure with walls 10 ft (3 m) high covering about 40 acres (16.2 ha). The octagonal enclosure has eight gateways, each about 15 ft (4.5 m) wide with a small mound just inside each gateway. The small mounds are 4 ft (1.2 m) longer than the gateways are wide, and set inside the fort by 8–10 ft (2.4–3 m). Atwater believed the mounds were built to defend the gateways. He also says that soil has been collected so carefully from the surrounding area that there is no evidence of pit or ditch near the enclosure. Atwater also described a "round fort" of 22 acres (54 ha) that is connected to the Octagon by two parallel walls of earth of equal height and length. At the opposite side of the circular enclosure from the parallel walls was an "Observatory platform" built of earth and stone. Atwater did not understand the celestial significance of these features, and despite the recent discoveries pertaining to Newark and Hopewell cosmology (Hively and Horn 2006; 2010), more insights may yet come to light.

The octagon and circle (Fig. 4.2) were not the only major enclosures Atwater found at Newark. He also mapped and described another large circular enclosure with walls 25–30 ft (7.5–10 m) high enclosing about 26 acres (10.5 ha). Inside the great circular wall was a large interior ditch. There was also a square fort (known today as Wright Earthworks), covering about 20 acres (8.1 ha) with walls similar in height and width to the Octagon. Atwater also depicted parallel walls that connect all of the major enclosures and also connect the Octagon and the Wright Earthworks to the Licking River. A parallel set of walls extends south from the Newark Earthworks for an undetermined distance.

Squier and Davis (1848) used the Whittlesey map as the basis for their subsequent study and added a number of mounds and other features to the complex (Fig. 4.2). The pioneering archaeologists provided substantial details about the features they observed. They noted that the major earthen features were built on an alluvial terrace situated between two small streams with a large natural pond in the middle of the earthwork complex. They also noted that a "large portion of the more complicated division of the group has, within the past few years, been almost completely demolished, so that the lines can no longer be satisfactorily traced" (Squier and Davis 1848: 67). Although they certainly did not identify all the earth and stone features at Newark, they did describe quite a few important features for the first time. They also noted the similarity of the size and shape of the various enclosures to places they had mapped near Chillicothe in the Scioto River valley. They made particular note of the similarity between the Newark Octagon and the octagonal enclosure at the High Bank Works south of Chillicothe. The similarity between these two amazing earthen features continues to stimulate discussion, hypotheses and models today.

In the years following the publication of *Ancient Monuments of the Mississippi Valley* by Squier and Davis (1848), two additional and very important maps were made of the archaeological landscape at Newark (Lepper 2002). David Wyrick (1866), a Licking County surveyor, prepared a detailed map of the site in 1860. In 1862 James and Charles Salisbury prepared an even more extensive map of the earthworks that adds details to our understanding of the size, relationship, complexity, and detail of the earth and stone features that comprised the Newark Earthworks. Over the next century and a half urban growth and agriculture has gradually degraded all

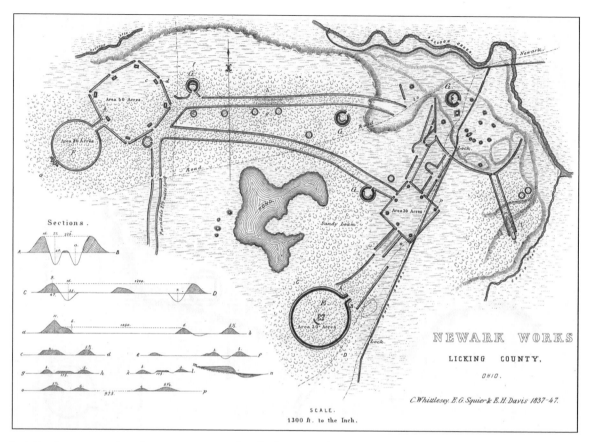

but the largest earthen features associated with the Newark Earthworks.

Shortly after the publication of *Ancient Monuments*, the Licking County Agricultural Society purchased the Great Circle from the owner, Nathan Seymour, who had never allowed the interior of the great monument to be plowed (Lepper 2002). The land became the home for the Licking County Fairgrounds, which included a racetrack inside the circular earthen wall and interior ditch, a grandstand for spectators, and buildings for livestock and other entertainment. The site hosted a number of important events (Lepper 2002) in the late 19th century and then became an amusement park in 1898. In 1933, the Great Circle and surrounding land was given to the Ohio Historical Society who removed the fairgrounds and other recent facilities and restored the site to its early 19th century appearance.

The Octagon Earthworks lay largely untouched until 1848 when farmers began plowing over sections of the wall (see Lepper 2002 for a more complete history). The city of Newark eventually stepped in, purchased the earthworks, and gave them to the Ohio State Militia (National Guard) to use for their base. Between 1893 and 1895 the earthworks became a camp for soldiers on summer training duty. When the militia outgrew the property it was returned to the city and eventually leased for the construction and maintenance as the Moundbuilders Country Club in 1911 (Fig. 4.3). Ownership of the Octagon Earthworks was transferred to the Ohio Historical Society in 1933.

Fig. 4.2. Charles Whittlesey, with assistance from a young Edwin Hamilton Davis prepared this map of the Newark Earthworks in 1836. The map was enhanced and published by Squier and Davis (1848: pl. xxv).

With the exception of a fragment of the Newark Square and some parallel walls, most of the remaining landscape that once formed the Newark Earthworks has disappeared under the railroads, roads, and buildings of the city of Newark. Most of what we know about the Earthworks today is due to the on-going efforts of Bradley T. Lepper of the Ohio Historical Society. His thorough documentary studies have led to the rediscovery of several critically important unpublished manuscripts, most notably that by James and Charles Salisbury. He has also poured through local newspaper accounts and archival records to attempt to relocate features that were leveled many decades ago. His field research provides important insights into the various components that form the Newark Earthworks and provides the context for understanding what is certainly the largest, and likely the most important, of all Ohio Hopewell ceremonial landscapes.

Octagon Earthworks is a remarkable earthen monument that was built almost certainly, at least in part, to serve as a prehistoric observatory (Hively and Horn 2006). This is not an observatory in the modern sense, but a place to recognize the knowledge of the skies that had been accumulated by many ancestral generations. The Octagon Earthworks consists of a circular enclosure and an octagonal enclosure connected by a short section of parallel walls. Repeated surveys have shown that the circle is nearly perfect to within 4 ft (1.2 m) of its 1054 ft (321 m) diameter. The area of the Circle is about 20 acres (8.1 ha). An earthen platform that is known as the Observatory mound is located along the south-western perimeter of the circle, opposite the opening to the Octagon. The Observatory mound is an elongated platform about 170 ft (51 m) long and 12 ft (3.6 m) high. It was apparently built across a gateway or opening in the circle that included a short section of parallel walls. Lepper (2002) reports that on July 4, 1836 the Calliopean Society of Granville Literary and Theological Institution (now Denison University) excavated into the south-west side of the Observatory in an effort to discover what many commentators thought was an archway that had collapsed. The excavators failed

Octagon and Circle Mounds, Newark, Ohio

Fig. 4.3. Aerial view of the Newark Circle and Octagon. Undated early 20th century post-card.

to find any evidence for an archway but did find that the exterior side of the Observatory mound or platform had been faced with limestone slabs.

The walls of the Octagon are each 550 ft (165 m) long and 5–6 ft (1.5–1.8 m) high. Gateways were built between each of the eight wall sections and varied from 50–90 ft (15–27 m) in width. An oblong platform mound was built partially blocking each opening. Each mound was about 100 × 80 ft (30–24 m) and 5–6 ft (1.5–1.8 m) high. Lepper (2010a) reports that a gravel-filled pit adjacent to one of the mounds produced radiocarbon dates of 1650±80 BP (Beta 769080) and 1770±80 BP (Beta-76909). It is unclear how this pit relates to the mound within the gateway and the construction of the Octagon itself.

The Octagon enclosure covers about 50 acres (20.2 ha) and was very carefully built. While many potential solar and lunar alignments have been proposed for Ohio Hopewell earthen enclosures, the work of Ray Hively and Robert Horn at Newark has shown that the Octagon Earthwork complex was built to a high level of precision for viewing a wide range of lunar events (Hively and Horn 2013).

The Great Circle Earthworks is a circular enclosure formed by a giant earthen wall 1200 ft (366 m) in diameter and up to 16 ft (5 m) high. An interior ditch, about 10ft (3 m) deep, encircles the enclosure and is only broken at the north-east facing entrance to the circle. Walls enclose about 30 acres (12.1 ha) and the circular wall varied from 5 ft to 14 ft (1.5–4.2 m) in height with a ditch encircling the interior of the wall. The ditch is deepest and the embankment walls are highest adjacent to the north-east facing gateway opening. The massive walls and interior ditch are clearly designed to make walls look higher and more impressive from the inside, where special activities were likely conducted. This massive circular enclosure was used as the county fairgrounds from 1854 to 1933 and included a racetrack that circled the interior of the enclosure (Figs 4.4 and 4.5).

At center of the Great Circle is a large mound called Eagle Mound. To some observers, the outline of the mound is reminiscent of a bird in flight. Reports of effigy mounds in the shapes of bears, birds, lizards, and other animals in Wisconsin and what was then the north-west states contributed greatly to the early study of such mounds and earthworks in the Midwestern United States (Lapham 1855). Although early scholars in Ohio apparently thought this mound was similar to those in Wisconsin, the mound appears to be a series of conjoined mounds

Left: **Fig. 4.4.** Gateway in the embankment and ditch looking into the Newark Fairgrounds Circle (photo courtesy of the Ohio History Connection).

Right: **Fig. 4.5.** The prominent embankment wall and interior ditch are visible in this photo of the Fairground Circle racetrack, (photo courtesy of the Ohio History Connection).

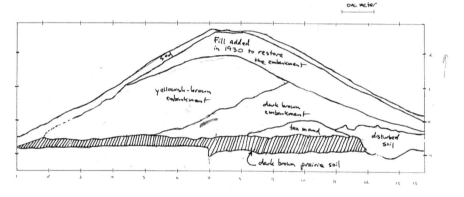

Clockwise from top left:
Fig. 4.6. Excavation of a trench across the embankment wall of the Newark Fairgrounds Circle revealed that the wall was built in two stages on top of an established prairie soil (photo courtesy of Bradley T. Lepper).

Fig. 4.7. Newark Fairground Circle wall profile showing two stages of construction resting on top of an established A horizon (photo courtesy of Bradley T. Lepper).

Fig. 4.8. Profile plan of Newark Fairground Circle wall (image courtesy of Bradley T. Lepper).

rather than a specific effigy form. Emerson Greenman directed excavation of the mound in 1928. Although Greenman never published a report on this excavation, Lepper has reviewed his fieldnotes and provides the following summary. The 1928 excavations revealed that the conjoined mounds cover a rectangular pattern of post-holes roughly 100 × 25 ft (30 × 7.5 m). A depressed, rectangular fire-hardened clay basin was found at the center of building and built into the prepared floor. These types of features were called altars or crematories by the early excavators of Ohio Hopewell mounds, but Greenman found no bones associated with this feature.

In 1992, Bradley Lepper and a team of archaeologists excavated a trench across the embankment wall that forms the Great Circle. The trench revealed that wall was built in stages (Fig. 4.6–4.8):

> "Initially, a circular arrangement of low mounds may have been built to provide the framework for the Great Circle. The Hopewell builders then dug the ditch inside the ring of mounds and placed the dark brown earth from their excavations over the small mounds, forming a circular embankment separated from the ditch by about fourteen feet. Finally, Hopewell workers dug deep pits, still visible east of

the Great Circle, to uncover the yellowish-brown, gravelly subsoil. They used this distinctive earth to fill the gap between the ditch and the top of the dark brown earthwork. The finished earthwork would have been dark brown on the exterior and yellowish-brown on the interior surface, reflecting the different soils used in the construction of the embankment." (Lepper 2002: 11–12)

Although Lepper acknowledges that what limited evidence now exists indicates the wall was built in stages, he does not believe that construction of the giant wall occurred over a substantial period of time (Lepper 2004).

A single radiocarbon date has been obtained from a buried soil horizon underlying the Great Circle wall. Carbon in the soil was dated to 2110±80 BP (Beta-58449). Pollen and phytoliths in the paleosol suggest that the local area was a prairie environment at the time of wall construction (Lepper 2010a). Recognizing that this single trench may not represent how all the monumental earthen features at Newark were built, the existing data indicate that embankment construction did not include stripping away the A horizon prior to construction.

The Newark Square or Wright Earthworks is a near perfect square enclosure with sides ranging from 940 ft to 950 ft (282–285 m) in length, and enclosing about 20 acres (8.1 ha). Only fragments of this enclosure remain. Parallel walls once connected it to the Octagon and Great Circle enclosures, and also connected Wright to a less well-defined oval enclosure along valley edge of Raccoon Creek.

The Cherry Valley Mound complex consisted of a dozen mounds of various sizes, mostly 12–18 m in diameter and 1–1.5 m high. The mounds were surrounded by a low oval enclosure wall about 550 m in diameter. Lepper (1998) has studied historical records relating to this mound group and notes that Newark was founded on the east side of Raccoon Creek and expanded westward into the Newark Earthworks. The Cherry Valley mounds were first to be impacted by urban development.

Construction of the Ohio Canal in 1827 destroyed at least one mound. A local individual told Squier and Davis that 14 skeletons were found about 4 ft (1.2 m) below the surface. The grave(s) were covered by a large quantity of mica sheets that he estimated at 15–20 bushels in volume. Lepper (1998) reports that the central mound of Cherry Valley group was a cluster of conjoined mounds that were destroyed by the construction of the Central Ohio Railroad between 1862 and 1865. This conjoined cluster was about 43 m long, 12 m wide and the tallest mound was about 6 m high. The exterior perimeter of the mound cluster was outlined by a stone pavement about 2.5 m wide.

Citing a local antiquarian, J. N. Wilson (1868), Lepper (1998) notes that Wilson observed the excavation of several skeletons and saw several post-molds indicative of the presence of a structure. Wilson also noted that the mound was built with alternating layers of black loam, blue clay, sand, and cobblestones with intermittent episodes of burning and burial present in the mound fill. Artifacts found within the mound are strongly suggestive of Hopewell origins. Although Wilson's collection has been lost, a mound remnant at this same location, many years later produced the famous Wray figurine – representing a Hopewell shaman (Dragoo and Wray 1964). Remaining mounds in the Cherry Valley group were leveled for construction fill for various other historic features in the late 19th century.

In addition to the four primary enclosures at Newark, there are a wide range of additional archaeological sites in the area around the earthworks. Lepper (1998) found documentary evidence for a rectangular earthwork with a small attached circle which he calls the Salisbury Square in the unpublished Salisbury brothers' manuscript. According to this manuscript, the square was 740 × 760 ft (226 × 232 m and the circle was 140 ft (43 m) in diameter. The enclosures are no longer extant and its location cannot be projected with any precision. The Salisbury brothers reported that a deposit of 194 leaf-shaped bifaces of Flint Ridge flint was found below the surface of the earthen wall forming the Salisbury Square. Lepper (2010a) reports that in 1970 a deposit of 150 blade cores and many bladelets discovered in a locality where the enclosure might have been.

Evidence for habitation in association with the Newark Earthworks is limited. Pacheco (1997) surveyed 50 ha and found four dense artifact clusters and five low-density clusters, which he numbered Murphy III–VI. Four Middle Woodland habitation sites have been identified fairly close to Newark. The Hale House site (33Li252) is the best documented of this group and is located just outside the Cherry Valley mounds oval (Lepper and Yerkes 1997). During salvage excavations at the site, excavators found post-holes suggesting a rectangular structure with a prepared floor, hearth, earth oven, refuse pit, and an hourglass-shaped basin lined with pebbles and covered with sheets of mica (Lepper and Yerkes 1997). An early Woodland radiocarbon date of 2670±70 BP (Beta-27446) is reported from the earth oven. Middle Woodland dates were obtained from a shallow basin, 1845±60 BP (Beta-28062/ETH.4593) and an hourglass-shaped pit dated 1640±90 BP (Beta 58450). Three other sites in the vicinity are recorded from surface collections. Somewhat farther from Newark, William Dancey (1991) has conducted extensive investigations at the Murphy site which he interprets to be a Hopewell farmstead.

In addition to the major enclosures at Newark, the earthwork complex includes parallel walls that connect the major enclosures with one another and also to the nearby water sources. The parallel walls seem to logically represent formalized routes to guide people into the enclosures. Parallel walls are known at other Ohio Hopewell ceremonial landscapes (e.g. Hopeton, Fort Ancient), but the sheer number and scale of these constructions at Newark are highly impressive. There is no evidence from Newark regarding the chronology of the parallel walls. Were they built first to emphasize the ceremony associated with the construction of the major enclosures, or were they built after the enclosures to enhance, and presumably direct, the ceremonial experience associated with visiting the enclosures and the activities conducted inside them?

In his examination of documentary evidence relating to the Newark Earthwork complex, Bradley Lepper (1995; 1996; 1998; 2010a) found evidence that one of the parallel walls seemed to extend for 90 km to the south toward the Chillicothe area and the great concentration of Hopewell enclosure sites in that region. He has named this hypothetical routeway the Great Hopewell Road. Lepper's argument draws strength from the fragmentary documentary sources that report the presence of parallel walls at varying distances from Newark (Atwater 1820; Salisbury and Salisbury 1862: 15). Lepper also notes that, in 1930, a private pilot named Warren Weiant Jr used an airplane to trace these parallel walls from

Newark about 17 km south to Millersport, a line of travel which, if extended, would ultimately arrive in the Chillicothe area. Newark and Chillicothe are the two most impressive concentrations of Hopewell constructed landscapes in Ohio and some connection between the two seems totally logical. The connection seems even stronger when we consider the amazing similarity between the High Bank Works and Octagon Earthworks at Newark. While most Hopewell enclosure sites seem to have been built so as to be different from every other enclosure site in southern Ohio, High Bank and Octagon have many similarities.

When Lepper first proposed the Great Hopewell Road model, informal discussion among scholars seemed to reject it as implausible. As he has continued to make his argument, the notion of some type of pathway or route from Chillicothe to Newark seems to be gaining greater acceptance. It is, at a minimum, a testable hypothesis. Testable hypotheses are often buried beneath the numerous great models that have been offered interpreting Ohio Hopewell culture, but too many Hopewell models and hypotheses are unfortunately untestable.

One of the corollary arguments Lepper has offered in association with the Great Hopewell Road is that the ceremonial landscapes being built at Chillicothe and Newark may have represented pilgrimage centers. The construction of these monumental landscapes may have brought people from great distances to participate in what they believed was an important ceremonial and spiritual activity. This model certainly helps explain where the labor needed to build these vast landscapes was derived. It also may explain how such vast quantities of exotic material that were fashioned into amazing ceremonial objects arrived in southern Ohio. Whether it was copper from the northern Great Lakes, obsidian from the northern Rocky Mountains, shells and sharks teeth from the Gulf of Mexico, or mica from the Appalachian region, scholars have speculated for many decades about the mechanism that brought these items to Ohio. Pilgrimage as proposed by Lepper may be one mechanism, but personal power quests as discussed by Helms (1988; 1993) and Spielmann (2002; 2009) were also likely important factors.

There are many ideas about what is behind the design and configuration of the Newark Earthworks landscape. Martin Byers has proposed that the geometric earthworks of southern Ohio were created for world renewal rituals. Based on the morphology of the different combinations of circular and rectangular enclosures, Byers has identified a series of different patterns. He suggests that the pattern he calls the Paint Creek C-R Configuration reflects the power of the cosmos that is manifested in tracking solar movements, while the High Bank C-R Configuration reflects tracking lunar movements. The combination of these two earthen enclosure configurations is present at Newark, which he describes as:

> "a monumental iconic warrant constructed in order to embody the totality of the cosmos in accordance with its Solar/Lunar sacred temporal structuring and its vertical/horizontal Heavens/Underworld sacred spatial structuring." (Byers 2004: 101)

Bradley Lepper (2004, 2010) views Newark as a "ritual machine" that attracted participants from beyond central Ohio to contribute labor for the construction of the enclosures and other landscape elements, participate in the rituals, ceremonies and festivals, and witness the celestial events that the landscape was built to track and commemorate. Lepper argues persuasively that the sophisticated and integrated geometry exhibited by the various enclosure shapes and sizes indicates that the Newark landscape was built as an integrated plan, rather than a series of elements that were sequentially tacked together. This view has also been championed by others who have studied the Newark landscape (Romain 2000; Marshall 1996).

The search for astronomical alignments has become a passion among Ohio Hopewell scholars and there is little doubt that at least some of the landscapes that were built incorporated lunar and solar movement into their design and construction. Through the careful work of Ray Hively and Robert Horn (2006) we now know that the alignments of constructed landscape elements within the Newark Earthwork complex were almost certainly built to mark celestial events. Combining careful survey and statistical analysis of the Newark data, Hively and Horn found five alignments to major and minor lunar standstills at Octagon and Circle. Four alignments are along the Octagon walls, and one is along the avenue axis that connects the Octagon with the adjoining Observatory Circle.

Even more remarkable, Hively and Horn (2006: 306) calculated that the combination of astronomical and geometric regularity recorded at Newark is only possible within a relatively narrow range of latitude (44.5 km) that includes the Newark locality. The geometry exhibited at Newark would not accurately mark the lunar standstills if precisely the same embankments were built outside the narrow north–south band, and this revelation about the role of latitude in the design of the enclosure may explain why there are clear differences in the High Bank Works, where the same earthwork shapes would not have produced comparable accuracy in marking lunar events (Hively and Horn 2006: 307; 2010).

Questions about construction chronology are at the center of all debates about the interpretation of the Newark ceremonial landscape. These same questions apply to virtually all the other geometric Hopewell enclosure sites in Ohio. Do the various combinations of circular and rectangular embankments represent a single design or an accretion of elements built over time? Martin Byers (1987) and Warren DeBoer (1997) have argued that the circular enclosure form, which appears in temporally earlier sites, preceded the rectangular enclosure form. Byers (1987: 280) argues specifically that the Newark Octagon was built after its paired Observatory Circle. With the more recent revelations about the precision of the Newark geometry with specific lunar alignments, the argument for accretive growth seems less plausible. However, the issue of the length of time spent in building the Newark Earthworks is far from resolved.

Lepper (2004; 2010a) has suggested that the landscape at Newark was constructed in a relatively short period of time, perhaps a single human lifespan. Evidence reviewed in this chapter from sites in the Scioto and Miami/Little Miami drainages indicates that some of those landscapes were built in stages over time, and more likely represent slower construction sustained by stable and committed communities. Certainly there are great similarities in the landscapes that were built across southern Ohio in the period between AD 1 and AD 400, but there are also major differences too. There is a great deal yet to learn about how and when the landscape features at Newark were built, and it would be inappropriate to expect that the same construction rules and principles that were in effect in the Scioto area or south-west Ohio to apply to the construction at Newark.

Marietta

Marietta, Ohio was built at the mouth of the Muskingum River, where it enters the Ohio River. The city of Marietta, now part of Washington County, is an old town that developed in the early days of westward expansion. Rufus Putnam and two partners purchased a fairly substantial piece of land under their ownership of the Ohio Company. A visit to their new investment led to preparation of a sketch map by Putnam in 1788 of the largely untouched Marietta Earthworks. Although this did not lead to more substantial archaeological investigations, it does offer an early picture of the character and size of one of the few major Ohio Hopewell ceremonial landscapes in the Muskingum River valley. Caleb Atwater (1820) provided a later map and detailed description of the site based upon reports from several correspondents who resided in south-east Ohio.

The Directors of the Ohio Company recognized the importance of the Marietta Earthworks and planned the town and its features so as to preserve the ancient landscape and gave the mounds and landscape features classical names. Squier and Davis (1848) published a map of the site that was attributed to Charles Whittlesey in 1837, although James L. Murphy (1977) argues that the map was actually made by General Samuel R. Curtis. MacLean (1879) also provides an extensive description of the site. The Whittlesey map depicts two rectangular enclosures with multiple gateways and five fairly substantial mounds.

The larger of the two enclosures covered about 40 acres (16.2 ha) and was connected to the eastern bank of the Muskingum River by a large "graded way" or *Sacra Via*. The larger enclosure had 16 gateways with four pyramidal mounds inside the enclosure. Walls of both enclosures were about 6 ft (1.8 m) high and 25 ft (7.5 m) wide at the base. Inside the large enclosure were two large mounds in the shape of truncated pyramids (Quadranaou and Capitolium). The smaller rectangular enclosure encompassed about 27 acres (10.9 ha) and had a series of small mounds built within or near the ten gateways. A single embankment wall stretched from the smaller rectangular enclosure to the south-east where it met a small circular enclosure that was filled by a large conical mound (Conus) that has been pictured on many postcards (Fig. 4.9). The Sacra Via was a sloping roadway with parallel walls lining each side of the passage from the enclosure to the river. It was 155 ft (46.5 m) wide and 680 ft (204 m) long.

Squier and Davis also describe the presence of several "dug holes" or "wells" which they believed were quarries to procure building materials for the mounds and earthen walls. MacLean (1879) reported that numerous stone mounds were present on the bluffs on the opposite side of the Muskingum River. Marietta has been one of the most recognized of all Ohio Hopewell constructed landscapes because it was the subject of an early lithograph by Charles Sullivan and was used by Squier and Davis as the frontispiece in *Ancient Monuments of the Mississippi Valley* (1848).

Fig. 4.9. The Conus mound was one of the prominent features within the Marietta Works and is shown in this plate from Ancient Monuments of the Mississippi Valley by Squier and Davis (1848: pl. xlv). This mound has survived as a feature in the historic cemetery for the City of Marietta, Ohio.

Despite the intention of the Ohio Company to design the town of Marietta around the earthworks, more than two centuries of historic activities have largely leveled all but a few of the earthen features. Modern archaeological studies at Marietta have been limited. William Romain (2000) has spent considerable time and energy showing the potential alignment of the Quadranaou and Capitolium Mounds and Sacra Via with the winter solstice sunset. Romain has also found that parts of the parallel walls that lined the Sacra Via are still intact. However, at this time there is insufficient information to determine if the winter solstice sunset alignment was significant, or a product of other prehistoric cultural preferences.

The only well documented excavation of any of the constructed landscape at Marietta was conducted in 1990 when N'omi Greber directed excavations at the Capitolium Mound in advance of plans to expand the Washington County Public Library which had been built on it. The excavation exposed parts of two different lobes of the mound, with each lobe exhibiting evidence of superimposed surfaces covered by traditional layers of mound fill. A report of the investigation of the south lobe by William Pickard (1996) describes and documents the very complex series of strata that contributed to the construction of this mound.

Platform mounds are not commonly associated with Ohio Hopewell ceremonial landscapes, but they have been documented here at Marietta, at the Mann site in Indiana (Kellar 1979), and the Pinson Mounds (Mainfort 1988a, 196) in Tennessee and at other localities. The Capitolium Mound was generally oriented north-west to south-east and had at least three earthen ramps leading up to the flat mound summit. The 1990 excavations examined only about 3% of the horizontal mound surface, but produced enough evidence for the excavators to conclude that the south lobe was an extension that had been added to a pre-existing mound. Despite substantial disturbance from construction of the library, they were able to discern the basic sequence of construction.

Construction of the south lobe was begun by removing vegetation and the A horizon to expose the B horizon. On the surface of the exposed subsoil a series of sand layers was spread, 5 cm or less in thickness, to form the mound base. On top of these, the builders placed a series of thin gravel layers, each less than 10 cm in thickness. Near the center of this sand and gravel base, a layer of mottled clayey-sand was added, which was then covered by layers of sands and gravels like the lower floor. Several post-holes were found at this level, with the posts being removed and post-holes filled with bright red and yellow clays. After this point, red, sandy clay became the major building material. Red colored soils and intermixed layers of gravel are common components of Ohio Hopewell earthwork construction. Pickard (1996) provides excellent documentation of the complex stratigraphy reflecting the construction of the upper part of the south lobe of the mound.

For example, he describes a sloping stratum designated Feature 36. The outer half of this layer was comprised of a series of superimposed clays, 5–10 cm in thickness, and separated by very thin layers of pea gravel. The inner half of this layer of the mound was a single continuous unit of clay that showed evidence of burning in places. Feature 51 was another area with complex stratigraphy. Several post-holes originated at this level and two concentrations of pottery were found. Apparently the surface of this layer of yellow silty sand was at one time a platform or activity surface that was eventually covered by subsequent mound fill. Unfortunately, the spatial limits of the excavations and the significant disturbance to the mound during initial construction of the library prohibit any greater understanding of the complex character of this mound's construction.

Greber (2003) reports the results of four radiocarbon dates from samples collected during the 1991 excavations at the *Capitolium* Mound. The dates range in age from 1660± 60 BP (Beta-78014) to 1880±70 (Beta-67234) and Greber expresses frustration at the internal inconsistency of the dates in relationship to their stratigraphic order. However, as she notes, when standard deviations at one sigma are factored into the results, the internal stratigraphic consistency is no longer relevant. Since these are the only dating results from Marietta, and the 1991 excavations at the Capitolium Mound are the only systematic excavations that have been reported, it is very difficult to estimate the age of the other earthen features at Marietta or the span of time in which the site was being built or used.

Scioto River valley

The Scioto River originates in Hardin County, Ohio, and generally runs from north to south in south-central Ohio where it empties into the Ohio River at Portsmouth. The northern reaches of the Scioto flow through lands that were heavily impacted by glaciation, but near Chillicothe the river enters the unglaciated Appalachian highlands. Chillicothe, which is widely regarded as home to the largest concentration of geometric earthen enclosures in North America, rests on the eco-tone of these two important physiographic provinces.

Much of what we know about the number and distribution of geometric and other earthen enclosures in this drainage was fairly well established with the publication of the *Archaeological Atlas of Ohio* by William C. Mills in 1914. The effort to locate and map mounds and earthworks in Ohio was begun by Col. Charles Whittlesey, President of the Western Reserve Historical Society in the 1870s. In 1891, Cyrus Thomas included a map showing the known mounds of Ohio in his summary report on the work of the Division of Mound Exploration. Four years later in 1895, Warren K. Moorehead began a systematic survey of the state to fully document the number and distribution of archaeological monuments. After Moorehead's resignation in 1897, the work was continued under William

C. Mills and eventually published as the now well-known atlas. Discoveries of new earthworks have, however, occurred since 1914 (see Anderson 1980), but as agriculture and urban development continued to change the face of the landscape these have become rare.

Drawing directly from Mills' 1914 *Atlas of Ohio Archaeology*, there are eight counties in the Scioto River Drainage. From north to south they are Hardin, Marion, Delaware, Franklin, Pickaway, Ross, Pike, and Scioto. The largest number of mounds and earthworks are found in Ross (see Fig. 4.1), but significant numbers are found in almost all of the Counties from Delaware to the south. Mills reported 140 enclosures and 864 mounds. Since publication of the 1914 *Atlas*, it is likely that a handful of additional enclosures and quite a few mounds have been discovered, but certainly these numbers convey the impressive density of earthen landscape construction in the Scioto drainage.

The notoriety of the Scioto River is, in part, due to the great density of mounds and earthworks attributed to Ohio Hopewell societies. However, even more important is the number of sites where excavations have yielded impressive numbers and varieties of artifacts. Major excavations in the late 19th and early 20th centuries at Mound City (Mills 1922a; 1922b), Hopewell Mound Group (Moorehead 1922), Tremper (Mills 1916), Seip Earthwork (Mills 1909a; 1909b; Shetrone and Greenman 1931); Adena Mound (Mills 1902a; 1902b), and many others yielded many artifacts which helped define Ohio Hopewell as an archaeological taxonomic unit, with exotic artifacts so impressive that they have become iconic symbols of the achievements of the people who built these vast earthen monuments. There can be no question about the importance of sites like Newark, Marietta, Turner, and Fort Ancient in the surrounding drainages, but the early study of Ohio Hopewell focused on sites in the Chillicothe area in the Scioto River valley and knowledge about this prehistoric era was built on those studies.

The mound and enclosure sites in the Scioto valley are not well known based solely on their vast numbers. They are impressive in size and diversity as well. Geometric enclosures are particularly numerous and they come in a dazzling variety of combinations and sizes. The forms range from individual circles (small and large sizes) and squares, to combinations of two or more of these geometric shapes conjoined into a larger unit. Several of the sites also include parallel walls, or "graded ways" as they are called in the early literature. The most unique geometric form found in the Scioto valley is the Octagon enclosure at the High Bank Works. The Octagon at High Bank and a similar one at Newark are the only known examples of this shape of geometric enclosure.

On the basis of past excavations and the unique finds reported from early Ohio Hopewell research, Mound City, Hopewell, Tremper, and Seip are probably the most famous sites in this drainage. The Hopeton Earthworks and High Bank Works have experienced most study in recent years, and consequently have produced substantial new information about earthen construction. The five Tripartite earthworks (Seip, Baum, Frankfort, Works East, and Liberty) are the largest enclosures in the Scioto valley and their unique character, combined with their similarity of size and form, have inspired considerable thought, hypotheses, and speculation in the archaeological literature.

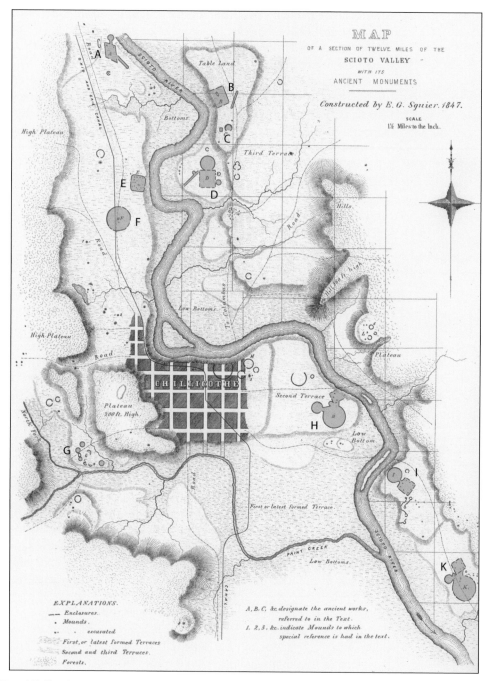

Fig. 4.10. Map of Chilllicothe, Ohio in about 1846 showing the high density of large geometric earthworks in this region. The publications and papers of Squier and Davis include several different versions of this map. The map illustrates the number and variety of mounds and earthen enclosures in a 12 mile (19.3 km) stretch of the Scioto River. (Squier and Davis 1848, pl. ii).

Key:

A	Dunlap's Works	E	Mound City	H	Works East
B–C	Cedar-Bank Works	F	Shriver Circle	I	High Bank
D	Hopeton	G	Junction Group	K	Liberty

The purpose of this discussion is to review the research that has been conducted at major earthwork sites in the Scioto River valley, and to articulate what has been learned about how these ceremonial landscapes were built. Chronological evidence about when the landscapes were built, and associated features that may give insights into what activities were performed at these monumental constructions will also be considered.

Information about the construction of the Hopeton Earthworks was presented in the previous chapter and forms an important basis for comparison with data gathered from other sites in the Scioto River drainage. Through the investigations at Hopeton, we have learned that the construction of at least one of these great earthen monuments consisted of far more than simply the process of piling up soil to form walls of geometric enclosures. The research at Hopeton demonstrates that vast amounts of soil were removed as part of the construction process and the builders were skilled and careful in the selection and placement of soil materials used to build the large enclosure walls. Although none of the other sites in the Scioto River valley has been subjected to the same types and the intensity of landscape research as were employed at Hopeton, important comparisons may be drawn from reviewing the studies of landscape construction methods at Mound City, Hopewell Mound Group, Seip Earthworks, High Bank Works, Anderson Earthworks, and the Shriver Circle (Figs 4.10 and 4.11).

Seip

The Seip Earthworks have been well known in the archaeological literature for nearly two centuries. Located east of Bainbridge, Ohio, in the Paint Creek valley, the site was initially described and mapped by Caleb Atwater (1820), although more recent publications use the map made by Squier and Davis (1848; Fig. 4.11, A). The Atwater map (1820) illustrates the general shape of the tripartite enclosure, but Squier and Davis (1848, pl. xxi: no. 2) illustrated the embankment walls with greater precision and added details such as associated smaller mounds and borrow pits.

Seip Earthworks comprises a large circular central enclosure with a smaller

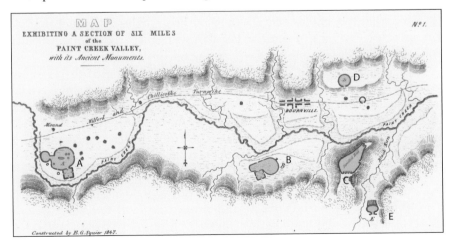

Fig. 4.11. Map of earthworks in the Paint Creek valley around Bourneville to the south-west of Chillicothe (Squier and Davis 1848, pl. iii).

Key:
A   Seip
B   Baum
C   Spruce Hill
D   Bourneville Circle
E   Bear Claw

circular enclosure attached on the west and a rectangular enclosure attached on the south-east. Atwater observed that the larger central enclosure was about 77.1 acres (31.2 ha) in extent and the walls had ten gateways. The square enclosure has eight gateways and is about 27 acres (10.9 ha) in extent. The smaller circular enclosure is about '60 poles' (i.e. 990 ft/301.8 m) in diameter with walls about 4 ft (1.2 m) in height. Borrow pits, which Atwater called "wells", are located outside the perimeter of the irregular central enclosure. Both Atwater and Squier and Davis (1848) paid particular attention to a large elliptical mound near the center of the central enclosure. The mound was estimated at 25 ft (7.5 m) (Atwater) to 30 ft (9 m) (Squier and Davis) in height and covered nearly two-thirds of an acre (0.27 ha). The mound was built of earth, but was covered by a layer of stones and pebbles. This mound was later called the Seip-Pricer Mound. A somewhat smaller, but still substantial, group of conjoined mounds known as the Seip Mound was located to the east. Both of these separate mounds, Seip-Pricer and the Seip Mound, have been the subject of important early 20th century excavations.

Squier and Davis (1848) recorded the Seip mound as three separate mounds, but William C. Mills (1909a; 1909b) considered it to be one mound made from three separate ones. At the west end of the mound, Mills measured the height as 18 ft (9.7 m) but noted that it rose to 20 ft 1 in (6 m); when excavations revealed the original base of the mound it had been covered by redeposited soil that had washed off the mound. The other two sections of the mound were measured at 11 ft 10 in (3.6 m), and 6 ft (1.8 m) high. Conjoined mounds of this type have been reported at other sites in the Scioto River valley.

During his excavation of the mound (Fig. 4.12a), Mills observed that it was comprised mainly of loamy soils but the tip section of the larger mound was composed of clay and limestone gravel (that had become cemented together over time). On the north side, excavators found a series of flat stones (averaging 25–36 cm) set in the side of the mound forming steps from the base to the summit. A large deposit of well-sorted gravel had been placed at the periphery of the mound base, up to 0.75 m deep and 1.5–2.1 m wide.

Three separate sub-mound structures were found at the base of the mound. Each was a circular pattern of post-molds, some with charred wood at the top of the mold. Numerous burials were placed on the floors of these structures, and all burials were cremations. Inhumation burials were found in the fill of the mound above the base, but only one had a prepared grave.

Mills observed that the "surface soil, which had been removed almost to the gravel, had been used in the construction of the large Pricer Mound, which is only a few hundred yards away (1909a: 281)." Post-holes (0.75 ft/0.23 m deep) reflected an oval structure built on the subsoil, 60 ft (20 m) east–west and 72 ft (21.6 m) north–south. Wall posts were spaced about 2.5 ft (0.75 m) apart. Entrances were noted on the north-west and east sides of the building:

> "The entrance to the northwest was of peculiar construction, and made by the walls overlapping each other, forming a passageway, or hall, about 3 ft [0.9 m] in width, and 7 ft [2.1 m] in length. The passageway was covered with fine sand varying in thickness from two inches to one-half inch [57–6 mm], and so firmly packed as to have the appearance of coarse sand-stone." (Mills 1909a: 281)

Fig. 4.12. a. Excavation of the Seip mound showing burial features at the floor of the mound and at least three stages of mound construction in the profile (photo courtesy of the the Ohio Historical Society and Hopewell Culture National Historical Park); b. The Seip-Pricer mound is one of the largest Hopewell mounds constructed anywhere. After excavations by H.C. Shetrone the mound was reconstructed and is preserved in a public park. The mound is visible in the distance with the Seip embankment wall in foreground (photo: author, June 2013).

The east entrance was a short passageway that connected to the second circular building. The passageway was 3 ft (0.9 m) wide and 2.5 ft (0.75) long. The floor was covered with fine sand. The second circular building was 43 ft (12.9 m) east–west and 32 ft (9.6 m) north–south. Posts forming the north side of this building were larger than those of structure 1, but the rest of the posts in the building were similar in size to the first structure. The building had two entrances: one leading to the first structure, and the second leading to the third section with practically no passageway. The third structure was oblong, 22.5 ft (6.75 m) north–south and 15 ft (4.5 m) east–west. The floor had been prepared and leveled. Posts for this building were smaller than the other two. The structures described by Mills are similar to "great houses" found beneath larger Hopewell mounds in the Scioto River drainage (Greber and Shane 2009).

Although Mills provides only very limited information about the structure of the Seip Mound, he noted that the soil under the mound had been stripped down to the subsoil. He assumed the topsoil removal was done to construct the nearby Seip-Pricer mound, but soil stripping prior to construction of an earthen feature is common, if not universal, in the Scioto River valley.

The central and largest mound was originally that on the Pricer farm and is now often called the Seip-Pricer Mound (Fig. 4.12b) , although it is called Seip Mound Number 1 by Shetrone and Greenman (1931) in their report on excavations conducted from 1925 to 1928 at the Seip Earthworks. Mills had previously designated the smaller conjoined Seip mound as mound #1 at the Seip Earthworks, Shetrone chose to later assign Mound #1 to the Seip-Pricer mound, apparently due to its larger size. Seip-Pricer is the largest mound in the Paint Creek valley at 250 ft (75 m) long, 150 ft (45 m) wide, with a maximum height of 32 ft (9.6 m). Shetrone and Greenman provide important information about the structure of the giant mound, which reflects how it was built.

Prior to the start of mound construction, the topsoil was stripped away to a depth of 6–12 in (15–30 cm) exposing the coarse clay and gravel subsoil. A layer of dark clay or muck was placed on the exposed surface in the shape of the mound base. The clay layer varied from 6–12 in (15–30 cm) in thickness and was hardened and colored in some places by fire. A layer of sand varying from 0.25–1 in (19–25 mm) in thickness was then placed on top of the clay floor:

> "The only constructions extending beneath the floor-level were the so-called crematory basins; holes formerly occupied by posts and stakes of wood, which had decayed; irregular depressions, apparently prepared for the reception of offerings of a special nature; and pits which contained refuse material, ashes and charcoal". (Shetrone and Greenman 1931: 364)

Excavators recorded crematory basins, depressions, pits, a large deposit of heavily burned artifacts, a cache of copper artifacts, post molds and burial platforms that had been built on top of the floor at the base of the mound. A Great House that served as a focus for a range of Hopewell ritual and ceremonial activities was built on the sub-mound floor. These buildings were eventually dismantled before the mound covering was placed over the floor.

One of the most substantial features constructed on the floor of the mound was a log chamber that had been covered by woven fabric at the western end beneath the largest lobe of the primary mound. The burial chamber had collapsed after the mound was built, filling it with earth. The void that was created by the collapse was subsequently filled. Six extended burials were originally placed in the tomb with their heads to the east. They have been identified as four adults and two infants. The burial chamber was built of logs and measured 12 ft (3.6 m) N–S and 15 ft (15.3 m) E–W. Stones had been used to hold the logs in place, particularly on the inside of the chamber. The low original vault was no more than 2 ft (0.6 m) high. The chamber was covered by a fabric canopy that was held in place by 100 or more bone skewers. These skewers or pegs were 6–12 in (15–30 cm) long and made from deer leg bones. During the process of mound construction, the canopy was covered by a thin layer of bark or fabric and sand.

> "The four adult burials at the west end of the vault were not upon small platforms as were the great majority of burials, but lay directly upon the top of the clay and gravel platform which rose between three and one-half and four feet above the floor. This eminence may itself be regarded as a common platform for the four interments, differing only in size from the usual type of platform found in Hopewell mounds. The four skeletons lay parallel and each was separated from the next by a small log, of which nothing remained by the mold or impression in the clay and a thin layer of white ash-like material." (Shetrone and Greenman 1931: 372)

The four adult burials were outlined with thousands of pearl beads. Excavators found five large ceremonial pipes of micaceous steatite in the mound soil above the burial chamber. Two are bird effigies – a squatting owl and a bird with outstretched wings. The other three are animals – a dog eating a human head, another dog, and a tubular pipe with the front end in the shape of a bear.

The floor and associated features was eventually covered by the original or primary mound, which comprised three conjoined lobes of earth. The primary earthen mound was then covered by a stratum of heavy gravel ranging from 6 in to 2 ft (15–60 cm) in thickness. The gravel stratum spread out beyond the base of the earthen primary mound and spilled beyond the edges by 8–10 ft (2.4–3 m). The margin of the mound at the its base was outlined by an outer ring of flat angular slabs of sandstone and limestone that served as the foot of an outer retaining wall composed of heavy gravel about 10 ft (3 m) thick at the bottom. The gravel extended about three-quarters of the distance up the sides of the mound, and its thickness diminished with height (Shetrone and Greenman 1931).

Of the three lobes forming the primary mound, the west lobe was the largest. Each lobe was comprised of earth that had a high clay content and was lighter brown in color, while earth above the primary mounds was made of darker colored soils:

> "intermixed with humus, charcoal and ashes and quantities of animal bones and other refuse materials, including an occasional artifact. In view of the nature of the soil and of the artifacts found in it, this portion of the mound appears to have been removed from the surface in the immediate vicinity upon which the builders had lived." (Shetrone and Greenman 1931: 359)

Re-deposited materials were found on the east end of the primary mound, probably resulting from erosion before the secondary or capping strata had been deposited.

The two oval rings of stone or retaining walls served to catch materials washing off the sides of the mound:

> "The pavement of stone slabs forming the base of the outer retaining wall was on the floor of the mound at its outer margin. The slabs forming this base were not all laid flat, and there was tendency for those on the outer edge to be in a perpendicular position. This pavement consisted for the most part of blocks of sandstone ranging from six to 100 pounds [2.7–45.5 kg] in weight. At some points they were piled on top of one another to a height of a foot or two [30–90 cm]. Above this base, forming a retaining wall proper and conforming to the slope of the surface of the mound, heavy gravel was piled. At the base the thickness of this gravel was generally the same as that of the stone pavement beneath, from eight to ten feet [2.4–3.0 m]; it decreased in thickness as it extended up the sides of the mound and disappeared about 15 feet [4.6m] from the apex excepting at certain points where it continued over the top of the mound to form a complete covering. It is apparent that gravel originally covered the entire mound and was partly washed down during the centuries following its erection. This retaining wall was covered at all points by a foot or two of earth which was thicker at the base of the mound than at the top, where at some points the gravel was at the surface. There can be little doubt that the height of this retaining wall, like that over the primary, was kept equal with that of the earth above the primary as it was built up, to prevent undoing by the elements of the arduous labor of the builders." (Shetrone and Greenman 1931: 362–3)

Shetrone and Greenman also excavated two smaller mounds, but offer little detail about the structure or construction of those mounds. In a discussion of the ceramics from the Seip investigations, they make reference to an excavation through the embankment wall. They note 80 sherds were collected from an excavation of a portion of the wall. They observe that the sherds were found "at a depth of two feet in an ash deposit" (Shetrone and Greenman 1931: 438). Shetrone apparently had little interest in the construction of the Seip enclosure wall, and he devoted even less attention to this part of his excavation than his excavation of the enclosure wall at the Hopewell Mound Group.

In 1966, Martha Potter Otto conducted a series of excavations to provide interpretive materials for wayside exhibits at the Seip State Memorial. Otto and three workers excavated a trench 80 ft (24.2 m) by 10 ft (3 m) across a section of embankment wall that had been reconstructed following Shetrone and Greenman's 1925–1928 excavations at the site (Otto 2009). Otto found that the base of the original embankment wall was still present and measured 50 ft (15.2 m) in width at the point of their excavation. She observed that the wall was built upon subsoil that was "compact, clayey reddish-brown mixed with small pebbles" and the wall fill was:

> "yellowish soil mixed with organic material and capped with a narrow ridge of dark earth that likely was the most visible part of the embankment wall at the time of Shetone's excavations. Lying against the inner flank of the wall and extending south for a distance of approximately 5.3 m (17 ft.) was a layer of dark soil identified in the field notes and profile map as 'midden'." (Otto 2009: 13)

Otto recorded that yellow-brown slope wash from the original embankment wall covered the north edge of the wall and the adjacent midden.

Although this brief account is the only report now available about how the walls at Seip were built, it contains some very useful information. Much as has been observed at other sites in the Scioto River valley, the Seip wall was built on top of truncated subsoil. Apparently, the A horizon had been removed and wall fill was placed directly on top of the exposed subsoil. Although the upper parts of the embankment wall had been removed by erosion from historic period activities, the 1966 excavation revealed the presence of at least two different types of soil that were placed to form the wall. This pattern has also been observed in many other Scioto River valley sites where investigators have examined the construction evidence within embankment walls.

Unrelated to the construction of the Seip Earthworks, but likely of great importance in understanding how this massive landscape was used, is an area of intense ceremonial activity between the Seip-Pricer mound and the enclosure wall to the north. The 1966 excavations by Martha Potter Otto revealed the presence of a Hopewell midden just inside the embankment wall. In addition to this trench, one of three test units placed between the embankment wall and the Seip-Pricer mound revealed the presence of a dark midden that was covered by a gravel layer. In 1971, Raymond Baby led an excavation by the Ohio Historical Society and Ohio State University in that area that exposed a series of post-holes from a structure adjacent to the 1966 excavation. Several years of subsequent excavations revealed additional structures in areas immediately contiguous to the first building. Additional research by Nomi Greber and Katherine Spielmann has documented one of the most intensely utilized areas at any Ohio Hopewell site. Further consideration of this research at the Seip Earthworks will be discussed in Chapter 5.

Excavations of the large Seip-Pricer mound and the trench across the embankment wall revealed that these earthen features were built on places where the A-horizon had been removed and the B-horizon was exposed. This is certainly consistent with earthen constructions at other sites in this region, but we are left wondering if this practice had been extended to the entire area within the three large Seip enclosures. Since there is evidence in the construction of the large Seip-Pricer mound that it was built in stages (Shetrone and Greenman 1931), it would be of considerable interest to know the chronological relationship between the various mounds, the multiple wooden buildings (Baby and Langlois 1979; Greber 2009b; Spielmann *et al.* 2005), and the geometric enclosure walls. Seip Earthwork is one of the larger ceremonial landscapes constructed by the Hopewell people in the Scioto River valley, and the work that has been undertaken at this important site barely scratches the surface of its potential.

High Bank Earthwork

High Bank is one of the most important and unique geometric enclosures in southern Ohio (Figs 4.10, I; 4.13). The earthworks comprised of a rare octagonal enclosure attached to a large circle by a narrow neck. Squier and Davis (1848: pl. xvi) illustrate four additional smaller circular enclosures and two long walls forming a wide avenue. The various enclosures cover more than 50 ha on High Bank terrace, which is 17 m above Scioto River floodplain. During the mid-19th century the octagon walls were 12 ft (3.7 m) high and the Great Circle wall was 5 ft (1.5 m) high. Agriculture has reduced the octagon walls to about 5 ft (1.5 m) and Great Circle is barely visible after two centuries of intensive cultivation

The importance of the earthen walls and the associated ceremonial landscape has been emphasized by the revelation by Ray Hively and Robert Horn that the High Bank walls align with "a combination of solar and lunar extreme rise/set points at its latitude" (Hively and Horn 2010: 139). They point out that the builders of the High Bank Works, unlike the Circle-Octagon at Newark, failed "to encode that astronomical design on the most prominent feature, its long axis" (Hively and Horn 2010: 139). Due to its unique form, and the celestial alignments that have been identified, it seems apparent that the embankment walls were built to a carefully established design.

What is known about the construction of the High Bank Earthwork is primarily a result of investigations conducted by Orin C. Shane III in 1972 and through ongoing research by N'omi Greber of the Cleveland Museum of Natural History (1994–present). Both of these investigators have invested substantial time and effort in the study of the earthen walls at High Bank (Greber and Shane 2009). In 1972, Shane and his students excavated three trenches across the Octagon walls and two across Great Circle walls. During her fieldwork between 1994 and 2002,

Hopewellian Grave goods and exotic artifacts I

Unfortunately, the majority of Hopewell burials were excavated before modern techniques of excavation and recording so that very few grave plans or photographs survive. The textbox in Chapter 2 describes the main form of burials and associated structures. A striking array of grave goods made from a range of exotic, imported raw materials such as copper, pipestone, shell, mica, various lithic materials including colored flints and obsidian, as well as pottery, wood, bone and antler, was interred with many burials, both inhumation and cremation. For example, one of the cremation burials under Mound 10 at Mound City, was accompanied by parts of a copper headdress, and the other with burnt shell and pearl beads, a single sherd of pottery, a copper headdress fragment and a copper adze in a twillwork bag. The undisturbed skeleton from the Haslett Mound was accompanied by classic Hopewell artifacts comprising an unusually large cross-shaped copper gorget placed under the head, and the deceased wore copper ear spools. A shell bead necklace was worn and near the right arm a copper-covered wooden object was found, possibly a knife. An ornament crafted from the lower jaw of a gray wolf was held in the left hand.

Bear/dog headdress. Made from hammered sheets of copper. The jaw and ears are moveable (photo: Pete Topping).

The discovery of metallic artifacts in association with Ohio Hopewell burials and ceremonial features led early antiquarians to believe those items were left by a lost race who were overwhelmed by the Native Indians who lived in the Ohio River valley. Early accounts described these items in terms of the material culture used by Europeans in the late 18th and early 19th centuries. They were unaware that prehistoric Native Americans quarried almost pure copper from mines in the area of Lake Superior in the Western Great Lakes up to 7000 years ago. The native copper could be obtained in small lumps from large veins in these quarries and could be either heated and pounded or cold hammered into the various ornaments and tools found in the archaeological record. Copper artifacts are well documented in Middle Archaic (*ca.* 7000–3700 BC) sites in the Great Lakes area, but copper work seems to have reached its most artistic levels during the Ohio Hopewell era. While copper artifacts are found across the Midwestern States, these highly stylized forms are recorded mainly in Hopewellian ceremonial deposits across Eastern North America, suggesting they were made and used by people associated with Hopewell ceremonial practices, or the Hopewell Interaction Sphere.

Thin copper plate in the form of a flying Peregrine Falcon.

Copper plate with scroll or cut-out work based on a central bird head motif.

Mushroom wand. The shaft is made from wood covered with a thin layer of copper inserted into a mushroom effigy copper head.

All artifacts from the excavations of Mills and Shetrone at Mound City (1920–1) (photos 2–4 courtesy of the Ohio History Connection and Hopewell Culture National Historical Park.

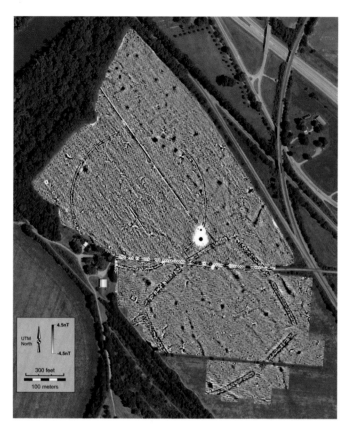

Fig. 4.13. Magnetic data shown on an aerial photograph, High Bank Earthworks (image courtesy of Jarrod Burks and Robert Cook).

Greber conducted geophysical mapping, plus excavation of two trenches south of the farm lane through the wall of the Great Circle, and a third trench across from the center of the neck joining the two large enclosures.

In all three trenches excavated by Shane the A horizon had been removed prior to construction and wall fill material was placed directly on the exposed subsoil. Wall fill was comprised of a variety of "sandy loams, clays, sandy clays, sands, gravelly-sands, and loose gravels" Greber and Shane 2009: 27). Basket-load deposits of sediments were frequently visible in the wall fill, and the investigators suggest the wall materials were likely collected from "dug holes" identified by Squier and Davis from just west of Octagon wall segment VII. The color of the sediments in Trenches I and III were similar, but the Trench IV sediments were composed of brighter red and yellow hues with higher sand and clay content.

Kent State University, under Shane, and the Cleveland Museum of Natural History, under Greber, combined to excavate five trenches across different parts of the wall forming the Great Circle enclosure. Annual cultivation had reduced the height of the earthen walls during the interval between the 1972 and subsequent (1994–present) excavations by more than 15 cm. In four of the five trenches, research revealed that the A horizon had been removed and the wall was built on the surface of the exposed B horizon. Greber and Shane (2009) recognized two construction phases in the exposed wall sections and observed that, while there were similarities between the wall sections that were examined, variations were also present. Wall fills comprised 2–3 different types of matrix, including thin layers of gravel with alternating color, coarse gravels, sands and pebbles, yellow silty clay loess, and reddish clay loam. The top layer in all areas examined was a silty clay loam.

Of considerable interest in three of these trenches was the presence of a fence of oak posts that had been closely set in a narrow trench during the early stages of wall construction. Trench III was located across from the midpoint of the neck that connects the Octagon and the Great Circle. The fence was later dismantled, partially burned and then covered by wall fill. Four AMS dates from a line of burned posts in Trench II produced an average age of 1860±80 years (at 2 sigma). Two dates on a post found under the embankment wall yielded a substantially earlier, pre-Hopewell date for the feature. It is unclear if dating oak posts may have encountered "old wood" that might have skewed these dates. Unfortunately, wood charcoal seems to be the most common organic material preserved at Hopewell embankment sites, and the Hopewell preference for hardwood in construction of embankment features, and wooden structures makes it difficult to find more suitable samples for dating.

The final trench was excavated to examine a magnetic anomaly and the northern wall of the Great Circle. The anomaly was generally circular and 14 m in diameter and located immediately outside the embankment wall. Excavation of a 2 × 18 m trench revealed that the A horizon had been stripped away and also much of the B horizon, to within about 20 cm of the basal sands and gravel that form the body of the terrace. About 200 circular features of varying diameters were exposed at the base of the embankment wall. No pattern was discernable, and the investigators attributed the features to posts that had been set in place and removed prior to the placement of sediments associate with construction of the Great Circle wall.

Greber and Shane (2009) observed that the trenches through the Great Circle wall revealed a deliberate use of contrasting colored construction materials. The CMNH trenches revealed the reddish, clayey soil on which the cobble layer was placed was overlain by yellow, silty clay loess that occurs in local spots as a result of Wisconsin glaciation. In the trenches that exposed the wooden fence (KSU Trench II and CMNH Trench II), alternating colored gravel layers mantled the subsoil just north of the decommissioned fence. Bright red and yellow clay-rich soils were used in building the Octagon walls, but these did not appear to be carefully separated during embankment construction. Although the work by Greber and Shane at High Bank has been limited to only a few areas of the walls forming this important geometric enclosure site, their data suggest that there were some important differences in the methods of sediment placement in constructing the two enclosures. The reason(s) behind these differences are unknown, but hopefully on-going research will attempt to identify explanations for this interesting construction variability.

Anderson Earthwork

Most of the major earthworks of Ross County, Ohio were recorded and mapped during surveys in the 19th and early 20th centuries. Although there is a possibility that the Anderson Earthworks were known and simply overlooked in the *Archaeological Atlas of Ohio* published by W. C. Mills in 1914 (Pickard and Weinberger 2009: 68–70), it was not until 1980 that this important earthen monument began to receive the attention it deserves.

In 1975, Jerrel Anderson discovered an interesting rectangular enclosure while examining the 1938 USDA aerial photographs for Ross County. Using more recent aerial photographs and ground surveys, he produced a map of a roughly square enclosure, located east of the Hopewell Mound Group (Anderson 1980). The enclosure wall was rectangular with rounded corners. A rounded node or circle was incorporated into the north and south walls of the enclosure.

A significant part of the Anderson Earthwork was purchased in 1993 by developers, and their plans to sub-divide the parcel and build houses represented a threat to the recently discovered site. William Pickard and some colleagues therefore began a program of surface collection and testing on the property in an effort to gather information about the site before it would be damaged or destroyed (Pickard and Weinberger 2009). They excavated two trenches across the west and north walls of the rectangular enclosure.

Their research indicated that the walls may have been 1–1.5 m high prior to being subjected to historic agricultural practices. At the time of their excavations, they observed that the A horizon had been stripped away before construction of the embankment wall. The exposed B horizon was then covered with "a layer of fine angular gravel in a silty clay matrix" (Pickard and Weinberger 2009: 71) that was 5–8 cm thick and up to 7 m wide. This layer was then covered by red sandy clay, which does not occur naturally on the landform where the Anderson Earthwork was built.

Pickard and Weinberger (2009) reported that four features were identified during excavation of the two trenches. Three of these were post-holes and the fourth was a lens of gravel in the red sandy clay fill of the wall, which they attributed to a stray basket-load of matrix that was deposited during wall construction. One of the post-holes contained the charred remains of a post (30 cm in diameter and extending 50 cm down into the subsoil). The wood in the post was identified as hickory (*Carya*), and an AMS date of 2010±60 BP (Beta 68758, CAMS 10484) was obtained.

The tract of land investigated by Pickard and Weinberger has been substantially altered and the potential for future study of a major part of the Anderson Earthwork is now limited to those remnants of the enclosure that remain on adjacent land.

Mound City

Mound City is one of the most important and readily recognized archaeological sites in North America. The site consists of at least 24 mounds within a geometric enclosure formed by a low embankment wall (Fig. 4.10 E). Widespread interest in the site developed following the publication of *Ancient Monuments of the Mississippi Valley* by Squier and Davis in 1848. Squier and Davis described the excavation of several mounds at Mound City and the unique, rich and complex mortuary and ceremonial remains they discovered under the mounds. Excavations by the Ohio Archaeological and Historical Society in the early 1920s (Mills 1922a; 1922b) produced additional information about the mounds and features they covered. Both studies described crematory basins, prepared clay altars, and other features resting on floors at the base of the mounds. Large numbers of beautiful and artistic objects made from exotic materials from as far away as the Rocky Mountains, Great Lakes, and the Gulf of Mexico were found in and around the features. The spectacular character of the mortuary-ceremonial mounds at Mound City, and nearby sites like Hopewell, Tremper, and Seip, has profoundly affected the approaches that archaeologists have since used in the study of Middle Woodland cultural developments and our interpretations about Ohio Hopewell.

Sometime after Squier and Davis published their landmark book, the owner of the Mound City property cut the trees and brought the land under cultivation (Fig. 4.14). The site was farmed by the Shriver family until 1917, when it was purchased by the Federal government to establish Camp Sherman for the U.S. Army. Construction at Camp Sherman was rapid, and 5000 men built nearly 2000 structures prior to the opening of the Camp on September 5, 1917 (Cockrell 1999). As the site was being prepared for construction, Henry C. Shetrone of the Ohio Archaeological and Historical Society was able to convince the Camp Commander to re-arrange the positions of the road and barracks to avoid the largest mound in the group (Mound 7; Cockrell 1999). Unfortunately, all the other earthen features

that comprise Mound City were severely affected by the building and operation of Camp Sherman. Mounds and the embankment wall were graded down, and borrow pits were filled (Fig. 4.15).

During the period when the site was under cultivation, the mounds and embankment walls were seriously degraded. Mound 7 was reduced in height by 60% between 1845 and 1920, and the south-east borrow pit had filled with sediments by the time Camp Sherman was constructed (Brown 1994: 3). Ownership of Mound City changed again in June 1917, when the site was leased by the War Department for the purpose of constructing a U.S. Army training base. The process of building and operating Camp Sherman further damaged Mound City, but archaeological investigations have shown that the impact was less severe than anticipated (e.g. Mills 1922a; 1922b; Brown and Baby 1966). With the coming of Armistice on November 11, 1918, soldiers at Camp Sherman began to receive discharges, and by 1920 the Army no longer had use for the facilities. At the same time, the Ohio Archaeological and Historical Society made plans for salvage excavations. Between 1920 and 1922, William C. Mills (1922) directed extensive excavations of the remaining mounds at the site. Custody of 57 acres (23 ha) at Mound City passed from the War Department to the Ohio Archaeological and Historical Society with a Presidential Proclamation on March 2, 1923 and was transferred back to Federal stewardship (National Park Service) on August 1, 1946.

Excavations by Squier and Davis (1848) and Mills (1922) provide some limited information about the structure and construction of the mounds they investigated (Fig. 4.16). Among the limited documentation that has been published, there is evidence that all excavated mounds showed clear indications of being built in stages. These studies also shown that the artifacts and features associated with Hopewell mortuary and ceremonial rituals were found on the floors of buildings that were covered by the fill layers that form the mounds. Although the methods used by Squier and Davis seem primitive by current standards, the mound profiles they recorded during their excavations

Fig. 4.14. This is the earliest photo of Mound City showing the mounds in cultivation. This undated photo must have been made sometime in the late 19th or early 20th century (photo courtesy of the Ohio History Connection and Hopewell Culture National Historical Park).

Fig. 4.15. Mound 23 seen under a barrack building at Camp Sherman (photo courtesy of the Ohio History Connectiony and Hopewell Culture National Historical Park).

Fig. 4.16. Profile drawing showing construction stages of Mound 7, Mound City (reproduced from Squier and Davis 1848, fig. 41).

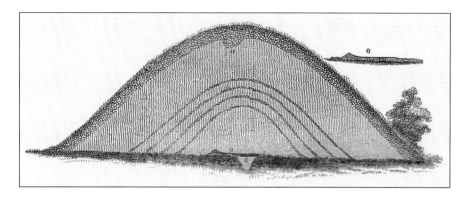

are very important to our understanding of mound construction. By the time Mills came to Mound City, only Mound 7 was remotely close to its 19th century height, but photographs, drawings and textual descriptions of the basal mound remnants also provide additional information about mound structure.

Despite the devastation associated with having an Army camp built on top of it, Mills' (1922) excavations at Mound City revealed that a surprising amount of sub-mound archaeology remained intact. There is no doubt that the building of Camp Sherman resulted in the truncation of all but one of the mounds, but in many cases the mound bases were preserved intact. Mills' excavations uncovered a wondrous array of ceremonial and mortuary features and some of the most amazing artifacts found anywhere in North America. But more important to the purpose of this discussion, the basal remnants of some of the mounds were still sufficiently intact to recognize that all of the mounds were built in stages (Fig. 4.17). Unfortunately, Mills paid little attention to mound construction and did not focus on the post-holes and other features that were the remains of the sub-mound buildings. Much of what we know about this is derived from photographs of the excavations.

Fig. 4.17. Photograph of Mound 7 during 1920–1 excavation showing multiple stages of construction. Fine sand layers separate larger layers of loam fill (photo courtesy of the Ohio History Connection and Hopewell Culture National Historical Park).

The Ohio Historical Society returned to Mound City again in 1963, and James A. Brown directed excavation of the south-eastern borrow pit, eastern, south-eastern and southern embankment wall, Mound 10, and Mounds 12 and 13 (Brown and Baby 1966; Brown 1994; 2012). The 1963 research devoted considerable effort to relocating the original south wall alignment. During the post-Camp Sherman reconstruction of Mound City, the south embankment wall was reconstructed in a different position relative to the mounds and other enclosure walls than shown in the Squier and Davis map (1848). Brown's 1963 research documented that the reconstructed south wall was not in its proper location, and the east embankment wall was intact in its appropriate and original alignment. Fortunately, Brown discovered that remnants of the south embankment wall were still sufficiently extant to identify its original alignment, and the wall was subsequently relocated to its current position (Fig. 4.18).

Prior to the 1963 excavations, no effort had been made to document the construction characteristics of the embankment wall. The 1963 excavations uncovered a series of profiles exposing different sections of it. Excavators were able to recognize the exterior slope of the south embankment wall:

> "over a distance of 220 feet [66 m] on the east end and 165 feet [49.5 m] on the west. The center section was obliterated by an early access road into the rear of the park. The outer slope was the edge mostly found, but three instances of an original inner slope was sufficient to determine the average width of the embankment. The discovery of vestiges of the original earthwork clearly demonstrated that the walls were slightly excurvate and that the corners curved gently from the sides. The shape of the enclosure that this information points to reveals one very close to that mapped by Squier and Davis (1848). However, the orientation of the south and east walls differs slightly from the old map." (Brown 1994, 38–9)

Brown's 1963 study found that midden deposits had been incorporated into two sections of the southern embankment wall. That study also documented the presence of a sheet midden that had been scraped up and incorporated in the wall in the south-east corner of the embankment (Brown 1994: 39). In 1966, NPS archaeologist Lee Hanson excavated a section of the east embankment wall (Hanson 1966). His study documented that the base of the embankment wall was still intact in this area, and he was able to relocate the east gateway.

The Midwest Archeological Center, under the direction of the author, with assistance from Rolfe Mandel, James Brown, Bret Ruby, Steven De Vore, and Ann Bauermeister is conducting on-going research at Mound City in an effort to better understand when and how the landscape at this important site was built. In 2009 and 2010, Center archeologists exposed sections of the south-east and east enclosure wall to document how it had been constructed. In 2011 and 2012 research was conducted inside the enclosure to determine the extent to which the non-mound areas inside the enclosure had been modified during the Hopewell era.

The 2009 excavation trench was placed along the edge of the backfill from the 1963 excavations. The 20 m trench exposed the original embankment wall in cross-section (Fig. 4.19). This profile was recorded and studied using geoarchaeological and geophysical techniques. Analysis of this data indicated that, prior to construction of the embankment wall, the A

Right: **Fig. 4.18.** 1963 excavations at Mound City exposed the original south-east borrow pit and embankment wall (photo courtesy of the Ohio History Connection and Hopewell Culture National Historical Park).

Fig. 4.19. Excavations in 2009 exposed a segment of the original Mound City south-east embankment wall (photo: author, September 2009).

horizon and most of the B horizon were removed from this location. At least 0.5 m of soil was removed from the area where the south-east embankment wall and borrow pit are located. As James Brown reported from the 1963 research, the 2009 excavation also found that the base of the embankment wall was made from fill containing numerous small artifacts. The color and character of this fill suggested that it was from a midden or occupation area. Although charcoal was abundant, it was not suitable for dating because its original context was not known. The 2009 research also showed that the south-east embankment wall and the south-east borrow pit were contiguous and were probably built at the same time. Careful design of both earthen features and careful selection and placement of construction material was necessary to keep the embankment wall from eroding into the borrow pit.

The 2010 study of the east embankment wall was conducted by excavating a 1 × 6 m trench perpendicular to the wall, roughly 20 m north of the east gateway. At the apex of the wall, the upper 80 cm of the current wall fill was comprised of historic fills from the restoration work following the Camp Sherman-era. The restoration fills included four primary lenses and contained numerous nails, coal, and other historic items. The remains of the original embankment is at most 38 cm tall at this point of the wall, and the wall fill is a homogeneous silty clay loam. Careful shovel skimming of this entire layer resulted in the collection of a single flint flake and a possible fire-cracked rock. The original embankment wall is 3.9 m wide in the exposed cross-section and rests on a prehistoric fill layer of poorly sorted gravelly loam. This layer extends across the entire width of the trench and appears to be a prehistoric fill, and may have been placed here to level the landscape surface prior to wall construction. This first layer of cultural fill rests on top of a loam with far less gravel, which is apparently the bottom of the B horizon. Only about 30 cm of B horizon remains at this point, and this unit rests on top of sand and gravel of undetermined depth.

Eight borrow pits have been identified surrounding the exterior side of the enclosure wall. The south-east borrow pit was identified and excavated under the direction of James Brown in 1963. All of the other borrow pits were excavated as part of restoration activities with much of the work being done with heavy equipment in the 1960s and 1970s. All of the borrow pits are sufficiently deep that they were excavated into the sand and gravels of the outwash terrace upon which the enclosure and mounds were built. These outwash sands and gravels are loose and unconsolidated and highly subject to erosion when exposed to weathering. Since many of the borrow pits are immediately adjacent to the embankment wall, test excavations in 2009, 2010, and 2011 were conducted to determine how the borrow pits were constructed. Test units in the south-west, south-east and east borrow pits confirmed that they penetrated into the loose outwash sediments of the terrace. The test units in the south-east and east features also confirmed that the borrow pits were lined with a clay loam that has maintained their shape over many centuries. Testing in the gigantic south-west borrow pit in 2011 suggested it was heavily impacted by Camp Sherman and subsequent restoration of this feature. No evidence of any original structure was observed in a 1 × 4 m trench into the east side of the borrow pit, midway between the embankment wall and the bottom of the pit.

The 2009 trench across the northern end of the south-east borrow pit revealed the presence of steps that were cut into the sands and gravels along its north-west edge, and these steps were covered by clay loam sediments (Fig. 4.20). Buried in the clay loam layer was a small area of burned soil and charcoal (pine) that appears to have been the result of a brief burning episode. Three AMS dates from this feature yielded conventional radiocarbon ages of 1630±40 BP (Beta-268507), 1590±40 BP (Beta-268508), and 1720±40 BP (Beta-268509). The three have a weighted average of 1607 BP±23 or a calibrated age of cal AD 465±23 (CalPal Online Radiocarbon Calibration 2007). This provides the first direct evidence for the age of the borrow pits at Mound City, and since the south-east borrow pit was built immediately adjacent to the embankment wall, this relatively late date supports Brown's (1994) interpretation that the embankment wall represents one of the final monumental features to be built at the site.

Borrow pits in association with enclosure walls are uncommon in the Scioto River valley. At Mound City there are eight prominent borrow pits in close proximity or adjacent to the enclosure wall. Despite the interpretive character of the nature of these prominent architectural features, their placement is more likely integral to the purpose of the site, rather than as localities to acquire building materials. If the borrow pits were simply quarries to acquire building material for other earthen features, it is unlikely that the builders would have gone to the trouble of lining them with clay loam. It is also worth noting that the poorly sorted sands and gravels that would have comprised the bulk of the material derived from the borrow pits has not been recorded in the fill of any of the mounds. The fill from the borrow pits would only have been a fraction of the material used in the building the approximately 26 mounds inside the enclosure. Furthermore, sands and gravels are plentiful within this entire landform, and could be easily obtained from the Scioto River channel that has never been a great distance from the site. The only reason the borrow pits needed to be adjacent to the embankment wall is because they were an integral part of the overall landscape design. The clay loam lining was certainly necessary to stabilize their size and shape, but it may also have been intended to hold water for short periods of time.

Opposite, top to bottom:

Fig. 4.20. Excavation in 2009 revealed that the south-east borrow pit at Mound City was constructed with a series of steps. Since the borrow pit was excavated into unconsolidated glacial outwash, the builders of the feature lined the borrow pit and the steps with a clay-rich loam. Geo-engineering approaches like this have been documented at the Shriver Circle and Hopewell Mound Group (photo: author, September 2009).

Fig. 4.21. Excavations in 1963 exposed the floor of Mound 10. Subsequent research by the author and James Brown, who excavated Mound 10 in 1963, suggest the floor of the sub-mound structure was built on a truncated B horizon surface (photo courtesy of the Ohio Historical Society and Hopewell Culture National Historical Park).

Fig. 4.22. Post-holes from the sub-mound structure at Mound 10 are seen penetrating into outwash (C horizon). Comparison to unmodified soil profiles suggest that perhaps 0.5 m or more soil was removed before the sub-mound building was constructed (photo courtesy of the Ohio Historical Society and Hopewell Culture National Historical Park).

Fig. 4.23. In 2011 and 2012 test excavations around the south-west side of Mound 7 uncovered the prepared sub-mound floor exposed by Mills in the 1920–1 excavations. The floor can be seen in profile as a band of lighter clay at the top of the photo scale. The fill above the floor is from Mills' old excavations and there is a thin A horizon immediately below the floor. The thin A horizon developed on a truncated B horizon surface (photo: author).

Brown (2004; 2012) has pointed out that the shape of the enclosure wall is comparable to the shape of many sub-mound buildings. This shape is may also mimic many of the prepared clay altars found on the sub-mound floors. Brown (2012) also suggests that the borrow pits may also simulate the whelk shell vessels placed around the perimeter of the clay burial platform on the floor of the second sub-mound structure under Mound 7 (Brown 2012). Considering the relationship between the embankment wall and the borrow pits, it is very likely that these were planned and carefully constructed features.

Previous investigations by Brown (Brown and Baby 1966) and others have provided evidence that prior to mound building, the area covered by the mounds was stripped of topsoil and floors for sub-mound structures. Although none of those investigations actually makes note of the truncation of the soil profile prior to mound construction, this is fairly apparent in photographs and notes where information about post-hole profiles is provided. Brown's excavations at Mounds 10 and 13 provide photographic evidence that sub-mound floors were built on truncated B horizons and post-holes from these structures clearly penetrate the glacial outwash or at least the B-C horizon at those locations (Figs 14.21 and 4.22). It is very difficult to determine if this practice was common to all mounds, because later investigations usually present only the horizontal pattern of post-holes without data on their depths or the matrix into which they were excavated.

In 2011, the author and National Park Service archaeologists excavated a test unit along the south side of Mound 7. In his investigations of Mounds 10 and 13, Brown observed that a halo of cobbles surrounded the mounds, presumably from the original mound covering and had been displaced by agriculture or other historic activities. As no excavations had been conducted at Mound 7 (the largest mound at Mound City) since Mills completed excavation of that mound in 1920, we hoped we might find a similar cobble zone there. If so, we could assume that the soil profile below it pre-dated cultivation and Camp Sherman activities.

The 2011 test unit was placed about 3 m to the south of the edge of Mound 7. The upper 78–85 cm of the deposit was obviously a recent fill and contained an assortment of Camp Sherman-era artifacts, including nails, window glass, and mortar. We also collected a sample of cobbles ranging in size from golf balls to baseballs which seem likely to have been from the "gravel" covering the mound described by Squire and Davis (1848). Below this mottled fill, we came upon a sandy but compact layer from which the fill easily peeled away. Observation of the surface of this horizon, which covered the floor of the test unit, suggested that this was similar to the sub-mound prepared floor described by Mills (1922 b: 403–4):

> "The true floor of the mound was easily disclosed, and proved to be very marked in character. It had been constructed of puddled clay, with a light covering of fine sand. Apparently this sand covering had been renewed from time to time as it became trampled into the clay beneath. A peculiar cement-like layer had resulted which, in our examination, was removed in pieces often one foot or more across, and resembling slabs of sandstone."

After clearing this surface across the entire test unit, it seemed that although we were at least 3 m south of the reconstructed Mound 7, we had in fact encountered a remnant of sub-mound floor that likely had been exposed by Mills in 1920 (Fig. 4.23). Since he reported that he had excavated the entire surface of the sub-mound structure floor, we then realized the fill we had found above it was likely backfill from his excavations. The indurated sand layer we encountered ranged from reddish to tan on the surface and was only 2–3 cm in thickness. We observed that it was dark on the bottom, and after removing this from the unit we saw a dark loamy horizon that appeared to be an A horizon. Initially, we assumed this was the original surface A horizon, but we were puzzled by how much deeper it seemed than the current ground surface. Later observation by Rolfe Mandel confirmed that it was indeed an A horizon, but thin (only about 5–8 cm thick), immature, and appeared to have developed on a truncated B horizon surface. We collected a soil sample from this thin buried A horizon and the presence of phytoliths in this soil has been confirmed (Laura Murphy, pers. comm.).

After the discovery of a buried soil under Mound 7, we decided to explore the periphery of Mound 18 to determine if any similar evidence might be present in that area. The magnetic survey data collected by Steve De Vore showed a magnetic high circling much of Mound 18, much like can be seen surrounding Mound 7. We hypothesized that this halo of magnetic high material was likely cobbles that had covered the mound when it was recorded by Squier and Davis (1848). Subsequent agriculture had pulled the cobble layer off the mound and spread it around its periphery. A 1 × 2 m test unit on the south side of Mound 18 confirmed that this is likely the source of the magnetic high readings, and a significant number of large cobbles were recorded in the upper 40–45 cm of the test unit. This test unit also revealed that the upper 40–45 cm consists of fill, probably from the agricultural period and Camp Sherman episode.

In an effort to better determine if stripping the upper parts of the natural soil profile was undertaken across the entire area within the enclosure, we compared the map of Camp Sherman and the magnetic survey data collected by Steve De Vore. We were specifically looking for an area that had no known Camp Sherman features, and no magnetic anomalies. We selected an area to the north-west of Mound 2. Another 1 × 2 m test unit was excavated and the sand and gravel outwash deposit (C horizon) was encountered at about 65 cm below surface. The B horizon extended upward to about 25 cm below the surface. This particular test unit was nearly devoid of artifacts with only a nail and a piece of turtle shell being collected. Normally, in comparable soils in this area, the C horizon would be expected to be 1.0–1.5 m below surface, so it seemed likely that much of the non-mound areas within the Mound City enclosure were stripped during the construction of this ceremonial landscape. However, the only places we can be certain that the removal of topsoil occurred during the Hopewell era, as opposed to during the Camp Sherman or subsequent park era, is in those test units that penetrate through intact prehistoric features. Fortunately, we have so far been able to record truncated soils under three different sub-mound structures and two places under the embankment wall.

Hopewell Mound Group

The Hopewell Mound Group is one of the most famous and well-known earthen enclosures in Ohio. With more than 40 mounds and 4 km of earth and stone embankment walls, the site is clearly worthy of being the "type site" for this famous episode of the North American archaeological record (Fig. 4.24). Although the site has been subjected to two centuries of cultivation and three major archaeological excavations, it retains tremendous potential for archaeological research.

Caleb Atwater (1820) provided the first description of the Hopewell Mound Group, and he estimated that the large enclosure wall encompassed 110 acres (44.5 ha). He reported that the wall is:

> "generally twelve feet [3.7 m] from the bottom to the summit of the wall, which is of earth. The ditch is about twenty feet [6.1 m] wide, and the base of the wall the same. There is no ditch on the side next to the river. The small work, on the east side, contains sixteen acres [6.5 ha], and the walls are like those of the larger work, but there is no ditch. The largest circular work, which consists of a wall and ditch like those already described, is a sacred enclosure, including within it six mounds, which have been used as cemeteries." (Atwater 1820: 183)

Squier and Davis (1848: 26–29) called the site "Clark's Work" and classified it among their "Works of Defence." They described the main enclosure as a parallelogram, 2800 × 1800 ft (840 × 540 m) with one rounded corner. The wall along the creek lacked a ditch, was 4 ft (1.2 m) high and followed the creek bank and contained a lot of water-worn cobbles. The walls of the main enclosure were 6 ft (1.8 m) high and 35 ft (10.5 m) wide, and the adjacent ditch was of similar dimensions. On the east end of the large enclosure was a square enclosure with walls of similar size but lacking the exterior ditch.

Warren K. Moorehead conducted excavations in 1891 and 1892 in many of the mounds of the Hopewell Mound Group for the purpose of gathering artifacts to exhibit at the World's Columbian Exposition in Chicago. Although Moorehead's report of the excavations was not published until many years later (1922), brief published notes (Moorehead 1896) shortly after the fieldwork generated considerable interest in the discoveries of the expedition.

The 1891–92 field investigations focused on mound excavations, but also included photographs of the site as it appeared at that time (Fig. 4.25). The photographs are limited in number, but they are certainly a time capsule in recording the condition of the embankment wall and mounds at the end of the 19th century. Artifacts, photographs, and records from Moorehead's excavations are housed at the Field Museum of Natural History in Chicago.

The Ohio Archaeological and Historical Society, under the direction of Henry C. Shetrone, returned to the Hopewell Mound Group and conducted excavations from 1922 through 1925. Most of Shetrone's work, like Moorehead's before him, focused on mound excavation. Sadly, neither made much effort to study or record the structure of the mounds, but simply removed them to expose the rich mortuary and ceremonial features buried on the floors of the mounds. A few field photographs from Shetrone's excavations show lenses of soil within the mound fill that may represent basket-loading (Fig. 4.26), but little discussion is offered.

Prior to conducting his work at the Hopewell Mound Group, Shetrone took note that Frederick Ward Putnam had found burials and other features incorporated into and under the embankment walls at the Turner Works near Cincinnati. Consequently, Shetrone decided to explore the embankment wall at the Hopewell Mound Group. He excavated 200 ft (70 m) of the east wall of the main enclosure but was disappointed in the results. He reported: "Upon the original surface were found several unimportant and not well defined fire-beds, which apparently were only incidental to occupation previous to the erection of the wall. Tests at other points revealed nothing" (Shetrone 1926: 112). The exact nature of "not well defined fire-beds" observed by Shetrone is unknown, but similar small features have proven to be invaluable in generating chronological information about wall construction at the Hopeton Earthworks. Perhaps future studies will revisit the embankment wall at the Hopewell Mound Group and expose more of these burned features for potential AMS or radiocarbon dating.

Fig. 4.24. Caleb Atwater made the earliest known map of the Hopewell Mound Group, but excavations by Squier and Davis produced some amazing artifacts and a much improved map of the site. This image of the Hopewell Mound Group during a storm was created by CERHAS, University of Cincinnati/CERHAS: www.ancientohiotrail.org.

The author, with assistance from Rolfe Mandel and students from a University of Nebraska field school, conducted research to better understand how the main embankment wall was built. A geophysical study by Arlo McKee (2005) of the area around and east of Mound 23 at the Hopewell Mound Group produced a clear image of the remains of the east embankment wall and ditch. The geophysical map was used to select a location for a test trench that was excavated in the summer of 2006 (Lynott 2006).

The east–west trench was 44 m long and 2 m wide and cross-cut the east embankment wall and ditch north-east of Mound 23. No features relating to wall construction were observed during excavations but fortunately basal remnants of the embankment wall were found to be still intact.

Unfortunately, agricultural activities over the last two centuries have severely truncated the embankment wall, limiting observations about its construction to evidence from only the remnant basal components. As noted at many other sites in the Scioto River valley, the embankment wall was built directly on top of a truncated B horizon, with the A horizon and upper B horizon apparently being removed in preparation for wall construction (Fig. 4.27). The primary intact material forming the core of the wall is a yellow-brown loam. This rests on the subsoil and itself has been truncated at the top by years of cultivation. Consequently, it is impossible to determine if this formed the bulk of the wall fill or just the foundation.

At the western end of the wall fill, there was a small area of intact wall fill that was comprised of red-brown silt loam containing much gravel. Gravel and silt loam do not often occur together in natural sedentary deposits, so this may represent a mixing of different sediments by the wall builders. This layer was quite distinct from the yellow-brown wall fill, and the sharp boundary between the two was consistent with the methods of construction that have been observed at other Scioto valley geometric enclosure sites. We cannot determine if this small remnant of red soil once formed a larger deposit that covered the interior of the embankment wall surface, but this would be consistent with construction approaches at other earthen enclosures in this region.

Along the western margin of the wall, a dark organic gray loam with gravel was observed. This was probably a soil that formed on the wall surface and was subsequently covered by displaced wall fill after cultivation was initiated in the 19th century. This soil layer rose from west to east and was truncated near the surface by the plowzone. A corresponding layer on the east side of the wall would have merged with the exterior ditch, but it was apparently destroyed by plowing.

The exterior ditch is visible as a slight depression on the surface, and is very distinct in geophysical data. The width and depth of the ditch are consistent with dimensions reported by Atwater (1820) and Squier and Davis (1848). Examination of the feature in profile revealed that it had been excavated down into the sands and gravels (glacial outwash) that form the base of this alluvial terrace. These sands and gravels are very loose and unconsolidated. To prevent the sides of the ditch from slumping and to avoid undercutting the embankment wall, the builders used a brown clay loam to line the sides and bottom. This was a very tight and stable surface. A dark organic gray loam with charcoal flecks gradually developed in the bottom of the ditch, and was likely a result of materials washing into the ditch from the embankment wall. Once cultivation of the site began, the ditch filled rapidly with re-deposited sediments from the wall and surrounding site surface (Fig. 4.28).

This limited study of earthen feature construction at the Hopewell Mound Group has produced a few important observations. First, the removal of the topsoil prior to building the embankment wall is a characteristic that is very common among Scioto River valley geometric enclosure sites. Although only a small amount of the original wall is still present, it appears to have been built with at least two different types of soil and these soils were placed so as to avoid mixing them. Some remains of an A horizon that formed on the embankment wall

Top: **Fig. 4.25.** Warren K. Moorehead brought a team of excavators to the Hopewell Mound Group in 1891 and 1892 to collect artifacts to exhibit at the Worlds Columbian Expedition in Chicago. Mound 25, even after almost a century of being plowed, was still the largest Hopewell mound ever constructed (photo courtesy of the Field Museum, Chicago).

Bottom: **Fig. 4.26.** 1926 excavation of Mound 25 showing lenses of soil near the base of the mound, Hopewell Mound Group (photo courtesy of the Ohio History Connection).

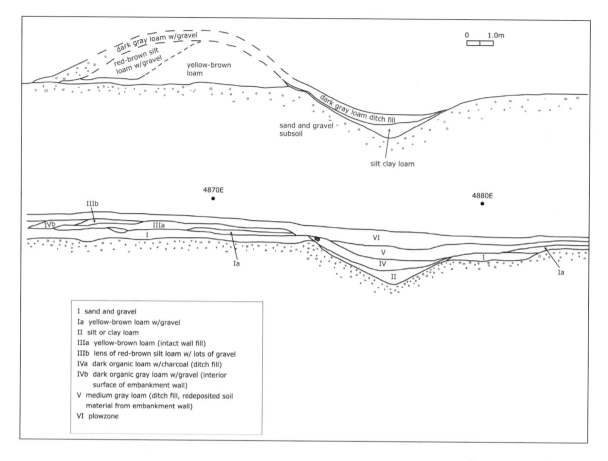

is still present on the inner side of the wall and it has been preserved by wall spill that has been re-deposited on top of it during cultivation. The exterior ditch is still well preserved and has been filled with sediments re-deposited mainly during the last 200 years. The clay loam used to line the sides and bottom of the ditch are another example of geo-engineering strategies used by the embankment builders to create a monumental landscape, both in terms of scale and longevity.

The clay-lined ditch is very similar in appearance to the ditch recorded at the Shriver Circle (Cowan *et al.* 2006; Picklesimer *et al.* 2006). Cowan suggested that these linings may have been intended to hold water during certain times of the year, and this may be the case for the ditch at the Hopewell Mound Group. Squier and Davis (1848) speculated that the builders of the earthen walls may have redirected the flow of a stream channel to flow into the ditch of the west wall of the main enclosure. Small springs were present at the base of the hill on the north side of the main enclosure in 1848 and one or more of these may have been directed to flow in the ditch along the east wall of the enclosure.

Hopewell earthen enclosures in southern Ohio exhibit many different shapes and the walls occur in a wide range of sizes and configurations. Early scholars assumed that walls were built with earth quarried from adjacent ditches and borrow pits. This may have been the case at some sites, but not at the Hopewell

Fig. 4.27. In 2006 the author directed excavation of a trench exposing the east wall and ditch of the main enclosure at the Hopewell Mound Group. This profile drawing shows the current condition of the wall and ditch and a hypothetical reconstruction based upon archaeological data and historical observations (image courtesy of the Ohio History Connection).

Fig. 4.28. The exterior ditch was excavated into unconsolidated sand and gravel and the builders lined the bottom and sides of the ditch with clay-rich loam to stabilize the loose C horizon (photo: author).

Mound Group. While the ditch fill may have been used somewhere during earthen construction at the site, the materials used in the walls appear to have been carefully selected and placed to avoid mixing the different soil materials.

The absence of any datable features associated with wall construction makes it impossible to determine the absolute age of the embankment wall and ditch. It also raises the question as to the chronological relationship between the various mounds at the Hopewell Mound Group and the different embankment walls. The evidence for stripping of the A horizon beneath the eastern embankment wall also raises the question as to whether it may have been removed from the entire site as part of the construction of this giant ceremonial landscape.

Shriver Circle

Like so many sites in Ross County, Ohio, the Shriver Circle earthwork was brought to the attention of the scholarly community by the work of Squier and Davis (1848; Fig. 4.10, F). The famous authors noted that the Shriver Circle is unusual among the circular enclosures in this area of Ohio. It is composed of an embankment wall surrounded by a circular ditch with a mound near the center of the enclosure. The enclosure wall and ditch are not truly circular and have diameters that range from 1220 ft (372 m) to 1152 ft (351 m). The embankment wall was measured in 1846 to be 5 ft (1.5 m) high and 25 ft (7.6 m) wide at its base. The exterior ditch was 4 ft (1.2 m) deep and 20 ft (6 m) wide. The wall and ditch were broken by six gateways. The enclosure is located slightly more than 700 m south of the Mound City enclosure.

Squier and Davis recognized and highlighted the unusual character of the Shriver Circle:

"Unlike the works obviously of sacred origin, which, if they possess a ditch at all, have it interior to the wall, this has an outer fosse; a circumstance which would seem to favor the suggestion of a defensive origin. On the other hand, it has a mound, very nearly if not exactly in the centre, which was clearly a place of sacrifice. It was found, upon excavation, to contain an altar singularly constructed of small stones, carefully imbedded in sand, forming a paved concavity, upon were the usual traces of fire, and the remains of the sacrifice." (Squier and Davis 1848: 55)

From 1848, following the publication of Ancient Monuments of the Mississippi Valley, the Shriver Circle was regularly subjected to cultivation, and received little further attention from the archaeological community. In 1917, it was purchased, along with Mound City, by the U.S. Army for the construction of Camp Sherman. It is unclear how the Army modified the mound, enclosure wall, and ditch, but after World War I the site was transferred to the Justice Department, where a federal prison was constructed, and the Shriver Circle and other surrounding land was then used as prison farm land. The land and facilities were transferred to the State of Ohio in 1966. Those parts of the Shriver Circle not in the Highway 104 right-of-way are owned by the Ross Correctional Institute.

Small circular enclosures are fairly common in southern Ohio and northern Kentucky and have been associated with the Adena culture. The Adena Mound, type site for the Adena culture, is located about 3 km south of the Shriver Circle. However, Squier and Davis (1848) and subsequent archaeologists have noted that the large size of the Shriver Circle was more typical of later Ohio Hopewell enclosures. What makes the Shriver Circle unusual is that it is an individual circular enclosure, and most of the other large circles (e.g. Hopeton, High Bank, Junction) are associated with additional large geometric enclosures (Fig. 4.29).

Mark Seeman (1981b) and students from Kent State University conducted a surface survey of the prison property in 1980. They used 1938 aerial photo to identify the approximate location of the enclosure wall and ditch. During the surface survey they were able to recognize an undulation of about 75 cm in the topography that appeared to be associated with the embankment wall and ditch.

Archaeological interest in the Shriver Circle was regenerated by a proposal to expand State Route 104 from two lanes to four, which would potentially impact upon whatever might remain of the enclosure and surrounding ditch. Compliance-driven surface survey by Warner and Stone in 1995 and shovel

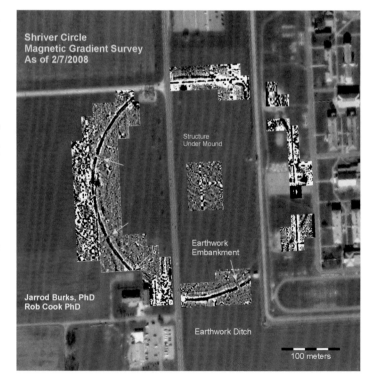

Fig. 4.29. Despite the impact of having a four lane highway and a State Prison partly built over it, the Shriver Circle is still detectable in magnetic survey data. The large circle being seen in the image is the exterior ditch that was excavated into the glacial outwash (C horizon) and lined with clay to stabilize the sides and bottom of the ditch (image courtesy of Jarrod Burks).

Shriver Circle
Magnetic Gradient Survey
As of 2/7/2008

Structure
Under Mound

Earthwork
Embankment

Jarrod Burks, PhD
Rob Cook PhD

Earthwork Ditch

100 meters

testing (Walter and Coleman 2001) failed to find evidence of the embankment wall and ditch. Jennifer Pederson and Jarrod Burks, from the neighboring Hopewell Culture National Historical Park, also conducted a magnetic survey of portions of this enclosure. Their research, and additional geophysical survey by Burks and Robert Cook, documented that much of the exterior ditch was still intact, and other potential prehistoric features might be present (Pederson and Burks 2002). Subsequent magnetic and electrical conductivity survey by R. Berle Clay (2002) provided further evidence that portions of the Shriver Circle might still survive intact.

Prior to expansion of the highway, additional investigations were conducted by Gray & Pape, Inc. (Picklesimer *et al.* 2006). Geophysical investigations, including magnetic gradient survey and electrical resistance survey, were conducted at close intervals and produced valuable information about the exterior ditch and historic utilities that have disturbed the site. The geophysical data indicated that the fill of the ditch was comprised of two separate types of fill, and this was confirmed when a segment of the ditch was excavated. Numerous smaller anomalies, many of them historic metal, were also noted.

Excavation of two trenches produced valuable information about the construction of the embankment wall and exterior ditch. Only a small remnant of the wall was visible in the trench profile, but it is apparent that the wall fill was placed on top of a B horizon that had been exposed after removal of the surface A horizon. Unfortunately, not enough of the wall fill was exposed to permit further observations about its construction.

Both trenches provided excellent cross-sections of the exterior ditch and revealed that this feature was built to be about 7.6 m wide and 2.4 m deep (including almost a meter of historic fill covering the feature). The depth of the ditch was sufficient to penetrate into the C-horizon, which at this location is unconsolidated sand and gravel deposited as glacial outwash. To stabilize and shape the ditch, the builders lined the feature with a clay-rich fine sand or clay loam. The investigators suggest that this not only served as a geo-engineering solution to the unconsolidated basal sediments, but may have served to hold water for brief intervals (Picklesimer *et al.* 2006).

As part of the highway project, the investigators stripped two large blocks off the surface adjacent to S.R. 104. A total of 620.3 sq m were scraped and only three cultural features were observed, all associated with Camp Sherman and the early 20th century. Like many Hopewell enclosure sites in the Scioto River valley, investigators only found a relatively low density of prehistoric artifacts in association with the enclosure.

Four radiocarbon dates were processed as part of the highway investigations, but only two of these shed any light on the age of the embankment and ditch. Samples collected from the clay ditch liner were calculated at 1470±40 BP (Beta-217913) and 1760±40 BP (Beta-221003) and are consistent with dates from nearby Mound City and the hypothesized Hopewell construction of this feature. Since these samples were collected from larger soil samples from the clay lining of the ditch, and cannot be linked to a specific burning episode, it is possible that the carbon being dated entered the ditch after it was built. This would suggest that

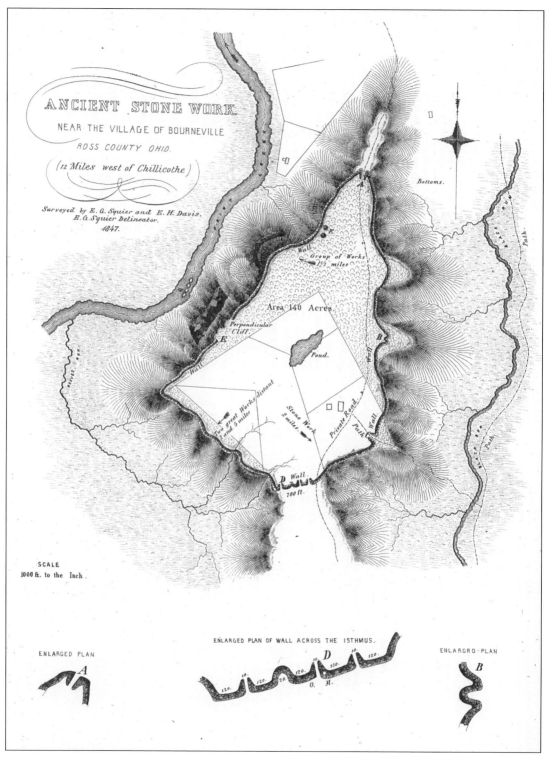

Fig. 4.30. Spruce Hill works (Squier and Davis 1848, pl. iv).

Fig. 4.31. Profile of
gateways at Spruce Hill,
courtesy of Bret Ruby
(2009).

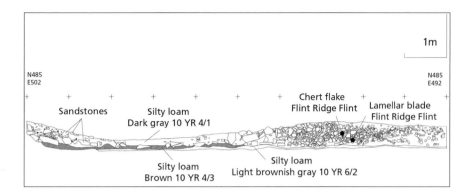

Spruce Hill

Spruce Hill Earthworks is located in south-west Ross County, on a steep mesa-like landform on the southern edge of the Paint Creek Valley (Figs 4.11, C; 4.30). The mesa-like landform is capped by 7–12 m of hard Berea sandstone that rests on top of much softer shales. The surface of the mesa is relatively flat and situated roughly 400 ft (120 m) above the valley floor. The edge of the landform is roughly triangular in shape and is encircled by a stone wall that is about 2.25 miles (3.75 km) in length and encloses about 140 acres (56.7 ha) (Squier and Davis 1848: 11–15 and pl. vi). Early observers noted that the rock-built wall was constructed of dry-laid stone with an average basal width of 8–10 ft (2.4–3.0 m), and an average height of 6–8 ft (1.8–2.4 m) (Randall 1908). The walls were highest and widest at the north and south ends of the site where gateways opened on to the more gently sloping hillside which provided the main entrance to the enclosure. A pond about 2 acres (0.8 ha) in size was present inside this enclosure.

construction of the ditch may have occurred somewhat earlier in the Middle Woodland period.

The imposing nature of the Spruce Hill Earthworks was recognized by early residents and travelers in the Paint Creek valley (Joynes 1902). Squier and Davis (1848, 12) reported the presence of areas of intense burning, that they attributed to signal fires. Test excavations by Emerson Greenman in 1943 revealed the presence of what he called "slag" at one of the gateways on the south side of Spruce Hill. Subsequent research by Mallery (1951) recorded the presence of what he interpreted to be Iron Age furnaces on Spruce Hill, which suggested that northern Europeans had been in this area roughly 1000 years before the voyages of Christopher Columbus. Subsequent studies have documented many other possible iron furnaces in southern Ohio (Conner 2009). Many scholars have examined the slag from these unusual features, and there is no question that it was produced by extremely high temperatures. However, the dating of these simple furnace sites is still uncertain and they may be the remains of an 18th century exploration of this region by European colonists. Ruby (2009) presents a more detailed summary of the evidence and interpretation about these interesting features.

Bret Ruby conducted a series of investigations at Spruce Hill in 1995–96 that carefully documented the intact and largely prehistoric age of this large and important hilltop enclosure. Ruby (2009: 54) observed that:

> "the stone wall today appears as a broad (10–15 m) band or low heap of undressed sandstone blocks running just below the brow of the hill. The stones average 20–30 cm in maximum dimension. The feature is difficult to trace in places and rarely, if ever, attains the 'three to four feet in height' cited by Squier and Davis (1848: 11)."

Ruby did note that at the gateways on either end of the enclosure, the stones are still piled sufficiently high to be readily recognizable (Fig. 4.31). Ruby also notes that conversations with individuals who farmed the interior of the hilltop enclosure for many years indicated that the area is largely devoid of rocks.

Ruby (2009) conducted test excavations at the southern gateway to the enclosure, which is labeled "D" and called "The Isthmus" by Squier and Davis (1848, pl. iv). The 1995–96 research included a surface collection that revealed the presence of burned and vitrified soil, fire-cracked rock, and glazed rock. They also collected a Hopewell blade made from Flint Ridge flint and a non-diagnostic nutting stone.

Ruby also excavated five test units and 36 shovel tests around the three gateways at the southern end of the site. These data indicate that at the southern gateways the wall consists of sandstone rubble heaped:

> "on top of the natural silt loam ground surface. The non-random size in distribution of stones within the wall provides further evidence of an anthropogenic origin. The largest stones, often tabular, line the outer surface of the feature, particularly along the interior edges of the gateway. This may reflect an intentional design intended either to shore up the wall and prevent collapse or for aesthetic purposes." (Ruby 2009: 57)

Ruby observes that everywhere he excavated, he found the much older Berea Sandstone rubble wall resting on more recent loess soil.

Ruby also found evidence of burned soil and rock within Gateways 1 and 2. The nature of the burning and the pattern of the burned soil suggested that these might have been the product of a wattle and daub structure that had burned, but might also simply be the product of a hot fire where burning wood came in contact with clay-rich sediments.

A range of prehistoric artifacts were collected from the various excavation units, including "diagnostic Hopewellian stone tools, prehistoric ceramics, and chert debitage both in and around the complex of stone walls and gateways *in the area of 'the Isthmus'*" (Ruby 2009: 61). The research conducted by Ruby provides conclusive evidence that the stone embankment wall and gateways at the south end of Spruce Hill were built during the prehistoric era, and they most likely were built as part of the vast program of landscape construction undertaken during the Hopewell era. Spruce Hill is particularly noteworthy as the only hilltop enclosure built in the Scioto River-Paint Creek region, which is dominated by geometric enclosures built in the wide valley bottoms.

South-west Ohio – Brush Creek, the Great Miami and Little Miami River drainages

From the Dayton area south to the Ohio River, south-west Ohio is heavily dissected terrain. The rivers and streams flow through deeply incised valleys between heavily wooded upland remnants that form the northern and western limits of the Appalachian highlands. The region is best known for the numerous and various hilltop enclosures that Ohio Hopewell people built on the flat summits of the high hills overlooking the deep valleys. Early antiquarians from Cincinnati were quick to report on what they perceived to be ancient "forts" and because of their locations they certainly give that defensive impression. Atwater (1820), Squier and Davis (1848), and somewhat later scholars like MacLean (1879) and Randall (1908) provided maps and then photos to document these forts of the mound-builders.

Hillforts are not the only ceremonial landscapes built by the Hopewell in southern Ohio. Geometric enclosures have also been mapped and studied in the larger floodplains of the Little Miami River. Turner and Stubbs are discussed here because they are very important to understanding the great diversity of landscapes construction conducted by Ohio Hopewell people. Many less well known enclosures have disappeared under the urban sprawl of Cincinnati, where early antiquarian accounts (Drake 1815) offer hints about the large number of mounds and enclosures that were once present at this key place on the north side of the Ohio River.

Most of the enclosures in south-west Ohio were built within the drainages of the Great Miami and the Little Miami Rivers. Also included in this section is the small river drainage named Brush Creek which originates in Highland County and flows south through Adams County before joining the Ohio to the east of Cincinnati, and the Great and Little Miami Rivers. From an archaeological perspective, Brush Creek is best known because of the presence of the Great Serpent Mound. Frederic Ward Putnam raised interest and funds to preserve this fantastic earthen monument over a century ago, and it is visited by thousands of people every year. Research continues to better understand the age and purpose of the Serpent Mound, but current data indicate it was built after the Hopewell era (Lepper 2005).

One other less well known site in the upper Brush Creek drainage was built by the Hopewell and fits easily alongside the hilltop enclosures of south-west Ohio. Fort Hill has been managed as a park for a considerable period of time, and although less well known than Serpent Mound, it is an important part of this discussion.

Fort Hill, Highland County

Fort Hill (33Hi1) is located in Brush Township in south-west Highland County, about 30 miles (50 km) south-west of Chillicothe. The hillfort-style enclosure sits atop a 500 ft (150 m) high mesa in the upper reaches of Brush Creek. The site was initially described by Locke (1838), and became well known after it was mapped and described in detail by Squier and Davis (1848) in their landmark volume. A subsequent survey and account of the site by Shepherd (1887) in 1878, and a series of early photographs and a description by Randall (1908) in the early years of the

Fig. 4.32. Fort Hill is built on edges of this mesa-like physiographic feature south-west of Bourneville, Ohio (early 20th century post-card).

20th century indicate that it is one of the best preserved of the hilltop enclosures in southern Ohio.

Fort Hill is unusual among these hilltop enclosures because it sits atop an isolated mesa with unusually steep sides (Fig. 4.32). Brush Creek is a relatively small drainage system that lies between the valleys of the Miami and Little Miami to the west and the Scioto to the east. The rugged topography of the Brushy Creek valley is known from the Serpent Mound, to the south in Adams County. The closest major Hopewell enclosures are in the Paint Creek Valley east of Bainbridge, approximately 16 km to the north-east.

In the 19th century, the site was covered by primary forest with many large hardwood trees growing on the walls and ditch that form the enclosure. Squier and Davis (1848: 14) described a chestnut and an oak tree that were, respectively, 21 ft (6.3 m) and 23 ft (6.9 m) in circumference, and growing on the embankment wall. Based on tree-ring estimates for these living monarchs, the authors and subsequent scholars calculated that the embankment wall must have been constructed at least 1000 years ago. Archaeological evidence providing somewhat more precise estimates of the age of the site is discussed later in this narrative.

Early survey records generally agree that the vertical distance from the base of the Fort Hill mesa to its summit is about 500 ft (150 m), and the flat area on top of the summit is 48–50 acres (20 ha) in extent. The embankment wall was built around the perimeter of the summit, and including gateways is measured at 8606 ft (2592 m) (Shepherd 1887: 26). The wall, composed of rock and stone, built on the upper slope of the mesa was generally 6–10 ft (1.8–3 m) high and it generally averaged 40 ft (12 m) in width. On the interior side of the wall was an interior ditch that averages 50 ft (15 m) in width and in places had to be excavated into bedrock that forms the mesa top. Thirty-eight gateways were present in the wall and 11 of these had corresponding causeways that interrupted the interior ditch. Three fairly large and noteworthy ponds are present in the interior of the enclosure, and may have served as quarries for construction materials for the embankment wall. Early observers saw these as water supplies for defenders during times of siege.

The northern end of the enclosure has been of particular interest to early scholars and is sometimes called the "citadel" (Locke 1838). In this location, a 200 ft (61 m) wide bluff rises about 20 ft (6 m) above the enclosure wall and forms the most prominent vantage point on the mesa. Early explorers of the site reported "strong evidences of the action of fire on the rocks" (Randall 1908: 34), suggesting the location may have served as a signal beacon.

Fort Hill State Memorial was established in 1932 with the purchase of 273 acres (110.5 ha), and subsequent land purchases enlarged the park to about 1200 acres (486 ha) (Morgan 1946). Visitor facilities consisting of a parking area, shelter house, museum, and service buildings were built by the Civilian Conservation Corps. Although the site received little attention from archaeologists until the 1950s, it is a popular, scenic location that has encouraged the imagination of curious visitors for decades.

During the summers of 1952–54, Ohio Historical Society archaeologists conducted excavations at an area along the southern base of Fort Hill where two small circular earthworks and surface evidence of Hopewell occupation had been identified. Only a brief report of these investigations is available (Baby 1954) but that narrative, in association with examination of fieldnotes from the project, permit an overview of the three seasons of field investigations.

Excavations in 1952 consisted of six exploratory trenches designed to determine the nature and extent of the site deposit. Excavations uncovered two small hearths, a row of posts from a building, and a row of posts under one of the circular earthworks. Pottery, mica, and flint artifacts were characteristic of Ohio Hopewell.

Excavations in 1954 returned to the row of posts exposed in 1952 and found evidence for a large rectangular structure with rounded corners. The building was estimated to be 120 × 60 ft (36 × 18 m) and it was uncertain whether it represented a stockade or a roofed structure.

Part of the 1952 field season and all of the 1953 season were dedicated to the exploration of one of the two small circular earthworks. The enclosure they chose to explore (33Hi9, William Reynolds enclosure) had a diameter of 174 ft (52.2 m) and the embankment wall was 2–3 ft (0.3–0.6 m) high. Excavations consisted of one long trench from the center of the enclosure south and through the embankment wall. Three shorter trenches were excavated to transect the embankment wall at roughly the cardinal directions.

Very little information about the embankment wall fill is recorded in the fieldnotes of William Sassaman, Field Director for the Ohio Historical Society excavations at this site. He did note, however, that the soil inside the enclosure was different from that on the outside:

> "The difference lies in the almost total absence of stones and the darkness of the soil. The profiles show 'lensing', which indicates the soil was brought into the area enclosed by the circular earthwork in small loads which overlap each other where they fell. This makes it appear as if the ground within the enclosure area had been screed to keep out stones and other impurities." (Sassaman 1952 fieldnotes: 15)

In his brief summary of the excavations, Raymond Baby (1954) reported that the embankment wall covered two circles of post-holes (Fig. 4.33):

> "The post-hole pattern, which was covered by the earthen wall, consisted of two rows of postmolds averaging ten feet [ca. 3m] between the rows. The inner series of postmolds was made up of alternate large and small molds spaced 1.5 feet [0.45 m] apart. The posts, averaging 8 and 4 inches in diameter [20 mm/10 mm], were set

in the ground to a depth of three feet [0.9 m] and were sloped inward. The outer molds, arranged in groups of three, were smaller and sloped outward. Flint chips and pottery and mica fragments were found on the floor of the structure as well as in the fill of the earthen embankment." (Baby 1954: 85)

Photographs from the excavations, and the fieldnotes recorded by Sassaman (1952; 1953) indicate that excavators encountered piles of stones at intervals under the embankment wall. Further examination indicated that these were stones inside post-holes that formed the two circular rows of posts of the sub-wall structure. A diorama reconstructing this unusual structure depicts a circular building with a roof enclosing a ceremonial space.

The William Reynolds enclosure and the large rectangular structure excavated in 1954 are in close proximity to Fort Hill, and provide ample evidence of Ohio Hopewell ceremonial activities. Unfortunately, the nature of the 1952–53 excavations and an absence of observations about the nature of the earthen wall construction leaves many questions about the nature and character of this unusual site. It is noteworthy that, even at a significant distance from the geometric enclosures of the Scioto River drainage and the numerous hilltop enclosures of the Miami River valley, Ohio Hopewell people were actively modifying the landscape and creating ceremonial earthen monuments. Since very few of these relatively small circular enclosures have been excavated and reported, it is uncertain whether the William Reynolds enclosure is typical of smaller circular enclosures in southern Ohio, or an isolated and unusual Hopewell earthen monument.

In 1964, Olaf Prufer spent a week directing the excavation of a trench across the embankment wall at Fort Hill, directly north of the circular enclosure and village area (33Hi9) at the bottom of the mesa. The 1964 trench was 1.5 m wide, and excavated in 1.5 m sections through the wall and ditch at an angle of 22° east of north. Prufer observed that the wall was built on a bedrock ledge that slopes towards the exterior of the enclosure. Two phases of construction were observed.

The initial phase of wall construction comprised of colluvium, dark humus, and large blocks of local Berea sandstone piled onto a surface of small rocky debris and clay. The surface upon which the wall was constructed also contained many small pieces of charcoal. Basket loads of buff-colored earth could be seen in parts of this primary wall core. The inner side of the wall was then covered "by a single layer of large, more-or-less dressed, flat sandstone slabs" (Prufer 1997: 317). Many of the large slabs had to be broken to be moved during excavation.

> "After this primary core wall had apparently fallen into disuse, an inner retaining wall, or 'ring' entirely 'composed of large slabs that were well fitted and having between their junctions a deposit of highly gumbotil material ... much harder and of a[n] entirely different character than any of the soils in the area' was encountered (field note, June 11, 1964). This retaining wall rested directly on the natural surface of the mesa and was partly leaning against the interior edge of the primary core wall that had been laterally truncated in order to accommodate the retaining wall. The latter also partly impinged on (and thus modified) the profile of the original interior ditch." (Prufer 1997: 318)

This inner stone ring and the primary wall core were then covered with buff-colored colluvium and irregular blocks of sandstone, and a thin layer of this fill

Left: **Fig. 4.33.** Excavations in the 1960s at the William Reynolds enclosure south-west of Fort Hill revealed the presence of two large rows of circular post-holes. After the posts were pulled from the holes, a circular earthen embankment was built over them (photo courtesy of the Ohio History Connection).

Right: **Fig. 4.34.** Excavations by Olaf Prufer at Fort Hill revealed that the embankment wall was built in at least two stages, with limestone slabs covering the surface of the wall in the final construction stage (photo courtesy of the Ohio History Connection).

spilled down into the interior ditch. Basket-loads were visible in this fill, and tiny specks of charcoal were also observed. The earthen fill was then covered by a layer of large sandstone slabs (2 in–2 ft 7 in/5–78 cm in maximum dimension) that appeared to be carefully placed to form a pavement. The pavement formed a covering ranging from three to four slabs in thickness. The interior ditch was not present at this location, because the embankment wall was built directly upon a bedrock ledge (Fig. 4.34).

The relationship between the Fort Hill enclosure and the smaller circular enclosures and wooden structures located to the south at the base of the mesa remains conjectural. Prufer (1968) observed that ceramics from the latter site appeared to be similar to ceramics that occur late in the Ohio Hopewell sequence. An obsidian hydration date from a biface collected from a post-hole from the large rectangular structure at the southern base of the Fort Hill mesa was measured at AD 306 (Lepper *et al.* 1998), which is consistent with Prufer's observation about the ceramics. Unfortunately, neither of these age determinations relate directly to the construction of either stage of the Fort Hill embankment wall and ditch or the circular enclosure wall (William Reynolds enclosure) at the southern base of the mesa.

Fort Ancient

In a region filled with iconic ancient earthworks, Fort Ancient stands out as one of the best known, if not best understood. Located in Warren County, about 40 miles (66.7 km) north-east of the confluence of the Little Miami and Ohio rivers it is situated on a steep-sided prominence, about 80 m above and overlooking the Little Miami (Fig. 4.35, A). The earthwork is surrounded by steep hills cut by deep ravines, except on the north-east, where a narrow neck of flat land connects Fort Ancient to a larger upland plateau.

Fort Ancient is probably the best preserved of all the major Hopewell enclosure

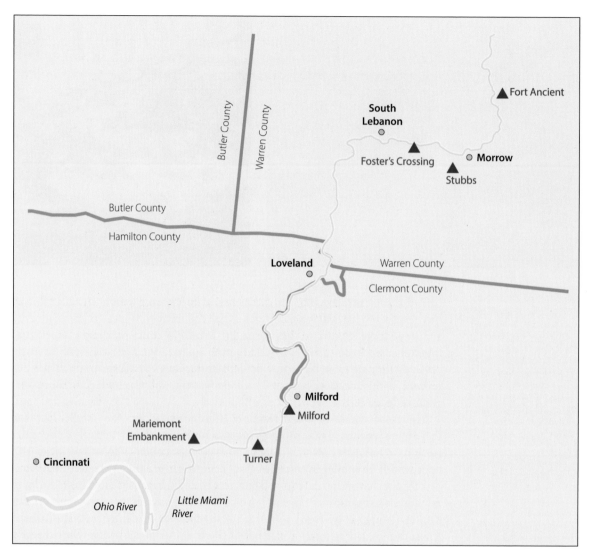

Fort Ancient

South
Lebanon

Foster's Crossing

Morrow

Stubbs

Butler County

Warren County

Butler County

Hamilton County

Loveland

Warren County

Clermont County

Milford

Milford

Mariemont
Embankment

Turner

Cincinnati

Ohio River

Little Miami
River

Fig. 4.35. Map of major earthwork sites in *ca.* 35 mile (56 km) stretch of the Little Miami River valley north-east of Cincinnati.

sites in southern Ohio. The first map of the site and the name "Fort Ancient" appeared in the *Port Folio* in 1809, submitted by an anonymous author (Moorehead 1890). More detailed early maps were subsequently published by Atwater (1820), Locke (1843), and Squier and Davis (1848). Warren K. Moorehead began excavations at the site in the early 1880s and his subsequent report (Moorehead 1892) brought even great public curiosity and scientific attention to the site. Moorehead was the first to express concern about the degradation of the site, and his writing (and speeches) led the Ohio legislature to appropriate funds in 1891 for the purchase of Fort Ancient under the stewardship of the Ohio Archaeological and Historical Society (Otto 2004).

Fort Ancient served as a popular picnic and day use area throughout much of the early 20th century. A railway station at the foot of the steep bluff below the site provided easy access for visitors from the nearby cities of Cincinnati and

Columbus to spend a day and explore the ancient earthen monument. Scholars affiliated with the American Association for the Advancement of Science (1898) and the International Congress of Americanists (1902) even made field trips to the site (Randall 1908). The popularity of Fort Ancient is seen in a series of guidebooks (Randall 1908; Mills 1920; Morgan 1946; Blosser and Glotzhober 1995) that were written to inform visitors about the earthworks under their feet.

The enclosure is formed by 5.7 km of embankment walls, which vary in height from 1.5 m to 7.0 m in height, and form three separate enclosures (Fig. 4.36). The embankment walls are broken by a large number of gateways. Various authors differ on the precise number of these, but Mills (1920) estimated about 70. The complexity of tracing the wall in places due to the subsequent formation of gullies and slumps along the steep ravines led Moorehead to caution:

> "the reader must not infer that every opening is a gateway. We use the term gateway because we have not a better one. It is probable that wood-work was built around the outside portion of the openings and they were used for additional defense, somewhat like bastions in a modern fort." (Moorehead 1890: 11)

The South Fort (Fig. 4.37) is widely believed to have been the first enclosure constructed at Fort Ancient (Moorehead 1890), and is often called the Old Fort in early reports. The walls of the South Fort are generally built along the lip of the plateau. Moorehead (1890; 1908) notes that the edge of the plateau on which Fort Ancient was constructed is irregular with many small and large spurs created by gullies of varying size. The embankment wall was built across most of the smaller gullies, but stops at the edge of the larger and deeper ones. Subsequent erosion has affected the wall at several of these places. The walls vary in height from 4 ft to 23 ft (1.2–6.9 m) with the larger walls being in the North Fort and the shorter ones in the Middle Fort.

Much of the early research at Fort Ancient focused on the South Fort, and Moorehead recorded an extensive cemetery consisting of stone graves near the center of the enclosure. He also observed circular depressions 20–30 ft (6–9 m) in diameter with reddish soil in the interior. This is in strong contrast to surrounding soil, and he suggested the depressions were the remains of lodges. On several modified terraces on the west side of South Fort, outside the embankment on the steep slope overlooking the Little Miami River, Moorehead found a scattering of graves. Like most graves at Fort Ancient, the graves on the exterior terraces were mostly covered by piles of stone. One of these was a mass grave with at least 20 individuals. Pottery, a slate pendant, projectile points, and a

Fig. 4.36. Squier and Davis and Moorehead published maps of Fort Ancient that helped the site become one of the most famous earthworks in North America. This image of Fort Ancient during a storm was created by CERHAS, University of Cincinnaiti University of Cincinnati /CERHAS: www.ancientohiotrail.org.

stone celt (axe) were found among the human remains.

The South Fort opens to the north through what has been called the Great Gateway (#55a). Most of what is known about this important earthen architectural complex is derived from Moorehead's excavations in the 1880s (Moorehead 1890; 1908) and has been nicely synthesized by Connolly *et al.* (2004). The Great Gateway complex comprised of two conical mounds that are connected by a ramp about 1 m high between the mounds which

slopes gradually to the plateau surface on both the north and south (Fig. 4.38a). The north side of the gateway leads to the isthmus or Middle Fort. The south gateway ramp contains an ossuary that is flanked by a pond or ditches. There is a burial mound west of the south ramp and a limestone slab pavement "lines the ditch that follows the interior of Wall 55 for approximately 46 m" (Connolly *et al.* 2004: 57). Another limestone pavement of similar length begins at the small conical mound and continues on a straight line south into the interior of South Fort.

The Middle Fort is built on a narrow neck of flat land, sometimes called the Isthmus that connects the South Fort to the plateau upon which the North Fort was built. The Isthmus varies from roughly 60 m to 100 m in width and the earthen walls that line its sides are notably shorter than those of the North and South Forts. Near the center of the Middle Fort there are two crescent-shaped embankments that serve as a funnel device for entry into the Great Gateway complex and South Fort. A small stone slab mound (containing two burials) is recorded on the interior curve of the east crescent embankment.

The North Fort, often called New Fort, is largest of the three enclosures with the most dramatic earthen walls (Fig. 4.38b). Most visitors to Fort Ancient enter the enclosure through State Route 350, which is an old historic road that connected Chillicothe with Lebanon, Ohio. The road passes through gateways in the embankment wall that have been enlarged to accommodate modern day

Fig. 4.37. The earthen walls of South, or Old, Fort, are easily seen in this early 20th century post-card of Fort Ancient.

Fig. 4.38. a. The Great Gateway is formed by two large embankments on a narrow neck that connects the South Fort with the Middle Fort; b. the massive walls of North Fort or New Fort (photos from Moorehead 1908).

automobiles. The embankment walls at this gateway are the largest at the site, being 23 ft (6.9 m) high and 70 ft (21 m) wide at the base. The walls on the opposite side of North Fort, where S.R. 350 descends downward toward the Little Miami River, though only 19 ft (5.7 m) high, are still impressive. Wall sections form the east side of the New Fort, and range from 85 ft to 160 ft (25.5–48 m) in length. A ditch or moat is present on the exterior side of the embankment wall on the north and east sides of North Fort. The ditch is continuous and connects with ravines leading to Cowan Run on the east and Randall Run on the north.

In regard to this ditch/moat, Moorehead wrote:

> "Its purpose is, first, for protection; second, to obtain material for the construction of the fortification. Nearly all the earth for the formation of the embankments was taken from the interior of the inclosure. The ground inclosed is somewhat lower than that outside; the clay layer is very thin, as if it had nearly all been dug up. In some places the loam or surface soil rests upon the limestone, there being but a few inches of clay remaining. Having exhausted nearly all the soil inside, the moat was dug to furnish sufficient to complete the wall and also to serve as additional protection." (Moorehead 1890: 8)

A number of landscape features were constructed within and surrounding the New Fort. A crescent-shaped earthen wall was leveled with the construction of the Chillicothe–Lebanon road (S.R. 350). Four small mounds were built within the North Fort enclosure forming a rough square. Survey of these mounds by William Romain (2004) indicate that while the placement of the mounds is close to being at 90° to one another, the distances between the mounds vary from 509 ft 6 in to 524 ft 10 in (152.9–157.5 m). Romain proposes that the average distance between the four mounds is very close to being one-half of what he proposes to be a Standard Unit of Measure for Ohio Hopewell of 1053 ft (315.9 m).

On the north-east side of Fort Ancient, two large mounds (the Twin Mounds) stand like sentries just outside a gateway opening that has been widened to accommodate the S.R. 350. Beyond the Twin Mounds, two parallel earthen walls extended for nearly a kilometer and terminated in an enclosure around a small mound (Cowan *et al.* 1997). Four to six additional mounds are present on a narrow section of plateau to the south of the New Fort.

Fort Ancient is, without question, the most impressive of all the hilltop enclosures in southern Ohio. Some of the earliest published accounts of the site raised the question of how such a large and complex set of enclosures could be built. As Warren K. Moorehead observed in the first extensive report on the site:

> "When we consider the magnitude of the walls of Fort Ancient, the immense amount of labor involved in their erection, and the construction of the miles of terraces connected with them, we realize all this required a long period of time or a large number of workers: perhaps, when we bear in mind the primitive methods of the builders, we are even justified in believing that it represents the prolonged and continuous industry of a numerous population." (Moorehead 1908: 99)

Moorehead was the first archaeologist to conduct extensive excavations and attempt to address how the earthen features at the site were constructed. Much of his work was clearly aimed at artifact recovery, but he was a tireless advocate for the preservation of the site and provided some of the first useful information about construction methods. In an examination of a slump of a section of west wall in the New Fort, Moorhead observed that the wall appeared to have been built in two stages:

> "at any rate, some time must have elapsed, after the completion of the lower layer, before the upper layer of stones and earth was placed upon it. Some vegetable matter has accumulated between the two layers. It seems quite evident that grass and small sprouts grew upon the lower stratum before the higher one was placed upon it. The line of division is a dark one, clearly marked, and is precisely such as would result from the decay of vegetable matter. It is half an inch in thickness.
>
> In the earth below, the prevailing color is yellow, with streaks and patches of darker soil. This is probably due to the locality from which it was taken, some of it being loam gathered from the surface, while other portions came from a greater depth, and were in consequence, yellow clay. Not a little blue clay appears. This the builders probably took from limestone beds and from the hollows. In many places, there are small quantities of colored earth, as much as would fill, perhaps, a half-bushel measure. This fact, we believe, indicates the size of the loads which the builders carried; and the variety of color in the earth used arises from the difference of locality whence it was taken." (Moorehead 1890: 31–2)

Moorehead (1890; 1908) also observed that the west wall of the South Fort has a layer of stone under it and suggested this was done to prevent landslides into the various gullies and ravines. He also notes that stones are visible in every gateway and that, while limestone slabs from ravine exposures were frequently used in building features at Fort Ancient, there are also water-worn cobbles that likely were collected from the creek and river bottoms below:

> "The amount of stone and its position indicates that the builders constructed a stone backbone entirely around the enclosure. This varied, but usually it lay near the center of the embankment. It is quite likely that on the exterior stones were laid up forming a wall sloping slightly backwards – as they naturally would lying against the curve of the embankment." (Moorehead 1908: 81–2)

Left: **Fig. 4.39.** Richard Morgan excavated a trench near Gateway 31A in the early 1940s which illustrates that the embankment is comprised of numerous soil layers reflecting construction episodes and subsequent soil development (photo courtesy of the Ohio History Connection).

Right: **Fig. 4.40.** Patricia Essenpries reopened Morgan's trench near Gateway 31 A and expanded it. The data she collected indicated that the embankment was built in a series of stages (photo courtesy of the Ohio History Connection).

Fig. 4.41. In the Trench Essenpreis excavated near Gateway 31, she recorded a Buried A horizon which indicates that wall construction was halted long enough for this soil to form on the wall (photo courtesy of the Ohio History Connection)..

In the 1940s, Richard Morgan began an excavation program at Fort Ancient that had the potential to increase significantly understanding about the construction and use of the built landscape. Unfortunately, Morgan's employment at the Ohio Historical Society was terminated before publications about his research were ever completed. Using Morgan's fieldnotes in the 1980s, Patricia Essenpreis re-opened some of his trenches to examine more closely the stratigraphy, and collected artifacts and samples for radiocarbon dating. Unfortunately, illness terminated both her work and life before she could bring it to a published format. More recently, Robert Connolly has re-examined the work of both Morgan and Essenpreis and directed his own excavations aimed at understanding landscape construction. His writing (Connolly 1996; 2004a; 2004b; Connolly and Lepper 2004; Connolly and Sunderhaus 2004) represents a major step in understanding when and how Fort Ancient was built and how it was used.

Richard Morgan began direct study of the embankment wall construction at Fort Ancient when he excavated a trench 5 ft (1.5 m) wide across wall north of Gateway 31A in the South Fort in 1940 (Fig. 4.39), which was partly re-opened by Patricia Essenpreis in 1986 (Fig. 4.40). Connolly's re-examination of fieldnotes and reports from both of these excavations indicated that Morgan and Essenpreis recognized differences in soil color and texture of wall fill. Essenpreis identified three construction stages (Fig. 4.41). Level 1 is the basal stratum and is culturally sterile. Level 2 consists of the first layer of wall fill and is comprised of alternating layers of yellow–brown and light gray soil of varying thickness. The gray soil is derived from maintaining pond features. A buried A horizon formed on top of Level 2, indicating that a period of some time elapsed before the final wall fill was added and covered the developing soil horizon (Fig. 4.41). Soils used to build this section of wall were generally devoid of artifacts and showed no evidence of being re-deposited midden. Connolly reported:

> "all lines of evidence from both the Morgan and Essenpreis excavations of Embankment Wall 31 suggest an accretive development toward the final architectural form. The development is marked by distinct changes in embankment wall form and construction material." (Connolly 2004a: 38)

At Embankment Wall 58, Essenpreis excavated a 5 × 30 ft (1.5 × 9 m) trench across the wall and interior ditch into the interior of Middle Fort in 1988. Connolly reports that her notes indicate wall construction patterns and materials were similar to Wall 31. Connnolly (2004a) reports that Essenpreis observed that Middle Fort was built in stages and, like South Fort, the interior wall was much more vertical than today. She was unable to expose the base of the wall. Connolly says she "estimated the unmodified pre-embankment ground surface was at least 40 cm below the lowest excavation level." Wall 58 showed no evidence of alternate soil layering above Level 1. Single, more homogeneous layers of soil were added to increase wall height. Level 1 of Wall 58 is similar to Level 2 of Wall 31, including use of soil from nearby ponds. Connolly notes that Essenpreis field profile has post-holes "suggesting a palisade-type structure was in place in the early construction sequence of Embankment Wall 58 (Connolly 2004a: 40)."

In the North Fort, Connolly (2004a; Sieg and Connolly 1997) excavated a 1 × 20 m trench in 1995 to produce a cross-section of embankment wall at Gateway 84. This excavation produced the first complete cross-section of a North Fort wall and the associated external ditch. The excavation demonstrated that the final configuration of the wall reflected multiple and complex construction events. Connolly recognized three stages of wall construction, all of which were preceded by the builders laying a clay floor deposit on the surface and covering a number of pits and other features.

Connolly calls the first construction stage Form 1, which is marked by "alternating layers of colored soils with some lenses of carbon" (2004a: 41). These were placed on the clay floor in three parallel sections of low wall. Form 2 was a rounded deposit that was placed on top of the first stage and was comprised of alternating layers of orange and dark gray soil on both the interior and exterior sides of the wall. Excavators observed pockets of different colored clay, carbon lenses, and 18 prehistoric features within the deposits comprising this stage of wall construction. The top of Form 2 was comprised of a limestone pavement that was placed on the exterior surface of the upper wall and a stacked row of limestone footers was placed on the exterior base of the wall. A variety of artifacts that Connolly attributes to ceremonial activities were found on the limestone pavement and in the fill around it. The final stage of wall construction was a covering of homogeneous brown–gray silts with a limestone buttress around the exterior perimeter of the wall and a second limestone paving.

Most early writers contributed to the overall description of Fort Ancient, and those descriptions have become important as natural erosion and historic human activities have degraded the embankment walls and associated features. Of particular importance is Caleb Atwater's description of the gateway flanked by Twin Mounds in the eastern wall of the North Fort:

> "At about twenty poles [330 ft/110.6 m] east from the gate, through which the state road runs, are two mounds, about ten feet eight inches [3.2 m] high, the road running between them nearly equidistant from each. From these mounds are gutters [ditches] running nearly north and south that appear to be artificial, and made to communicate with the branches on each side. Northeast from the mounds, on the plain, are two roads [earthen walls], B. each about one pole [16 ft 6 in/5 m] wide, elevated about three feet [0.9 m], and which run nearly parallel, about one fourth of a mile [0.4 km], and then form an irregular semicircle round a small mound Atwater." (1820: 157)

Moorehead (1890) observed the parallel walls in the 1880s and noted they were made entirely of earth, and due to cultivation they were only 1 ft (0.3 m) high. Annual plowing had spread out the walls to about 12 ft (4 m) in width, and they were reported to be 120 ft (36 m) apart. Moorehead noted the soil forming them had been burnt red in places. Moorehead also described the excavation of a stone pavement at the western end of parallel walls where they meet the Twin Mounds. The pavement was built of limestone slabs, roughly 12 × 6 in (15 ×30 cm) and 2.5 in (6.25 cm) thick. The pavement had been set on top of a clay surface and fine gravel had been put between the stones to cover an area of at least 130 × 500 ft (39 × 150 m) between the Twin Mounds and parallel walls.

In 1996 the Cincinnati Museum Center conducted studies of a planned housing area on the Gregory Farm north-east of the Fort Ancient enclosures (Cowan *et al.* 2004). Surface collection, checking exposures created by construction activities, and limited testing produced evidence for specialized lithic use and production areas. Unfortunately, the salvage nature of the research did not permit systematic collection and recording for the entire area. Overall, the Gregory Field data suggest diverse uses with distinct activity areas. Some residential activities are possible, particularly tied to select artifact concentrations. The researchers recorded wooden architecture in construction exposures at several locations, but all of these lacked cooking or storage features and did not exhibit the diverse artifact assemblages associated with residential localities.

The Cincinnati Museum Center work on the east side of the Fort Ancient enclosures provided important evidence that ritual/ceremonial activities were not restricted to the interiors of the earthen enclosures. Cowan *et al.* (2004) make an excellent case that water as well as earthen walls are boundaries for separating sacred and secular space. They note that the parallel walls extend from the Twin Mounds to the south-east where they terminated in a small enclosure. This enclosure, although no longer visible today, was apparently built on the ridge that separates the headwaters of Cowan Run and Randall Run, which flow into the Little Miami and form boundaries for Fort Ancient. Cowan and colleagues note that at least three large caches of Hopewell artifacts have been found near this small terminal enclosure. Their research has significantly expanded archaeological perspectives on the nature and location of activities in and around Fort Ancient.

Archaeologists from Moorehead to Morgan, Essenpries, and Connolly who have excavated at Fort Ancient have come to accept the model that the complex began with the construction of South Fort, and was expanded northwards with the construction of Middle Fort and North Fort, and finally the complex of earthen features associated with the parallel walls. In several places where they have examined the construction of the earth and stone walls there is evidence that early stages of walls were exposed long enough for an A horizon to form on the wall surface. This soil was then covered by fill that enlarged those particular sections of embankment wall. Connolly (2004b) has compiled the radiometric evidence for dating activities at Fort Ancient and proposes that Ohio Hopewell people occupied the site from 100 cal BC to cal AD 350. Later occupation associated with the Fort Ancient culture did not seem to have altered the earthen features built during the Hopewell era.

One unfortunate aspect of the excavations conducted thus far at Fort Ancient is that only the 1995 trench excavated by Robert Connolly penetrated deep enough to determine what type of surface preparation might have been applied prior to the beginning of the enclosure wall construction. In the area of Gateway 84, Sieg and Connolly (1997) found that earlier features were covered by a clay layer that served as the foundation for subsequent wall construction materials. It would be useful to know if this method of establishing a wall foundation was used throughout Fort Ancient, or if earlier wall construction utilized soil stripping to prepare a surface for constructing an earthen wall, as is typical of the geometric enclosures of the Scioto River valley.

Fig. 4.42. Some of the mounds at Fort Ancient were built with substantial amounts of stone. This slab covered mound is located in the North or New Fort (photo: author, 2006).

There is abundant evidence for the use of earth and stone in building the Fort Ancient ceremonial landscape (Fig. 4.42). Moorehead reported the use of limestone blocks as footers in many parts of the walls, and subsequent scholars have recorded limestone slabs as pavements on wall surfaces. Connolly (2004a) says there are differences between the wall construction methods used in building the South Fort and North Fort. He suggests that expansion to the north included fewer discrete construction episodes, and that the different use of soils in the initial phase at Gateway 84 suggests an increase in the tempo and complexity of North Fort construction. Essenpreis (Essenpries and Mosely 1984) considered that this implies greater central planning and standardization through time.

Traditional interpretations of Fort Ancient have proposed that the South Fort, like most hilltop enclosures in south-west Ohio, was built to follow the physiographic edge of the plateau on which it is built. This would seem likely, but analysis of all three enclosures suggests that the placement of gateways, ponds, mounds, and other earthen walls was non-random (Connolly 1998; Connolly and Sunderhaus 2004). Current data indicate that, not only did the area enclosed within earthen walls grow with the addition of the Middle Fort and North Fort, but the rules for placement of features and construction of walls also changed. The reason(s) for the changes in Fort Ancient over time are as yet to be determined, but ongoing research by Wright State University under Robert Riordan continues to demonstrate that even sites that have been subjected to the work of archaeologists for more than a century can still have many secrets remaining to be revealed (see Chapter 5).

Foster's Crossing

This hilltop enclosure was explored by Frederick W. Putnam of the Peabody Museum during the summer of 1879. The site is situated on a high plateau adjacent to the Little Miami River near the station called Foster's (Fig. 4.35, C). Putnam (1890c) reports that the enclosure is more than 0.5 miles (0.3 km) in length, with the highest sections of wall being on the north where he estimated it to be 9–12 ft (2.7 × 3.6 m) high and 55 ft (16.5 m) wide. The south-east side of the enclosure is only a few meters high and the wall on the western side is barely visible. Putnam's brief paper provides only limited information about their research at this site,

Hopewellian Grave goods and exotic artifacts 2

Among the wide range of raw materials used for Hopewell ceremonial objects are mica, chlorite and quartz crystals from the Appalachian highlands; obsidian and grizzly bear teeth from the Rocky Mountains; copper and silver nuggets from the Great Lakes region; galena from north-west Illinois or Missouri; shark and aligator teeth from the Florida Gulf Coast; marine shells from the coastal areas of the south-east; and flint and cherts from various localities in Ohio but also from more distant sources as far away as North Dakota and the upper Missouri. Finished objects were also imported, most notably beautifully carved stone effigy pipes from north-west Illinois. However, curiously, the exotic raw materials and crafted artifacts appear to have mostly remained in the Hopewell core areas and were not often 'exported' back to the distant, peripheral locations from where the materials had originated, despite the fact that Hopewell traditions and influences did spread outwards beyond the core areas.

Early scholars thought these items arrived in Ohio through a trade network that was an important element in what has become known as the Hopewell Interaction Sphere. However, since very few of these objects have been found between Ohio and their source areas, current scholars believe the raw materials were likely brought by pilgrims coming to the great ceremonial sites in Ohio, or obtained by Ohio Hopewell people who travelled great distances to obtain exotic materials on power quests. The key factor seems to be that these valuable, exotic artifacts were integral to the activities, or ceremonialism, which was played out at and around the earthen enclosures and burial mounds of Ohio, and as such became purposefully deposited in important places and thus remained at the core of Hopewellian cultural influence.

Probably the most iconic and beautiful objects are the thin, almost translucent mica sheets carved into hands, disks, animal and anthropomorphic forms, and the so-called 'claw' shown here with projecting talons (alongside a mica bear tooth) which demonstrates the artistry of the Hopewell artisans. Both artifacts from the Hopewell Mound Group in Ross County (Photo: Pete Topping).

Obsidian, essentially volcanic glass, was prized by many prehistoric cultures around the world at different times for its beautifully glossy, often black, colour, superb flaking qualities and incredible sharpness. Hopewell obsidian artifacts mainly comprise large projectile points and spearheads, whose size suggests that they were likely ceremonial rather than functional, a point reinforced by their frequent deposition in rich grave assemblages (Photo: courtesy of the Ohio History Connection and Hopewell Culture National Historical Park).

Sharks teeth originated from the Gulf Coast and were an important part of the Hopewell assemblages. Some are perforated for suspension and were likely worn, strung on hide thongs, around the neck as some kind of talisman or status symbol (Photo: courtesy of the Ohio History Connection and Hopewell Culture National Historical Park).

Animal effigy platform smoking pipes are another classic Hopewell artifact type. These sculpted effigies have been recovered from several Hopewell sites but especially Mound City and Tremper Mound, where large caches of over 100 examples were excavated by Mills and Shetrone in the 1920s. The pipes take many forms: owls, ravens and a variety of other birds, toads, frogs, beavers, otters, racoons – and may represent the spirit guides of shamans who smoked the pipes to induce a trance-like state. An interesting feature is that, in most cases, the animal would be facing the smoker. Although pipestone occurs locally in the Scioto river valley, chemical analysis of the Tremper Mound pipes shows them to have been made from Illinois pipestone (Photo: courtesy of the Ohio History Connection and Hopewell Culture National Historical Park).

but some of his comments seem to echo observations made at other south-west Ohio hilltop enclosures:

> "The whole circumvallation is made up to a carefully laid wall of flat stones along the outer side several feet in height; behind this are loose stones, both large and small, making nearly half the structure; and behind an over these stones a mass of clay burnt to all degrees of hardness, from that only slightly burnt to great masses of slag, showing that the clay had been subject to very great heat, in places forming a vitreous surface over the slag, which resembles that from a blast furnace. In many places the limestone had been burnt in varying degree, and here and there large quantities of pure lime were found. Large pieces of charcoal and beds of ashes were discovered in many parts of the structure. At one place on the north side, where the burnt material runs out in the form of a low mound nearly one hundred feet long and eighty feet wide, there was a larger quantity of charcoal and ashes than in other parts of the work explored. Here was also uncovered a singular wall of small stones about six feet long and two feet high. At very part of the work through which a trench was dug the same story was told, – burnt stones and clay, ashes and charcoal, and the mass of stones, faced on the outer side by a good stone wall." (Putnam 1890c: 136–7)

The investigators found small amounts of flint flakes, projectile points, and pottery in the northern portion of the enclosure, and although parts of the interior of the enclosure had been plowed, they were surprised by the lack of evidence for more intensive occupation. Like most scholars of the time, Putnam must have believed the hilltop enclosure was built for defensive purposes, and he assumed the village would be inside the enclosure for protection and that the graves of the inhabitants would be located nearby. However, Putnam was not fully convinced of the defensive character of the fortifications and noted:

> "It is locally known as 'The Fort,' but although well situated it does not seem at all to answer the requirements of a fortification; and, apparently, if such was intended, a bank could have been made of ordinary clay with a retaining stone-wall that would have answered the purpose as well without all this labor of burning."

The very brief account of Putnam's study of the hilltop enclosure at Foster's Crossing documents once again that careful observers who saw these sites before they were heavily impacted by development or agriculture frequently observed strong signs of fire in the earth and stone that form the embankment walls. Robert Riordan (1996) has also documented a significant burning event at the Pollock Works and has noted the evidence for major conflagrations at other hilltop enclosures in south-west Ohio.

Pollock Works

The Pollock Works, west of Cedarville, in Greene County, Ohio is one of the most important Ohio Hopewell sites because it has been the subject of careful and sustained research by Robert Riordan of Wright State University for about two decades (Riordan 1995; 1996; 1998; 2006; 2010b). Through the efforts of Riordan and his students, we know more about the construction and use of the Pollock Works than any other Hopewell hilltop enclosure site in Ohio.

Pollock Works is situated on a 5.5 ha mesa that was formed by the downcutting of Massie's Creek through the local limestone bedrock. The mesa is marked by sharp, steep (3–15 m) bluffs on the north, west, and south sides of the landform, and its builders constructed a series of earth, stone and timber embankments on the more gradual western slope. The site was mapped by Squier and Davis (1848) and has only been slightly impacted by subsequent human activities (Fig. 4.43). The primary embankment is called the Barrier Wall and it has three gateways or openings. The wall is 3 m high and 10 m wide and 90 m long. The walls do not fully encircle the circumference of the plateau. To the west and downslope from the Barrier Wall, Squier and Davis mapped four crescent-shaped embankments and three mounds that blocked access to the openings in the Barrier Wall. Riordan (1998) reports that these landscape features to the west of the enclosure are no longer extant, and were likely destroyed during limestone quarrying activities. To the north and west of this main embankment is a lower "Perimeter Wall". It was 1 m high and 210 m long, from the north side of the mesa to the east where a steep limestone outcrop forms the mesa edge. The Perimeter Wall has been heavily impacted by plowing and is barely visible in most places.

Riordan and Wright State University students excavated 15 trenches and a number of cores to better understand how this system of walls was built. Through his long commitment to this project, Riordan has been able to identify five stages in the construction, modification, and use of these landscape features. The excavations have also produced a series of radiocarbon dates that, in combination with the archaeological and geoarchaeological evidence, permit a fairly accurate chronology for the construction history of the Pollock Works.

Riordan (1995) estimates that the first Barrier Wall was built sometime in first half of the 1st century AD. This was a broad, low earthen wall comprised of four segments and three gateways that connected the cliff at the south-west corner of the plateau with the edge of the bluff above Massie's Creek. The wall was 1–1.7 m tall and 6 m wide at the base and was built with basket-loads of earth, very likely collected from within the mesa-top enclosure. At the base of this initial wall Riordan found a "prepared layer of light-colored silty clay" (1995: 66). Excavators found no evidence of a palisade or post-holes at this level, and Riordan believes the wall probably served to define space on the mesa top and had no real defensive purpose. It is worth reminding ourselves that Robert Connolly

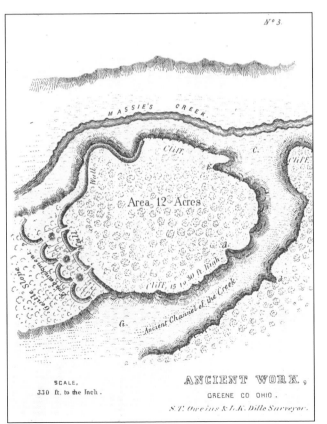

Fig. 4.43. The first map of the Pollock Works appeared in Ancient Monuments of the Mississippi Valley (Squier and Davis 1848, pl. xii).

(2004a) reported a clay layer being placed on the original surface at the base of the embankment wall at Gateway 84 at Fort Ancient (see above).

Riordan is unable to determine confidently when the three gateways became part of the embankment wall. He notes that during this first stage, the presence of a central gateway is unclear. If an open gateway was part of the original embankment wall, it was likely wider than the present gateway, which has been narrowed by the subsequent addition of soil mantles to the adjacent embankments (Riordan 1995). The Central and North Gateways become apparent during the Stage 2 and 3 additions to the wall. These wall openings were formed as builders intentionally left these areas free of the new soil deposits. The South Gateway did not become apparent until the fifth and final wall construction phase. It is uncertain when the external crescent walls and mounds were built, but Riordan logically notes that, since they are aligned with these three gateways, it is plausible that they were also built during Stage 2 or 3.

During Stages 2 and 3, the embankment wall between the south and central and the Central and North gateways was increased in height and width by addition of at least two soil layers. These layers were 20–60 cm thick, and the first was deposited with clear evidence of basket-loading, while later additions were built by a broadcast method of spreading earth onto the wall. There is some variability in the structure of the wall during these stages. In Trench L, eight thin layers of soil were added to the original wall stage, while in Trench B, the stage 3 surface exhibits "limited development of an A soil horizon, possibly signifying a pause in construction activities" (Riordan 1995: 65). Some limestone rubble may also have been added to the exterior side of the wall at the end of Stage 3 (Fig. 4.44). There are no radiocarbon dates directly dating Stages 2–3 of construction but, other than the slight development on the surface of the wall at the end of Stage 3, the geoarchaeological evidence suggests that relatively little time elapsed between the first three construction stages.

Left: **Fig. 4.44.** The third stage of embankment construction at the Pollock Works (Riordan 1995) involved the use of substantial amounts of large rock to enlarge the wall (photo courtesy of Robert Riordan).

Right: **Fig. 4.45.** A palisade wall that had been constructed on the less precipitous slope of the Pollock Works as part of the perimeter wall was consumed by fire and never rebuilt. The burned palisade remains were then covered by earth (photo courtesy of Robert Riordan).

Stage 4 represents a dramatic change in the character of the Barrier Wall. A lightly built fence was constructed on top of the embankment wall at the end of Stage 3 on either side of the Central gateway. Post-holes observed in Trenches B and H reveal widely separated upright posts, estimated to be 1–2 m high with horizontal timbers laced between the uprights. The character of the fence is clear in burned remnants of wood structure in several trenches. The fence was linked to a stockade that was built on the bluff overlooking Massie's Creek. A weighted average of four radiocarbon dates on burned remnants of this fence yielded a calibrated average range and slope intercept of cal AD. 78 (130) 212 at one sigma, cal AD 63 (130) 231 at 2 sigma (Riordan 1995).

During Stage 4 the Perimeter Wall was built, which begins where the Barrier Wall ends at the bluff edge above Massie's Creek,. This long low wall is difficult to trace today. Riordan excavated seven trenches and explored the wall at intervals with soil cores and found consistent evidence for construction of a timber stockade under the entire embankment. Large post-holes, 19–40 cm in diameter, often exhibited evidence that they had been braced with limestone. Like the fence on the Barrier Wall, the stockade under the Perimeter Wall was built with horizontal timbers woven between the vertical upright posts. Post-holes vary from 19–44 cm in diameter and 22–60 cm deep, spaced 55–65 cm apart. Riordan estimates that this palisade was 3–4 m high and the bottom was plastered with mud. A buttress of limestone was piled against the exterior base of the wall. When the stockade later burned, mud plaster was baked and left a red color that was easily identified (Fig. 4.45). Nine radiocarbon dates from timber features associated with the stockade indicate that the Barrier Wall fence and Perimeter Wall stockade were contemporary in Stage 4.

The fifth and final stage of construction consisted of simply adding additional earth and stone to the Barrier and Perimeter Walls and effectively covering the charred remains of the earlier stockade and fence (Fig. 4.46). No evidence of post-holes from a second fence or palisade was noted anywhere in the Wright State University excavations. After nearly two decades of study, Riordan (2006) estimates a timespan of perhaps three centuries from the start of construction until the fifth and final stage of wall construction at the Pollock Works was completed. Artifacts in general, and evidence for habitation in particular, have never been discovered at this site.

What makes the evidence from Pollock particularly notable is that it clearly indicates that the enclosure walls were built in several stages and that their nature and likely purpose changed with time Riordan (2006). After clearing vegetation and placing a 2 cm thick layer of silty clay on the surface, the initial Barrier Wall was built with basket-loads of soil to a height of 1–1.3 m and width of 8–9 m. More soil was added to make the wall about 80 cm higher and slightly wider in Stage 2. The third stage involved deposition of more homogeneous strata totaling 20 cm in thickness on top of the wall which did not increase its width. Then a thin layer of additional soil was added to the interior side of the wall and 20–30 cm of additional soil was added on top of the wall. A final mantle of soil (40 cm thick) was added on both sides. The surface today is humus.

During all stages of construction, stone played an important role in the

Opposite: **Fig. 4.46.** Trench U was excavated into Section 3, the central section of the Barrier Wall and shows the multiple construction stages identified by Riordan (1995; 2006). This section of embankment was built with large quantities of earth (photo courtesy of Robert Riordan).

construction and appearance of the primary Barrier Wall at Pollock. In Trench U, Riordan (2010a) and his students removed 1400 stones that weighted almost 4.6 tons (Fig. 4.43). The average stone weighed nearly 3 kg, and there were 120 stones that weighed 10 kg or more. It is believed that these blocks of limestone were quarried from exposures in the Massie's Creek canyon 0.5–1.0 km upstream. Riordan believes the rock was set in place on the exterior surface of the embankment during every phase of construction to create a rock-faced wall that joined to the rocky cliff that borders it.

Construction of the fence on the Barrier Wall and the robust stockade on the palisade appear to represent a substantive change in how the enclosure was used, or at least how the site was viewed by local residents. Riordan (1996) makes a good case that the initial use of the Pollock Works as a ritual/ceremonial space may have changed around the 3rd century AD when the addition of wooden architecture gave the site a more military or defensive appearance. He also notes that the burning of the wooden structures following the enhancement of the earthen walls may reflect a return to the original purpose of the site.

About 2 km to the west of Pollock is the Bull Works (Squier and Davis 1848: pl. iv, no. 3). It is a rectangular enclosure built on the closest low and flat place in the valley. Riordan (2010a) has suggested that Pollock and Bull were contemporary and the two were built as a circular/rectangular pair that may have symbolised the sky and earth for the people who built these landscapes. The data from Pollock is the best available for any hilltop enclosure in southern Ohio. Perhaps as data accumulate at other sites it will be possible to determine if the patterns identified by Robert Riordan have a wider and more regional character.

Miami Fort

On a narrow, flat, ridge overlooking the confluence of the Great Miami and Ohio Rivers is a hilltop enclosure that was studied, mapped, and described by William H. Harrison (1838). Squier and Davis (1848: pl. ix, no.2) used Harrison's sketch map to depict this small but important site now located within the boundaries of Shawnee Lookout County Park. The flat narrow ridge on which Miami Fort was built is 250–290 ft (60–87 m) above the valley floors. The topographic setting provides extensive view-sheds of the states of Indiana to the west and Kentucky to the south.

Warren K. Moorehead visited the site in the late 19th century and provided a brief but detailed description of the site and its condition:

> "The embankment is about the same average size as that at Fort Ancient. It is carried around the brow of the hill, probably the distance of over a mile [1.6 km]. The gateways are similar to those at Fort Ancient, and there is a great deal of stone in them. The area inclosed about 40 acres [16 ha]. The ditch in all places is on the interior of the wall; in some places it reaches a depth of three feet [0.9 m]. The average height of the embankment is seven feet [2.1 m]; in one or two places it has reached an altitude of 12 feet [3.6 m]. The ends of the embankment in some of the gateways show burning to a considerable depth. It seems as if block-houses or bastions of wood had been burned down when once protecting the gateway." (Moorehead 1890: 102–3)

Moorehead excavated at various places to examine the possible evidence of burning and found the soil to be brick-red in color and very hard, which led him to conclude that a wooden structure that once stood on and along the walls must have burned. Moorehead also observed large blocks of limestone in some of the gateways, and reported that a small area of flat ground to the west of Miami Fort had been recently cultivated. There was a conical mound in this field and he noted the presence of several stone covered graves that had been partially exposed by the plowing.

The first well-documented study of Miami Fort and its surroundings was directed by Fred Fisher, who led University of Cincinnati field schools in limited excavations at the site in 1965 and 1966. Fisher also conducted an intensive survey to locate sites in the vicinity and directed excavations at the nearby Twin Mounds site (Fischer 1968; 1969; 1970). In his study of Miami Fort, he reported extensive evidence of occupation by Early and Middle Woodland people. He also excavated the largest of three conical mounds located immediately west of the enclosure walls.

When Fischer (1965) began work at Miami Fort he reported that the earth and stone embankment wall was not, and probably never was, continuous. He noted that in places where the natural slope below the fort was steepest the earthen wall was either low or non-existent. The wall was largest and best defined in places where the fort is exposed to a gradual slope outside it. The area within the enclosure is roughly 1150 ft (345 m) E–W and 560 ft (168 m) N–S. The embankment wall, like many other hilltop enclosures, was built slightly below the topographic lip of the landform. The walls are 10–12 ft (3–3.6 m) high on the western end of the enclosure and 12–15 ft (3.6–4.5 m) high on the eastern end where the ridge continues toward the east. Lower embankments are present on the north and south sides of the enclosure where the valley walls are particularly steep. There are two carefully constructed gateways at the north-east and south-east corners of the enclosure. There are also breaks in the north and south walls, but it is uncertain if these sections were ever built or if subsequent erosion has created the breaks.

During the 1965 season, Fisher excavated the embankment wall in two places to develop a better understanding of how they were built constructed. A 5 ×15 ft (1.5 × 4.5 m) trench was dug into the inner side of the embankment at the extreme west end of the site. The embankment wall is about 12 ft (2.6 m) high at that location. Fischer (1965) provides few details about the nature of the embankment wall deposit, but notes they exposed the "old humus" at 9.7 ft (2.9 m) below the present top of the embankment. The presence of this buried soil surface suggests that the wall was built without significant soil stripping or surface preparation.

In his efforts to trace the embankment wall around the perimeter of the site, Fisher saw the same red, seemingly burned-clay, chunks that were originally described by Moorehead (1908) along the north portion of the wall. He excavated a 5 × 3.5 ft (1.5 × 1.05 m) test unit into the wall to examine this more closely. The excavators observed an:

> "irregular zone of burnt red clay from about two feet to almost five feet below surface. The upper portion of the zone is composed of rather small particles of burned earth. Particle size increases with depth and the base of the zone is made

up of very irregular chunks of brick-hard burned clay. Stick and twig molds are common in these lumps. A thin layer of vegetal material is present just below the burned clay, and is apparently on the pre-earthwork surface." (Fischer 1965: 5)

Fisher suggests the red, clay-burned zone represents a wood and clay daub structure that had been built on the original surface as part of the enclosure wall. At some point the wood burned and the charred remains collapsed and left a low mound of clay and charcoal debris. This was subsequently covered by a large amount of soil material to form the present wall. This interpretive scenario has strong similarities to the situation reported by Robert Riordan (1995; 2006) at the Pollock Works.

On an extension of the same ridge on the western side of Miami Fort there were three conical mounds, ranging from 3–4 ft (0.9–1.2 m) high and 30–60 ft (9–18 m) in diameter. The westernmost mound had been thoroughly vandalized when Fisher began work, but the other two seemed largely intact. Fisher excavated a trench into the largest mound in 1966. Although he eventually discovered that the central core had been excavated and refilled long ago, he was able to gather some very useful information about the structure and construction of the mound.

Fischer (1966) reported that the upper mound fill was composed of brown humic soil from an occupation area. He found lithic debris, potsherds, fire-cracked rock, and broken stone tools throughout the mound fill, and noted that the pottery and projectile points were indicative of both Adena and late Middle Woodland occupation. Under the mound the excavators discovered what has been interpreted to be a low primary mound, comprised of orange–yellow clay about 1 ft (0.3 m) high and 20–30 ft (6–9 m) in diameter. At the base of the mound they encountered a brown humus resting on sterile yellow clay subsoil. The sub-mound humus also contained occupation debris.

Most of Fischer's work in 1965 and some work in 1966 was aimed at locating and evaluating evidence for habitation in association with the enclosure. Although he was unable to find any buildings, he did identify three limestone hearths, a concentration of fire-cracked rock, and a pit filled with refuse and artifacts he attributed to Adena and Hopewell occupation.

A single radiocarbon date has been reported for Miami Fort from the charred remains found under the north embankment wall. The date of AD 270±150 (Fischer 1968: 19) was the first date reported for an Ohio hilltop enclosure and documents the Middle Woodland origin of the embankment wall. It seems likely that the charred remains found at the base of the wall were from a fence or stockade, and suggests that the Miami Fort enclosure very likely was built in at least two stages – a wooden structure that burned and was covered by an earthen wall.

Recent research at Miami Fort has questioned the defensive character of the hilltop enclosure and proposed that the earthworks were built as part of a water management system to provide adequate water resources for people and crops during an increasingly dry climate (Ballantyne 2009). During a survey of the earthworks, three reservoirs were recorded with a potential capacity of more than 1.2 million liters. The reservoirs are connected by a series of raceways that permit management of stored water. Some of the walls of the enclosure are believed to be dams built of stone, earth, and timber.

Three radiocarbon samples collected from soil cores in the embankment walls have produced dates that range from Middle Woodland through Late Prehistoric in age (Ballantyne 2009, 35). Since the samples were collected from soil cores in earthen walls, the contexts of these samples are not well documented and it is hard to determine how to best interpret this array of dates. The 2008 University of Cincinnati field school excavations at the nearby Twin Mounds site collected a sample of bear bone that has yielded a Middle Woodland date of cal BC 160–AD 60 (Beta 247820, at two sigma). Another sample of wood charcoal collected by Robert Riordan from beneath the North Wall at Miami Fort yielded a date of cal AD 77–617 (M1869, at two sigma). Three additional dates from wood charcoal collected from soil cores by Ballantyne during the 2008 field investigations suggest that at least some of the earthen walls contain charred wood that is more recent than the Hopewell era. These new data suggest the possibility that the construction and use of Miami Fort may have started in the Hopewell era, but was re-used and even witnessed new construction in the late prehistoric era. More research is certainly needed to better understand what seems to be a complex architectural history of this important site.

Turner Group of Earthworks

The Turner Group of Earthworks in Hamilton County, east of Cincinnati, is one of the most impressive and unusual geometric enclosure sites in all of southern Ohio (Figs 4.35, D; 4.47 and 4.48). It did not draw the attention of Squier and Davis (1848) in their landmark account, but was brought to public attention by Charles Whittlesey (1851) a few years later. It has been suggested that the failure of Squier and Davis to recognize the Turner site has resulted in this amazing site being undervalued by archaeological scholars (Tankersley 2007), but this seems to be more hyperbole than fact. Whittlesey published the first map (Fig. 4.47) and description of the Turner site in the same Smithsonian Institution publication series that printed Squier and Davis' *Ancient Monuments*, and his brief but graphic description must have drawn some attention from the mound and earthwork scholars of that day. Excavations by the Peabody Museum of Harvard University from 1882 through 1908 were among the most extensive that were undertaken at any Ohio Hopewell site. N'omi Greber, who is very familiar with the Turner site data and its records has suggested that early appreciation for the site was affected by the dense vegetative cover. She also notes that the excavation records housed at the Peabody Museum are among the best available for any of the earlier excavations (Greber, pers. comm. 2014).

Charles Whittlesey was one of the most experienced and widely traveled of all the scholars who mapped and reported mound and enclosure sites in the Ohio River valley. He was clearly impressed by what he saw at the Turner Works and wrote:

> "Among the curious structures of the mound-builders, there are none more difficult to explain than this. On a detached ridge, composed of limestone gravel, covered with a clay loam, is a low wall, averaging two feet high and fifteen feet broad [0.6 × 4.5 m], nearly in the form of a circle; although its north and south diameter is about twenty-five feet [7.6 m] the longer. The average diameter of the circle is four

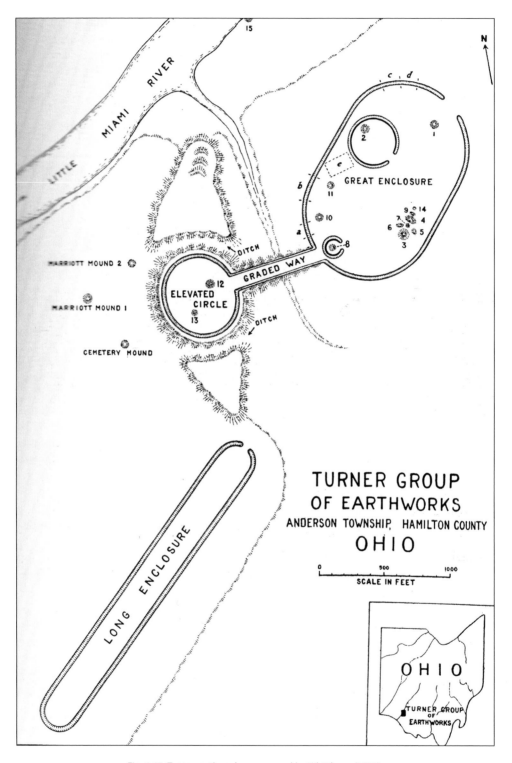

Fig. 4.47. Turner earthworks as mapped by Whittlesey (1851).

hundred and seventy feet [143 m]. The flat ridge on which the figure A is situated, is about twenty-five feet [7.6 m] higher than the adjacent plain; which is from twenty-five to thirty-five feet [7.6–10.7 m] above the Little Miami River. Outside of the circular figure, there is a space from twenty to thirty feet [8.1–8.8 m] wide, on the natural surface of the ground. On the two opposite sides of the circle, where it occupies the height of the ridge, is an external ditch, or excavation, enclosing about half the figure. It is from seventy to eighty-five feet [21.3–25.9 m] broad at the top, and from twelve to eighteen feet [3.6–5.5 m] deep. The bottom of this trench is not smooth, and is from seven to ten feet [21.–3.0 m] higher than the adjacent plain. Its sides are as steep as the gravel and earth will lie. On the east, in the direction of c g, is an embankment or grade, extending by a gradual slope, from the enclosure A to the plain. It is one hundred and sixty-eight feet [51 m] wide at the neck, where it joins A, and has, at the edges, raised side-walls, like those made for pavements in cities, with a drain or gutter inside. The space between the side-ways is rounded like a turnpike, as represented in the section d e. Its length is six hundred feet [183 m], and the side-ways are connected with a low and now almost obliterated wall, turning outwards each way at i, i. Some distance to the north-east is another traceable fragment f, f; and this may, with I, I have been portions of a large ellipse, now destroyed by time and cultivation." (Whittlesey 1851: 9)

Whittlesey's brief but graphic description of the site drew the interest of Frederick W. Putnam of the Peabody Museum, who hired Dr Charles Metz to direct excavations at Turner in 1882 and for a number of subsequent years. The excavations were outstanding in comparison to others of that time, but unfortunately the results were never fully published until many years later when Charles Willoughby used the fieldnotes, maps, and artifacts to produce a summary of what had been accomplished (Willoughby and Hooton 1922). Subsequently,

Fig. 4.48. The Turner Group of earthworks, created by CERHAS, the University of Cincinnati University of Cincinnati / CERHAS: www.ancientohiotrail.org.

several competent scholars have reviewed the records and collections and added their thoughts about the importance of the Turner Works (Greber 1976; Byers 2010; Starr 1960), but additional field investigations at the site have not been undertaken. Whether this is, as Tankersley (2007) claimed, due to the false rumors that the site was destroyed by gravel quarry activities, is unknown. Sadly, the Turner Works like most Ohio Hopewell Ceremonial landscapes has been greatly degraded by historic activities and it is very difficult to fully appreciate the nature and scale of landscape construction that was conducted at this location by the Ohio Hopewell people.

Although the site had suffered some degradation from cultivation during the years between Whittlesey's time at the site and beginning of the Peabody Museum excavations, most of the earthen construction features were still sufficiently visible to produce a map that conveys the extent of the landscape building activities.

Tankersley (2007) has noted that earthen features at the Turner site were built on three different quaternary landform surfaces. A least one mound (#15) and an occupation site were on the T-0, which is the floodplain of the Little Miami River. The majority of constructed landscape features, including the Great Enclosure, Elongated Enclosure, three circular enclosures, and at least 14 conical mounds – plus portions of an occupation area – were located on the large T-1 terrace. This terrace was formed during the Late Woodfordian period of the Pleistocene and is composed of outwash gravels and has been extensively mined in historic times. Also present at this location is a higher terrace remnant (T-2) that dates to the Early Woodfordian period, and rises about 16 m above the surrounding Little Miami River valley. The use and modification of this natural landform by the builders of the Turner Works is what makes this site unique and highly noteworthy. The top and sides of this landform were modified to build the Elevated Circle, adjacent deep ditches, and the Graded Way. At least four conical mounds were on the T-2 landform.

The elevated circle was formed by a circular earthen wall that was separated from the remainder of the landform by two deeply excavated ditches on the north and south sides of the circle. As can be seen from the quotation above, Whittlesey (1851: 9) estimated that these ditches were 75–85 ft (22.5–25.5 m) wide and 12–18 ft (3.6–5.4 m) deep, and he believed the earth taken during their excavation was used to build the Elevated Circle. Within the Elevated Circle were two mounds and the circle opened to the east. From the eastern opening, a broad earthen ramp, called a Graded Way was built to slope downward to the T-1 terrace below. This ramp was 168 ft (50.4 m) wide where it exited the Elevated Circle with raised edges like the curbs of modern streets. The Graded Way extended at a gradual downward slope for 600 ft (183 m) where it merged with the Great Enclosure. He even noted that the graded way had been built across a small stream, and the builders had included some type of culvert or sluice to allow the intermittent passage of rain water down the rivulet without damaging the graded way.

Much of the excavation work conducted by Putnam, Metz, and other archaeologists from the Peabody Museum concentrated on the mounds and the area forming the Great Enclosure. Willoughby reported that the:

"embankment forming the great enclosure could be traced practically throughout its length. Beginning at the foot of the graded way, about one-half of the northwestern section was well defined except in one place, the average height being about 2 feet [0.6 m] and the width approximately 20 feet [6.1 m]. Beyond this, for a space of about 500 feet [152 m], the embankment was just perceptible; the remaining portion, extending to the northeastern gateway, was about 1 foot [0.3 m] high and 25 feet [5.7 m] wide." (Willoughby and Hooton 1922: 6)

There was no evidence of a ditch on either side of the embankment wall.

Like most of the excavations conducted at this time, the Metz and the Peabody team focused their attention on mounds and cemetery areas. Unlike other archaeological work in the late 19th century, they carefully recorded the stratigraphy in the mounds they examined, and the profile drawings clearly indicate that mounds were built with different materials and included multiple stages of construction. The practice of stripping mound fill with horse or mule teams to examine the base of the mounds was in wide use by Warren Moorehead and his contemporaries, but the data left by the Peabody for Turner show clearly that the mounds were more than just piles of dirt covering human graves. This can be inferred from the complex mortuary remains found under many Ohio Hopewell mounds, but the details provided for the Turner mounds show that they were all built using carefully selected and placed mixtures of earth and stone.

Mound 3 was probably the most complex and interesting of the mounds excavated by Charles Metz (Fig. 4.49). Mound 3 was located in the south-eastern section of the Great Enclosure and like all of the mounds in that group, it was surrounded by a low stone wall. The wall was 2 ft (0.6 m) high and 4 ft (1.2 m) wide on the south side, but expanded to 3.5 ft (1.05 m) high and 15 ft (4.5 m) wide on the eastern side of the mound. The floor of the mound, like most of the mounds at Turner, was constructed of a mixture of clay, sand, and gravel that Metz called "concrete" in his field notes. Willoughby suggested these compact and hard prepared floors derived their character from the inclusion of lime derived from burned limestone, which is found at many places on the site. The term "Hopewell concrete" is widely used now to describe the hardened surfaces found associated with the remains of buildings throughout southern Ohio.

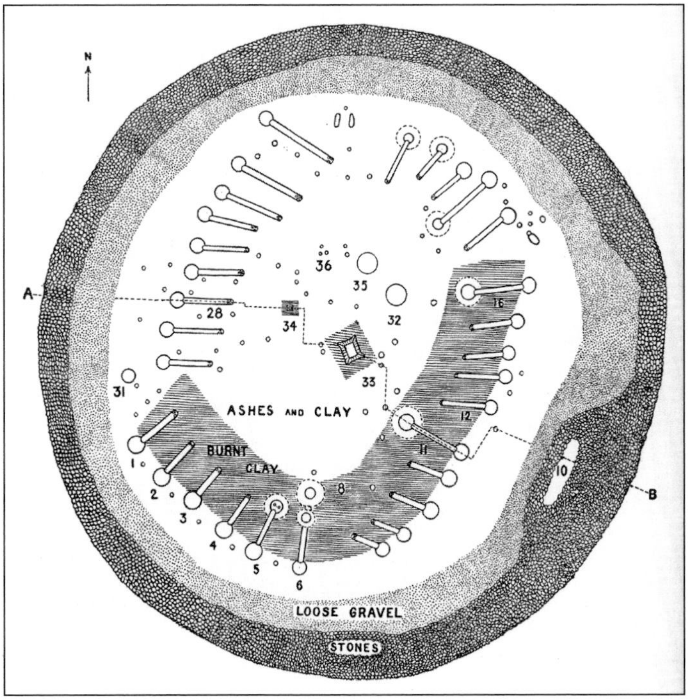

Metz reported the presence of five distinct soil layers resting on top of the "concrete" mound floor. From top to bottom these were a topsoil layer, clay

Fig. 4.49. Mound 3, Turner floor map (from Willoughby and Hooten 1922).

with specks of charcoal and ash, clay, a mixture of gravel and clay, and yellow clay with a thin covering of sand.

The wide stone wall on the eastern side of the mound was connected to a low vaulted stone chamber. Willoughby quoted from Metz's field notes:

> "When the stones were remove from its front side, an oblong oval-shaped recess was discovered filled with irregular layers of ashes, sand, and clay burned red, the lower stratum being of black ashes and charcoal, 2 to 4 inches [5–10 cm] in thickness and 18 inches [46 cm] in width. In this stratum many fragments of burnt bone were found, and resting on the ashes was a large marine shell with it open side up, and a carved piece of deer horn representing a species of fish.
>
> The cavity in which these were found was 30 inches [0.8 m] high, 2 feet [0.6 m] wide, and 10 feet [3.0 m] long. The layer of black ashes extended eastward 10 feet [3.0 m] beyond the arched cavity, into and between the layers of stone forming the wall.
>
> The floor of the recess was composed of three layers of large flat river stones, the top layer showing marked evidence of having been expose to the action of fire. The lowest of the three layers of stone which formed the covering of the recess was much burned, and the middle layer also showed evidence of direct contact with the fire. No flue or chimney was found leading from this recess.
>
> Below the stone floor of the recess was a bed of clay, 2 ft [0.6 m] wide, and 15 ft [4.5 m] in length. The wall extended but a short distance beyond the recess into the mound." (Willoughby and Hooton 1922: 35)

This stone funerary crypt was not the only unique feature found in Mound 3. Under the compact floor at the base of the mound, Metz discovered a complex system of pits and vents that were built around the perimeter of the mound under the large central altar. These unusual features were composed of vertical and horizontal tubes about 1 ft (0.3 m) in diameter and about 8 ft (2.4 m) long that connected somewhat larger pits with the floor of the mound. The horizontal tunnels and vertical chimneys were made of yellow clay. Where the chimneys opened on the surface of the mound floor, Metz noted they were "each covered with a hood of clay showing evidences of having come in contact with fire at their tops (Willoughby and Hooton 1922: 39)." Willoughby proposed that the tunnel and chimneys may have been used for storage, and he observes that the central hearth likely was built after the tunnels and flues were in place. The central altar in Mound 3 contained a massive deposit of artifacts, including some of the most detailed and impressive objects found in any Ohio Hopewell site.

Mound 3 was unique in both its elaborate construction and amazing content, but all of the mounds described from the Turner site appear to have been built over a compacted floor that almost certainly was part of a building. Post-holes are reported from many of the floors, but recognition of sub-mound structures was not a strength of the Peabody excavations. Mound 3 was part of a group of seven mounds that shared their stone perimeter wall with one or more mounds, and it seems likely that each of these mounds covered the floor of an important building. It would be very interesting to know if these were all contemporary of if they were built in succession to replace a building that had been decommissioned and covered by mantles of soil. This grouping of seven, almost conjoined mounds,

Fig. 4.50. Plan map of features under embankment wall at Turner (from Willoughby and Hooten 1922).

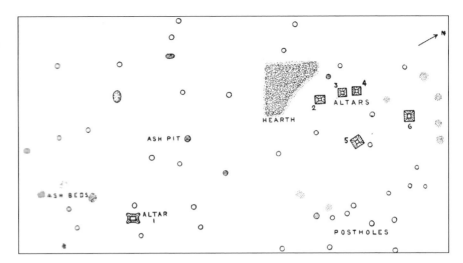

is very unusual (Greber 1996, 157). However, in the Scioto River, it is likely that conjoined mounds were enlarged into some of the truly giant mounds found at sites like the Hopewell Mound Group and Seip Earthworks.

In addition to mound and cemetery explorations, Charles Metz excavated a series of trenches parallel to the walls of the Great Enclosure. His trenches were just slightly wider than the width of the embankment wall. Metz excavated four trenches at various places in the enclosure wall, and unfortunately, if he recorded information about how the wall was constructed, Willoughby did not include it in his summary of the Peabody Museum research. What Willoughby did share is that everywhere Metz excavated he found the embankment wall covered a large number and series of features including hearths, ash beds, graves, clay altars, post-holes and large numbers of artifacts (Fig. 4.50). N'omi Greber (pers. comm. 2014) has commented that the field notes indicate that the features and artifacts were placed on a stone pavement, which in turn had been placed on a low earthen wall, and this low earthen wall covered a series of post-holes. Although Willoughby does not report the length of Trench C, it is reasonable to estimate from the length of the other trenches that Metz excavated about 600 ft (180 m) of the walls of the Great Enclosure. The density of features found under, and possibly within, the wall fill is remarkable in comparison to other Ohio Hopewell ceremonial constructed landscapes.

The features and artifacts in Trench A are particularly noteworthy. The trench was excavated in 1898 and was located just north of the Graded Way. The trench was 100 ft (30 m) long and 50 ft (15 m) wide, which was slightly wider than the embankment. At the base of the wall, excavators found 37 post-holes, a few small ash-beds and pits, six altars, and a large hearth built of flat limestone. Post-holes were 3–12 in (7.6–30.5 cm) in diameter and found at the base of the embankment, roughly 30 inches (76 cm) below the surface. The majority were 18–24 in (46–61 cm) deep and filled with dark earth mixed with ashes and charcoal. Several small ash beds were found at a depth of about 30 inches (76 cm) below the surface, and some of these may have been post-holes filled with ash. The small pits under the embankment in Trench A were filled with black soil, charcoal, ashes, potsherds, animal bones, and an occasional flake knife fragment.

A large triangular hearth made with flat limestone slabs was found only about 6 in (15 cm) below the surface. The soil around the limestone slabs was mixed with charcoal and ashes, and many of the slabs appeared to have been exposed to fire. Similar hearths were found in other parts of the embankment.

Six small clay altars were found only 6–7 in (15–18 cm) below the surface. Only two were deep enough to have escaped damage from plowing. Altar 1 was 36 × 25 in (91 × 64 cm) and contained ashes, perforated animal canine teeth, bone, copper beads, copper buttons, copper ear ornaments, shark teeth, flint blade, mica, and fragments of carved bone, all having been subjected to fire. The carved bone included two beautifully incised long bones with raptorial bird motifs. Both bones were human, one a femur and the other an ulna. These artifacts are highly stylized and have been the subject of recent iconographic and symbolic analysis (Carr and McCord 2013). Altar 5 was filled with ash, charcoal, burned bone, perforated shark teeth, 17 shell beads, 4 pearl beads, a broken projectile point, and fragments of bone and antler implements.

Willoughby suggests that a structure was present at this location prior to the construction of the embankment, possibly an earth-covered building. He believes the embankment may have subsequently covered a series of such structures, and notes that his interpretive model follows an earlier one offered by Lewis Henry Morgan (1881). Willoughby encouraged additional embankment wall excavations and recommended that his hypothesis should be tested at other earthwork sites.

The Turner Works is one of the most unusual and impressive of all the Ohio Hopewell ceremonial landscapes. As we have noted, recent studies of viewsheds associated with geometric enclosures suggest that the location and orientation of many of these sites may include views of and from surrounding topographic high points (Hively and Horn 2010; DeBoer 2010). At Turner and the Hopewell Mound Group near Chillicothe, enclosures and mounds are built on two different alluvial terrace surfaces with different elevations. The association of these two sites in two different drainage systems has generated considerable discussion and debate among archaeologists working in this region (Byers 2010).

Stubbs Earthwork

Although ignored by Squier and Davis in their landmark compendium of earthworks in the Mississippi River Valley, the Stubbs Earthwork (Fig. 4.35, B) was visited by Charles Whittlesey (1851) who provided a brief description and map of the geometric enclosure. Whittlesey did not appear to be overly impressed by the site and observed that it is generally similar to other Ohio earthen enclosure sites, except that Part D is built on a raised terrace that looks down on the remainder of the earthen construction. Whittlesey had apparently been told that the mound designated Part D on his map had some resemblance to the effigy mounds of Wisconsin. The land had been cultivated for a number of years when visited in 1839, but he could not see any resemblance to the effigy mounds of the north-west. Whittlesey described a very distinct graded way from the elevated plane to the river terrace, and most of the embankment walls were readily visible. He reports that his map was basically a sketch made without any measurements since he was surprised by a snow storm.

The Stubbs Earthwork is probably best described as a geometric enclosure consisting of a somewhat rectangular enclosure attached to a circular enclosure. Two pairs of long walls that may form an entrance to the site are present to the east, and Whittlesey noted that these were low but distinct. Within the enclosure are two mounds, two arched semi-circular walls, and the supposed effigy figure. In 1837 the walls of the large rectangular enclosure were low and without ditches. Like many of the great enclosures of southern Ohio that were described in mid-19th century accounts like Squier and Davis (1848) or Whittlesey (1851), further attention to Stubbs Earthwork would wait for many years.

Robert Genheimer (1997) of the Cincinnati Museum of Natural History conducted an intensive survey of the area around the Stubbs Earthworks in 1979–80. He recorded more than two dozen Middle Woodland sites in the vicinity of the earthworks and noted that this was the first research at the site since Whittlesey had visited there in 1839.

In 1998 and 1999, Genheimer, Frank Cowan, Ted Sunderhaus, and a large number of volunteers returned to Stubbs to conduct salvage excavations prior to the construction of a new school. The team excavated nearly 4000 sq m mostly in areas outside the earthworks. They discovered a large number of Middle Woodland buildings and found evidence for very intensive use. Of particular importance, they discovered the presence of a giant circle of posts that can only represent a wooden ceremonial architecture. This discovery by itself made Hopewell archaeologists reconsider their ideas regarding the large earthen ceremonial landscapes and how they may have been built and used. The primary contribution of the work conducted at the Stubbs Earthwork is about the features, artifacts, and the activities that produced them. They will be discussed in greater detail in Chapter 5.

5

What do we know about Hopewell ceremonial landscapes?

In the last two to three decades, considerable research has been conducted on Ohio Hopewell ceremonial landscapes. This research is very diverse and ranges from studies that examine how the landscapes were built, to those that try to explain why they were built in a specific place and to a specific configuration and orientation. Unfortunately, much of this work remains unpublished or unassimilated into the literature, making it difficult for scholars to assess the data that are available. However, considering the large number of sites that were built between AD 1 and AD 450 in southern Ohio, only a very small number of these sites have received more than cursory attention from the archaeological community. What we know about the age, construction, and use of the great Hopewell ceremonial centers is extrapolated from the limited research that has been conducted at a small number of sites.

The relative proportion of investigated sites is also sadly limited. Testing has produced some data from a handful of sites in the Scioto–Paint Creek region and in south-west Ohio, but there is very little data from large and important sites like Newark and Marietta in the Muskingum River drainage. In the previous chapter we reviewed the data from sites in these regions that raise questions like are the differences in construction methods due to different building strategies by different societies, or do these differences represent technological changes that evolved though time?

The development of geoarchaeological and geophysical methods has provided the necessary procedures to investigate large constructed Hopewell landscapes more effectively. However, despite the availability of these new and highly effective methods, answering some of the most basic questions about the construction of Hopewell landscapes cannot be accomplished in a single field season or through limited testing projects. Most of what we have learned about the construction of Ohio Hopewell landscapes is derived from the work of scholars who have devoted long-term and persistent commitments to examining and interpreting the data from one or two sites.

Robert Riordan has spent nearly two decades investigating how the Pollock Works near Dayton, Ohio were built. His careful and persistent study has provided clear evidence that the embankments forming this hilltop enclosure evolved through time. Riordan's excavations suggest that the nature and purpose of the embankments and associated wooden stockade wall changed several times during the roughly two centuries the site was in use. The excavations produced evidence for major fires, which have also been reported at several other hilltop enclosures in south-west Ohio (Riordan 1996). Traditional interpretations that hilltop enclosures were defensive can point to this information as evidence for warfare in the Hopewell era. While Riordan does not rule out this possibility, he notes that after the Pollock Earthworks palisade was burned, the earth and stone walls were repaired and the enclosure again seems to have assumed its ceremonial function. The unequivocal evidence from the Pollock Works, much as we have argued for the Hopeton Earthworks, strongly suggests that the local society that built and modified the landscape at Pollock was stable and committed to this important ceremonial center for quite a few generations.

As discussed in Chapter 3, nearly a decade of research at the Hopeton Earthworks has also produced an important set of data about how that ceremonial landscape was constructed. Through the use of geophysical and geoarchaeological studies in association with strategic archaeological excavations, there is strong evidence that as much as 40 acres (16 ha) comprising the two largest enclosures, plus the two "sacred circles" along the eastern wall of the rectangular enclosure, were subjected to removal of the A-horizon prior to the beginning of any earthen wall construction. The embankment walls were then built from subsoil quarried from within the two larger enclosures. The Hopeton Earthworks Project succeeded because the investigators followed a long-term research plan, and employed a multidisciplinary approach to answering questions about the construction of the ceremonial landscape.

Through the combined work of this author, James Brown, and a team of archaeologists, geophysicists, and geoarchaeologists at Mound City, we have also collected evidence of substantial surface preparation prior to earthen landmark construction. Although the Mound City study is still ongoing, there is strong evidence that the area within the enclosure wall was heavily stripped before any mounds were built. In places at Mound City, more than 0.5 m of the upper soil profile appears to have been removed. It is unclear where this large quantity of soil may have been redeposited. It is also apparent from radiometric and stratigraphic evidence that the embankment wall and associated borrow pits were likely the last landscape features constructed at Mound City. The evidence from Mound City, like the data from Hopeton and Pollock, suggests the site was used for multiple centuries. This implies it was built, maintained, and expanded by a stable local society. This does not, however, imply continuous or constant use by Hopewell people. At Mound City and most large Hopewell ceremonial sites, activities such as mound or embankment construction or augmentation, dances, games, rituals, burials, and ceremonies were likely episodic. Some activities may have been annual, seasonal, or scheduled by celestial events. The main point here is that the construction and use of at least some of these large Hopewell sites spanned multiple generations, but use of the sites was not constant.

Before we review the evidence associated with the construction of the various Hopewell ceremonial landscapes, it is important to remember that Hopewell sites, features, and artifacts may be characterized as diverse and unique. While there are certainly similarities in the sizes of the different geometric enclosures, the great variety of shapes and forms that were used in different combinations implies that the builders made a concerted effort to create unique and lasting monuments. Due to this very heavy emphasis on creating unique forms, we must be cautious in simply extrapolating what may have been learned at Pollock, Hopeton, or Mound City to other similar ceremonial sites in the region. We have learned a great deal about how the Hopewell people built the large ceremonial landscapes that characterize the Middle Woodland period in southern Ohio, but each site is unique and each society that built one of these landscapes was autonomous. Ruby *et al.* (2005) make a strong argument that the density of large earthen enclosures in the central Scioto River valley makes it unlikely that each site was built and maintained by a separate group of people. Their argument that communities were organized at several levels represents the best explanation for the current data in this area. Participation in the Hopewell Interaction Sphere likely signals participation in a shared ideology or belief system, but it does not imply hereditary leadership or political controls. This raises the question, just how did small-scale tribal societies manage to build and maintain so many ceremonial landscapes in the southern Ohio region during the period AD 1 to about AD 450?

Constructed landscapes, site preparation and planning

Even a cursory look at the *Archaeological Atlas of Ohio*, compiled by William C. Mills and published in 1914, makes it apparent that there were a large number of mounds and earthen enclosures in southern Ohio. We have already noted that the two largest concentrations occur in the Scioto–Paint Creek region of south-central Ohio and in the rugged hilly region of south-west Ohio. For more than a century the archaeological literature has been absorbed with hypotheses and ideas about how these giant landscapes were used. Recently, scholars have turned their attention to the questions concerning how were the locations for these sites selected, and how were individual landscapes built?

How were sites selected for landscape construction? Were localities chosen to highlight alignments with the heavens, local landmarks, or other sites? Papers by William Romain (2004), Ray Hively and Robert Horn (2010), and Warren DeBoer (2010) have noted that whether they are viewed individually or in groups, the large ceremonial landscapes seem to align to different features of the Hopewell world. Thus far, the careful analysis conducted by Hively and Horn for Newark, High Bank and sites in the central Scioto region appear to be the most convincing in revealing patterns of construction related to celestial events and site interconnections. However, the shared ideas of these scholars serve to raise the very important question: if sites were placed in specific locations and planned to align or orient toward other sites in the Scioto River Valley, was there a grand plan from which the locations for individual earthen monuments were selected? This implies a level of social organization and leadership that is more centralized and structured than anything currently being proposed for Ohio Hopewell societies today. Lacking temporal control over the start and end of construction for virtually all of these sites makes evaluation of these larger, more centralized hypotheses difficult. It does not eliminate the growing impression that the locations for individual Hopewell ceremonial landscapes were not randomly selected.

Throughout this discussion, we have attempted to emphasize how little data exist pertaining to how Hopewell earthen landscapes were constructed. Most of what we know comes from efforts at a few sites. In the Scioto–Paint Creek region, we have fairly comprehensive data from the Hopeton Earthworks and useful information from High Bank, Anderson, Mound City, Seip, Shriver Circle, and the Hopewell Mound Group. The available data from these sites indicate that soil stripping was an important element of site preparation and planning, with the A horizon and upper B horizon being scraped away and removed from under the areas where walls were later built. Data from Hopeton, High Bank, and Mound City, where investigations have been conducted to discover how the landscape was built, indicate that the soil scraping was more extensive and likely involved all areas that were eventually included within the major enclosures. Could this have been accomplished in small pieces, with builders stripping an area and then building on top of it before moving on to the next segment of the landscape? It certainly could, but in almost any construction scenario that is proposed, it seems likely that the plan and alignment of the earthen walls had to have been established before large-scale construction began. We must also remember that the construction of large enclosures required large landforms, and the alluvial terraces of southern Ohio were heavily forested. At least some forest-clearing must have been done in association with the design and laying-out of large enclosures, unless they were constructed in pre-existing clearings, natural or otherwise, that were already occupied at least on a seasonal basis. Such a scenario has recently been discussed in relation to the Neolithic of southern England (Allen and Gardiner 2012).

A. Martin Byers (1987; 2004) and Warren DeBoer (1997) proposed that large circular enclosures developed from the smaller Adena sacred circles and both of these preceded the construction of rectangular enclosures. Byers (2004) used the Hopeton Earthworks as his example for this seriation of enclosure forms. He based his sequence on the maps published in Squier and Davis (1848). Test trenches excavated at Hopeton in the only point where the two large enclosures intersect have been described in Chapter 3. Those trenches failed to show any evidence for overlapping construction and, in fact, revealed soil strata that would have been part of both large earthen features, which suggests they were likely built about the same time. There is nothing in the radiocarbon evidence from wall construction at Hopeton to suggest the large circle preceded the rectangular enclosure. The current evidence, which of course may change with additional research, suggests the large enclosure features and parallel walls were planned and built in segments over 4–6 generations. It is certainly possible that either large geometric enclosure was built first and partially dismantled to accommodate construction of the other large enclosure. However, current radiocarbon and stratigraphic evidence do not support this scenario.

Would this sequence still have appeared logical if the more accurate geophysical maps being produced today were available? What if they had known that the area under both of the large Hopeton enclosures had been stripped of topsoil? Hindsight is always better, but certainly even the limited data that are now available shed different light on our assumptions and interpretations about these prehistoric landscapes.

Considerable research is still needed to determine if the vast scale of soil stripping observed at the Hopeton Earthworks was applied at other sites in the Scioto–Paint Creek region. The limited testing at Mound City suggests that soil profiles in both the areas under and between the mounds have been heavily truncated by topsoil removal. Could this have been a part of the building of the much larger centers like the Hopewell Mound Group, Seip, Baum, and Liberty? Is it really possible that all the sites in the Scioto–Paint Creek region were prepared in this manner? This changes the calculations for labor required to accomplish construction by a significant degree. It also impacts estimates for the length of time involved in landscape construction and the number of people needed to accomplish the work. More data will be needed from a wider number of sites to seriously test these hypotheses. The research approach used at Hopeton could certainly be implemented at these sites too, but until we have more data these interpretive ideas remain hypothetical.

In south-west Ohio, the evidence for preparation of the surface of individual ceremonial landscapes is less apparent. The best construction data from this region is derived from Riordan's work at Pollock, and the excavations of Morgan, Essenpries, and Connolly at Fort Ancient. At these sites, investigators found some soil had been added to the original land surface prior to construction, but no large scale soil stripping has been reported. Fischer (1965) reported the presence of an intact A horizon at the base of the embankment wall at Miami Fort, and the wall excavations at the Turner Earthwork exposed a high density of features, many of which contained important ceremonial objects or prestige goods (Willoughby and Hooten 1922). The construction of an earthen wall over a large number of ceremonial features is unique to sites in south-west Ohio. Connolly (Seig and Connolly 1997; Connolly 1998) also reported that sections of walls at Fort Ancient were built over features from earlier activities at the site, but these were hardly as impressive as the ones recorded at Turner.

At the Newark Earthworks, the only effort to examine wall construction revealed that the embankment forming the Fairground Circle was built on top of a well established soil (Lepper 2010). While this represents fairly limited data from the many potential kilometers of walls at Newark, it does at least suggest that the extensive site preparations that have been observed in the Scioto–Paint Creek area were not utilized in the building of Newark. Brad Lepper (2010) has suggested that Newark may have been built in a single human lifespan, and that might have been possible if the more extensive site preparation steps had not been used for the giant earthworks here and sufficient numbers of people were available.

Although our current evidence is far from definitive, it does suggest that monument building and landscape construction differed to some extent from Newark to the Scioto–Paint Creek and into south-west Ohio. Are these differences due to time? Radiocarbon is not sufficiently accurate to identify the specific decade in which a feature was built, but there seems to be sufficient overlap in the radiocarbon dates to assume that at least some of the landscape construction in these three regions was contemporary. If that is correct, then it seems likely that the differences that have been observed in site preparation were due to local cultural preferences for appropriate practices. Local autonomy could also help explain the wide degree of variation that is observed in the materials and methods used to build the visible earthen features of these landscapes.

Material selection and the placement of material: art or engineering?

In Chapters 3 and 4 we reviewed the available data on the materials that were used in building embankment walls at a number of different sites across southern Ohio. Although detailed soil analysis has only been conducted for a limited number of these investigations, it is apparent that, in almost all cases, embankment walls were built with materials that were locally available. Certainly it is likely that, in some important locations or features, soils or rock from non-local settings were incorporated into the embankment. However, of the sites that have been studied to date, there is no real evidence that builders ventured great distances to obtain building materials. In the Scioto–Paint Creek area, soils used in wall construction are generally available within a few hundred meters or less from the location where they were eventually placed as fills. The limestone used in the hilltop enclosures of south-west Ohio is available along the sides of the mesas on which the landscapes were built. This does not imply that it did not take great effort to obtain these materials.

Although the builders may not have travelled great distances to obtain the materials they used for landscape construction, they did demonstrate a good knowledge of the properties of the building materials they chose to use for specific features and purposes. In Chapter 3 we noted that in most of the places examined at the Hopeton Earthworks, the earthen walls were built with homogeneous materials that had been carefully selected and placed. Builders used caution to avoid mixing two types of soil materials, and while multiple layers of material were observed in every wall cross-section that was examined, the boundaries between the different soils were sharp and distinct even after nearly 2000 years. Soils with reddish colors tended to be used on the outer side of the enclosure wall, but not in all circumstances. Similar patterns have been observed at other sites in the Scioto–Paint Creek area, and attention to material selection and care in placing those materials is also reflected in the trench profile that was excavated across the Fairground Circle wall at Newark (Lepper 2005; 2010).

Soil selection and placement at the hilltop enclosures in south-west Ohio seems to be more individualistic in terms of actual construction. All of these sites use some combination of soil and stone to form the walls, and in several instances larger stone slabs were placed on the walls to anchor soil, inhibit erosion, or both. Moorehead (1890; 1908) reported major use of some stone in construction of parts of the Fort Ancient enclosure. Builders of the Pollock Works used soil, stone, and wood for a palisade or fence during different construction of the various phases identified by Riordan (2010a). At virtually all of these sites, wall construction appears to have been done in stages. There is some evidence, particularly at Fort Ancient and Pollock, that construction sometimes paused long enough for a natural soil to form on the embankment wall. Wall builders then covered those soils with materials from the next building phase. Placement of all of these building materials along the precipitous edges of these hilltop landforms demonstrates considerable skill and knowledge of materials and geo-engineering principles.

The use of specialized soils to stabilize constructed slopes and possibly inhibit plant growth or hold water can be seen in many places among these constructed landscapes. Clay-rich soils were used to line the ditches that penetrated into outwash gravels at the base of alluvial terraces at the Shriver Circle (Picklesimer *et al.* 2006) and the Hopewell Mound Group (Lynott 2006). Clay-rich soil was also used to line the borrow pit at Mound City where they penetrated into the same underlying sands and gravels (Lynott *et al.* 2010; Benson 2012). The selection and use of these materials in these situations demonstrate excellent knowledge of the geo-engineering properties of the soils, but also a desire to build monumental features that were intended to last through time. At several hilltop enclosures, the use of large blocks of limestone and then infilling between them with soil and stone rubble may also have been designed to create a lasting and permanent architectural feature. Less durable architectural features have been noted in the form of palisade walls, post-circles, and wooden great houses. Most sub-mound buildings reported from Hopewell contexts in Ohio tend to have been dismantled before they were covered by the various soil layers that eventually formed the mound. Quite a few mounds were built over log crypts, however, at the Hazlett Mound on Flint Ridge (Mills 1921), excavations revealed a substantial stone wall or crypt that formed the core of the mound.

At this point, our knowledge about the range of materials used in landscape construction and the purpose of their placement is limited and definitely biased by the few places where more intensive studies have been conducted. One thing is clear in the building of the various monumental landscapes. Builders used a wide range of materials and demonstrated knowledge of the properties of those materials in their placement. This is not at all surprising, because people in Eastern North America had been constructing earthen monuments for several millennia prior to the beginning of the Hopewell building era (Gibson 2000; Ortmann and Kidder 2012; Saunders *et al.* 2005).

Landscape features – unique and diverse

One thing that all the constructed ceremonial landscapes associated with Ohio Hopewell have in common is the construction of monumental earthen features. In some instances, these are simply mounds (e.g. Chillicothe North-west Group). In other instances, they are earthen enclosures without mounds (Hopeton and High Bank). Some sites combine these features and include a vast array of additional features ranging from ditches or borrow pits, to post-circles, pavements, and palisades. We must almost certainly expect that, like more recent North American Indians, the people of the Hopewell era likely built a wide range of smaller and less permanent shrines and ceremonial features that have been destroyed or obscured by the forces of nature and modern historic activities. The discussion in this volume has devoted considerable attention to the *process* of building the large earthen enclosure walls. Some further mention of the other types of features found within these ceremonial landscapes seems appropriate.

Long parallel walls or processional ways have been recorded at Newark, Hopeton, Fort Ancient, Portsmouth, and several other sites. These must have been important landscape features and whether they were formal entrances or served some other functions in uncertain. We have noted that Bradley Lepper (2006) has proposed that one of these, which he calls the Great Hopewell Road, was built to connect the concentration of ceremonial landscapes in the Scioto–Paint Creek region with the largest Hopewell landscape ever built, at Newark. While this hypothesis cannot be confirmed or denied at this time, the presence of these parallel walls as potential routeways cannot be ignored.

Mounds are the best known and most basic of all earthen monuments, and studies across the Eastern United States are demonstrating that they are important elements of prehistoric constructed landscapes. Ohio Hopewell mounds tend to be conical in form, but they also occur in a very diverse range of shapes and size, including elongated, flat-topped pyramidal, conjoined, and possibly even effigy mounds. None of the mounds built by Hopewell people in the Ohio Valley rivals the giant Mississippian mounds, like Monk's Mound at Cahokia in East St Louis, IL. However, Mound 25 at the Hopewell Mound Group, the Seip-Pricer mound at the Seip Earthworks, the Edwin Harness mound at the Liberty Earthworks, and the Mount Vernon mound and the largest mound at the Mann site in Indiana are massive constructions by any form of measurement. It must always be recalled that the Hopewell mounds appear to have been built with a great deal of care by small-scale societies that lacked the higher population density that was common in later Mississippian societies.

Most Ohio Hopewell mounds tend to occur as part of a group of mounds or in association with an earthen enclosure. Although they vary greatly in size, form, and content, mounds represent monumental earthen construction. Most Ohio Hopewell mounds are earthen covers over the remains of dismantled ceremonial buildings. Early excavations paid little attention to the patterns of post-holes that were found on the floors beneath mounds and focused recovery and recording efforts on the impressive deposits of mortuary and ceremonial artifacts that were buried there. It did not take archaeologists long to recognize that the vast majority of artifacts and features they sought were buried at the base of Ohio Hopewell mounds and not in the mantles of soil that covered these deposits. Consequently, these early excavations often paid little attention to the different soil layers that comprised the mound itself.

There are some exceptions, such as the early and very rough profiles provided by Squier and Davis (1848), showing the different strata they encountered within the mounds they excavated and reported. These drawings are very crude and it is almost certain that fine strata and subtle changes in soils went unnoticed. More careful recording of mound structure appears in the excavations conducted by the Peabody Museum at Harvard at the Turner Group in the late 19th century. Mound profiles reported by Willoughby and Hooton (1922) include substantial detail and depict many construction layers and fine strata. However, N'omi Greber, who has carefully studied the records from the Turner Earthworks, advises that the unpublished fieldnotes offer a more accurate account of the strata (Greber, pers. comm. 2014). Mills (1922) spent little time addressing the strata of the mound remnants he encountered after Camp Sherman closed and the site became available for excavations in 1920. However, he does illustrate the basal strata of Mound 18 where at least four and possibly five fine gravel strata are visible in the mound profile photograph (Fig. 5.1).

Virtually every mound, for which there is construction data, appears to have been built in two or more stages. The careful selection and placement of fills to add successive soil mantles must have some important ritual or ceremonial meaning. Virtually all Hopewell scholars recognize that the features and artifacts found under and at the base of mounds are ritually charged and reflect important ceremonial and ritual activities. James A. Brown (2012) has suggested that the mounds and their contents may be like important ceremonial bundles, and activities conducted at or around a mound may necessitate that it be mantled with earthen material, much like a ceremonial bundle is carefully wrapped in a very specific manner after its contents have been used in a ceremony or ritual.

Most Hopewell mounds seem to be an accumulation of individual layers of earthen mantle, and the interpretation offered by Brown is the best explanation for these activities offered to date. However, at this point it is uncertain how often different soil mantles were added to mounds. Could these have been added in association with seasonal ceremonies, yearly ceremonies, or even lunar cycles? At this point there is little evidence to refine this interpretation. The time spans between mantling episodes cannot be too long, because no evidence of soil formation on any of these layers has been reported from Ohio mounds. However, we must note that early mound excavation methods and lack of interest in structure may have led early excavators to fail to recognize subtle soil layers buried deeply within a mound. At Cotiga Mound in West Virginia, investigators recognized ten lithological

Fig. 5.1. Mound 18 at Mound City is exposed in profile under Camp Sherman barracks building. Five construction layers are clearly visible with thin sand layers separating darker layers of loam (photo courtesy of (photo courtesy of the Ohio History Connection and Hopewell Culture National Historical Park).

strata, with the first nine representing stages in mound construction (Cremeens *et al.* 1997). Micromorphological analysis indicates that the interfaces between individual basket-load layers display sharp, irregular contacts with very little evidence of pedoturbation, which likely reflects rapid construction (Cremeens 2004). Since most Ohio Hopewell mounds were excavated well before such contemporary geoarchaeological methods were developed, it is uncertain how these results might compare to the few sites where internal mound construction data was recorded.

The use of large gravel and small cobbles to cap some Hopewell mounds in Ohio may indicate that ceremonial activities that led to successive soil mantle layers had been completed. At Mound City, Squier and Davis (1848) reported deep layers of gravel, from 12–20 in (0.3–0.5 m) in thickness, covering Mound 7 and most of the other larger mounds at the site. Remnants of those cobble layers are still present, even after destruction and reconstruction, as rings around the periphery of the mounds, which are visible in geophysical survey data and have been confirmed in test excavations (Fig. 5.2). Examination of these cobbles show that individual clasts range from golf balls to softballs in size. The larger gravels and cobbles at Mound City Mound 7 were likely hand selected from poorly sorted outwash deposits in the nearby Scioto River valley.

Mills (1909a) recorded large quantities of gravel surrounding the Seip Mound, and Shetrone and Greenman (1931) reported similar gravel covering at the Seip-Pricer mound. Shetrone and Greenman (1931) recorded that a gravel covering was on the initial mound that mantled the sub-mound structure and other features. This initial mound was later covered by large amounts of earth and then covered with the final gravel cap. Seip-Pricer, which is one of the largest of all Ohio Hopewell mounds, had a ring of limestone slabs set vertically around its base, presumably to help anchor the gravel layer on the mound surface. Shetrone (1926) recorded significant deposits of large gravel with Mound 25 at the Hopewell Mound Group (Fig. 5.3). It seems reasonable to assume that if the gravel was the final mantling or wrapping of a mound, it likely meant that regular construction ceremonies at the mound were concluded. Few Ohio Hopewell mounds exhibit layers of gravel of

Left: **Fig. 5.2.** Squier and Davis reported the larger mounds at Mound City were covered by a thick layer of gravel. Excavations at Mound 7 in 2011 and, here, in 2012 exposed remnants of the gravel, which are more like cobbles, in a ring or halo around the perimeter of the mound (photo: author).

Right: **Fig. 5.3.** Gravel deposits Mound 25, Hopewell Mound Group (photo: author).

this size in any location except as the cap resting on the final surface of the mound. Several mounds at Fort Ancient were covered with stone slabs, which is probably the Little Miami drainage equivalent of capping a mound with large cobbles.

It is unclear how many mounds once existed in southern Ohio. Most of the larger mounds were recognized and recorded by the various survey programs of the Ohio Historical Society by 1910 (Mills 1914). However, many smaller mounds were likely plowed down by early agriculture before any systematic effort was launched to record these prehistoric landscape features. Due largely to the extremely impressive funerary remains and features found beneath them, Ohio Hopewell mounds have become the popular symbol for this important prehistoric manifestation.

Details of mound structure, materials used in mound construction, and number of layers used in construction are highly variable within and between sites. This is very likely further evidence that, while Ohio Hopewell people shared a common general ideology, local people were very autonomous and individualistic in their interpretation of rituals, ceremonies, and in the construction of earthen monuments and landscapes.

Early descriptions of ditches associated with embankment walls and borrow pits associated with mounds and other landscape features made the assumption that these prehistoric excavations were quarries rather than landscape features. More recent research involving North American Indian belief systems suggests that these features were likely used to separate sacred space from the more secular world. Robert Hall (1997) has provided substantial documentation for the incorporation of symbols and belief systems in all aspects of the archaeological record, and some of these symbols likely served to link societies throughout the Hopewell Interaction Sphere.

Many early writers speculated that embankment walls were built as fortifications and may have also included timber palisades to make them even more formidable barriers. As the interpretation of these large landscape features shifted away from defensive constructions, less attention was paid to possible wooden features that may have been part of the ceremonial landscape. Recent discoveries and increasing use of geophysical survey is raising interest in wooden constructions that were dismantled, decomposed, or covered by larger earthen features.

We have already mentioned in Chapter 4 the discovery of the Great Post Circle at the Stubbs Earthwork (Cowan and Genheimer 2010). Review of current and former excavation combined with geophysical survey has raised the possibility of a similar but smaller post-circle at the Seip Earthworks (Spielmann and Burks 2011). We must also recall that excavations at the Pollock Works have shown that a palisade wall of large timbers was built during one stage in the landscape history (Riordan 2006). Considering the large expanses of constructed landscape that have received little or no archaeological attention to date, it seems highly likely that additional timber-built features will be discovered in the years ahead. One final timber-built element deserves mention at this point, specifically the wooden buildings that have been found under many Hopewell mounds. These wooden buildings certainly served a variety of ceremonial purposes and they may have been important elements of the landscape for several decades before they were dismantled and covered by earthen mounds. Particularly prominent among these pre-mound constructions were large

Clockwise from top left:
Fig. 5.4. The Harness Mound was partially excavated by Frederick W. Putnam, followed by W. K. Moorehead and then W. C. Mills. This photo of excavations under Mills show how little attention was being paid to the structure of the mound (photo courtesy of the Ohio History Connection).

Fig. 5.5. Aerial view of the Harness Mound showing the Great House excavated by N'omi Greber (photo courtesy of Cleveland Museum of Natural History).

Fig. 5.6. Stone pavement exposed by Warren K. Moorehead near Twin Mounds on the east exterior of the New Fort, Fort Ancient (photo courtesy of the Ohio History Connection).

wooden Great Houses that have been found in association with the largest of the Ohio Hopewell mounds. The best-known Great House structure was excavated and reported by N'omi Greber (1983a) from beneath the Edwin Harness mound (Figs 5.4 and 5.5). These and other wooden structures must have been impressive and important elements at virtually all of the Ohio Hopewell ceremonial landscape sites.

One additional type of landscape feature deserves mention. During excavations at Fort Ancient, Warren K. Moorehead (1890) encountered a substantial pavement of limestone slabs at the western end of parallel walls where they meet the Twin Mounds. The pavement was built of slabs, roughly 12 × 6 in and 2.5 in thick (30 × 15 × 6.3 cm) that had been set on top of a clay surface. Fine gravel had been put between the stones to cover an area of at least 130 × 500 ft (39.5 × 152.4 m) between the Twin Mounds and parallel walls (Fig. 5.6). The pavement was covered by about 12 in (30 cm) of soil. A stone pavement has also been discovered in association with the entrance to the Moorehead Circle at Fort Ancient. While this is certainly the most impressive of all the hilltop enclosures in southwest Ohio, it seems quite possible that future research will identify similar features at other Hopewell sites. Clay floors, stone pavements and wooden architecture were likely important structural elements of most Ohio Hopewell ceremonial landscapes.

Time and landscape construction

The earthen monuments that were built in southern Ohio by the people of the Middle Woodland period cannot be fully understood without developing a more precise chronology for their construction and use. The work at the Hopeton Earthworks has demonstrated that these sites were carefully planned and constructed, and built by several generations of people. Considering the planned characteristics of individual mounds and earthen enclosures, it seems likely that one or more of these monumental earthen features may have been linked into a larger cultural landscape. Unfortunately, any chronological relationship between sites is at this time largely hypothetical. Every issue relating to the construction and use of Ohio Hopewell ceremonial landscapes is in some way tied to problems with intra-site and inter-site chronology, relationships and associations.

Only two sites have sufficient direct dates from ceremonial landscape features to begin to discuss when construction started and how long it continued. The data from Hopeton and Pollock provide strong evidence that construction occurred over multiple generations. While radiocarbon dates alone might be enough to support this conclusion, there is also good geoarchaeological data from Pollock and Fort Ancient, where construction ceased long enough for a soil horizon to develop on the wall. At this point it is uncertain how much time had elapsed while these soils were forming but the shallow soils were eventually covered by fills from succeeding wall stages. While these minor points may seem somewhat trivial, they undermine interpretive models that suggest the great Hopewell ceremonial landscapes were built relatively quickly and then left unaltered. While it is still possible that some enclosure walls were built quite rapidly, we must note that almost every wall that has been examined in Ohio shows evidence of being built in two or more stages. There was definitely a distinct process to wall construction, and it may have been at least as important as the final earthen landmark itself (Bernardini 2004).

In his comprehensive model of the Ohio Hopewell era, Martin Byers (2004) has argued that the builders of ceremonial earthwork centers lived by what he calls the principle of sacred earth. Byers argues that once a basket of soil has been put in place as part of the construction of a sacred monumental features (mound or wall), then that soil could not be modified. He does say that mound-building principles might have permitted the earth to be covered by additional earth, but a wall or mound cannot be altered or removed. Once again, there is some evidence at Pollock and Hopeton that this behavioral assumption is not always supported by archaeological evidence.

In the situation at Hopeton, we noted that Trench 4 through the north-east corner of the rectangular enclosure exposed two separate features that have been radiocarbon dated to about AD 1000. While it is often fashionable in archaeology to dismiss such dates due to contamination or laboratory error, this would not be logical in this instance. First, it will be recalled that the samples that were dated were found in two distinctly different parts of the wall and they are two very different types of features. Second, the radiocarbon results from the two samples only differ from each other by 10 radiocarbon years, making them internally consistent and statistically indistinguishable. Finally, these dates are not the only evidence that people were present and creating another phase of the archaeological record at this point in time. Temporally diagnostic projectile points from this time period have been found in excavated contexts and on the surface at the site, and features with comparable radiocarbon results have been excavated at the Red Wing and Triangle sites immediately south-east of the large enclosures.

Riordan's (1995; 2006) work at the Pollock Works provides the most convincing evidence for changes to the height, configuration, and likely purpose of the enclosure wall over time. Over about three centuries, successive soil layers were added to the barrier wall raising the wall from 1.3 m to 3.0 m in height and widening the base of the wall by 10+ m. Riordan identified three stages of construction in the barrier wall, but they did not change the basic character of the enclosure or its shape. At the north end of the barrier wall where it meets the perimeter wall, excavations revealed evidence of a burned stockade on the original ground surface in one locality and on top of the embankment soil in another. Riordan considers the construction of the stockade as evidence for a shift in the use of the enclosure from ritual to defense. He estimates the stockade was 4–5 m tall on the bluff and 2 m high on the barrier wall. Post-holes are about 0.5 m apart and were tied together with horizontally woven branches. Daub covered the bottom 2 m of the wall. Riordan believes the stockade was deliberately burned and covered by soil along the perimeter embankment. The central gateway into the enclosure was paved with carefully fitted stones to form a flat surfaced ramp. Riordan's excavations revealed two large post-holes from the stockade under this pavement, and both posts appear to have been pulled when the stockade was burned and dismantled.

The possibility that people may have modified, altered, or repaired these giant earthen monuments as much as six to eight centuries after they were originally built has obvious implications for research aimed at the identification and interpretation of original wall alignments and purpose. While the evidence for modification of enclosure walls over time is limited, we must emphasize again that our knowledge about ceremonial landscape constructions is also still very limited. More research is needed to learn whether the evidence from Hopeton and Pollock represent anomalies, or whether they are more typical of all the large ceremonial landscapes of the Hopewell era.

How were ceremonial landscapes used?

The large earthen enclosures and their associated landscapes appear to have been multi-functional places where people perhaps met for games, ceremonies, rituals, trade, or to share news. Based upon the vast amount of energy that was needed to build these large and complex centers, it is likely that the construction and subsequent use of the landscapes involved non-local populations. Regularly scheduled events may have led to mate-exchange agreements and other social mechanisms that linked various groups across the Ohio Valley and possibly across much of Eastern North America. While these small-scale societies may have been linked by common ideologies or belief systems, their local autonomy is clearly visible in the great diversity seen in landscape construction and the features associated with the large enclosures. Perhaps this is best illustrated by a discussion of some recent research.

Ritual refuse pits at the Riverside site, Hopewell Mound Group

The Riverside site (33Ro1059) is located immediately south of the square enclosure at the Hopewell Mound Group between the North Fork Paint Creek and an abandoned railway line that has been converted to a bike trail. The site is situated on a high terrace that is being eroded by the northward migration of a meander loop of North Fork Paint Creek. In 2006 National Park Service archaeologists under the direction of Ann Bauermeister conducted excavations along North Fork Paint Creek to mitigate the potential damage to the archaeological site by the active erosion of the creek.

As we have seen, the Hopewell Mound Group has received considerable attention since it was featured prominently in Squier and Davis's (1848) landmark book. Subsequent intensive excavation by Warren K. Moorehead in 1891–92 gave the site considerable notoriety. Henry C. Shetrone (1926) spent parts of several years conducting more intensive and extensive excavations. While all of these early studies focused heavily on the excavation of mounds, they also identified non-mound features that documented that the archaeological record at Hopewell Mound Group included more than simply mounds and earthen walls.

Mark Seeman (1981a) conducted an extensive survey of the Hopewell Mound Group and surrounding lands, and William Dancey (1991) conducted another survey aimed at the catchment area surrounding the famous mound group. Jennifer Pederson Weinberger (2007) conducted an intensive geophysical survey and some limited testing inside the enclosure to better understand the non-mound areas of the site. None of these studies identified any strong evidence for a large village associated with the Hopewell Mound Group, but they did identify sites and features that were likely important in understanding how this famous site was used.

The Pederson Weinberger study randomly selected eighteen 40 × 40 m units within the enclosures which did not contain any mound remnants. Each of these grid blocks was surveyed using magnetic and soil resistivity instruments. In association with the geophysical surveys, Pederson-Weinberger also excavated nine shovel tests for each 40 × 40 m grid block. A total of 155 shovel tests were completed and artifacts were found in 122 of these units. Using this combination of techniques, and excavating test units at selected anomalies identified in the geophysical surveys, considerable non-mound data from inside the large enclosure was recovered. Particularly noteworthy was the discovery of a previously unrecorded ring-ditch. The feature is not visible in the current topography, but was readily observed in the geophysical data. The study indicates that non-mound areas within the enclosure were used for ceremonies and corporate activities. Limited test excavations showed that the non-mound areas of the Hopewell Mound Group were used by both earlier and later people. Use of the site about AD 900–1000 is reflected in sub-surface features and surface artifacts and was likely the evidence that led earlier scholars to suggest the Hopewell occupation included a village area.

The National Park Service study began research at the Riverside site with a careful surface examination of the area threatened by erosion along the north bank of Paint Creek. This was followed by more extensive geophysical survey and some limited strategic testing (Bauermeister 2010). This provided sufficient evidence that significant resources were being lost to erosion and that continuing erosion would make it difficult to understand how the Riverside site was used in association with the Hopewell Mound Group. After a consideration of all alternatives, the

Fig. 5.7. Riverside site 2006, excavation of pit with ceramic vessels and food remains (photo: author).

Fig. 5.8. Excavation of pit features, Riverside site, 2006 (photo: author).

National Park Service decided to conduct excavations in an area that might be affected by continuing erosion.

The 2006 project (Bauermeister 2010) included excavation of four 20 × 20 m blocks using a backhoe to strip away the plowzone. Three of the excavation blocks were placed in areas with numerous magnetic anomalies, while the fourth block was placed in an area with no obvious magnetic anomalies. The most important part of this project is that it exposed 13 archaeological features. Most of these were either small pits or post-holes, but no structural pattern was detected. The study also identified two larger pits, roughly 6–7 m apart, and filled with charcoal, pottery, bladelets, bone tools, calcined bone, lithic debris, mica, and a pitted stone (Figs 5.7 and 5.8). The dense quantity and variety of artifacts found in these two pits was quite dramatic, particularly in regard to the large number of ceramic sherds in the pit fill. Subsequent analysis has shown that at least six vessels are represented in the two pits, including at least three partially restorable tetrapod examples (Fig. 5.9). Careful efforts to restore these led to the discovery that parts of the different ceramic vessels had been discarded in the different pits, suggesting that the vessels were deliberately broken and purposefully placed in separate pits. The disposal of ceramic vessels in separate pits is somewhat reminiscent of Feature 9 at the Hopeton Earthworks, where large quantities of pottery and mica were carefully placed in a large pit and covered with a sterile fill before another group of pottery and mica were placed in the same pit.

The pits, pots, and other artifacts at the Riverside site are found in close proximity to one of the largest and most important of all Ohio Hopewell ceremonial centers. The three reconstructed vessels (Fig. 5.9) have tetrapodal bases, a form of vessel that has been found in ritual contexts under mounds at sites like Mound City. The ceramics from Feature 9 at Hopeton also included tetrapod vessels, but that feature lacked the relatively large quantity of calcined bone found in Features 7 and 8 at the Riverside site. At both the Hopeton Earthworks and the Hopewell Mound Group, these larger refuse pits were found outside the embankment walls, and outside the sacred space that is framed by those large monumental earthen walls. It seems likely that the materials in the pits do not represent ordinary household refuse, but probably include debris and deliberately broken objects

used in ceremonies or rituals. It is important to emphasize that this practice of the deliberate breakage of objects is well established also in sub-mound deposits at many Ohio Hopewell sites. Further studies to locate, identify, and examine features inside versus outside Hopewell embankments are needed to help understand more specifically how the great enclosures were used internally and externally.

Fig. 5.9. Three reconstructed ceramic vessels from Riverside site, 2006 (photos courtesy of Ann Bauermester, Midwest Archeological Center, Lincoln, Nebraska).

There is much yet to be learned about the Hopewell Mound Group and how it was used during the Hopewell era. A variety of features related to ceremonies, rituals, and non-domestic activities are to be expected. Many of these seem to be the products of feasting or ceremonies, and some may include refuse from materials created to be included in the many sub-mound deposits found at this site. Hopefully, future research will also learn if the large area within the two large enclosures was stripped of topsoil as has been documented at Hopeton and Mound City. It will also be interesting to learn whether the perimeter walls and ditch features were built early in the sites history, or if they were later additions, as has been interpreted for Mound City. One thing is clear in the current Hopewell Mound Group data, there is no evidence that the site was used for long-term residential activities during the Hopewell era.

The Moorehead Circle, Fort Ancient

Fort Ancient is one of the most famous and most impressive of all Ohio Hopewell ceremonial constructions. Due to its relatively remote location on the top of a precipitous mesa and its early development as a tourist center, the site has seen considerable archaeological activity but has not been subjected to the ravages of agriculture and urban development that has damaged or destroyed so many of the other great Hopewell sites. Fort Ancient State Memorial is part of a group of Ohio Hopewell earthen monuments being nominated for recognition as a World Heritage Site by the United Nations Educational Scientific and Cultural Organization (UNESCO). Efforts to preserve and protect the site are balanced with the need to make it available to Ohio residents for appreciation of its historical importance and its scenic beauty.

The Moorehead Circle was discovered in 2005 by a geophysical survey that was conducted across the interior of the North Fort in an effort to find a route

Hopewell lithic procurement

The Hopewell used a wide range of both local and more distant stone sources from which they crafted tools both for everyday subsistence activities and special artifacts they required for rituals and in burial ceremonialism. In Ohio there are at least 18 known sources of flints or cherts scattered across the southern and central parts of the state, ranging from the well known Flint Ridge varieties to the unusually-named Upper Mercer Bird Dropping Variety, but not all of them were utilised by the Hopewell. Only 9 sources seem to have been exploited by the Hopewell communities, especially Flint Ridge and the Upper Mercer sites (DeRegnaucourt & Georgiady 1998).

That stone was an important raw material to the Hopewell communities is illustrated by the range of tools and artifacts they created. Although meteoric iron and Great Lakes copper were occasionally used, most Hopewell cutting implements, drilling tools and projectile points were knapped from stone. At the Harness Mound Group, Licking County, a range of small tools were crafted from Flint Ridge flints – alongside other regional and exotic types of stone – by striking blades from a heat-treated core. Such small bladelets appear to have been the dominant cutting tools and discrete workshop areas for their production are found beside many major earthwork complexes.

Distinctive projectile points occur, often of multi-colored flints and cherts, At Mound 25 at Hopewell itself exotic large bifaces knapped into extravagant forms of projectile point were produced from Knife River chalcedony from the Dakotas and obsidian from the northern Rockies. Such exotica, however, are quite rare, and the Hopewell site is one of few places to have produced such items. Extravagance could also be demonstrated by artifact quantity. Excavations in Mound2 at Hopewell discovered 7000+ ovoid bifaces made from Wyandotte chert from southern Indiana/northern Kentucky, distributed between two separate mound deposits which helped to reinforce the richness of the burial assemblage.

The Hopewell also used stone to craft various ornaments and personal adornments. Gorgets of various geometric and other elaborate forms could be made from shale (Tremper Mound), or probably Ohio pipestone (Mound 17, Hopewell), for example. The superbly carved effigy tobacco pipes (see Chapter 4) stand alongside the finest mica sheet cut-outs and copper plaques as examples of the quality and competency of Hopewell artistic achievement. At the Hopewell site, amongst the 40 or so forms of platform and elbow pipes, was a particularly fine example carved from a solid piece of fire clay depicting a large-billed bird (possibly a Roseate Spoonbill) grasping a big fish, which was found on Altar 2 (Moorehead 1922, 140–2 & pl. lxxviii; Greber & Ruhl 2000, 168–75).

Many of the stone quarries occur where bands of the toolstone were exposed along river banks or on steep hilldsides. Flint Ridge, Licking County, is probably the best known site, where the remains of quarries can still be seen as deep depressions, lying a few meters apart, interspersed with waste dumps. The fact that Flint Ridge, like many other Midwestern stone sources, was utilised for thousands of years by successive cultures and communities, demonstrates the importance of stone as a medium for both mundane, everyday tool making, but also its significance for the manufacture of artifacts which helped to underpin ritual and ceremonial life and define status, thus creating identities in stone.

Photos by Pete Topping

A mannequin of a flint knapper crafting a biface, alongside examples of the many tool types created with Flint Ridge flint.

A quarry at Flint Ridge with a waste dump mounded immediately behind the pit.

A Hopewell stone axe, or celt, found at Mound City and now curated at the site museum.

Some of the 7000+ Wyandotte chert bifaces discovered in Mound 2 at the Hopewell site and now curated in the Field Museum, Chicago.

to permit heavy equipment and materials to be transported across the enclosure to stabilize the eroding earthen walls along the perimeter of the landform. The geophysical survey, conducted by Jarrod Burks, identified a number of potentially interesting smaller anomalies and a large circular anomaly that resembled a small circular enclosure.

More intensive study of the Moorehead Circle began in 2006 under the direction of Robert Riordan (2006). As discussed in Chapter 4, Riordan led Wright State University archaeology field schools at the Pollock Works for more than 20 years before turning his attention to this amazing feature at Fort Ancient. In 2006 and each subsequent season, Riordan has uncovered evidence of one of the most complex Ohio Hopewell non-mound features ever identified. Riordan gave the name Moorehead Circle to this feature to honor the research and preservation efforts of Warren K. Moorehead, whose work led to the site being purchased by the State of Ohio for preservation as the first state park in 1891. Since the research at this site is ongoing, the brief description provided here is drawn from preliminary reports, conference papers, and communications with Dr Riordan (Riordan 2007; 2009; 2010b; Anonymous 2010).

The Moorehead Circle is comprised of a variety of different architectural elements. The shape of the feature is formed by three incomplete concentric rings of large posts that were formed by large post-holes, many of which were filled with chunks of limestone. The outer ring may be comprised of as many as 200 posts, and is about 60 m in diameter. Individual post-holes are about 30 cm in diameter and 1 m deep, and the posts that resided in these holes likely stood another 3 m above ground. Sections of two additional post-rings have been identified. It is unclear if these represent three separate post-circles, or if there was some form of roof or ramada connecting the post-rings.

At the center of the circle is a large pit filled with bright red soil and broken Hopewell ceramics. The central pit is roughly 4.7 m N–S and 4 m E–W and 80 cm deep. An intrusive trough or shallow ditch was subsequently excavated around the perimeter of the central feature, and evidence of extensive burning was seen in the fill on the east side of the trough. The red soil is highly magnetic and was clearly the source of the magnetic anomaly identified in 2005. Research is ongoing to determine if the red soil has been burned or if represents naturally red soil that was quarried at an unknown location and used to form this central feature.

An opening in the post-rings faces southeast and is formed by a well-fitted pavement of limestone slabs (Fig. 5.10). Computer models indicate that, on summer solstice, the sunrise may be seen from the center of the Moorehead Circle aligning along the rock pavement with a stone mound and an opening in the east wall of the North Fort (Anonymous 2010). The floor of a small structure (40 × 50 ft/12.2 × 15.2 m) is located next to the central feature and a series of trenches and prepared floors were built in arcs across the southern half of the Circle.

Fig. 5.10. Annual excavation beginning in 2006 by Robert Riordan and Wright State University at the Moorehead Circle at Fort Ancient has revealed an extremely complex ceremonial feature that must have been a major part of the constructed Fort Ancient landscape. This photo shows a stone pavement which forms the entrance into the Moorehead Circle (photo courtesy of Robert Riordan).

While much remains to be learned about the construction and use of this large and complex architectural feature, it is clear that a substantial amount of labor was invested in its construction and maintenance. The latter is implied by the observation that several post-holes exhibit evidence that the original posts had been removed and replaced, before the entire structure was dismantled and covered by a layer of gravel. Radiocarbon dates from different elements of the Circle suggest it was used for a century or more.

Craft houses and other wooden structures

The Seip Earthwork consists of three large contiguous earthen enclosures on the north side of Paint Creek, east of Bainbridge, Ohio. As described in Chapter 4, the central enclosure at this site is a combination of a rectangular form on the south side and a circular form on the north side. A circular enclosure is attached to this central enclosure on the west and a rectangular enclosure on the south-east. The main attraction of this large earthen monument for early archaeologists was two large mounds near the center of the central enclosure. The very large Seip-Pricer mound was excavated by H. C. Shetrone (Shetrone and Greenman 1931), while the somewhat smaller mound (Seip, formed of three conjoined mounds) was excavated by W. C. Mills (1909a). The Seip mound was reconstructed after excavations and is part of a narrow strip of land, including a section of the north embankment wall for the central enclosure that comprises the Seip Mound State Memorial.

Raymond Baby directed a series of excavations at the site in 1966, including a test unit on a low rise roughly midway between the Seip Mound and the north embankment wall. The test excavation revealed the presence of about 30 cm of dense dark midden containing Hopewell artifacts. Baby returned to the location in 1971, and excavations exposed parts of a Hopewell structure. Subsequent excavations through 1977 exposed the remains of seven additional houses and the corner of an eighth. The rectangular structures varied in size, ranging from 7 m on a side up to 14 m on a side. Most exhibited rows of double posts on two sides and single line of posts on the opposite sides. Baby and Langois (1979) reported that the structures lacked evidence of interior hearths, mortuary or charnel-house features, and food remains consistent with domestic activities. They reported that individual buildings contained unique combinations of specialized tools, debris, and features suggesting they represented workshops of craft specialists.

Unfortunately, Baby never published a full report on his excavations among the Seip structures, but his interpretation of the use of the buildings continued to affect the interpretation of Hopewell social organization. Workshop-scale craft production is not widely anticipated among small-scale societies and tends to be practised in more complex economic and political systems. Consequently, interpretation of the data from the excavation of the buildings at Seip has major implications for understanding Hopewell societies.

N'omi Greber (2009a; 2009b) and a team of colleagues (Greber *et al.* 2009), having some familiarity with the Seip Earthworks, decided to study the extant collections and records from Baby's research. Careful examination of the actual data from the 1966–77 excavations failed to produce any evidence of tools, raw materials, or waste materials that might be interpreted to represent specific craft production activities.

Katherine Spielmann directed an Arizona State University Summer Archaeological Field School at Seip in 2005 (Spielmann *et al.* 2005). She recognized that the excavation procedures that Baby applied on seven buildings in the 1970s were fairly coarse and she planned more careful excavations at an eighth structure that Baby recorded but never excavated. The purpose of her research was to open the floor of the building and record artifacts and features on a more precise scale to determine whether evidence of craft production debris was present. Unfortunately, when they reopened the area where Baby had recorded the eighth structure, the row of post-holes he described consisted of only a single post-hole and some aluminum tent pegs marking where additional post-holes might have been. While several features were located, none of these appeared to be positioned within a structure. They did identify what appeared to be some large post-pits, that when combined with features reported from the earlier excavations, formed part of an arc and may represent a post-circle. Geophysical survey and subsequent, very limited, test excavation produced evidence of at least one additional post-pit, but the existence of a post-circle has yet to be confirmed (Spielmann and Burks 2011).

Since recent research has rejected the hypothesis that the concentration of buildings inside the embankment wall at Seip represents craft workshops, the obvious question that arises is what was their function? Greber (2009b) makes the important point that we do not know if these buildings were contemporaries, or represent a succession of structures. Certainly the location must have been of some importance, and each house was dismantled and then covered with a layer of gravel and or soil. The dismantling of ceremonial buildings, as opposed to burning them, is a common characteristic of Hopewell buildings across southern Ohio.

When Baby excavated the concentration of buildings at Seip, remains of structures that had not been used as charnel houses were uncommon in Hopewell archaeology. This is certainly no longer the case. The building described in Chapter 3 from just outside the Hopeton enclosure wall exhibits no evidence that it was used for preparing bodies for burial. Unfortunately, the floor of the Hopeton structure was destroyed by plowing, but most of the same types of artifacts found in the Seip buildings were also found at Hopeton. The Seip buildings were significantly larger and the walls were more regular than the Hopeton structure, but the location of all of these buildings inside or near a large geometric enclosure suggests they were used in association with activities specific to the enclosure.

Research at the other Hopewell sites has shown that concentrations of buildings in association with large enclosures are not uncommon. Lazazzera (2004) has summarized information about all the different buildings that have been encountered at the Fort Ancient site. Most notable was an arc-shaped cluster of ten structures that were exposed by excavation in preparation for construction of the Visitor Center and Museum. Unlike the Seip structures, this cluster of buildings also had interior and exterior storage and cooking pits, and extensive and stratified midden deposits. Lazazzera's analysis of these and other structures at Fort Ancient indicates that both domestic and ceremonial activities occurred at the same time in association with these structures. She also distinguishes three different types of household context in association with these sites: "general domestic (for residential use), specialized domestic (used for short term habitation and special production activities), and specialized ceremonial (non-residential structures related exclusively to ritual activity)" (Lazazzera 2004: 105). Fort Ancient is the only large earthen enclosure where significant evidence of residential activities has been recorded.

A great post-circle and many buildings

Charles Whittlesey (1851) mapped the Stubbs Earthworks in 1839, and noted that since the site had already been in cultivation for many years, parts of the earthworks had been significantly degraded even at that early date. Whittlesey found little about the conjoined rectangular and circular enclosures to distinguish the site from other geometric earthworks in Ohio. However, he was intrigued by a mound with an amorphic shape that he felt might represent an animal effigy. Whittlesey also recorded a low, open, circular enclosure outside the main enclosure to the south.

We noted at the end of Chapter 4 that the excavations at the Stubbs Earthworks are a perfect example of archaeologists working against time to save information from the archaeological record before all was lost to the demands of modern development. Salvage excavations by Frank Cowan, Robert Genheimer, and Ted Sunderhaus of the Cincinnati Science Museum in 1998 and 1999 exposed 15 structures in four different excavation areas (Cowan *et al.* 1998; 1999; 2000; 2003; Cowan 2006). The buildings were positioned from just outside the embankment wall to 300 m from the enclosure. All the Stubbs structures were built in shallow basins and most of them with wall trenches, a technique where rows of post were set into shallow trenches leaving post-holes in the bottoms. This type of construction has not been documented at other Ohio Hopewell sites. Some of the Stubbs buildings were circular, others rectangular (with rounded corners), and many either overlapped or were superimposed. Cowan (2006) attributed this density of buildings to long-term use, and the radiocarbon dates reflect several centuries of activities. The buildings at Stubbs do not seem to represent domestic or residential structures, because associated refuse and storage features as well as lost and discarded artifacts and refuse, occur in only small quantities around these buildings. Radiocarbon dates from these structures reflect use in the 1st through the 3rd centuries, possibly as late as the 5th century AD (Cowan and Sunderhaus 2001).

Not far from the Stubbs Earthworks, salvage excavations at the Smith site (Sunderhaus *et al.* 2001; Cowan 2006), located on a high terrace overlooking the Stubbs Earthworks, revealed the presence of two more houses. The absence of artifacts and features normally associated with residential sites is notable at these buildings as well. The investigators believe these structures were only used for a short period of time. The Smith site, like many other sites recorded in what is called the Stubbs Cluster (Genheimer 1997), seem to reflect more of what Lazazzera (2004) would classify as non-residential structures. Cowan (2006) has suggested these buildings may have served as temporary quarters for pilgrims from other areas who visited the Stubbs Earthworks to participate in ceremonies or landscape construction activities.

Left: **Fig. 5.11.** Excavations by Frank Cowan, Bob Genheimer and colleagues discovered an amazing Circle of large posts while conducting salvage excavations at the Stubbs Earthwork. The Great Post circle as seen in this aerial view must have been a very important part of the constructed landscape at Stubbs (photo courtesy of Frank Cowan).

Right: **Fig. 5.12.** View of the individual post-holes that form the Great Post Circle at the Stubbs Earthwork. The posts were pulled out of their holes an the holes filled with darker soil that contained artifacts, and then the entire circle was covered by an embankment wall (photo courtesy of Frank Cowan).

By far the most important landscape feature discovered at the Stubbs Earthwork is a Great Post Circle (Cowan and Genheimer 2010). This was discovered by the investigators while stripping plowzone from an area to the south of the main enclosure. The area they were searching was the approximate locality of the open-circle or C-shaped small enclosure that Whittlesey (1851: pl. ii) identified as 'Figure E'. Examination of early maps indicates these small circles are fairly common in association with large geometric enclosures, and Cowan and Genheimer were attempting to discover if any of the features could be detected.

What they found was a series of large post-holes that can be described as a woodhenge (Figs 5.11 and 5.12). The giant timber feature was formed of 172 posts, 30–50 cm in diameter and set into the ground 60 cm or more. Excavation of some of the post-holes revealed that the posts had been slid into place using ramps from one side and then made sturdy by packing soil and limestone rocks into the margins of the hole around them. The woodhenge had evidently been dismantled, because excavators found the post-holes filled with artifacts and midden refuse. Three radiocarbon dates from samples collected from widely separated post-holes yielded an average radiocarbon age calibrated to around cal AD 180 (Cowan and Sunderhaus 2001; Cowan and Genheimer 2010).

When Charles Whittlesey visited the Stubbs Earthworks in 1839, it did not appear to be any way exceptional compared with the many other geometric enclosures he was seeing in his survey of Ohio earthworks. The discovery of several groups of wooden buildings and a Great Post Circle during salvage archaeological excavations appears to have changed that view. But has it really? We know a lot about the construction of wooden architecture at Stubbs because the site was endangered and large-scale stripping of the surface revealed features that had not been previously seen by Hopewell archaeologists. However, there is little doubt that similar features, and likely many different forms of wooden architecture, have yet to be discovered in and around the large geometric enclosures that still remain in southern Ohio.

Beyond the enclosure at Mound City

In 1982 I led a team of archaeologists from the Midwest Archeological Center in a survey and evaluation of a tract of land (about 40 acres/*ca.* 16 ha) immediately north of Mound City. The land was owned by another federal agency and they were prepared to offer the property to the National Park Service. Before NPS could accept the land, they had to determine if there were any significant resources within the tract. We planned a week-long pedestrian surface survey and limited test excavations to assess any archaeological resources that might be present. Although the tract had been cultivated for some time, the absence of rain left the surface dusty and made it very hard to see artifacts. Despite this difficulty, we were able to locate and record a prehistoric artifact scatter and three historic period sites. Since bladelets were found at the prehistoric site, it was assumed that it must have been used during the Middle Woodland era (Lynott and Monk 1985). The data from the project helped the NPS decide to accept the land transfer, and the property called the "North 40" is now part of the Mound City unit of Hopewell Culture National Historical Park.

In 2007, Kathleen Brady and a group of archaeologists and volunteers from Hopewell Culture NHP began a more intensive study of the North 40 tract (Brady and Pederson Weinberger 2009; 2010). Their project began with a fluxgate gradiometer survey that identified a number of potential sub-surface anomalies. Rather than assume that they could interpret each anomaly from the magnetic data alone, the archaeologists used soil cores to interpret the character of the sub-surface archaeology associated with each feature. They found prehistoric artifacts in 11 of the 17 soil coils extracted from magnetic anomalies. Using these data, they developed a plan to conduct more extensive test excavations to better evaluate the nature and character of the subsurface archaeological deposits.

One test unit exposed a series of post-holes. That excavation was subsequently expanded to reveal the partial outline of a building. Some of the post-holes were excavated into a deposit of heavy gravel that appears to represent a fill layer placed in this location during the Middle Woodland era. A number of bladelets and bladlelet fragments were found in the fill from the structure. The magnetic data indicates that some internal features may be present within the building. Charcoal collected from three of the post-holes produced dates of 1940±40 BP, 1920 BP, and 2010±40 BP.

Magnetic survey also identified five linear-aligned anomalies near the structure. Test units placed over two of these anomalies revealed the presence of two pits at the base of the plowzone. One of the features was a large circular pit, 2 m in diameter and 0.83 m deep. About half of the feature was excavated and revealed the presence of a cordmarked body sherd, some fire-cracked rock, and a large quantity of fragmentary and a few complete ovate bifaces and chert debitage. The bifaces and debitage include flint from multiple sources. Analysis of the lithic artifacts indicates that the debitage represents a series of different knapping episodes. The bifaces exhibit no evidence of use wear and analysis by Richard Yerkes indicates these items were discarded due to some manufacturing error. A radiocarbon date of 1890±40 BP was obtained from charcoal in the pit fill. The second excavated pit was irregular in shape and up to 4 m wide. The fill of the pit contained hundreds of potsherds, fire-cracked rock, chert debitage and biface fragments, and several pieces of mica.

National Park Service geophysical survey and testing have been conducted at a variety of other locations around the Mound City enclosure. Several features have been exposed, but most have not been extensively excavated. None of these features is indicative of ordinary habitation activities, but they appear more indicative of specialized activities that may relate to the sub-mound structures and their internal features. The radiocarbon dates from the North 40 test excavations indicate that a large structure and features of a non-residential nature were in use sometime around turn of the 1st centuries BC/AD. This would be consistent with the widely held belief that Mound City was in use at the beginning of the Hopewell era. Field investigations in the areas surrounding Mound City have not been systematic or comprehensive and it is reasonable to expect that additional features will be detected and a better understanding of the non-mound aspects of the site will be developed in the future.

Some additional thoughts

The excavations at the Hopeton Earthworks, Hopewell Mound Group, Mound City, and many other sites in southern Ohio have revealed evidence for a complex constructional history reflecting planned construction and movement of massive quantities of soil. While we cannot confirm that topsoil removal was a universal element of all Ohio Hopewell landscape construction, it is certainly a common practice in the central Scioto River valley and appears to be a fundamental practice at the geometric earthen enclosure sites in this region (e.g. Greber and Shane 2009; Pickard and Weinberger 2009; Lynott 2006; Lynott et al. 2010; Lynott and Mandel 2009). The amount of soil removed from the top of the natural soil profile is difficult to estimate, but based upon our work at Hopeton, Hopewell, and Mound City, 15–25 cm must be considered a minimum estimate. Beneath the East Embankment Wall at Mound City, only about 25 cm of the lower B horizon was still present, suggesting that perhaps 50–80 cm of the upper soil profile had been removed at that location. Quantification of the amount of soil that has been removed from each of these sites will be difficult due to the cumulative impact of historic agriculture, but it may be possible to build more precise interpretive models with careful coring of the enclosures and their surrounding landforms. Many of these enclosures are quite large, and stripping topsoil from hectares of land represents a vast and significant commitment of labor. Considering the carefully planned and constructed characteristics of individual mounds and earthen enclosures, is seems likely that one or more of these monumental earthen features may have been linked in a larger cultural landscape.

From our examination of construction methods of earthen features at Hopeton Earthworks, Hopewell Mound Group, and Mound City, it is very clear that the monumental earthen features at these sites are not simply masses of soil that were randomly acquired and piled up to create a pre-determined form. Almost every earthen feature we have examined reflects the careful selection and placement of soil. In some instances this practice is clearly for geo-engineering purposes aimed at creating long-term landscape stability, as in lining borrow pits and ditches excavated into sandy sediments with more stable clay layers. In other instances, the use of homogeneous soils for wall construction probably does not reflect practical engineering concerns. The careful selection and placement of soils within earthen walls was not a structural necessity, and probably reflects ritualistic behavior and a strong sense of discipline and order in landscape construction. The careful selection (for color and texture) and placement of soil strongly implies that, although wooden monumental construction may have preceded earthen walls, as proposed by Cowen *et al.* (2000) and DeBoer (2010: 201), there was nothing passive about the construction of monumental earthen walls. As Bernardini (2004) has proposed, studies of Ohio Hopewell earthen wall construction clearly indicate that the process of constructing these ancient landscapes was at least as important as the final earthen enclosures they form.

Geoengineering to create stable long-term landscape features has a deep history in the Eastern United States and is well documented at Poverty Point. Gibson (2000) documents the use of clay to cap earthen walls that were largely built of loess. Loess is easily eroded, and in a land with high annual rainfall, monument construction required an erosion-resistant layer of clay to protect the earthen wall structure. Knowledge of the construction qualities of various soil types was undoubtedly developed over centuries of mound and earthen construction, but specific evidence of the care and knowledge associated with Ohio Hopewell monumental earthen landscapes has only recently become the subject of direct studies.

Excavations at the Hopeton Earthworks have also documented the presence of small burned features that were buried under and within large earthen walls. The frequency of these brief burning episodes at the Hopeton Earthworks indicates they were a routine, if not important, aspect of preparation for earthen wall construction. Greber and Shane (2009) also report evidence for pre-wall construction ritual features at the High Bank Works. In combination with the geoarchaeological evidence that walls were built of soils that were carefully selected and placed, these small burned features provide further evidence that the process of landscape construction was regulated and conducted with the same care toward details as has been observed for Ohio Hopewell mortuary features.

We must also remember that, in virtually every instance where a significant area inside or near a large enclosure site has been investigated, investigators have found some remnants of wooden architecture. The very monumental character of the earthworks has, since their discovery by European settlers and explorers, dominated our consideration of these important ceremonial centers. Recent research at Hopeton Earthworks and other sites is demonstrating that these sites must be viewed as large constructed landscapes that were built mainly for ceremonial uses. The vast earthen enclosures in this region may look empty today, but they were most likely crowded places at special times, with numerous temporary wooden structures. The sites probably served multiple functions, perhaps being places where people met for games, ceremonies, and periodic rituals. Activities at these centers, including construction, likely involved non-local populations and may have led to mate-exchange and other social mechanisms that linked various groups across the Ohio Valley. While there are many aspects about Ohio Hopewell ceremonial landscapes that suggest the people who built them shared a common ideology or world view, there is great diversity in how the landscapes were built and possibly used, reflecting an emphasis on a level of local autonomy.

6

Some final thoughts: what we still need to learn

During the course of conducting research for this book, it has become apparent that archaeologists have collected a wide variety of data about the construction of earthworks and landscape features associated with Ohio Hopewell centers. Data from the Scioto River–Paint Creek region have suggested that removing topsoil was an important element of site planning and preparation. However, more data are needed to confirm this hypothesis and to assess whether it is applicable to other Hopewell regions.

Much of the current Hopewell literature concerns the presentation of interpretive models developed from the study of existing data, mainly from sub-mound contexts. In these studies, hypotheses or ideas are examined under the light of information that was collected by archaeologists often half a century or more ago. While the legacy data may help support an interpretive model, it is hardly ever of the same quality as data that might be obtained by fieldwork conducted in the last decade. The application of logical or structural inferences can produce an impressively detailed model, but readers must be careful to avoid accepting such hypothetical constructions as factual interpretations of the data. Most of the more powerful interpretive models offered to explain the Ohio Hopewell world are truly hypothetical constructions, and deserve to be tested by future generations of scholars.

We believe that one of the main factors in the successes achieved in the Hopeton Earthworks Project has been the participation of technical experts who can more readily interpret the subtle variations in the archaeological record. Throughout the project, we were particularly fortunate to have the enthusiastic participation and support of John Weymouth, Bruce Bevan, and Rinita Dalan in the selection, application, and interpretation of geophysical studies. Some of the approaches that were attempted were experimental and not all of them were successful. Particularly noteworthy were the studies that focused on open excavation units and attempted to better explain the results obtained during surface geophysical surveys. These studies are available only in manuscript form at this time, but they will be made available to a wider audience in the near future.

Another major factor in the success of the Hopeton Earthworks Project was the participation of Rolfe Mandel, Kansas Geological Survey. Rolfe brought considerable experience in geoarchaeology to the Hopeton study, and his ability to identify many of the subtle nuances of the larger constructed landscape was essential to understanding what the builders had done to create the landscape. Rolfe recognized that earthen constructions are difficult to understand because they represent soil materials that have developed at another location and then have been dug up and relocated into an earthen feature elsewhere. The soil materials that were piled up to form the earthen feature have then subsequently been subjected to nearly two millennia of soil formation processes, which may have altered the color, chemistry, and granular composition of the different construction layers. Geoarchaeological approaches and specialized tools such as soil micromorphology can be extremely valuable in the study of earthen construction (Van Ness *et al.* 2001), but the participation of geoarchaeologists in the study of Hopewell earthworks is a relatively new development. Considering what we have learned at Hopeton, future studies must be alert to the possibility that, in addition to the construction of walls, mounds, ditches, and borrow pits, it is possible that builders of these monumental landscapes moved many hectares of topsoil to achieve their desired landscape setting.

We must, however, caution against the acceptance of broad generalizations about landscape construction at this time. The Ohio Hopewell archaeological record strongly suggests that all aspects of that world were products of societies that accepted and likely encouraged diversity in ceremonial matters. The existing landscape data, as described in this volume, suggest that landscape preparation differed between Newark, the Scioto–Paint Creek region, and south-west Ohio. More research is needed to determine if the differences that have been observed are valid, and if so, if they represent differences due to time of construction or in the views of local populations. One thing that appears certain, there is as much diversity in landscape construction as there is in the types and varieties of Hopewell ceremonial artifacts.

We have at various points in this discussion encouraged readers to be aware that many hypothetical models and interpretations about Ohio Hopewell features and sites are too often presented as factual statements. For example, the suggestion by Baby and Langlois (1979) that the cluster of buildings found inside the earthen enclosure at Seip Earthworks represent craft workshops became "engrained in the 'common wisdom' of North American archaeology for a generation" (Greber 2009a: 171). Careful examination of the data from the seven buildings revealed that there is very little existing evidence to support the original interpretive claim. The literature of Ohio Hopewell is filled with examples where a scholar suggests that archaeological data reflects some type of social organization, alignment, or connections between different sites. There are far too few instances where researchers are actively trying to evaluate these hypotheses. What we are finding is that when an idea becomes enmeshed in the Hopewell literature, it all too often becomes part of what our colleague N'omi Greber (2009a) calls the "common wisdom" of Hopewell archaeology. We encourage readers to remember that despite nearly two centuries of study and speculation, the real study of Ohio Hopewell ceremonial landscapes is just beginning.

Landscapes and time

Throughout the course of this volume we have noted that almost every question about Hopewell archaeology has a component that is rooted in our inability to understand the subtle temporal difference between artifacts, features, and sites. At the root of this problem is that Hopewell archaeology is highly dependent upon radiocarbon and AMS dating to estimate the age of different elements within the archaeological record. At a time when our hypotheses and models are evolving to propose questions that require temporal control at the generational level, we are relying on methods that are only accurate under the best terms to the century.

We must also remember that not all radiocarbon dates are equal in their interpretive value. At Hopeton, the best samples we submitted for dating were selected from features that by all evidence were produced by a single burning episode and then were buried and sealed without the potential to be contaminated by later burning episodes. In some instances we selected charcoal from a post-hole or pit where the material being dated likely originated somewhere nearby, but the sample was deliberately placed in the feature as part of decommissioning a structure or disposal of ritual refuse. We believe this care in sample selection and then identification of the sample being submitted (we selected samples that contained a single type of wood charcoal to lower the risk of dating multiple burning episodes), helped to make the suite of dates from the Hopeton Earthworks an accurate and reliable estimate of the age of the site features. We must also note here, that with the exception of Hopeton and the Pollock Works, very few sites have multiple dated samples associated with earthen wall construction. If we are ever to learn how long it took to build one of these earthen landscapes, we must obtain multiple dated samples from reliable contexts associated with earthen construction. This will take persistence and time at each site under consideration.

The Ohio Hopewell literature contains many examples where scholars have suggested that connections exist between pairs or even groups of sites. For example, Byers, Marshall, DeBoer, and even the Rev. Stephen D. Peet in 1903 have argued for the pairing of Mound City with Hopeton on the opposite side of the Scioto River to the east. Based upon what we think we know, and new information can certainly change this observation, Mound City was likely in use at least a century before earthen construction began at Hopeton, and the borrow pits and embankment wall at Mound City were not built until at least a century after most earthen construction at Hopeton had ceased. As we have noted earlier in this volume, the radiocarbon chronology for Hopeton is among the better ones currently available for Ohio Hopewell sites, while the suite of dates for Mound City raises more questions than it answers. That being said, it is fairly clear that the two sites may have been in *use* at the same time, but their construction episodes likely differ by decades if not centuries. We would also like to know if the two sites were built by the same people, and were other sites around Mound City and Hopeton (Shriver, Dunbar, Cedar Bank) part of a larger landscape plan?

Another example of assumed temporal contemporaneity is the tripartite geometric earthworks in the Scioto–Paint Creek area. These are widely believed by scholars working in this field to be among the last of the great enclosures built in this region of southern Ohio. Carr (2005b) proposes that the five tripartite sites and the Hopewell Mound Group actually represent three different local allied communities, comprised of Hopewell-Frankfort, Seip-Baum, and Works East-Liberty. Unfortunately, despite the logic of this argument and what appears to be widespread acceptance of the contemporaneity of the sites, there are no radiocarbon dates linked to any of the construction episodes at any of the earthen features at any of these six sites! This proposal must be evaluated by continued study of existing collections and new research at the sites that are still intact. While most of the above-ground evidence at Works East, Liberty, Baum, and Frankfort are no longer visible, geophysical studies and perhaps yet to be developed technologies may make it possible to locate sub-surface features that will help evaluate this proposal.

Carr (2005a) and others believe that the smaller and simpler earthen enclosure sites of Mound City, Tremper, and Hopeton all pre-date the more complex and larger tripartite enclosure sites. While this may be true, the argument ignores the fact that existing radiocarbon dates (some with less than excellent context) from Mound City and the Hopewell Mound Group indicate that both of these sites were in use over four or even five centuries. Geoarchaeological and stratigraphic evidence combined with dates on a single feature associated with borrow pit construction strongly suggests the embankment and borrow pits were the last landscape features built at Mound City (Brown 1994; 2012; Lynott *et al.* 2010; 2012). Can we ignore the possibility that the Hopewell Mound Group was also a very large group of mounds, and the ditch and enclosure wall were not built until toward the end of their use? We must also recall that the radiocarbon dates from the Hopewell Mound Group suggest that activities were being conducted there at the same time that Hopewell activities were beginning at Mound City and Hopeton. The research reported in this volume has shown that it is possible to learn a great deal from the ceremonial sites that have survived. Future research will likely find ways to better test issues of contemporaneity and shared function.

Time also plays an important role in understanding the energy investment in constructing one of these large ceremonial landscapes. Estimates of labor can be mathematically calculated without time, but the temporal span of construction is important in assessing the potential role of non-local labor in earthwork construction. The sometime, contentious arguments about settlement types and subsistence strategies are also important in assessing the relative role of local versus non-local labor contributions. Considering the four to five centuries of Hopewell landscape construction in Ohio, it is very likely that all of these factors may have varied through time. Small-scale societies are much more flexible in their ability and willingness to adjust to changes in their natural and cultural worlds and a flexible subsistence and settlement approach may have allowed Hopewell societies to maintain their commitment to the construction and use of ceremonial landscapes.

Efforts to calculate the energy requirements for landscape construction are also complicated by our limited understanding of whether construction occurred as a single, perhaps prolonged event, or if the final form of a given earthwork was achieved by multiple stages of construction, modification and possibly even demolition and reuse. The evidence presented by Riordan (2006) for the Pollock Works is compelling, and demonstrated that at least one site was built and modified over multiple generations. The combined evidence from Hopeton, Pollock, and Fort Ancient strongly suggests these places were built by successive generations from committed local societies. The nature, size, and character of the societies that built these landscapes is yet to be determined, and we must also remember that the one thing that is most consistent about Ohio Hopewell landscape construction is the variability between different regions in southern Ohio. Perhaps Bradley Lepper (2010) is correct and the great Newark Earthworks was built during a single lifetime with substantial help from pilgrims who traveled there from other regions. Lepper fully understands this is a hypothesis that must be tested, and we all hope that future years will see substantial research at Newark to address this and other questions about the largest of all Ohio Hopewell ceremonial landscapes.

Southern Ohio before monument construction

There is abundant evidence in the archaeological record of Eastern North America for earthen monument building prior to the Ohio Hopewell era. Joe Saunders and colleagues (Saunders *et al.* 2007) have documented the construction of mounds organized around a plaza during the Middle Archaic period at Watson Brake (*ca.* 4500 BC). Poverty Point in north-east Louisiana was the first truly monumental earthen construction (Gibson 2000; Ortmann and Kidder 2012) dating to about 1000 BC. Sometime in the Early Woodland period, residents of the Ohio River valley began building mounds that were surrounded by circular embankments and ditches. These Adena monuments are fairly widespread in Midwest, Southeast and even to some extent the Northeastern United States. We have discussed the problems in interpreting the relationship between Adena, which is generally earlier in time, and the Hopewell. What does appear to be clear at this time, is that some societies living in southern Ohio during the 1st century of the Christian era began to build earthen monuments on a much larger scale that at any time since the Poverty Point era.

We have noted that the region where this explosion of monument building occurred was heavily forested with isolated pockets of grassland prairie. Much of the discussion about the labor and duration of Hopewell ceremonial landscape construction has been limited to the movement of soil and rock. Very little discussion has been conducted on forest clearing. Did the people who designed the large earthen enclosures lay them out while they were still forested? In public lectures it has been suggested that the Hopewell only built in areas where forests might have been less dense. Considering the large numbers of these sites and their locations in places where trees thrive today when sites are left out of cultivation, this argument seems less plausible. This seems even less possible as proposals for alignment of constructed landscape features with celestial events, natural landmark features, and even other Hopewell sites are being offered and refined (DeBoer 2010; Hively and Horn 2010). From the surface soil stripping that has been recorded at the Hopeton Earthworks, most of the trees and other vegetation must have been removed to provide access for removal of topsoil and to quarry subsoil.

In the Scioto River–Paint Creek region, this would have required clearing large blocks of forest in a dozen or more locations. Would this impact have altered the pollen record for the region? Can paleoenvironmental data be gathered and used to help understand if all these clearings were created in a few decades or were they spread throughout the Hopewell era?

One study was conducted as an effort to detect changes in the pollen record for the central Scioto River valley (Snyder *et al.* 1991), but the study failed to find pollen that could be attributed to the Hopewell era. Additional pollen studies in concert with other paleoenvironmental techniques are needed to determine if the large scale of landscape construction may have altered the local environments in southern Ohio. Construction of ceremonial centers, villages, and corn fields have been detected during the Mississippian era (Delcourt and Delcourt 2008), and the large amount of landscape construction in parts of southern Ohio would also seem to be detectable.

The meaning behind landscape forms

One of the aspects of Hopewell earthen enclosures that fascinated early scholars was the use of geometric forms at some sites and great diversity of shapes and configurations that were found among the earthworks as a group. Hopewell scholars continue to speculate about what the different shapes mean.

Were the different shapes built at different times? Did the different shapes and configurations have different purposes and meanings, or does this diversity in enclosure form reflect another example of the unique character of Hopewell art?

Martin Byers conducted a morphological analysis of geometric earthen enclosures, based on the shapes and combination of shapes of sites in southern Ohio, and has suggested that they may be temporally seriated based on their attributes (Byers 1987; 2004). This mode of study has drawn considerable interest among Hopewell scholars. Byers has also suggested that the basic circular and rectangular earthwork forms are symbols of the Hopewell cosmos, while others have noted that these forms reflect the shapes of winter and summer houses of many Woodland Indians (Faulkner 1977). Romain (2000) proposes that square-shaped geometric enclosures represented the sky to their builders, while the circular enclosures represent earth. Any or all of these interpretations may have merit, but without solid geo-chronological data for the paired combinations, we must recognize that this is really an exercise in hypothesis building.

The discovery of the Great Post Circle at the Stubbs earthwork (Cowan and Genheimer 2010) highlighted the use of large timber-built architecture as part of ceremonial landscapes. Warren DeBoer (2010: 176) suggests that the earthen walls at the Hopeton Earthworks may have been preceded by rows of posts or fences. DeBoer (2010: 201) also suggests a more general model with timber-built structures representing the active phase of the landscape and the earthworks representing the passive and final phase of the monument. Certainly most Ohio Hopewell mounds were built over the site of one or more wooden structures, but in all these cases the timber posts were removed and the structural footprint covered by a mantle of soil. There is no evidence that the building was burned. With literally dozens of examples of Hopewell timber structures being dismantled rather than burned, it seems highly unlikely that the two instances of two burned posts found under the earthen wall at Hopeton would be from a ceremonial, pre-embankment active phase of the monument. The buried logs may simply be remnants of forest clearing and site preparation. With increasing use of geophysics, many more large timber-built features are likely to come to light in what now appear to be vacant spaces in and around the large earthen enclosures

Using the small bits of data that are currently available about landscape construction across southern Ohio during the Hopewell era, we have noted the possibility that at least some basic elements of the "architectural grammar" (Connolly 2004a; 2004b) may differ between these regions. We noted that all of the sites that have been studied in the Scioto reflect stripping of topsoil from the areas where earthen walls were later built, and possibly across entire enclosures. Comparable data are lacking for the many geometric enclosures of southern Ohio, but the hilltop enclosures in that region in some cases were built on top of established A horizons. The only data we have for the Newark Earthworks was a test trench across the Fairground Circle, and the data indicate that the great circular embankment was built on top of an established soil horizon. These variations in earthwork construction methods likely reflect construction by local groups with different construction methods, rather than variations in construction over time. However, this cannot be conclusively addressed without substantial new research.

Although most of the large earthen walls have been badly degraded, current research methods have allowed relocation of the base of some of them and revealed some of the materials used in their building. The development of geophysical methods also offers a way to address the vast size of these constructed landscapes and learn about less prominent structures that may have been built into the landscape. What remains difficult is interpreting how the earthworks were used. Were all earthworks used in the same way? Did functions change over time? These questions remain valid for virtually all Ohio Hopewell ceremonial landscapes.

Through the efforts of several Hopewell scholars, we are learning a great deal about the precision that has been incorporated into making earthwork features align with celestial events (Romain 2000; Hively and Horn 2013). Ray Hively and Robert Horn in particular have offered strong probability analysis to indicate that the alignment of features at Newark and High Bank with lunar events is unlikely due to chance. They have also suggested that some embankment features may be aligned with local landmarks and with other Hopewell landscape sites. At most sites, there are a large number of potential alignments. Were all Hopewell enclosure sites built to align with something? Are all embankment alignments intended to mark lunar or solar events? Geophysical maps of existing sites will provide more accurate data than can be obtained from the current degraded topography or from the old maps of the 19th century.

A recent paper by Warren DeBoer (2010) suggests that many of the Hopewell sites in the Scioto–Paint Creek region are aligned with one another. The alignments he identifies extend for kilometers and cross over river drainages. If these sites were actually built to create alignments with other monumental earthen sites, does this mean that all the sites are part of some "grand" plan, or did this desire to align landscapes evolve over generations and centuries? It does raise the question of what factors led to the selection of locations for landscape development and earthen construction. Elsewhere, we have suggested that variability in construction methods reflects autonomy among local groups, but perhaps there was less autonomy among groups in the Scioto–Paint Creek region. Some scholars privately refer to the mound deposits in this region as reflecting the "high church" aspect of Ohio Hopewell, and it is hard to argue with the large number of extremely impressive sub-mound mortuary/ceremonial deposits that have been found. There is an excellent database for comparison from the Turner Group in the Little Miami River valley, but sadly there is not much other systematic data for comparison from Newark or other geometric enclosure sites beyond the Scioto–Paint Creek region. How did changes through time affect these cultural developments? Four centuries is a long time for any society to remain committed to a plan for a massive scale of landscape construction.

Settlement sites and ceremonial landscapes

It is generally agreed that Ohio Hopewell people were organized in small-scale societies and lacked the hierarchical and hereditary leadership generally associated with chiefdoms in later prehistory. Study of sub-mound Ohio Hopewell deposits has demonstrated that some people attained status and power, as reflected in the elaborate mortuary objects associated with specific individual bodies. What still remains a topic of debate among Hopewell scholars is how these people organized themselves across the landscape and how deeply they were committed to food production to sustain their social organization and commitment to landscape construction and maintenance.

Earlier in this volume, we reviewed the general points that have led many scholars to argue for either dispersed sedentary communities or mobile communities. What makes this debate particularly interesting is that there is very little agreement on what we would expect a Hopewell hamlet to look like. The earliest statement of this model was derived from excavation of midden material at the McGraw site (Prufer 1965). Not far from the McGraw site, Paul Pacheco (Pacheco *et al.* 2006; 2009a; 2009b) and colleagues have excavated two sites with large square house floors in an area called Browns Bottom, not far from the Liberty or Harness Earthworks. Each of these structures contains four earth ovens or hearths and other features. Neither site has produced trash pits, storage pits, or a midden comparable to what Prufer identified at the McGraw site. The structures that are reflected by the post-hole patterns on the house floors were very substantial and it appears that they were dismantled and abandoned. Macrobotanical data suggests consumption of native cultigens along with wild plant and animal foods. These carefully excavated sites provide some of the best evidence for sedentary hamlets in the Scioto River valley, but two factors suggest to me that structures of this type were built as part of the ceremonial or ritual landscape.

In south-west Ohio, excavation inside and around the enclosure wall at Fort

Ancient has revealed the presence of habitation debris (Connolly 1997) and a cluster of structures oriented around a plaza (Lazazzera 2004). Features associated with the complex of structures included earth ovens, ash-filled pits, trash pits, and processing pits. The occupation area and features contained food remains, lithic debris, stone tools, bladelets, and ceramics. Also present were small quantities of copper, mica, galena, and obsidian. Three different types of household activities were interpreted: general residential/domestic, specialized domestic (short-term habitation and special production activities), and specialized ceremonial or non-domestic activities (Lazazzera 2004: 105).

One of the hallmarks of Ohio Hopewell ceremonialism in the Scioto River valley is the abundant record of wooden structures that were dismantled, and the floor of each structure was covered by successive mantles of earth to form mounds. Rich artistic and ceremonial deposits were often left on the floors of these structures. Many of the ceremonial artifact deposits were burned at very high temperatures, and then the heat-fractured fragments were collected and placed on the structure floors. In no instance, that I have discovered, has anyone reported that one of these sub-mound buildings was burned and then buried. Every building that has been reported was dismantled before its floor was covered with mound fills. Ceremonial structures that have been excavated at earthen enclosure sites, but not affiliated with mounds display this same pattern (Hopeton: see Chapter 3; Seip: Greber 2009; Stubbs: Cowan 2006; Cowan *et al.* 2000).

Burned structural remains are commonly associated with sedentary communities throughout Eastern North America. The presence of so many dismantled structures associated with Ohio Hopewell ceremonial sites raises the question as to whether it was a general practice of Ohio Hopewell communities to dismantle their buildings, or did they only dismantle community/ceremonial buildings? There is no answer to this question at this time. However, it may be useful to identify some aspects of a sedentary Hopewell hamlet or small village that we should reasonably expect to find in archaeological contexts.

First, if a family or extended family were going to live in one place for a decade or two, we would expect to find a structure built for shelter. The building would likely have an interior heat source and might also have pits for storage of food and other important necessities. A later farmstead site, such as the Mississippian period Gypsy Joint site in south-east Missouri (Smith 1978) may be used to model expectations. One important difference that must be kept in mind is that occupants of the later Gypsy Joint site were actively engaged in maize agriculture, and while cultivation of native starchy seeds may have provided substantial food for Hopewell people, the process of maize agriculture represents a much larger labor and subsistence commitment. This does, of course, also raise the question – just how sedentary were people who cultivated native plants?

Smith (1978) identified two small rectangular wall-trench structures that had been built in shallow basins at Gypsy Joint, 11 pits, a concentration of maize grains, and a Woodland period burial. Analysis of the spatial distribution of artifacts suggests that four of the pits were associated with activity areas. Both structures had been burned and the basins in which the houses were built contained considerable wood charcoal. Excavations produced a large number and diverse range of artifacts and food refuse. Smith interprets the site as a nuclear family homestead that was occupied for 3 years or less.

While a direct comparison between Ohio Hopewell and a later society that is more dependent upon agriculture may not be completely appropriate, it is fair to ask why Hopewell hamlets that are believed to be cultivating native plants and have been used for two to three generations seem to leave less of a footprint than does this Mississippian farmstead that was occupied for only a few years? There is one Ohio Hopewell site that seems to offer some alternative answers to that question.

The Patton site (33AT990) is a Middle Woodland habitation site in the Hocking River drainage in south-east Ohio (Weaver *et al.* 2011). The site is located on an unplowed river terrace and excavations by Ohio University over 2 years revealed the presence of a wattle and daub house with three superimposed floors, indicating the original building had been twice rebuilt on the same location. The final floor (3 × 6 m) showed strong evidence that the structure had burned. The stratified structure floors also included three central interior hearths, an exterior hearth outside the doorway, four pits (storage/refuse), and several miscellaneous post-holes in the area around the structure.

The Patton site was first occupied during the Early Woodland period, but separate radiocarbon dates from two of the superimposed hearths within the Middle Woodland structure indicate the building likely dates to the 1st century AD (Beta-218883, cal AD 50–230, 2 sigma; Beta-249733, cal AD 60–240, 2 sigma). The excavators (Weaver *et al.* 2011) indicate that 5–10 years after the first house was built, it was burned and the floor and burned remains were covered by a 15–20 cm thick layer of fresh soil. A new set of walls and roof were built on the same location. The hearth was partially re-excavated and some post-holes from the first structure may have been re-used. After another episode of occupation this process was repeated and a third house was built on this location and then finally burned. The excavators estimate the three houses occupied this locality for 15–30 years.

Earlier we noted that the Hocking valley is one of the few areas of southern Ohio that is characterized by the presence of only a limited number of earthen enclosures and none of the really large and complex enclosures that we believe represent ceremonial landscapes. Despite the absence of giant ceremonial earthen landscape features, the Patton site represents one of the best examples of the types of archaeological remains we would expect to find at a farmstead or family settlement.

Weaver *et al.* (2011) note that the evidence from Patton suggests that not all Middle Woodland houses were large constructions with deeply embedded posts. They observed that perhaps during the Middle Woodland period, some of the domestic structures might have been smaller buildings with shallow post-holes. The evidence at the Patton site also suggests that the discovery of residential sites may be pursued more productively by looking at somewhat greater distances from larger ceremonial centers.

Intensive archaeological investigations in the close proximity to large ceremonial centers has failed, at least up to this point, to locate unequivocal evidence of Ohio Hopewell settlement sites. There are definitely buildings and locations that offer suggestions of domestic activities, but they also offer indications that they may be part of the ceremonial or ritual landscapes. Perhaps the dense concentration of enclosure sites in the Scioto River–Paint Creek region was a large ceremonial district and most of the smaller Hopewell sites in this area will reflect both domestic and ritual uses. Future investigations that focus on good settlement localities that are at some distance from these large and complex centers may be a more productive direction for research.

When and why did the Hopewell era end?

In any study of the archaeological record, it is obvious that societies and cultures change through time. In regard to Ohio Hopewell, early scholars blamed their demise on the native savages that surrounded them. Such dramatic explanations are no longer widely held, but the question is still relevant. In the first two centuries AD, small-scale societies in much of southern Ohio began to participate in an intensification of rituals and ceremonies that included construction of monumental-scale landscapes. Despite conscious efforts, archaeologists have been unable to locate nucleated villages associated with these ceremonial centers. Current scholars are divided as to whether the populations retained their mobile foraging lifestyle or settled into a series of sedentary hamlets where they were engaged in an intensified horticulture growing native plants. Settlement sites from the Hopewell era in Ohio have proven to be somewhat elusive, so it is unclear whether the daily lives of people during this era went along unchanged, or whether there may have been a shift from the more mobile to the more sedentary lifestyle. Sometime in the 5th century AD it appears that activities at the large constructed landscapes diminished or ceased altogether. A few writers have addressed this process (Braun 1977; Dancey 1996), but this event has received far less attention than it deserves.

There is no evidence that people abandoned the river valleys of southern Ohio, but there does appear to be a lapse of several centuries before the monumental earthen landscapes began to be used again. Squier and Davis (1848) found several graves that had been dug into Hopewell mounds in the Ross County area. Subsequent archaeological studies found that Late Woodland people buried their dead in the existing Hopewell mounds and enclosure walls, and they were given the name Intrusive Mound Culture, and later the Cole Culture (Potter 1968).

Evidence from Hopeton and the Hopewell Mound Group indicates that humans returned to these sites about AD 1000 and, based upon the data from Hopeton, they may have either repaired or remodeled some of the earthen walls. It is unclear if this represents an obscure event, or if people in this Late Woodland period began to reshape existing ceremonial monuments to better serve the needs of their day. Were the people who returned to the large enclosures in the Scioto River–Paint Creek region descendants of the people who built the large earthen walls many centuries earlier? My own speculation is that some of them were, but it is also likely that new families and probably whole communities moved into southern Ohio and married and lived with the descendants Ohio Hopewell communities. Of course, the descendants of some of the people who lived in this region during the Ohio Hopewell era likely moved to other places in North America.

Efforts to understand the end of large-scale earthen monument construction in southern Ohio continue. While artifact styles may contain clues about human migration and population movements during and at the end of the Hopewell era, the most direct evidence comes from the skeletal biology of the Ohio Hopewell people, their neighbors, and their descendants. Case and Carr (2008) and their collaborators have compiled an admirable database of the human remains from the Scioto River–Paint Creek region. These data offer important insights about the people who were buried in mounds in this region.

One new avenue of research that is particularly exciting includes the study of ancient DNA and the chemical composition of human teeth. A doctoral dissertation by Lisa Mills (2003) on ancient DNA extracted from teeth discovered at the Hopewell Mound Group, and a study of ancient DNA from individuals buried at the Peter Klunk Mound Group in Illinois by Deborah Bolnick and David Glenn Smith (2007), provide genetic evidence of frequent migration and gene flow between Illinois and Ohio. What makes the studies fascinating is that the evidence indicates that migration and gene flow was largely unidirectional, *from* Illinois *to* Ohio. This is just the opposite of what archaeologists have proposed (Prufer 1964).

In another recent study, in this case of strontium isotopes from teeth of human burials at the Albany and Utica mound groups in Illinois and the Hopewell Mound Group in Ohio (Behr 2011), there is further evidence of non-local people being buried at the Hopewell Mound Group. Strontium-87 is a radiogenic isotope that originates from underlying bedrock geological formations and is absorbed by local plants. Just as bedrock formations vary from region to region, the strontium isotopes of animals and humans that consume the plants will also vary. In the Illinois populations that were examined, there was very little evidence (three of 43 individuals) that immigrants from another region were buried in the Albany and Utica mounds. On the contrary, seven of the 38 individuals examined from the Hopewell Mound Group may have lived in other regions before being buried at Hopewell. Although this must be considered preliminary in nature, this seems to support the proposal that construction of Ohio Hopewell ceremonial landscapes benefited from pilgrimages to southern Ohio from other areas of Eastern North America.

The study of human remains from archaeological contexts in the United States is controlled by a variety of federal and state legislation. Since the passage of the *Native American Graves Protection and Repatriation Act* in 1990, native tribes and descendant communities have had a substantial voice in studies that have been conducted. Belief systems about the appropriate and respectful treatment of human remains must be one major consideration in any future studies. However, if appropriate justifications are developed and necessary approvals are obtained, further studies such as those just outlined may provide important new data on who were the Ohio Hopewell people and where did they go when they stopped building and maintaining their large ceremonial centers.

Beyond southern Ohio

Many decades of archaeological study have provided strong evidence that people living in Ohio during the Hopewell era had a major impact upon people across much of Eastern North America and possibly most of the continent. The presence of beautifully made, often highly stylized objects created from exotic raw materials from regions that were great distances from Ohio has created the "WOW factor" for most people familiar with Hopewell archaeology. These prestige goods included vast amounts of obsidian from the Rocky Mountains, large caches of objects made from Lake Superior copper, a wide range of mica forms from quarries in the Appalachian region, and sharks teeth, shells, and other objects from the Gulf Coast and Florida peninsula. Less common exotic raw materials include grizzly bear teeth, meteorites, galena, silver, quartz crystals, plus a wide variety of flints and fossils, and ceramics with decorative techniques that reflect connections with the Southeast. In tandem with these exotic prestige goods being found in Ohio, archaeologists have found numerous examples of local Middle Woodland complexes in other areas or regions that exhibit strong Hopewell influence in mound-building, treatment of the dead, and the acquisition of prestige goods made of exotic raw materials.

In Chapter 2 we reviewed the geographic scope of the Hopewell Interaction Sphere, and although not every Middle Woodland society participated in the ceremonial practices associated with Hopewell, it did influence societies from all along the Mississippi River Valley and westward in the Missouri Valley as far as modern-day Kansas City. Hopewellian sites have been reported in Florida and the Gulf Coast states, and up the Atlantic coast to New York and southern New England.

Strong Hopewell influence is documented in the mounds and village sites of the Illinois River valley and in the Lower Ohio River valley, particularly in the Wabash and other southern Indiana drainage. Although dating for the cultural evolution of Hopewell is less certain than would be desired, most scholars accept that the earliest ceramics, mound burials with prestige goods and exotic raw materials that may be called Hopewell appear in the Illinois River valley. Perhaps a century later, the societies of southern Ohio, who were already building small-scale cultural landscapes, began to amplify ceremonial construction and acquisition of prestige goods in the era AD 1–450. This is the classic era of Ohio Hopewell where the construction of ceremonial landscapes, acquisition of prestige goods and exotic materials, and the potlatch-like destruction and burial of these items under mounds reached a level that is unmatched in the archaeological record of North America.

The vast number and large scale of the sites and ceremonial activities represented in Ohio Hopewell archaeology is beyond the level of anything that has been found elsewhere associated with the Middle Woodland period by a scale of magnitude. Throughout this presentation, we have tried to acknowledge this distinction by referring to the sites and activities in Ohio as Hopewell while the lesser Middle Woodland complexes are called Hopewellian. The ceremonial intensification reflected in Ohio Hopewell societies likely included a combination of power quests and pilgrimages.

What has widely been called the Hopewell Interaction Sphere likely began with people from southern Ohio making long trips to distant places to acquire raw materials that were converted into prestige objects (Spielmann 2002; 2009). During the course of these power quests, they told stories to communities along the way about the building of vast ceremonial landscapes and performance of ceremonies and rituals that required great power. Some of the people who heard these stories were sufficiently impressed to make pilgrimages to Ohio and possibly participate in the construction of ceremonial landscapes and other ceremonies and rituals (Lepper 2006). The pilgrims and the Ohio people who returned from power quests brought information about the cultural and natural worlds and this gradually made southern Ohio a center of knowledge. Using well-developed oral skills, details about the geography and cultural traditions of what was, to them, the known world began to coalesce among the Ohio Hopewell leaders. Many of the verbal records of how to travel to distant lands likely developed among indigenous peoples during the Hopewell era. The directions that Lewis and Clark received to guide them on their trip to the Pacific Ocean in 1804 probably can be traced to the power quests and pilgrimages of the Hopewell era.

Future studies and final thoughts

Improved understanding of how the great earthen landscapes associated with Ohio Hopewell archaeology were built will depend greatly upon our ability to model or reconstruct how individual sites have been altered by natural forces, agriculture, and modern urban growth. Geophysics and geoarchaeology have proven, thus far, to be extremely useful tools. In the United Kingdom, archaeologists grappling with this same problem in regard to locally constructed earthworks decided to launch an experimental earthwork project. In 1960, two experimental earthworks were built in different locations to reflect the different soil conditions associated with many earthworks in the southern United Kingdom (Bell *et al.* 1996). The research plan calls for systematic examination of the walls at intervals to measure things ranging from the organic decay of wood and textiles, to soil chemistry, particle size analysis, and soil compression.

Michael O'Neal and colleagues (2005) used a different approach at the Hopewell Mound Group to model changes that have occurred in the embankment wall and associated ditch. Their application of simple finite-differences models, which are more often used to model geomorphic changes in natural topography, suggest that the embankment wall was originally higher and the ditch was deeper. These projections have been confirmed in a preliminary study of these features in an area that has been impacted by farming in the vicinity of Mound 23 (Lynott 2006). Further studies of constructed landscape evolution are needed, in combination with geophysical mapping and geoarchaeological analysis of constructed earthen features. These studies will be important contributions in future efforts to assess how the landscapes were built and how much energy was invested in construction.

We know so little about some of the great Ohio Hopewell landscapes that it is hard to say much more about some of them than Squier and Davis did in 1848. The Cedar Bank Works is still largely intact, as is Junction in the Scioto River Valley.

Suggestions for future research: towards a draft research strategy

As in any sphere of landscape archaeology, this investigation of the Hopewell ceremonial landscapes reminds us that the more we learn the less we know. This chapter highlights some of the areas that should be addressed through future research and these bullet points summarize key objectives. It is, of course, acknowledged that some of these are more easily achievable than others.

- The continued adoption of multi-disciplinary approaches to excavation and field survey, especially geoarchaeology, geophysics, and other types of remote sensing such as LiDAR.
- The acquisition and analysis of paleoenvironmental datasets (especially pollen, charcoal, and plant macro-fossils) and development of paleoenvironmental sequences and local/regional models of landscape change, forest clearance and land-use to help model the setting of the ceremonial landscapes and identify domestic settlement locations and subsistence strategies.
- The acquisition of suites of radiocarbon dates and modeling of intra- and inter-site sequences.
- Further research into the cosmological aspects and inter-site alignments of the earthwork complexes.
- The detailed analysis of sequences of soil removal and earthwork construction.
- Further modeling of the likely labor investment required for construction of the major earthwork monuments and the implications for social organisation and the local economy.
- Spatial analysis of features and objects within settlement sites and earthwork enclosures in order to examine patterns of activity, artifact use, breakage and discard, and to examine the detailed relationship between domestic and non-domestic activities.
- The analysis of site sequences in terms of the dating, construction, use and destruction/decommissioning of timber buildings and associated features and their relationships with mortuary ceremonialism and the construction of overlying mounds.
- The detailed analysis of animal bone assemblages from future excavations as well as re-analysis of any existing ones from earlier research to model subsistence strategies and craft preferences.
- Detailed analysis of all aspects of the 'Hopewell Interaction Sphere', including extraction 'industries' and the movement of lithic material and artefacts, and the identification, sourcing and circulation of exotic non-local materials and substances.
- The modeling of site/landscape abandonment and the end of Hopewellian cultural influences across Ohio, Illinois and beyond.
- Continued development of good working relationships with national, state and local agencies at all levels in the development and application of good practices in the identification, interpretation, conservation, protection and presentation of Hopewell monuments.
- The continued engagement of public interest in Hopewell archaeology generally, and to build or further develop constructive working relationships with relevant national, regional and local conservation bodies to increase awareness and promote positive conservation outcomes for Hopewell archaeological sites and their preservation for future generations.
- Engagement with American Indian tribes that have links to the Hopewell, whether those links are biological, cultural or simply geographical. These tribes are the inheritors of the cultural legacy of the Hopewell and as such, they deserve to know about that legacy. Active relationships with the tribes can lead to research aimed at addressing questions they might like to have answered. In addition, NAGPRA requires a level of consultation on issues relating to the human remains and funerary objects of the Hopewell. If museums are to be able to retain the physical remains of these ancient people, which will allow scientists to continue to learn the stories contained in their bones, it is up to archaeologists and physical anthropologists to make the case that those stories are worth knowing.

Modern America, like many western countries, has had at times an uneasy and checkered relationship with its ancestral past. The demands of agricultural expansion, industrial development and urban growth have inevitably served to greatly reduce and even obliterate many important archaeological sites all across the country. This is, of course, a global problem, but it is incumbent upon us as archaeologists to continue to strive to record, interpret and assist in the conservation of ancient sites and landscapes to ensure that future generations are able to embrace them within their own cultural milieu and to appreciate the astonishing achievements of our native predecessors.

Ohio possesses some of the most impressive and cohesive archaeological landscapes in the USA. Ultimately, what is required is a comprehensive modern resource assessment of sites and landscapes and the development of an informed, inclusive research agenda for the Ohio Hopewell. Hopefully these objectives, and this volume as a whole, will contribute to the development of that agenda.

Works East is largely obliterated and two centuries of agriculture have flattened all earthworks at Liberty. The Dunlap Earthworks is now covered by the Ross County Fairgrounds, but it is unknown if any vestiges of that very unusual enclosure and associated embankments remain. In the Little Miami Valley, most of the geometric earthworks have been greatly reduced in visibility or totally destroyed. Tankersley (2007) has reported that portions of the Turner Group of Earthworks are still intact, although the site was reported to be destroyed more than a half century ago (Starr 1960: 35). If Tankersley is correct, further studies at Turner must be a priority for future Hopewell scholars. Despite over a century of study at Fort Ancient, the recent discovery of the Moorehead Circle has demonstrated that there is still much to learn at this important site. Romain (2000) has located remnants of the Marietta embankments, but other than the Capitoleum Mound (Pickard 1996) we have very little data about this impressive earthwork complex. Then there is Newark. This is the largest and most complex of all Ohio Hopewell ceremonial centers, and we have not learned much about this site in the last century. Bradley Lepper has mined the historical archives for every shred of data about Newark, but we need contemporary field data to really understand how this huge and impressive construction was built, when it was built, and how it was used.

Two recent events offer great hope for the future of Hopewell research. Unlike many other nations in the world, laws in the United States do not protect archaeological resources located on private land. Mounds and other earthworks have been flattened by years of agriculture or the desire to build modern facilities on ancient landscapes. In the last decade, the Spruce Hill Works and the Junction Works were offered for public sale by families that had owned the sites for many decades. In both cases, a coalition of preservation groups raised the necessary funds to purchase these sites and protect them for the benefit of future generations. The Spruce Hill site is described in Chapter 4. The Junction Works was recorded and mapped by Squier and Davis (1848). Although 150+ years of agriculture have reduced the earthen walls to the point where they are no longer apparent visually, magnetic survey has shown the subsurface aspects of the site are still present and represent an important record of Ohio Hopewell monument construction (Fig. 6.1).

This volume is just the beginning, not the final word on Hopewell landscape construction. It will be hard for any one person or institution to replicate the excellent long-term research conducted by Robert Riordan of Wright State University at the Pollock Works. However, with geophysical and geoarchaeological techniques, it may be possible to obtain important data more efficiently. As our knowledge about Hopewell earthen construction develops, we may be able to replace long trenches with more strategic test units, and perhaps standard-sized test units may eventually be replaced by soil cores. Certainly, we will need to continue to verify geophysical data with some type of strategic testing program, but as more and more archaeologists become comfortable using these techniques to study landscapes it will be possible to conduct our research more efficiently. This is absolutely essential because the Hopewell built on grand scales and their works demonstrate sufficient diversity to urge caution in extrapolating knowledge from one part of a giant site to the site as a whole.

In closing this discussion, it is very difficult to over-estimate the magnitude of

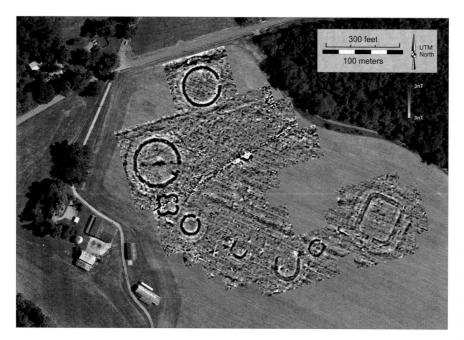

Fig. 6.1. The Junction Group earthworks (Fig. 4.11, G) lie on a terrace overlooking Paint Creek just south-west of Chillicothe. They were surveyed by Squier and Davis (1848, pl. xxii) but have been plowed flat. in 2005, when the site was being rapidly encroached upon by development, a detailed magnetometer survey was undertaken by N'omi Greber, Wesley Bernardini and Jarrod Burks. It revealed clearly the plowed out banks and ditches and also discovered that a small sub-square enclosure mapped by Squier and Davis is actually quatrefoil shaped – and so far unique among the Ohio Hopewell earthworks. In March 2014 the farm containing the site was put up for auction for development but, after a rapid appeal to the public, 192 acres (77.7 ha) including the 89 acres (36 ha) of the earthworks was bought for $1.1 million by the Arc of Appalachia Preserve System and will be developed into a park and nature preserve (image courtesy of Jarrod Burks).

the Ohio Hopewell archaeological record. Something truly amazing was happening in southern Ohio between roughly AD 1 and 450. Despite the construction of massive and complex ceremonial landscapes, and the ceremonial destruction of massive quantities of prestige goods, the people living in this area were organized in small-scale, tribal units with considerable local autonomy. It is hard to imagine how they maintained a stable social organization and commitment to monument building over so many generations. Certainly during the Ohio Hopewell era, both tradition and change must have been important parts of the lives of the people that planned, built, and maintained so many important sites. In the archaeological record of North America, this was likely the first time that the activities and accomplishments of people from a single region became known to people across much of the North American continent. Hopewell archaeology stimulated some of the first discussions and debates about the archaeological record of North America and it will likely hold our attention for the foreseeable future.

Appendix 1

A model of the construction chronology of the Hopeton Earthworks

Timothy Schilling

Recent, long-term investigations at the Hopeton Earthworks have yielded 22 radiocarbon dates that are relevant for understanding the construction chronology of the earthwork (Chapter 3). Twenty fall within the Hopewell period while two are clearly later and probably represent a Fort Ancient period occupation or rehabilitation of the earthwork. Hopewell period calibrated dates span a range from the early 2nd century cal BC to the middle 4th century cal AD. The broad span and imprecision of the radiometric database leads to multiple, competing models of the earthwork's construction chronology. Logically, interpretations of the construction chronology can be placed along a continuum. At one end, the data can be used to support a model where construction began early in the Hopewell period and continued incrementally over the span of many generations. At the other end, the data can also be used to support a model where Hopeton was built near the end of the Hopewell period, and was executed as a brief, intense undertaking, potentially spanning only a few months to several years. In between, estimates support interpretations that blend different aspects of these extremes. Although it will probably never be possible to state precisely when the earthwork at Hopeton was constructed, judgments about these temporal frameworks can and should be made since these construction chronologies are vital for evaluating demographic and social organizational models of Hopewellian society.

To evaluate which interpretation of the absolute chronology and construction span is the most consistent with the radiometric data, a series of Bayesian models were constructed in OxCal ver. 4.2. These models were designed to investigate which chronology, either the early, extended, or the late, abbreviated, is most appropriate, Typically, OxCal is used to model sequences of events using cross-cutting relationships to provide more accurate estimates of events. In this instance, observable stratigraphic superpositioning between and among the different wall segments has not been discovered. There is no *a priori* reason to indicate any kind of ordering within wall segments. Similarly, all of the radiocarbon dates come from materials recovered from contexts that are stratigraphically below mound construction sediments. Most were recovered from a layer that was probably deposited immediately before any construction (see Chapter 3). Consequently,

Bayesian modeling of radiocarbon dates

"The basic idea behind the Bayesian approach to the interpretation of data is encapsulated by Bayes' theorem (Bayes 1763). This approach is fundamentally probabilistic and contextual. It simply means that researchers analyse the new data collected about a problem ('the standardised likelihoods') in the context of existing experience and knowledge about that problem ('prior beliefs'). This enables archaeologists to arrive at a new understanding of the problem which incorporates both existing knowledge and new data (our 'posterior beliefs'). Today's posterior belief becomes tomorrow's prior belief, informing the collection of new data and their interpretation as the cycle repeats. In Bayesian modeling, scientists use formal probability theory, where these kinds of archaeological information are expressed as probability density functions. An accessible general introduction to the principles of Bayesian statistics is provided by Lindley (1985).

Bayesian modeling is an explicit, probabilistic method for estimating the dates when events happened in the past and for quantifying the uncertainties associated with these estimated dates. When constructing a Bayesian chronology, the calibrated radiocarbon dates form the 'standardised likelihoods' component of the model and archaeology provides the 'prior beliefs'. This means that the radiocarbon dates are reinterpreted in the light of the archaeological information, to provide new posterior beliefs about the most likely age of a dated sample. Bayesian modeling fundamentally shifts how archaeologists understand chronologies of past events. Independent, scientific radiocarbon dates were once heralded as providing 'good objective chronology' ... Bayesian chronologies are different. They are contextual and interpretative. They can and will change as more radiocarbon dates are obtained and incorporated into our models, and as archaeological information is viewed in new ways. Sometimes, a group of radiocarbon dates may be modeled in different ways to answer different questions ... Indeed, the construction and comparison of alternative models (known as 'sensitivity analyses') are a fundamental part of the Bayesian process." (Bayliss *et al.* 2011: 19–20).

Prior beliefs maybe 'uninformative' or 'informative'. The latter usual derive from the relative dating evidence provided by stratigraphic relationships between radiocarbon samples – if sample B was stratified above sample A and if both were contemporary with their contexts then B must be later than A – and the assumption that the events concerned occurred within a bounded phase (Bayliss & Bronk Ramsey 2004; Bayliss *et al.* 2011). The construction chronology of the Hopeton earthwork was created using informative prior beliefs based on the stratigraphic position of dated samples.

The 'standardised likelihoods' are normally the radiocarbon date though these may be supplemented by documentary/historical evidence or other forms of dating such as dendrochronology. Once the components of a Bayesian model have been assembled – the standardised likelihoods obtained and the prior beliefs explicitly defined – they can be combined using Bayes' theorem (Fig. 2.4). This is done using a Markov chain Monte Carlo (MCMC) random sampling technique. Modeling of the dates is then undertaken using the calibration program OxCal (Bronk Ramsey 1995; 1998; 2001; 2009).

'Two statistics are calculated by OxCal which aid the archaeologist in an assessment of the reliability of a model. The first of these is the individual index of agreement (A: Bronk Ramsey 1995, 429). This index provides a measure of how well any posterior density estimate agrees with the standardised likelihood from which it derives. If the posterior density estimate is situated in a high-probability region of the likelihood, the index of agreement is high; if it falls in a low-probability region, it is low. If the index of agreement falls below 60%, then the radiocarbon result may be in some way problematic. It should be noted that this threshold has been empirically derived, and in practice provides only an indication of when a date may be inconsistent with the model employed (about 1 in 20 dates will have a low index of agreement simply on statistical grounds). The index of agreement is not a quantitative measure of how well a date 'fits' the model...

The second statistic is the overall index of agreement, which is calculated from the individual agreement indices ($A_{overall}$: Bronk Ramsey 1995, 249). This provides a more general measure of the consistency between the prior information and the standardised likelihoods. Again, the overall index of agreement has a threshold value of 60%, and models which produce values lower than this should be subject to critical re-examination." (Bayliss *et al.* 2011: 34–5)

A general introduction to the application of the Bayesian approach to archaeological data is provided by Buck *et al.* (1996). More specific introductions to building Bayesian chronologies in archaeology are provided by Bayliss *et al.* (2007a) and Bronk Ramsey (2009).

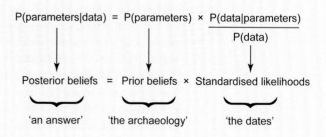

$$P(\text{parameters}|\text{data}) = P(\text{parameters}) \times \frac{P(\text{data}|\text{parameters})}{P(\text{data})}$$

Posterior beliefs = Prior beliefs × Standardised likelihoods

'an answer'   'the archaeology'   'the dates'

these dates are *termini post quem* for wall segment construction. The limits of their ages provide the best estimate of when construction began on each segment. There are no data from mound summit contexts so it is not possible to calculate the duration of construction but geoarchaeological observations indicate that there was not a substantial amount of time required to build each segment (Lynott and Mandel 2008: 176).

Modeling was based on three assumptions:

1. All of the dates are valid assessments of the proportion of C^{14} to C^{12} in the sample. The radiometric database from Hopeton has been produced in the last 20 years using standard techniques. All radiometric measurement have been corrected to standardized values. Dates were first calibrated using IntCal13 calibration curves (Reimer *et al.* 2013) and then modeled according to stratigraphic and associational relationships using OxCal ver.4.2 (Bronk Ramsey 2013)

2. All of the dates are reasonable indicators of the time period immediately before the construction of each segment. With the exception of materials from Trench 1, excavators indicate that samples were not exceptionally large charcoal fragments. They probably were twigs used for small fires. Samples were recovered from well-defined feature contexts. Geoarchaeological observations suggest that the pre-earthwork surface did not undergo *in situ* weathering and there was no buried humic or grass horizon. Presumably, each element was built on a surface that was stripped to sub-surface horizons removing all potential old wood and other earlier contaminates. None was believed to be old wood nor were any believed to be intrusive (see Chapter 3; Ruby 1997). Materials from Trench 1 were all recovered from a single large log and the treatment of these samples is discussed in more detail below.

3. Each segment was constructed independent of one another and each of the segments is assumed to be a single project. One of the goals of testing was to determine if segments were coeval or sequential. Segments were modeled with the potential to overlap in time. No *a priori* order was assumed.

The 20 Hopewell dates were modeled as eight overlapping phases that were in sequence with and earlier than a Fort Ancient phase that was represented by the two later dates. In the instances of Trench 2 and Trench 7, only one date exists from each context so the individual dates were used in the model as standalone events rather than creating a phase with a single event. Dates from the log in Trench 1 can be appropriately modeled as a phase. Excavators suggest that the samples from Trench 1 represent a mixture of growth rings that sample the entire age of the tree. Consequently, a phase model would represent a good estimation of the period of growth of the tree. Logically then, mound construction happened after the tree was cut and the end boundary of the age of the tree's growth is the best estimate of when construction of the overlying wall segment happened.

Archaeologically, this model is the most reasonable way to approach the dataset. It is the simplest and has the fewest *a priori* constraints. When the dates were calibrated within the model, test statistics (A_{model}=86, $A_{overall}$=79.7) demonstrated that the model is statistically valid and the radiocarbon dates probably

Sample no.	Determination (BP)	Standard error	δ¹³C/¹²C ratio	Calibrated date 2σ (95.4%)	Comments
Beta-147187	4850	80	-25.0	BC 3780–3390	F. 50, Triangle
Beta-147186	3660	60	-24.3	BC 2200–1890	F. 143-4, Triangle
Beta-147189	3529	60	-25.0	BC 2010–1690	F. 149, Triangle
Beta-147190	3260	40	-25.0	BC 1620–1440	F. 1, Triangle
Beta-147183	3180	40	-26.3	BC 1520–1390	F. 17, Triangle
Beta-249012	2130	40	-26.7	BC 350–50	F. 805, Trench 9
Beta-177506	2040	80	-25.0	BC 350–AD120	F. 6, Trench 1
Beta-176576	1990	130	-25.0	BC 370–AD 330	F. 6, Trench 1
Beta-177507	1990	70	-25.0	BC 170–AD 140	F, 6, Trench 1
Beta-249009	1940	40	-25.4	BC 30–AD 130	F. 801, Trench 9
Beta-147184	1960	50	-25.0	BC 50–AD 130	F. 64, Triangle
Beta-96598	1930	60	-25.0	BC 40–AD 235	Tr. 6, Ruby 1996
Beta-176579	1910	40	-24.5	AD 20–220	F. 14, Trench 3
Beta-176580	1910	40	-23.7	AD 20–220	F. 17, Trench 3
Beta-109963	1900	50	-25.0	AD 15–240	Red Wing, Ruby
Beta-197242	1900	40	-26.5	AD 30–220	F. 33, Structure 1
Beta-176581	1900	40	-26.3	AD 30–220	F. 23, Structure 1
Beta-233777	1900	40	-25.8	AD 20–220	F. 04-2, Trench 6
Beta-233775	1890	40	-24.8	AD 30–230	F. 05-2, Trench 8
Beta-233776	1870	40	-23.6	AD 60–240	F. 105, Trench 5
Beta-176578	1870	50	-26.7	AD 40–250	F. 9
Beta-198332	1860	40	-25.7	AD 70–240	F.04-2, Trench 6
Beta-109961	1850	70	-27.0	AD 25–370	Red Wing, Ruby
Beta-197241	1850	40	-25.2	AD 70–250	F. 34, Structure 1
Beta-198331	1840	40	-26.6	AD 80–250	F. 04-1, Trench 7
Beta-109962	1840	50	-25.0	AD 75–330	Tr. 6, Ruby 2003
Beta-249011	1830	40	-24.6	AD 80–310	F. 804, Trench 9
Beta-249010	1820	40	-23.6	AD 90–320	F. 803, Trench 9
Beta-213026	1790	40	-26.7	AD 130–350	Trench 8, F. 05-4
Beta-159033	1740	50	-25.0	AD 150–410	F.6, Trench 1
Beta-176577	1710	80	-25.0	AD 130–530	F.11, Trench 2
Beta-182632	1680	40	-23.6	AD 255–435	F. 105, Trench 5
Beta-109964	1150	40	-26.0	AD 790–990	Red Wing, Ruby
Beta-147188	1080	90	-25.0	AD 770–1160	F. 88, Triangle
Beta-182630	1010	40	-24.1	AD 980–1050	F. 107, Trench 4
Beta-182629	1000	40	-24.0	AD 980–1055	F. 100. Trench 4
Beta-197243	860	40	-25.6	AD 1040–1260	FS #141, Str. 1
Beta-213025	420	40	-26.8	AD 1420–1620	Trench 8, F. 05-8
Beta-182631	230	40	-26.2	AD 1530–1950	F. 112, Trench 4
Beta-176574	220	100	-25.0	AD 1450–1950	F.1, Level 4
Beta-213027	220	40	-24.9	AD 1640–1950	Trench 8, F. 05-10
Beta-176575	190	40	-25.0	AD 1650–1950	F. 1, Level 5
Beta-147185	190	40	-26.0	AD 1650–1700	F. 44, Triangle
Beta-213028	170	40	-23.5	AD 1650–1950	Trench 8, F. 6

Table 4: Hopeton radiocarbon dates. Calibrations were calculated using the University of Washington Quaternary Isotope Lab Radiocarbon Calibration Program Rev. 4.3, based on Stuiver and Reimer (1993) and Stuiver *et al.* (1998).

Fig. Appx1.1. End dates of each pre-mound phase. The open circle indicates the mean of the posterior probability distribution and the corresponding line represents 1 standard deviation around the mean. The lower line includes 95% of the probability distribution of each modeled time period. There dates are the best estimate when each segment was built.

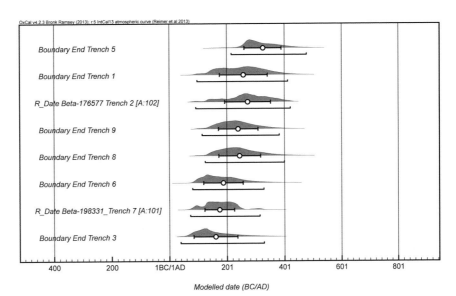

Fig. Appx 1.2. Probable length of time between the earliest and latest construction events.

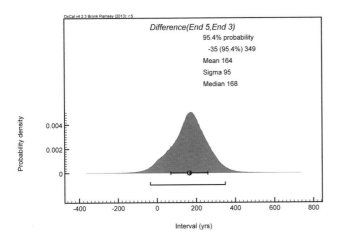

represent overlapping activities (Fig. Appx1). Sequences, one where the circle preceded the square and one where the square preceded the circle, were modeled. These were found to be statistically invalid and not supported by the radiocarbon data.

Even though all radiocarbon dates are *termini post quem* for their individual segments and overlap between the age ranges exists, multiple lines of evidence suggest it is unlikely all of the wall segments were constructed contemporaneously. Based on the most likely age of the modeled events, it is clear some elements were constructed earlier than others. The data can be ordered reasonably well (Table 4). Moreover, the span of time from the end of the earliest end date to the end of the latest end date is about 165 years, indicating that the mound segments were constructed over the course of perhaps around six generations. Yet, some appear contemporaneous or at least very close in time. Construction may have been planned but the implementation occurred sporadically or intermittently over the course of many life times.

Appendix 2

Ohio Hopewell ceremonial sites open to the public

As will have become clear from the preceding text, many formerly magnificent earthwork sites are now so reduced by agriculture, urban development and/or general neglect that there often remains little or nothing to see and explore. The following is a list of managed sites with public access or which can be viewed from public rights of way; all sites listed below have a reasonable level of preservation or have been reconstructed to a greater or lesser degree. Details are as correct as possible at the time of writing (August 2014). Please check locally for full details. A few of the larger Adena sites are also included here.

Central Ohio

Newark Earthworks, Licking County

The complex Newark earthworks (see text for details) are now encompassed by the city of Newark and it is very difficult to get a feel for their layout on the ground. The Great Circle, accessed from Hebron Road, is an open park with a small museum. Remnants of the Wright Earthwork may be viewed from James Street, a short distance from Grant Street and the State Route (SR) 79 interchange. The Octagon is on the grounds of the Moundbuilders Country Club, 125 North 33rd Street, and access is restricted (to non-members) to a car park and viewing platform. Access to all sites is free and they are open dawn to dusk.

The museum is open all year Monday–Friday: 8:30 am–5 pm; Memorial Day–Labor Day (last Monday May–first Monday September) Saturday: 10 am–4 pm, Sunday: 12–4 pm. there are restricted opening times on holidays.

Flint Ridge State Memorial, Licking County

Flint Ridge is one of the few easily accessible Native American quarries in the Midwest, spanning a ridge some 9 miles (14.5 km) long and up to 3 miles (4.8 km) wide in places. It is also one of the most important sources of flint in the region, with deposits of the Vanport Flint occurring in beds up to 12 ft (3.7 m) in thickness, and in a multitude of colors. The flint found here was extracted from the Paleoindian Period up to Historic times and even by Anglo-American settlers in the Muskingum Valley. It was traded extensively during the prehistoric period, and was the most important flint source for the Hopewell. The site now comprises numerous quarry hollows of varying sizes, often juxtaposed with waste dumps alongside. An interesting museum has been constructed over one of the quarries, and has informative displays explaining the significance of the site.

The site can be found at 15300 Flint Ridge Road, Glenford, Ohio 43739. The park grounds are open dawn till dusk all year; the Museum is open weekends only May to October (see website for times: www.flintridgeohio.org)

Shrum Mound (Campbell Mound), Franklin County

This flat-topped mound survives to a height of some 20 ft (6 m) with a diameter of ca. 100 ft (30 m). It is located on what was once a high bluff overlooking the Scioto River, on the west side of McKinley Avenue in the James E Campbell Park, Columbus, and is one of only a few Adena mounds in Columbus. Access to the mound is from McKinley Avenue.

Huffman Mound (Tippett Mound), Licking County

The Huffman Mound is located on the Taft Reserve on Flint Ridge Road on the south-east side of Newark, between Newark and I 70 on CR 312 . The Mound stands roughly 20 ft (6 m) high with a diameter of 197 ft (61 m). This mound was partly excavated by David Wyrick around 1860 who discovered multiple burials at the base of the mound which had been buried beneath layers of ash and charcoal. A tubular tobacco pipe was found near the center of the mound at a depth of some 6 ft (2 m). Taken together, the burial deposit and the site location both suggest that this mound was of Adena origin.

For further information see the website: http://www.lickingparkdistrict.com/

South-east Ohio

Marietta, Washington County

The Marietta Earthworks are located within the town of Marietta, at the confluence of the Muskingum and Ohio rivers in Washington County. Originally, the complex included a large square enclosure surrounding four flat-topped pyramidal mounds, another smaller square, and a circular enclosure with a large burial mound at its center representing both Adena and Hopewell monuments and possibly Late Prehistoric features. Three segments of the Marietta Earthworks are maintained as public parks today and can be visited free of charge: the Conus mound, lying inside the Mound Cemetery graveyard (entrances on 5th and Tipper Streets); the Capitolium mound on which sits the Washington County Public Library; and the Quadranaou in Quadranaou Park (Warren and 3rd Streets). The Via Sacre earthworks are no longer extant but its route is laid to grass, extending from the park down towards the Muskingum river.

All of the remaining fragments of the Marietta Earthworks can be viewed from public streets at any time. The Campus Martius Museum (601 2nd Street) places the earthworks in context and recounts the story of early settler attempts to preserve the sites.

Piketon Mounds, Pike County

The four conical mounds of the Piketon group are located upon a terrace overlooking the Scioto River The largest mound is 24 ft (7.6 m) high and 75 ft (23 m) in diameter, whereas the smaller mounds are only 2–5 ft (0.6–1.5 m) in height. Although these mounds are undated, the skeleton of a girl covered in bark hints at Adena or Hopewell burial practices, and nearby a Hopewell graded way aligned north–south adds to the suspicion that these mounds were associated with one or both of these cultural groups. Sadly the graded way has now been largely destroyed by modern developments. the mounds lie within the within Mound Cemetery, on CR 84 half a mile north of SR 124 and can be accessed off Mound Cemetery Road.

Straight Mound (Dunn Mound, New Marshfield Mound, Stright Mound), Athens County

Straight Mound is conical in form and roughly 6 ft (2 m) high with a circumference of 59 ft (18 m) and is located near the top of a ridge which separates two tributaries of the Raccoon Creek. Excavations on the summit of the mound in 1940 discovered an extended adult male skeleton accompanied by Adena grave goods. The mound lies in the Indian Mound Campground on the south-west side of New Marshfield at 7896 Roundhouse Road. The Campground, which apparently contains a small Native American museum, is open all year and the mound and can also be seen from CR 8 and Roundhouse Road.

Scioto River Valley

Hopewell Culture National Historical Park, Ross County

Six major earthwork sites are located and managed within the Hopewell Culture National Historical Park, which covers nearly 1200 acres (486 ha) in the area around Chillicothe and the confluence of the Paint Creek and Scioto rivers. These are: **Mound City Group**, **Hopeton Earthworks**, **Hopewell Mound Group**, **Seip Earthworks**, **High Bank Works** and **Spruce Hill** (see text for details).

Hopeton Earthworks and High Bank Works are closed to the public except during special events and access to Spruce Hill is limited and visitors must go to the Visitor Center to gain access. All the other sites are open dawn till dusk throughout the year. The Park's Visitor Center is situated at Mound City (16062 State Route 104, Chillicothe, OH 45601-8694) and is open 8:30 am to 5 pm seven days a week (closed January 1st, Thanksgiving Day, and December 25th).

Entry to the park and all sites is free.

Full details, including GPS co-ordinates for all the major sites can be found on the Park's website http://www.nps.gov/hocu/index.htm

Adena Mound, Ross County

The site of the Adena Mound now lies buried beneath a housing development at Lake Ellensmere on the south side of US 35 on the north-western edge of Chillicothe. The Adena Mound gave its name to the Adena Culture and lay 1.5 miles (2.4 km) north-west of Chillicothe, and was intervisible with the later Mound City Hopewell cemetery. Originally standing 26 ft (8.1 m) high and with a circumference of 445 ft (135.6 m), the mound appeared to have been constructed in two major phases with a sequence of elaborate burial deposits probably accumulating over several generations. The Mound also produced the iconic clay effigy pipe from a log-lined crypt containing burial #21 which depicts a stunted male figure featuring a stylized hair style, clothing and typical circular ear spools which have been taken as an accurate representation of the personal appearance of some Adena Indians. The mound lies on the corner of Appleton Drive and Orange Street.

Story Mound, Ross County

This mound lies on the east side of Delano Avenue, Chillicothe within a small park area. The Story Mound was originally about the same size as the Adena Mound which lay roughly 1 mile (1.6 km) to the north-west. Today this Adena mound survives some 20 ft (6 m) high and 95 ft (29 m) in diameter. It was excavated by Clarence Loveberry in 1897, who tunneled into the mound from the side and discovered an extended male skeleton with grave goods, but more importantly a series of post-molds of a circular building which was the first recorded instance of an Adena pre-mound structure.

South-west Ohio – Brush Creek, The Great Miami and Little Miami River drainages

Fort Hill, Highland County

Fort Hill is a major Hopewell hilltop enclosure constructed from earth and stone walling standing 6 ft (1.8 m) to 15 ft (4.5 m) high and up to 44 ft (13.7 m) wide which follow the contours of the terrain. It lies in woodland atop a 500 ft (150 m) high mesa in the upper reaches of Brush Creek in Brush Township, about 30 miles (50 km) south-west of Chillicothe. There are pleasant woodland walks and a small museum which is open on Saturdays May–October 12–5 pm.

There is free access to the site which is open all year, dawn to dusk, apart from a few days in winter when it is closed for hunting to control the deer population.

Full details are available at http://www.arcofappalachia.org/visit/fort-hill.html

Fort Ancient, Warren County

Fort Ancient is a spectacular example of a Hopewell hilltop enclosure whose earth and stone walls spanning some 3.5 miles (5.6 km) which enclose an area of 125 acres (50.5 ha). This enclosure lies 245 ft (75 m) above the Little Miami River, on SR 350, at Oregonia, about 35 miles (56 km) NE of Cincinnati. It is the largest and best preserved of the Hopewell complexes whose walls follow an erratic course delineating a figure-of-eight shaped enclosure or 'fort', and excavations have discovered evidence of Hopewell settlement within the site. There is an excellent museum, picnic areas and 2.5 miles (4 km) of hiking trails. Admssion fees apply for both the site only and the site with museum.

Museum opening hours are: April–November: Tuesday–Saturday 10 am–5 pm, Sunday 12–5 pm (closed Mondays);

December–March: Saturday 10 am–5 pm, Sunday 12–5 pm (closed Monday–Friday except by appointment)

Full details are available at: http://www.fortancient.org/

Pollock Works (Indian Mound Reserve), nr Cedarville, Greene County

This Hopewell enclosure followed the terrain of a limestone plateau, and was constructed between roughly AD 50 and AD 225, with five building phases. The enclosure has three entrances protected by elaborate outworks. The enclosure now lies in woodland and the earthworks are not very prominent.

The site lies south of Clifton village, on US 42, 1.4 miles off SR 72 towards Cedarville. From a parking area, a walking trail leads north to the large, conical, Adena era Williamson Mound.

To reach the Pollock Works follow another trail east which leads through a gate in the enclosure and onto a circular walk around the site.

Miami Fort, Hamilton County

Miami Fort lies near the confluence of the Ohio and Great Miami rivers on an elevated, irregularly-shaped peninsula within the Shawnee Lookout Park to the west of US 275 near Elizabethtown This Hopewell enclosure is defined by earthen walls ranging from 1ft (0.3m) to 12 ft (3.6 m) high, and enclosing an area of some 12 acres (4.8 ha). One construction phase has been dated to around AD 270, and settlement evidence (of unknown duration) has been discovered within the fort. Three mounds lie on a promontory to the south-west of the enclosure, and an Adena-Hopewell village site has also been excavated in this area.

Shawnee Lookout (2008 Lawrenceburg Rd. North Bend, OH 45052). is open year-round, dawn to dusk. For further details see the website http://greatparks.org/parks/shawnee-lookout

Orators Mound (Glen Helen Mound), Greene County

This truncated Adena conical mound was once topped by a pavilion and now survives to a height of 5 ft (1.5 m) with a diameter of 45 ft (13.7 m). Partial excavations revealed a burial deposit of 4–6 individuals accompanied by Adena projectile points and mica crescents.

The Orators Mound lies on property owned by Antioch University on the eastern side of Yellow Springs. A

Trailside Museum and parking lot is located on Corry Street south off US 68. The mound can be viewed from the self-guiding Inman Trail.

Stubbs Earthworks, Warren County

The Stubbs Earthworks was a Hopewell composite enclosure incorporating circular with rectangular elements with a detached small, circular enclosure lying to the south. A large W-shaped linear earthwork lay to the west, probably forming an embanked avenue or graded way. The circular enclosure was discovered to be a Woodhenge with 172 posts set in a circle of 73.1 m diameter, which was dismantled about AD 180 and an earthen bank built over it. Excavations in the interior of the main enclosure complex have discovered Hopewell houses, although they did not produce many finds, suggesting that this site was only periodically inhabited. Taken together with the adjacent Woodhenge, this implies that the Stubbs Earthworks may have had a temporary use tied into the annual cycle of rituals or seasonal ceremonies.

A fragment of the W-shaped linear earthwork is all that survives, and it can be found on the access route leading to Little Miami High School from Morrow-Cozaddale Road which leaves US 22 between Hopkinsville and Morrow.

Tremper Mound, Scioto County

This important site originally consisted of an ovoid enclosure of 400 × 479 ft (122 × 146 m), which enclosed a large amorphous mound. An entrance break lay in the south-west, protected by a short length of external bank. Excavations by Mills in 1915 discovered a complex oval building beneath the mound represented by 600+ post-molds defining an irregularly-shaped structure 200 ft (61.0 m) long by 100 ft (30.5 m) wide which paralleled the outline of the mound and appears to have been a Hopewell great house. Unusually, four communal graves estimated to contain 375 cremations, with their accompanying grave goods, were discovered in the charnel house. Overall a large assemblage of artifacts was recovered, including numerous tobacco pipes (many of Ohio pipestone) which had been broken as part of the burial ceremonialism which took place at this site.

This site is in private ownership, but can be viewed with caution from the roadside. It lies on the western side of where routes SR 73/104 converge to the north-west of Portsmouth.

Portsmouth Mound Park, Scioto County

This Hopewell complex was one of a cluster of three major groups of geometric earthworks – one in Ohio, the others in Kentucky – which focused around the confluence of the Scioto and Ohio Rivers. The Portsmouth earthworks comprise a pair of large U-shaped embanked features roughly 79 ft (24 m) long by 69 ft (21 m) wide which were located within an interrupted circular enclosure that had a small constellation of smaller semi-circular and circular enclosures scattered around the third terrace. At least four circular burial mounds were juxtaposed (one enclosed and probably Adena in origin), and a series of what appear to be embanked trackways led to and from various elements of the site. Sadly, little now survives of this complex, although the Park has preserved the eastern U-shaped feature, and other eroded elements are still just visible.

Portsmouth Mound Park lies three blocks north of US 52 on Hutchins Avenue.

Bibliography

Abrams, E. (1989) Architecture and energy: an evolutionary perspective. In *Archaeological Method and Theory*, ed. M. B. Schiffer, Vol. 1: 47–87. Academic Press, New York.

Alex, L. M. (2000) *Iowa's Archaeological Past*. University of Iowa Press, Iowa City, Iowa.

Alex, L. M. and Green, W. (1995) *Toolesboro Mounds National Historic Landmark Archaeological Analysis and Report*. Research Paper 20 No. 4. Office of the State Archaeologist, University of Iowa, Iowa City Iowa.

Anderson, J. C. (1980) A recent discovery – the Anderson Earthwork. *Ohio Archaeologist* 30 (1): 31–5.

Anonymous (2010) Wooden "Stonehenge" emerges from prehistoric Ohio. *National Geographic Daily News*, July 20, 2010. http://news.nationalgeographic.com/news/2010/07/100720-woodhenge-stonehenge-ohio-fort-ancient-science/

Applegate, D. and Mainfort, R. C. Jr (ed.) (2005) *Woodland Period Systematics in the Middle Ohio Valley*. University of Alabama Press, Tuscaloosa, AL.

Atwater, C. (1820) Description of the antiquities discovered in the State of Ohio and other western states. *Transactions and Collections of the American Antiquarian Society* 1: 105–267.

Aveni, A. F. (2004) An assessment of studies in Hopewell astronomy. In *The Fort Ancient Earthworks: Prehistoric Lifeways of the Hopewell Culture in Southwestern Ohio*, ed. R. P. Connolly, and B. T. Lepper: 243–58.

Aveni, A. F. (2008) *People and the Sky: Our Ancestors and the Cosmos*. Thames and Hudson, London.

Baby, R. S. (1954) Archaeological explorations at Fort Hill. *Museum Echoes* 27 (11): 86–7.

Baby, R. S. and Langlois, S. M. (1979) Seip Mound State Memorial: nonmortuary aspects of Hopewell. In Brose and Greber (ed.) 1979: 16–18.

Ballantyne, M. R. (2009) *Miami Fort: An Ancient Hydraulic Structure*. M.A. Thesis, University of Cincinnati, Department of Anthropology.

Baker, E. C., Griffin, J. B., Morgan, R. G., Neumann G. and Taylor J. L. B. (1941) Contributions to the Archaeology of the Illinois River Valley. *Transactions of the American Philosophical Society*, new series 1.

Barnhart, T. A. (1986) An American menagerie: the cabinet of Squier and Davis. *Timeline* 2 (6): 2–17.

Barnhart, T. A. (2005) *Ephraim George Squier and the Development of American Archaeology*. University of Nebraska Press, Lincoln, Nebraska.

Bartram, W. (1996) *Travels Through North and South Carolina, Georgia, East and West Florida, the Cherokee Country, the Extensive Territories of the Muscogulges or Creek Confederacy, and the Contry of the Chactaws*. Reprint of publication by The Library of America, New York.

Bauermeister, A. C. (2010) Feature finds from the Riverbank Site, 33RO1059, *Hopewell Archaeology: The Newsletter of Hopewell Archaeology in the Ohio River Valley* 7(2), chap. 5.

Bayes, T. R. (1763) An essay towards solving a problem in the doctrine of chances. *Philosophical Transactions of the Royal Society* 53: 370–418.

Bayliss, A. and Bronk Ramsey, C. (2004) Pragmatic Bayesians: a decade integrating radiocarbon dates into chronological models. In *Tools for Constructing Chronologies: Tools for Crossing Disciplinary Boundaries*, ed. C. E. Buck and A. R. Millard: 25–41. Springer, London.

Bayliss, A., Bronk Ramsey, C., Plicht, J. van der and Whittle, A. (2007). Bradshaw and Bayes: towards a timetable for the Neolithic. *Cambridge Journal of Archaeology* 17 (1), supplement: 1–28.

Bayliss, A., Plicht, J. van der; Bronk Ramsey, C., McCormac, G., Healy, F. and Whittle, A. (2011) Towards generational time-scales: the quantitative interpretation of archaeological chronologies. In Whittle *et al.* 2011: 16–49.

Beaubien, P. L. (1953) Some Hopewellian mounds at the Effigy Mounds National Monument, Iowa. *Wisconsin Archeologist* 34 (2): 125–38.

Bell, M., Fowler, P. J. and Hillson, S. W. (1996) *The Experimental Earthwork Project, 1960-1992*. Council for British Archaeology Research Report 100. Council for British Archaeology, York.

Behr, D. E. (2011) *Investigation of Middle Woodland Population Movement in the Midwestern United States Using Strontium Isotopes*. PhD dissertation, Department of Anthropology, University of Illinois at Urbana–Champaign, IL.

Benchley, E. D., Gregg, M. L. and Dudzik, M. J. (1977) Recent investigations at Albany Mounds Whiteside County, Illinois. *Illinois Archaeological Survey Circular 2*. Illinois State Museum, Springfield, IL.

Benn, D. W. (1978) The Woodland ceramic sequence in the culture history of northeastern Iowa. *Midcontinental Journal of Archaeology* 3: 215–83.

Benn, D. and Stadler, S. (2004) *Effigy Mounds National*

Monument Archeological Overview and Assessment. Unpubished manuscript on file Midwest Archeological Center, National Park Service, Lincoln, NE

Benson B. B. (2012) Geophysical investigations of the Mound City borrow pits, Ross County, Ohio. Master's Thesis, Department of Geology, University of Kansas.

Bernardini, W. (2004) Hopewell Geometric Earthworks: A Case Study in the Referential and Experimental Meaning of Monuments. *Journal of Anthropological Archaeology* 23: 331–356.

Bevan, B. D. (1997) Conductivity, Resistance and Radar Survey Over Mounds. In *Geophysical Surveys at Two Earthen Mound Sites*, Wright–Patterson Air Force Base, Ohio, ed. M. J. Lynott: III, 1–101. Midwest Archeological Center, National Park Service, Lincoln, NE.

Blank, J. E. (1985) *An Aerial Photogrammetrical Analysis of the Hopeton National Historic Landmark, Ross County, Ohio.* Report on file, National Park Service, Midwest Archeological Center, Lincoln, NE.

Blosser, J. and Glotzhober, R. C. (1995) *Fort Ancient: Citadel, Cemetery, Cathedral, or Calendar?* Ohio Historical Society, Columbus, OH.

Bohannon, C. F. (1972) *Excavations at the Pharr Mounds, Prentice and Itawamba Counties, Mississippi and Excavations at the Bear Creek Site, Tishomingo County, Mississippi.* unpublished report, U.S. Department of the Interior, National Park Service, Office of Archaeology and Historic Preservation, Division of Archaeology and Anthropology, Washington, DC.

Bolnick, D. A. and Smith, D. G. (2007) Migration and social structure among the Hopewell: evidence from ancient DNA. *American Antiquity* 72 (4): 627–44.

Bozell, J. R. (2000) *Faunal Remains from the Hopeton Triangle Site, Hopewell Culture National Historical Park, Ohio.* Unpublished report on file, National Park Service, Midwest Archeological Center, Lincoln, NE.

Brady, K. and Pederson Weinberger, J. (2006) *Phase I Archeological Survey of the Cryder Farm Site (33-Ro-810, 33-Ro-812-8) Impacted by Activities Related to the Development of Visitor Services for Hopewell Culture National Historical Park.* Unpublished report on file, Hopewell Culture National Historical Park, Chillicothe, OH.

Brady, K. and Pederson Weinberger, J. (2009) *Recent Investigations at the Mound City Group.* Unpublished paper given at the Ohio Archaeological Council Meeting, Newark, OH.

Brady, K. and Pederson Weinberger, J. (2010) Recent Investigations at the Mound City Group. *Hopewell Archeology* 7 (2): 3.

Brackenridge, H. M. (1814) *Views of Louisiana, Together with a Journal of a Voyage up the Missouri River in 1811.* New edition, 1962, Quadrangle Book, Chicago, IL.

Brashler, J. G., Hambacher, M., Martin, T., Parker, K. and Robertson, J. (2006). Middle Woodland occupation in the Grand River Basin of Michigan. In Charles and Buikstra (ed.) 2006: 261–84.

Braun, D. P. (1977) *Middle Woodland-Early Late Woodland Social Change in the Prehistoric Central Midwestern U.S.* Ph.D dissertation, Department of Anthropology, University of Michigan, University Microfilms, Ann Arbor, MI.

Brew, J. O. (1966) *Early Days of the Peabody Museum at Harvard University.* Museum Centennial, Peabody Museum at Harvard University. Cambridge, MA.

Bronk Ramsey, C. (1995) Radiocarbon calibration and analysis of stratigraphy: the OxCal program. *Radiocarbon* 37 (2): 425–30.

Bronk Ramsey, C. (1998) Probability and dating. *Radiocarbon* 40: 461–74.

Bronk Ramsey, C. (2001) Development of the radiocarbon calibration program Oxcal. *Radiocarbon* 43: 355–63.

Bronk Ramsey, C. (2009) Bayesian analysis of radiocarbon dates. *Radiocarbon* 51: 337–60

Brose, D. S. (1974) The Everett Knoll: A Late Hopewellian site in northeast Ohio. *Ohio Journal of Science* 74 (1): 36–46.

Brose, D. S. (1976) *An Historical and Archaeological Evaluation of the Hopeton Works, Ross County, Ohio.* Unpublished report submitted to the National Park Service in fulfillment of contract PX-6115-6-0141, Midwest Archeological Center, Lincoln, NE.

Brose, D. S. (1991) *Archeological Monitoring of the Chillicothe Sand and Gravel Company Ground Stripping at the Hopeton Works, Ross County, Ohio.* Unpublished report on file, National Park Service, Midwest Archeological Center, Lincoln, NE.

Brose, D. S. and Greber, N. (ed.) (1979) *Hopewell Archeology: The Chillicothe Conference.* Kent State University Press, Kent, OH.

Browman, D. L. (2002) Frederick Ward Putnam: contributions to the development of archaeological institutions and encouragement of women practitioners. In *New Perspectives on the Origins of Americanist Archaeology*, ed. D. L. Browman and S. Williams: 209–41. University of Alabama Press, Tusaloosa, AL.

Brown, E. H. (1949) Harvard and the Ohio Mounds. *New England Quarterly* 22 (2): 205–20.

Brown, J. A. (1979) Charnel houses and mortuary crypts: disposal of the dead in the Middle Woodland Period. In Brose and Greber (ed.) 1979: 211–9.

Brown, J. A. (1994) *Inventory and Integrative Analysis: Excavations of Mound City, Ross County, Ohio.* Unpublished manuscript, Midwest Archeological Center, National Park Service, Lincoln, NE.

Brown, J. A. (2004) Mound City and issues in the developmental history of Hopewell culture in the

Ross County Area of southern Ohio. In *Essays in Honor of Howard D. Winters,* ed. A.-M. Cantwell and L. Conrad: 147–68. Illinois State Museum Scientific Papers, Springfield, IL.

Brown, J. A. (2005) Reflections on taxonomic practice. In Applegate and Mainfort (ed.) 2005: 111–9.

Brown, J. A. (2006) The shamanistic element in Hopewellian period ritual. In Charles and Buikstra (ed.) 2006: 475–88.

Brown, J. A. (2012) *Mound City: The Archaeology of a Renown Ohio Hopewell Mound Center.* Midwest Archeological Center, National Park Service, Special Report 6, Lincoln, NE.

Brown J. A. and Baby, R. S. (1966) *Mound City Revisited.* Unpublished manuscript, Ohio Historical Society, Columbus, OH.

Buck, C. E., Cavanagh, W.G. and Litton, C. D. 1996. *Bayesian Approach to Interpreting Archaeological Data.* Wiley, Chichester.

Buikstra, J. E., Charles, D. K. and Rakita, G. F. M. (1998) *Staging Ritual: Hopewell Ceremonialism at the Mound House Site, Greene County, Illinois.* Kampsville Studies in Archaeology and History 1. Center for American Archaeology, Kampsville, IL.

Bullen, R. P. (1951) The Gard Site, Homosassa Springs, Florida. *Florida Anthropologist* 4: 27–31.

Bullen, R. P. (1953) The Famous Crystal River Site. *Florida Anthropologist* 6: 9–37.

Bullen, R. P. (1966) Stelae at the Crystal River Site, Florida. *American Antiquity* 31: 861–5.

Burks, J. (2010) Rediscovering prehistoric earthworks in Ohio, USA: it all starts in the archives. In *Landscapes Through the Lens, Aerial Photographs and Historic Environment,* ed. D. C. Cowley, R. A. Standring and M. J. Abicht: 77–87. Oxbow Books, Oxford.

Burks, J. (2013a) *HOCU Magnetic Survey 2012/2013.* Unpublished report 2012-52, Ohio Valley Archaeology Inc, OH.

Burks, J. (2013b) *The State of Ohio's Earthworks.* Unpublished paper presented at the Midwest Archaeological Conference, Columbus, OH.

Burks, J. (2014) Geophysical survey at Ohio earthworks: updating nineteenth century maps and filling the 'empty' spaces. *Archaeological Prospection* DOI: 10; 1002/arp. 1475.

Burks, J. and Cook, R. A. (2011) Beyond Squier and Davis: rediscovering Ohio's earthworks using geophysical remote sensing. *American Antiquity* 76 (4): 667–89.

Burks, J. and Gagliano, D. W. (2009) Hopewell occupation at the Hopeton earthworks: large scale survey using GPS technology. In Lynott (ed.) 2009b: 97–108.

Burks, J. and Pederson Weinberger, J. (2006) The place of nonmound debris at Hopewell Mound Group (33Ro27), Ross County, Ohio. In Charles and Buikstra (ed.) 2006: 376–401.

Burks, J. Pederson Weinberger, J., Willsey, L., Gagliano, D. W. and Brady–Rawlins, K. (2004) New discoveries right in our own front yard: preliminary results of recent research at Mound City Group. *Hopewell Archeology* 6 (1).

Byers, A. M. (1987) The Earthwork Enclosures of the Central Ohio Valley: A Temporal and Structural Analysis of Woodland Society and Culture. Ph.D. dissertation, State University of New York at Albany.

Byers, A. M. (2004) *The Ohio Hopewell Episode: Paradigm Lost, Paradigm Gained.* University of Akron Press, Akron, OH.

Byers, A. M. (2010) The Turner–Hopewell axis: exploring interaction through embankment form and mortuary patterning. In Byers and Wymer (ed.) 2010: 230–44.

Byers, A. M. (2011) *Sacred Games, Death, and Renewal in the Ancient Eastern Woodlands, The Ohio Hopewell System of Cult Sodality Heterarchies.* Alta Mira, Lanham, Maryland.

Byers, A. M. and Wymer, D. (ed.) (2010) *Hopewell Settlement Patterns, Subsistence, and Symbolic Landscapes.* University Press of Florida, Gainesville, FL.

Caldwell, J. R. (1964) Interaction spheres in prehistory. In Caldwell and Hall (ed.) 1964: 133–43.

Caldwell, J. R. and Hall, R. L (ed.) (1964) *Hopewellian Studies.* Scientific Papers, Illinois State Museum, Springfield, IL.

Carr, C. (2005a) Salient issues in the social and political organizations of northern Hopewellian people: contextualizing, personalizing, and generating Hopewell. In Carr and Case (ed.) 2005: 73–118.

Carr, C. (2005b) The tripartite ceremonial alliance among Scioto Hopewellian communities and the question of social ranking. In Carr and Case (ed.): 258–338.

Carr, C. and Case, D. T. (ed.) (2005) *Gathering Hopewell: Society, Ritual and Ritual Interaction.* Kluwer Academic/Plenum Publishers, New York.

Carr, C. and MacCord. R. (2013) Ohio Hopewell depictions of composite creatures, part I – biological identifications and ethnohistorical insights. *Midcontinental Journal of Archaeology* 38 (1): 5–82.

Case, D. T. and Carr, C. (2008) *The Scioto Hopewell an Their Neighbors.* Springer, New York.

Chapman, J. and Keel, B. C. (1979) Candy Creek–Connestee components in eastern Tennessee and western North Carolina and their relationship with Adena–Hopewell. In Brose and Greber (ed.) 1979: 157–61.

Charles, D. K. and Buikstra, J. E. (2002) Siting, sighting, and citing the dead. In *The Space and Place of Death,* ed. H. Silverman and D. Small: 1–21. Archaeological Papers 11, American Anthropological Association, Arlington, VA.

Charles, D. K. and Buikstra, J. E. (ed.) (2006) *Recreating Hopewell.* University Press of Florida, Gainesville, FL.

Clark, A. (1996) *Seeing Beneath the Soil: Prospecting Methods in Archaeology.* Batsford, London.

Clay, R. B. (1986) Adena ritual spaces. In *Early Woodland*

Archaeology, ed. K. B. Farnsworth and T. E. Emerson: 581–95. Center for American Archaeology, Kampsville, IL.

Clay, R. B. (1987) Circles and ovals: two types of Adena space. *Southeastern Archaeology* 6: 46–55.

Clay, R. B. (1988) Peter Village, an Adena enclosure. In Mainfort (ed.) 1988b: 19–30.

Clay, R. B. (1991) Adena ritual development: an organizational type in temporal perspective in the human landscape in Kentucky's past, ed. C. Stout and C. K. Hensley: 30–9. Kentucky Heritage Council, Frankfort, KY.

Clay, R. B. (1998) The essential features of Adena ritual and their implications. *Southeastern Archaeology* 17: 1–21.

Clay, R. B. (2001) Complementary geophysical survey techniques: why two ways are always better than one. *Southeastern Archaeology* 20: 31–43.

Clay, R. B. (2002) *Geophysical Survey at the Shriver Circle Earthwork, 33RO347, near Chillicothe, Ross County, Ohio.* Unpublished report: Cultural Resources Analysts Contract Publication Series 02–90. Prepared for MS Consultants, Inc., Canton, OH/Lexington, KY.

Clay, R. B. (2005) Adena: rest in peace. In Applegate and Mainfort (ed.) 2005: 94–110.

Clay R. B. (2006) Conductivity survey: A survival manual. In *Remote Sensing in Archaeology, An Explicitly North American Perspective*, ed. J. K. Johnson: 79–107. The University of Alabama Press, Tuscaloosa, AL.

Clay, R. B. and Niquette, C. M. (1992) Middle Woodland mortuary ritual in the Gallipolis Locks and Dam Vicinity, West Virginia. *West Virginia Archaeologist* 44 (1–2): 1–25.

Cockrell, R. (1999) *Amidst Ancient Monuments: The Administrative History of Mound City Group National Monument/Hopewell Culture National Historical Park.* National Park Service, Omaha, NE.

Cole, F.-C. and Deuel, T. (1937) *Rediscovering Illinois.* University of Chicago Press, Chicago, IL.

Colvin, G. H. (2011). The presence, source and use of fossil shark teeth from Ohio archaeological sites. *Ohio Archaeologist* 61 (4): 26–46.

Conner, W. D. (2004). *The Fort Ancient Earthworks: Prehistoric Lifeways of the Hopewell Culture in Southwestern Ohio.* Ohio Historical Society, Columbus, OH.

Conner, W. D. (2009) *Iron Age America Before Columbus.* Coachwhip Pulbications, Landisville, PA.

Connolly, R. P. (1996) Prehistoric land modification at the Fort Ancient hilltop enclosure: a model of formal and accretive development. In Pacheco (ed.) 1996: 258–73.

Connolly, R. P. (1997) The evidence for habitation at the Fort Ancient Earthworks, Warren County, Ohio. In Dancey and Pacheco (ed.) 1997: 251–81.

Connolly, R. P. (1998) Architectural grammar rules at the Fort Ancient Hilltop enclosure. In Mainfort and Sullivan (ed.) 1998: 85–113.

Connolly, R. P. (2004a) Evolution of Fort Ancient embankment wall form. In Connolly and Lepper (ed.) 2004: 35–50.

Connolly, R. P. (2004b) Time, space and function at Fort Ancient. In Connolly and Lepper (ed.) 2004: 217–22.

Connolly, R. P. and Lepper, B. T. (ed.) (2004) *The Fort Ancient Earthworks.* Ohio Historical Society, Columbus, OH.

Connolly, R. P. and Sunderhaus, T. S. (2004) Rules for "reading" Fort Ancient architecture. In Connolly and Lepper (ed.) 2004: 51–65.

Cooper, L. R. (1933) Red Cedar variant of the Wisconsin Hopewell Culture. *Bulletin of the Public Museum of the City of Milwaukee* 16: 47–108.

Cotter, J. L. and Corbett, J. M. (1951) Archaeology of the Bynum Mounds, Mississippi. *Archaeological Research Series* 1. National Park Service, US Department of the Interior, Washington, DC.

Coughlin, S. and Seeman M. (1997) Hopewell settlements at the Liberty Earthworks, Ross County, Ohio. In Dancey and Pacheco (ed.) 1997: 231–50.

Cowan, F. L. (2006) A mobile Hopewell? Questioning assumptions of Ohio Hopewell sedentism. In Charles and Buikstra (ed.) 2006: 26–49.

Cowan, F. L. and Genheimer, R. A. (2010) The Great Post Circle at the Stubbs Earthworks. Unpublished paper presented at the Midwest Archaeological Conference, Bloomington, IN.

Cowan, F. L. and Sunderhaus, T. S. (2001) Dating the Stubbs "woodworks." http://Ohioarchaeology.org, 1–7.

Cowan, F. L., Genheime, R. A. and Sunderhaus, T. S. (1997) Recent investigations at Fort Ancient's parallel walls. *Ohio Archaeological Council Newsletter* 9: 15–19.

Cowan, F. L., Picklesimer J. W. II, and Burks, J. (2006) The Shriver Circle Earthworks 160 years after Squier and Davis. Unpublished paper presented at the 52nd Annual Meeting of the Midwest Archaeological Conference, Urbana, IL.

Cowan, F. L., Sunderhaus, T. S. and Genheimer R. A. (1998) Notes from the field, an update from the Stubbs Earthworks. *Ohio Archaeological Council Newsletter* 10: 6–13.

Cowan, F. L., Sunderhaus, T. S. and Genheimer R. A. (1999) Notes from the field, 1999: more Hopewell "houses" at the Stubbs Earthwork Site. Ohio Archaeological Council Newsletter 10 (2): 6–13.

Cowan, F. L., Sunderhaus, T. S. and Genheimer R. A. (2000) *Wooden architecture in Ohio Hopewell sites: structural and spatial patterns at the Stubbs Earthworks site.* Unpublished paper presented at the 65th Annual Meeting of the Society for American Archaeology, Philadelphia, PA.

Cowan, F. L., Sunderhaus, T. S. and Genheimer R. A. (2003) Up-"dating" the Stubbs Cluster, Sort of... *Ohio Archaeological Council Newsletter* 15 (2): http://ohioarchaeology.org/cowan_10_2003.html.

Cowan, F. L., Sunderhaus, T. S. and Genheimer R. A. (2004) Earthwork peripheries: probing the margins of the Fort Ancient site. In Connolly and Lepper (ed.) 2004: 107–24.

Crawford, O. G. S. and Kieller, A. (1928) *Wessex From the Air*. Oxford University Press, Oxford.

Cremeens, D. L. (2004) Micromorphology of the Cotiga Mound, West Virginia. *Geoarchaeology* 20 (6): 581–97.

Cremeens, D. L., Landers, D. B. and Frankenberg, S. R. (1997) Geomorphic setting and stratigraphy of Cotiga Mound, Mingo County, West Virginia. *Geoarchaeology* 12: 459–77.

Dalan, R. A. (2007) A review of the role of magnetic susceptibility in archaeogeophysical studies in the USA: recent developments and prospects. *Archaeological Prospection* 15: 1–31.

Dancey, W. S. (1991) A Middle Woodland settlement in central Ohio: a preliminary report on the Murphy Site. *Pennsylvania Archaeologist* 61: 37–72.

Dancey, W. S. (1996) Putting an end to Ohio Hopewell. In Pacheco (ed.) 1996: 394–405.

Dancey, W. S. (2005) The Hopewell of the Eastern Woodlands. In *North American Archaeology*, ed. T. R. Pauketat and D. DiPaolo Loren: 108–37. Blackwell, Oxford.

Dancey, W. S. (2009) Overly, a Middle Woodland settlement near the Hopeton Earthwork, Ross County, Ohio. In Lynott (ed.) 2009b: 76–97.

Dancey, W. S. and Pacheco, P. J. (1997) A community model of Ohio Hopewell settlement. In Dancey and Pacheco (ed.) 1997: 3–40.

Dancey, W. S. and Pacheco, P. J. (ed.) (1997) *Ohio Hopewell Community Organization*. Kent State University Press, Kent, OH.

DeBoer, Warren R. (1997) Ceremonial centres from the Cayapas (Esmeraldas, Ecuador) to Chillicothe (Ohio, USA). *Cambridge Archaeological Journal* 7(2): 225–53.

DeBoer, Warren R. (2010) Strange sightings on the Scioto. In Byers and Wymer (ed.) 2010: 165–98.

Delcourt, P. A. and Delcourt, H. R. (2008) *Prehistoric Native Americans and Ecological Change: Human Ecosystems in Eastern North America Since the Pleistocene*. Cambridge University Press, Cambridge.

Dempsey, E. (2008) *Seeing through walls: magnetic susceptibility, geoarchaeology, and the Hopeton Earthworks (33RO2b)*. M.A. Thesis, University of Nebraska, Lincoln.

DeRegnaucourt, T. and Georgiady, J. (1998) *Prehistoric Chert Types of the Midwest*. Occasional Monographs Series of the Upper Miami Valley Archaeological Research Museum 7, Arcanum, Ohio.

De Vore, S. L. (2010) The initial phase of the magnetic investigations of the Mound City Group (32Ro32) at the Hopewell Culture National Historical Park, Ross County, Ohio. *Hopewell Archeology* 7 (2).

Dragoo, D. W. (1963) *Mounds for the Dead: An Analysis of the Adena Culture*. Annals of the Carnegie Museum 37, Pittsburgh, PA.

Dragoo, D. W. and Wray, C. F. (1964) Hopewell figurine rediscovered. *American Antiquity* 30: 195–9.

Drake, D. (1815) *Picture of Cincinnati and Miami Country*. Looker and Wallace, Cincinnati, OH.

Eddy, J. A. (1974) Astronomical alignment of the Big Horn Medicine Wheel. *Science* 184 (4141): 1035–43.

Emerson, T. E., Farnsworth, K. B., Wisseman, S. U. and Hughes R. E. (2013) the allure of the exotic: reexamining the use of local and distant pipeston quarries in Ohio Hopewell pipe caches. *American Antiquity* 78 (1): 48–67.

Erasmus, C. J. 1965 Monument building: some field experiments. *Southwestern Journal of Anthropology* 21 (4): 277–301.

Essenpreis, P. S. and Moseley, M. E. (1984) Fort Ancient: citadel or coliseum? *Field Museum of Natural History Bulletin* 55 (6): 5–10, 20–6.

Faulkner, C. H. (1968) *The Old Stone Fort: Exploring an Archaeological Mystery*. University of Tennessee Press, Knoxville, TN.

Faulkner, C. H. (1977) The winter house: an early Southeast tradition. *Midcontinental Journal of Archaeology* 2 (2): 141–59.

Faulkner, Charles H. (1988) Middle Woodland community and settlement patterns on the Eastern Highland Rim, Tennessee. In Mainfort (ed.) 1988b: 76–98.

Farnsworth, K. B. (2004) *Early Hopewell Mound Explorations: The First Fifty Years in the Illinois River Valley*. Illinois Transportation Archaeological Research Program, University of Illinois, Studies in Archaeology 3. University of Illinois Press, Urbana, IL.

Fischer, F. W. (1965) *Preliminary Report on 1965 Archaeological Investigations at Miami Fort*. Unpublished paper, on file, Hopewell Culture National Historical Park, OH.

Fischer, F. W. (1966) *Miami Fort Site, 1966 Preliminary Report*. Unpublished paper, on file, Hopewell Culture National Historical Park, OH.

Fischer, F. W. (1968) *A Survey of the Archaeological Remains of Shawnee Lookout Park*. Unpublished paper, Department of Sociology and Anthropology, University of Cincinnati, OH.

Fischer, F. W. (1969) *Preliminary Report on the University of Cincinnati Archeological Investigations, 1969, Part I*. Unpublished paper, Department of Sociology and Anthropology, University of Cincinnati, OH.

Fischer, F. W. (1970) Preliminary Report on the University of Cincinnati Archeological Investigations, *Preliminary Report on the University of Cincinnati Archeological Investigations, 1969, Part 2*. Unpublished paper, Department of Sociology and Anthropology, University of Cincinnati, OH.

Ford, J. A. (1963) Hopewell Culture burial mounds near Helena, Arkansas. *Anthropological Papers of the American Museum of Natural History* 50 (1): 1–56.

Ford, J. A. (1969) A comparison of formative cultures in the Americas. *Smithsonian Institution Contributions to Anthropology* 11. Washington, DC.

Ford, J. A. and Willey, G. (1940) *Crooks Site, a Marksville Period burial mound in LaSalle Parish, Louisiana. Department of Conservation, Louisiana Geological Survey.* Anthropological Studies 3. New Orleans.

Fowke, G. (1902) *Archaeological History of Ohio: The Mound Builders and Later Indians.* Ohio State Archaeological and Historical Society, Columbus, OH.

Fowke, G. (1927) Archaeological Work in Louisiana. *Smithsonian Miscellaneous Collections* 78 (7): 254–9.

Fowke, G. (1928) Archaeological Investigations – II: Explorations in the Red River Valley in Louisiana. *Forty Fourth Annual Report of the Bureau of American Ethnology*: 399–436

Garland, E. B. and Desjardins, A. L. (2006) Between Goodall and Norton: Middle Woodland settlement patterns and interactions networks in southwestern Michigan. In Charles and Buikstra (ed.) 2006: 227–60.

General Electric Company (1997) *Hopewell in Mt. Vernon. A Study of the Mt. Vernon Site.* General Electric Company.

Genheimer, R. A. (1997). The Stubbs Cluster. Hopewellian site dynamics at a forgotten Little Miami River settlement. In Dancey and Pacheco (ed.) 1997: 283–309.

Gibson, J. L. (2000) *The Ancient Mounds of Poverty Point: A Place of Rings.* University Press of Florida, Gainesville, FL.

Goodman, K. (1973). A Hopewell Burial Trait. *Ohio Archaeologist* 23 (1): 24–5.

Greber, N. B. (1976) *Within Ohio Hopewell: Analysis of Burial Patterns from Several Classic Sites.* Unpublished PhD dissertation, Case Western Reserve University, Cleveland, OH.

Greber, N. B. (1983a) *Recent Excavations at the Edwin Harness Mound; Liberty Works, Ross County, Ohio.* Midcontinental Journal of Archaeology Special Paper 5. Kent State University Press, Kent, OH.

Greber, N. B. (1983b) Recent excavations at the Edwin Harness Mound, Liberty Works, Ross County, Ohio. *Kirtlandia* 39: 1–93.

Greber, N. B. (1991) A study of continuity and contrast between central Scioto Adena and Hopewell sites. *West Virginia Archeologist* 43: 1–26.

Greber, N. B. (1996) A commentary on the contexts and contents of large to small Ohio Hopewell Deposits. In Pacheco (ed.) 1996: 150–73.

Greber, N. B. (1997) Two geometric enclosures in the Paint Creek Valley: an estimate of possible changes in community patterns through time. In Dancey and Pacheco (ed.) 1997: 207–29.

Greber, N. B. and Ruhl, K. C. (2000) *The Hopewell Site: A Contemporary Analysis Based on the Work of Charles C. Willoughby.* Eastern National. Fort Washington, Pennsylvania.

Greber, N. B. (2003) Chronological relationships among Ohio Hopewell sites: few dates and much complexity. In *Theory, Method, and Practice in Modern Archaeology*, ed. R. J. Jeske and D. K. Charles: 88–113. Praeger, Westport, CT.

Greber, N. B. (2005a) Adena and Hopewell in the Middle Ohio Valley: to be or not to be. In Applegate and Mainfort (ed.) 2005: 19–39.

Greber, N. B. (2005b) *Report to Hopewell Culture National Historical Park on 2005 Field Work at the High Bank Works.* Unpublished manuscript on file, Hopewell Culture National Historical Park, Chillicothe, OH.

Greber, N. B. (2009a) Final data and summary contents. In Greber 2009b: 171–86.

Greber, N. B. (ed.) (2009b) Re-interpretation of a group of Hopewell low mounds and structures, Seip Earthworks, Ross County, Ohio. *Midcontinental Journal of Archaeology* 34 (1): 5–186

Greber, N. B. and Ruhl, K. (1989) *The Hopewell Site.* Westview Press, Boulder, CO.

Greber, N. B. and Shane, O. C. III (2009) Field studies of the Octagon and Great Circle, High Bank Earthworks, Ross County, Ohio. In Lynott (ed.) 2009b: 23–48.

Greenman, E. F. (1932a) Excavation of the Coon Mound and an analysis of the Adena Culture. *Ohio State Archaeological and Historical Quarterly* 41: 366–523.

Greenman, E. F. (1932b) Origin and development of the burial mound. *American Anthropologist* 34: 286–95.

Griffin, J. B. (1941) Adena pottery. *American Antiquity* 7: 344–58.

Griffin, J. B. (1945) The ceramic affiliations of the Ohio Valley Adena Culture. In Webb and Snow 1945: 220–46.

Griffin, J. B. (1946) Cultural change and continuity in eastern United States archaeology, In *Man in Northeastern North America,* ed. F. Johnson: 37–95. Papers of the Roberts S. Peabody Foundation for Archaeology 3, Cambridge, MA.

Griffin, J. B. (1952a) *Archaeology of the Eastern United States.* University of Chicago Press, Chicago, IL.

Griffin, J. B. (1952b) Culture periods in eastern United States archaeology. In Griffin (ed.) 1952a: 352–64.

Griffin, J. B. (1958) *The Chronological Position of the Hopewellian Culture in the Eastern United States.* Anthropological papers, Museum of Anthropology, University of Michigan 12, Michigan, MI.

Griffin, J. B. (1967) Eastern North American archaeology: a summary. *Science* 156: 175–91.

Griffin, J. B. (1985) Formation of the Society for American Archaeology. *American Antiquity* 50 (2): 261–71.

Griffin, J. B. (1996) Hopewell housing shortage in Ohio, A.D. 1–350. In Dancey and Pacheco (ed.) 1996: 4–15.

Griffin, J. B., Flanders, R. E. and Titterington, P. F. (1970) *The Burial Complexes of the Knight and Norton Mounds in Illinois and Michigan.* Memoirs of the Museum of Anthropology, University of Michigan 2, Michigan, IL.

Griffin, J. B., Gordus, A. A. and Wright, G. A. (1969) Identification of the sources of Hopewellian obsidian in the Middle West. *American Antiquity* 34: 1–14.

Gunderson, J. N. (2012) X-ray diffraction analysis of pipes and pipe fragments from Mound City. In Brown (2012), Appendix B: 411–44.

Hall, R. L. (1976) Ghosts, water barriers, corn, and sacred enclosures in the Eastern woodlands. *American Antiquity* 41: 350–4.

Hall, R. L. (1997) *An Archaeology of the Soul: North American Indian Belief and Ritual.* University of Illinois Press, Urbana, IL

Hanson, L. H., Jr. (1966) *Excavation of the Borrow Pit, Section F, Mound City Group National Monument. National Park Service.* Manuscript on file at Midwest Archaeological Center, Lincoln NE.

Harrison, W. H. (1838) *A Discourse on the Aborigines of the Valley of the Ohio ...* Cincinnati Express, Cincinnati, OH.

Hatch, J. W., Michels, J. W., Stevenson, C. M., Scheetz, B. E. and Geidel, R. A. (1989) Hopewell obsidian studies: behavioral implications of recent sourcing and dating research. *American Antiquity* 55: 461–79.

Hawkins, J. S. (1965) *Stonehenge Decoded.* Doubleday, New York.

Hawkins, R. A. (1996) Revising the Ohio Middle Woodland ceramic typology: new information from the Twin Mounds West Site. In Pacheco (ed.) 1996: 70–91.

Haven, S. F. (1856) Archaeology of the United States. *Smithsonian Contributions to Knowledge* 8: 1–168. United States National Museum, Washington, DC.

Helms, M. W. (1988) *Ulysses' Sail: An Ethnographic Odyssey of Power, Knowledge, and Geographical Distance.* Princeton University Press, Princeton, NJ.

Helms, M. W. (1993) *Craft and the Kingly Ideal: Art, Trade, and Power.* University of Texas Press, Austin, TX.

Hemmings, E. T. (1984) Fairchance Mound and Village: an Early Middle Woodland settlement in the Upper Ohio Valley. *West Virginia Archeologist* 36: 3–68.

Herold, E. B. (1970) Hopewell burial mound builders. *Palimpsest* 51: 487–528.

Herold, E. B. (1971) The Indian mounds at Albany, Illinois. *Anthropological Papers* 1. Davenport Museum, Davenport, IA.

Hinsdale, W. B. (1931) *Archaeological Atlas of Michigan.* Michigan Handbook Series 4. University Museums, University of Michigan, Ann Arbor, Michigan, MI.

Hively, R. and Horn, R. (1982) Geometry and astronomy in prehistoric Ohio. *Archaeoastronomy* 4: S1–20.

Hively, R. and Horn, R. (1994) Hopewellian geometry and astronomy at High Bank. *Archaeoastronomy* 7: S85–100.

Hively, R. and Horn, R. (2006) A statistical study of lunar alignments at the Newark Earthworks. *Midcontinental Journal of Archaeology* 31 (2): 281–321.

Hively, R. and Horn, R. (2010) Hopewell cosmography at Newark and Chillicothe, Ohio. In Byers and Wymer (ed.) 2010: 128–64.

Hively, R. and Horn, R. (2013) A new and extended case for lunar (and solar) astronomy at the Newark Earthworks. *Midcontinental Journal of Archaeology* 38 (1): 83–118.

Hughes, R. E. (1992) Another look at Hopewell obsidian studies. *American Antiquity* 57: 515–23.

Hughes, R. E. (2006). The sources of Hopewell obsidian: Forty years after Griffin. In Charles and Buikstra (ed.) 2006: 361–75.

Jackson, H. E. 1998. The Little Spanish Fort: an Early Middle Woodland enclosure in the Lower Yazoo Basin, Mississippi. *Midcontinental Journal of Archaeology* 23 (2): 199–220.

Jefferies, R. W. (1976) *The Tunacunnhee Site: evidence of Hopewell interaction in Northwest Georgia.* Anthropological Papers of the University of Georgia 1, Athens, GA.

Jefferies, R. W. (1979) The Tunacunnhee Site: Hopewell in Northwest Georgia. In Brose and Greber (ed.) 1979: 162–70.

Jenkins, N. J. (1979) Miller Hopewell in the Tombigbee Drainage. In Brose and Greber (ed.) 1979: 171–80.

Jones, D. and Kuttruff, C. (1998) Prehistoric enclosures in Louisiana and the Marksville Site. In Mainfort and Sullivan (ed.) 1998: 31–56.

Johnson, A. E. (ed.) (1976) *Hopewellian Archaeology in the Lower Missouri River Valley.* Publications in Anthropology 8, University of Kansas, Lawrence, KS.

Johnson, A. E. (1979) Kansas City Hopewell. In Brose and Greber (ed.) 1979: 86–93.

Johnson, A. E. (1981) The Kansas City Hopewell subsistence and settlement system. *Missouri Archaeologist* 42: 69–76.

Johnston, R. B. (1964) Proton magnetometery and its application to archaeology, an evaluation at Angel Site. *Prehistory Research Series* 4 (2). Indiana Historical Society, Indianapolis, IN.

Joynes, T. R. (1902) Memoranda made by Thomas R. Joynes: on a journey to the States of Ohio and Kentucky, 1810. *William and Mary Quarterly* 10 (4): 221–32.

Keel, B. C. (1976) *Cherokee Archaeology, a Study on the Appalachian Summit.* University of Tennessee Press, Knoxville, TN.

Kellar, J. H. (1979) The Mann Site and "Hopewell" in the

Lower Wabash–Ohio Valley. In Brose and Greber (ed.) 1979: 100–7.

Kellar, J. H., Kelly, A. R. and McMichael, E. V. (1962) The Mandeville Site in southwest Georgia. *American Antiquity* 27: 336–55.

Knight, V. J. Jr (2001) Feasting and the emergence of platform mound ceremonialism in eastern North America. In *Feasts: Archaeological and Ethnographic Perspectives on Food, Politics, and Power*, ed. M. Dietler and B. Hayden: 311–33. Smithsonian Institution Press, Washington, DC.

King, J. L., Herrmann, J. T. and King, Jane E. (2013) *The Golden Eagle Site: A 21st Century Perspective.* Unpublished paper presented at the Annual Meeting, Midwest Archaeological Conference, Columbus, OH.

Lapham, I. A. (1855) *Antiquities of Wisconsin as Surveyed and Described.* Smithsonian Contributions to Knowledge, Smithsonian Institution, Washington, DC.

Larkin, F. (1880) *Ancient Man in North America, Including Works in Western New York and Portions of Others States Together With Structures in Central America.* Privately published by the author.

Lazazzera, A. (2004) Hopewell household variation at the Fort Ancient Site. In Connolly and Lepper (ed.) 2004: 84–106.

Leone, K. L. (2014) *Paleoethnobotanical Analysis of Soil Samples from the Hopeton Earthworks (33Ro26), Hopewell Culture National Historical Park, Ross County, Ohio: Results from the 2013 Field Season.* Unpublished report on file, Midwest Archeological Center, National Park Service, Lincoln, NE.

Lepper, B. T. (1995) Tracking Ohio's Great Hopewell Road. *Archaeology* 48: 52–6.

Lepper, B. T. (1996) The Newark Earthworks and the geometric enclosures of the Scioto Valley: connections and conjectures. In Pacheco (ed.) 1996: 224–41.

Lepper, B. T. (1998) The archaeology of the Newark Earthworks. In Mainfort and Sullivan (ed.) 1998: 114–34.

Lepper, B. T. (2002) *The Newark Earthworks, A Wonder of the Ancient World.* Ohio Historical Society, Columbus, OH.

Lepper, B. T. (2004) The Newark Earthworks: monumental geometry and astronomy at a Hopewell pilgrimage center. In *Hero, Hawk and Open Hand: American Indian Art of the Ancient Midwest and South*, ed. R. V. Townsend and R. V. Sharp: 72–81. Art Institute of Chicago and Yale University Press, New Haven, CT.

Lepper, B. T. (2005) *Ohio Archaeology: An Illustrated Chronicle of Ohio's Ancient American Indian Cultures.* Orange Frazer Press, Wilmington, OH.

Lepper, B. T. (2006) The Great Hopewell Road and the role of the pilgrimage in the Hopewell interaction sphere. In Charles and Buikstra (ed.) 2006: 122–33.

Lepper, B. T. (2010a) The ceremonial landscape of the Newark Earthworks and the Raccoon Creek Valley. In Byers and Wymer (ed.) 2010: 97–127.

Lepper, B. T. (2010b) The Adena pipe: icon of Ancient Ohio. *Timeline* 27 (1): 2–13.

Lepper, B. T. and Yerkes, R. W. (1997) Hopewellian occupations at the northern periphery of the Newark Earthworks: The Newark Expressway Sites revisited. In Dancey and Pacheco (ed.) 1997: 175–205.

Lepper, B. T., Skinner, C. E. and Stevenson, C. M. (1998) Analysis of an obsidian biface fragment from a Hopewell occupation associated with the Fort Hill (33Hi1) hill top enclosure in southern Ohio. *Archaeology of Eastern North America* 26: 33–9.

Lepper, B. T., Leoe, K. L., Jakes, K. A., Pansing, L.L. and Pickard, W. H. (2014) Radiocarbon dates on textile and bark samples from the central grave of the Adena Mound (33Ro1), Chillicothe, Ohio. *Midcontinental Journal of Archaeology* 39 (1): 1–21.

Lindley, D.V. (1985) *Making decisions* (second edition). London: Wiley.

Locke, J. (1838) Ancient work in Highland County. In *Second Annual Report on the Geological Survey of the State of Ohio*, ed. W. W. Mather *et al.*: 267–9.

Locke, J. (1843) Ancient earthworks in Ohio. *Association of American Geologists and Naturalists, Reports 1840–1842*: 229–38.

Logan, B. (1990) *Archaeological Investigations in the Plains Village Frontier, Northeastern Kansas.* Museum of Anthropology, Project Report Series 80. Lawrence, University of Kansas, KS.

Logan, B. (1993) *Quarry Creek: excavation, analysis, and prospects of a Kansas City Hopewell site, Fort Leavenworth, Kansas.* Museum of Anthropology, Project Report Series. Lawrence, University of Kansas, KS.

Logan, B. (2006) Kansas City Hopewell: Middle Woodland on the Western frontier. In Charles and Buikstra (ed.) 2006: 339–58.

Logan, W. D. (1976) *Woodland Complexes in Northeastern Iowa.* Publications in Archaeology 15. National Park Service, Washington, DC.

Long, A. and Rippeteau, B. (1973) Testing contemporaneity and averaging radiocarbon dates. *American Antiquity* 39 (2): 205–15.

Lynott, M. (1997) *Geophysical Surveys at Two Earthen Mound Sites, Wright-Patterson Air Force Base, Ohio.* Midwest Archeological Center, National Park Service, Lincoln, NE.

Lynott, M. (2001) The Hopeton Earthworks: an interim report. *Hopewell Archeology* 4 (2): 1–5.

Lynott, M. (2002) *Archaeological Research at the Hopeton Earthworks, Ross County, Ohio.* Unpublished paper presented at the 48th Midwest Archeological Conference, Columbus, OH.

Lynott, M. (2004) Earthwork construction and the organization of Hopewell society. *Hopewell Archeology* 6 (1): http://www.cr.nps.gov/mwac/hopewell/v6n1/six.htm.

Lynott, M. (2006) Excavation of the East embankment wall, Hopewell Mound Group: a preliminary report. *Hopewell Archeology* 7: (1): 1–6. http: //www.nps.gov/history/mwac/Hopewell/v7n1/one.htm.

Lynott, M. (2007) The Hopeton Earthworks Project: using new technologies to answer old questions. In *Seeking Our Past: An Introduction to North American Archaeology*, ed. Sarah W. Neusius and G. T. Gross: 550–9. Oxford University Press, New York.

Lynott, M. (2008) *Embankment Wall Construction at the Hopeton Earthworks.* Unpublished paper presented at the 2008 Midwest Archaeological Conference, Milwaukee, WI.

Lynott, M. (2009a) Searching for Hopewell settlements: the Triangle Site at the Hopeton Earthworks. In Lynott (ed.) 2009b: 1–12.

Lynott, M. (ed.) (2009b) *Footprints: In the Footprints of Squier and Davis: Archeological Fieldwork in Ross County, Ohio.* Midwest Archeological Center Special Report 5. National Park Service, Lincoln, NE.

Lynott, M. (2010) *Ditches, Walls, Mounds and Monuments: What do we really know about Ohio Hopewell Earthen Enclosures?* Unpublished paper presented at the 75th Annual Meeting of the Society for American Archaeology, St Louis, MO.

Lynott, M. and Mandel, R. D. (2006) *Geoarchaeological Study of an Ohio Hopewell Earthwork.* Unpublished paper presented at the Annual Meeting of the Geological Society of America, Philadelphia, PA.

Lynott, M. and Mandel, R. D. (2009) Archaeological and geoarcheologial study of the Hopeton Square. In Lynott (ed.) 2009b: 159–78,

Lynott, M. and Monk, S. M. (1985) *Mound City, Ohio, Archeological Investigations.* Midwest Archeological Center Occasional Studies in Anthropology 12. National Park Service, Midwest Archeological Center, Lincoln, NE.

Lynott, M. and Weymouth, J. (2001) *Investigations at the Hopeton Earthwork, Ross County, Ohio in the 2001 Season.* Unpublished report on file, National Park Service, Midwest Archeological Center, Lincoln, NE.

Lynott, M. and Weymouth, J. (2002) Preliminary report, 2001 investigations, Hopeton Earthworks. *Hopewell Archeology* 5 (1): 1–7.

Lynott, M., Mandel, R. D. and Brown, J. A. (2010) *Earthen Monument Construction at Mound City, Ohio: 2009-2010.* Unpublished paper presented at the 56th Annual Meeting of the Midwest Archeological Conference, Bloomington, IN.

Lynott, M., Mandel, R. D., Ruby, B. J., Bauermeister, A., De Vore, S. L. and Brown, J. A. (2012) *Earthen Monument Construction at Mound City, Ohio: 2009-2012 Investigations.* Unpublished report on file, Midwest Archaeological Center, National Park Service, Lincoln, NE.

MacLean, J. P. (1879) *The Mound Builders, Being an Account of a Remarkable People that Once Inhabited the Valleys of the Ohio and Mississippi, together with an Investigation into the Archaeology of Butler County, Ohio.* Robert Clarke and Company, Cincinnati, OH.

McClusky, S. (1977) The astronomy of the Hopi Indians. *Journal for the History of Astronomy* 8: 174–95.

McGimsey, C. (2003) The Rings of Marksville. *Southeastern Archaeology* 22 (1): 47–62.

McGregor, J. C. (1952) The Havana Site. In *Hopewellian Communities in Illinois. Scientific Papers,* ed. T. Deuel: 43–91. Illinois State Museum, Springfield, IL.

McKee, A. (2005) Geophysical investigations of the Hopewell Earthworks (33Ro27), Ross County, Ohio. *Hopewell Archeology: The Newsletter of Hopewell Archeology in the Ohio River Valley* 6: 2.

McKern, W. C. (1929) Ohio type of mounds in Wisconsin. *Yearbook of the Public Museum of the City of Milwaukee* 8: 7–21.

McKern, W. C. (1931) A Wisconsin variant of the Hopewell Culture. *Bulletin of the Public Museum of the City of Milwaukee* 10: 185–328.

McMichael, E. V. (1964) Veracruz, the Crystal River Complex, and the Hopewellian climax. In Caldwell and Hall (ed.) 1964: 123–32.

Mainfort, R. C. Jr (1980) *Archaeological investigations at Pinson Mounds State Archaeological Area: 1974, 1975, and 1978 field seasons.* Research Series 1, Tennessee Department of Conservation, Division of Archaeology, TN.

Mainfort, R. C. Jr (1986) *Pinson Mounds, a Middle Woodland ceremonial center.* Research Series 7, Tennessee Department of Conservation, Division of Archaeology, TN.

Mainfort, R. C. Jr (1988a) Pinson Mounds, internal chronology and external relationships. In Mainfort (ed.) 1988b, 132–46.

Mainfort, R. C. Jr (ed.) (1988b) *Middle Woodland Settlement and Ceremonialism in the Mid-South and Lower Mississippi Valley.* Mississippi Department of Archives and History, Archaeological Report 22.

Mainfort, R. C. Jr (1996) Pinson Mounds and the Middle Woodland Period in the Midsouth and Lower Mississippi Valley. In Pacheco (ed.) 1996: 370–91.

Mainfort, R. C. Jr (2005) Some comments on Woodland taxonomy in the Middle Ohio Valley. In Applegate and Mainfort (ed.) 2005: 221–30.

Mainfort, R. C. Jr (2013) *Pinson Mounds: Middle Woodland Ceremonialism in the Midsouth.* University of Arkansas Press, Fayetteville, AR.

Mainfort, R. C. Jr and McNutt, C. H. (2004) Calibrated radiocarbon chronology for Pinson Mounds and Middle Woodland in the Midsouth. *Southeastern Archaeology* 23 (1): 12–24.

Mainfort R. C. Jr and Sullivan, L. P. (ed.) (1998) *Ancient Earthen Enclosures of the Eastern Woodlands.* University Press of Florida, Gainesville, FL.

Mainfort, R. C. Jr and Walling, R. (1992) Excavation at Pinson Mounds: Ozier Mound. *Midcontinental Journal of Archaeology* 17: 112–35.

Mainfort, R. C. Jr, Cogswell, J. W., O'Brien, M. J., Neff, H. and Glascock, M. D. (1997) Neutron Activation Analysis from Pinson Mounds and nearby sites in western Kentucky: local production vs. long–distance importation. *Midcontinental Journal of Archaeology* 22: 43–68.

Mallory, A. H. (1951) *Lost America.* Overlook Company, Washington, DC.

Mandel, R. D., Arpin, T. L. and Goldberg, P. (2003) *Stratigraphy, Lithology, and Pedology of the South Wall at the Hopeton Earthworks, South-Central Ohio.* Unpublished, Kansas Geological Survey Open File Report 2003-46, Lawrence KS.

Mandel, R. D., Arpin, T. L. and Goldberg, P. (2010) Stratigraphy, *Lithology, and Pedology of the Hopeton Earthworks, South-central Ohio: Evaluation of Trench 9.* Unpublished report, Kansas Geological Survey. Lawrence, KS.

Mangold, W. L. and Schurr, M. R. (2006) The Goodall tradition: recent research and new perspectives. In Charles and Buikstra (ed.) 2006: 206–26.

Marshall, J. (1969) Engineering principles and the study of prehistoric structures: a substantive example. *American Antiquity* 34 (2): 166–71.

Marshall, J. (1978) American Indian geometry. *Ohio Archaeologist* 28 (1): 29–33.

Marshall, J. (1980) Geometry of the Hopewell Earthworks. *Ohio Archaeologist* 30 (2): 8–12.

Marshall, J. (1996) Towards a definition of the Ohio Hopewell core and periphery utilizing the geometric earthworks. In Pacheco (ed.) 1996: 210–20.

Maslowski, R. F., Niquette, C. M. and Wingfield, D. M (1995) The Kentucky, Ohio, and West Virginia radiocarbon database. *West Virginia Archaeologist* 47: 1–2.

Meltzer, D. J. (1998) Introduction: Ephraim Squier, Edwin Davis, and the Making of an Archaeological Classic. In *Ancient Monuments of the Mississippi Valley,* reprint edition: 1–97. Smithsonian Institution Press, Washington, DC.

Millon, R. F. (1967) Teotihuacan. *Scientific American* 216: 85–95.

Mills, L. (2003) *Mitochondrial DNA Analysis of the Ohio Hopewell of the Hopewell Mound Group.* Unpublished Ph.D. dissertation, Department of Anthropology, The Ohio State University, Columbus, OH.

Mills, W. C. (1902a) Excavations of the Adena Mound. *Ohio State Archaeological and Historical Quarterly* X: 451–79.

Mills, W. C. (1902b) Excavation of the Adena Mound. *Records of the Past* I: 131–49.

Mills, W. C. (1906a) Baum prehistoric village. *Ohio State Archaeological and Historical Quarterly* 15: 45–136.

Mills, W. C. (1906b) Prehistoric village site, Ross County, Ohio. *Records of the Past* 5: 303–13, 342–52.

Mills, W. C. (1907) Explorations of the Edwin Harness Mound. *Ohio State Archaeological and Historical Quarterly* XVI: 113–93.

Mills, W. C. (1909a) Explorations of the Seip Mound. *Ohio State Archaeological and Historical Quarterly* XVIII: 269–321.

Mills, W. C. (1909b) The Seip Mound. In *Putnam Anniversary Volume, Anthropological Essays:* 102–25.

Mills, W. C. (1914) *Archaeological Atlas of Ohio.* Ohio State Archaeological and Historical Society, Columbus, OH.

Mills, W. C. (1916) Explorations of the Tremper Mound. *Ohio Archaeological and Historical Quarterly* 25: 262–398.

Mills, W. C. (1917) Exploration of the Tremper Mound. *Certain Mound and Village Sites* 2 (3): 105–240.

Mills, W. C. (1920) *Map and Guide to Ft. Ancient, Warren County, Ohio.* F. J. Heer, Columbus, OH.

Mills, W. C. (1921) Flint Ridge. *Ohio Archaeological and Historical Society* 30: 91–161.

Mills, W. C. (1922a) Exploration of the Mound City Group. *Ohio Archaeological and Historical Quarterly* 31: 423–584.

Mills, W. C. (1922b) Exploration of the Mound City Group, Ross County, Ohio. *American Anthropologist* new series 24: 397–431.

Moore, C. B. (1903) Certain Aboriginal mounds of the Florida central west-coast. *Journal of the Academy of Natural Sciences of Philadelphia* XII: 360–494.

Moore, C. B. (1907) Crystal River revisited. *Journal of the Academy of Natural Sciences of Philadelphia* 13: 406–25.

Moorehead, W. K. (1890) *Fort Ancient. The Great Prehistoric Earthwork of Warren County, Ohio, Compiled from a Careful Survey with an Account of its Mounds and Graves.* Robert Clarke, Cincinnati, OH.

Moorehead, W. K. (1892) *Primitive Man in Ohio.* G. P. Putnam's Sons. New York.

Moorehead, W. K. (1893) *Report Upon the Work Done in Southern Ohio. Report to World's Columbian Exposition.* Manuscript on file: Department of Anthropology, Field Museum of Natural History, Chicago.

Moorehead, W. K. (1896) The Hopewell find. *American Antiquarian* XVIII: 58–62.

Moorehead, W. K. (1897a) Report of field work, carried on in the Muskingam, Scioto and Ohio Valleys during the season of 1895. *Ohio State Archaeological and Historical Quarterly* V: 165–274.

Moorehead, W. K. (1897b) The Hopewell Group. *Antiquarian*

1: 113–20, 153–8, 178–84, 208–14, 236–44, 254–64, 291–5, 312–16.

Moorehead, W. K. (1898) The Hopewell Group. *American Archaeologist* 2: 6–11.

Moorehead, W. K. (1899) Report of field work in various portions of Ohio. *Ohio State Archaeological and Historical Quarterly* VII: 110–203.

Moorehead, W. K. (1908) *Fort Ancient, the Great Prehistoric Earthwork of Warren County, Ohio*. Department of Archaeology Bulletin, Phillips Academy III: 35–163.

Moorehead, W. K. (1909) A study of primitive culture in Ohio. *Putnam Anniversary Volume*: 137–50.

Moorehead, W. K. (1922) *The Hopewell Mound Group of Ohio*. Field Museum of Natural History Publication 211, Anthropological Series. Field Museum of Natural History, Chicago, IL.

Moorehead, W. K. (1934) A forgotten tree ring record. *Science* LXXX: 16–17.

Morley, S. G. and Brainerd, G. W. 1956. *The Ancient Maya*. Stanford University Press Stanford

Morgan, L. H. (1881) *Houses and house-life of the American Aborigines*. Contributions to North American Ethnology IV. Department of Interior, US Geographical and Geological Survey of the Rocky Mountains.

Morgan, R. G. (1946) *Fort Ancient*. Ohio State Archaeological and Historical Society, Columbus, OH.

Morgan, R. (2008) *Boone, A Biography*. Algonquin Books, Chapel Hill NC.

Morse, D. F. (1986) Preliminary investigation of the Pinson Mound site: 1963 field season. In Mainfort (ed.) 1986: 96–119.

Munson, P. J. (1967) A Hopewell Enclosure in Illinois. *American Antiquity* 32 (3): 391–3.

Murphy, J. L. (1977) Authorship of Squier and Davis' map of the Marietta Earthworks: a belated correction. *Ohio Archaeologist* 27 (3): 20–2.

Neuman, R. W. (1962) A historical note on tree ring dating. *Plains Anthropologist* 7 (17): 188–9.

Neusius, S. W. and Gross, G. T. (2007) *Seeking Our Past: An Introduction to North American Archaeology*. Oxford University Press, New York.

O'Brien, M. J. and Wood, W. R. (1998) *The Prehistory of Missouri*. University of Missouri Press, Columbia, MO.

O'Neal, Michael A., O'Mansky, M. E. and McGregor, J. (2005) Modeling the natural degradation of earthworks. *Geoarchaeology* 20 (7): 739–48.

Otto, M. P. (2004) A brief history of archaeological investigations at Fort Ancient, Warren County, Ohio. In Connolly and Lepper (ed.) 2004: 3–13.

Otto, M. P. (2009) Historical introduction to the 1971–1977 Ohio Historical Society excavations. In Greber (ed.) 2009b: 9–18.

Ortmann, A. L. and Kidder, T. R. (2013) Building Mound A at Poverty Point, Louisiana: monumental public architecture, ritual practice, and implications for hunter–gatherer complexity. *Geoarchaeology* 28: 66–86.

Pacheco, P. J. (ed.) (1996) *A View from the Core: A Synthesis of Ohio Hopewell Archaeology*. Ohio Archaeological Council, Columbus, OH.

Pacheco, P. J. (1997) Ohio Middle Woodland intracommunity settlement variability: a case study from the Licking Valley. In Dancey and Pacheco (ed.) 1997: 41–84.

Pacheco, P. J. and Dancey, W. S. (2006) Integrating mortuary and settlement data on Ohio Hopewell society. In Charles and Buikstra (ed.) 2006: 3–25.

Pacheco, P. J., Burks, J. and WymerD. A (2006) Investigating Ohio Hopewell settlement patterns in central Ohio. www.ohioarchaeology.org/joomla/Index.php?option=com_content&task= view&id=103 &Itemid=32/; accessed April 4, 2009.

Pacheco, P. J., Burks, J. and Wymer D. A (2009a) The 2006 Archaeological Investigations at Brown's Bottom #1 (33RO1104). http://www.ohio archaeology.org/joomla/index.php?option=com_content&task=view&id= 268&Itemid=32; ac- cessed December 3, 2010.

Pacheco, P. J., Burks, J. and Wymer D. A (2009b) The 2007–2008 Archaeological Investigations at Lady's Run (33RO1105). http://www.ohioarchaeology.org/joomla/index.php?option= com_content&task=view&id=281&Itemid=32/; accessed December 3, 2010.

Pederson Weinberger, J. (2007) *Ohio Hopewell Earthworks: An Examination of Site Use from Non-Mound Space at the Hopewell Site*. Ph.D. Dissertation, Ohio State University, Columbus, OH.

Pederson, J. and Burks, J. (2002) Detecting the Shriver Circle Earthwork, Ross County, Ohio. *Hopewell Archaeology* 5: 10–11.

Peet, S. D. (1903) *The Mound Builders: Their Works and Relics*. Office of the American Antiquarian, Chicago, IL.

Petro, J. H., Shumate, W. H. and Tabb, M F. (1967) *Soil Survey of Ross County, Ohio*. Ohio Department of Natural Resources, Division of Lands and Soil, in cooperation with United States Department of Agriculture, Soil Conservation Service, and Ohio Agricultural Experiment Station, Washington, DC.

Phillips, P. (1970) Archaeological surveys in the Lower Yazoo Basin, Mississippi: 1949–1955. *Papers of the Peabody Museum of Archaeology and Ethnology* 60 (1, 2). Cambridge, MA.

Pickard, W. H. (1996) Excavation at Capitolium Mound (22WN31) Marietta, Washington County, Ohio: a working evaluation. In Pacheco (ed.) 1996: 274–85

Pickard, W. H. and Weinberger, J. W. (2009) Falling through

a crack in the core: the surprise and demise of Anderson Earthwork. In Lynott (ed.) 2009: 67–75.

Picklesimer, J. W. II., Cowan, F. L. and Burks, J. (2006) *Phase I Cultural Resources Survey for the ROS-104-14.26 (PID21250) Road Widening in the Scioto and Union Townships, Ross County, Ohio*. Unpublished report prepared for Ross County Engineers Office, Gray and Paper, Inc.

Pluckhahn, T. J., Thompson, V. D. and Weisman, B. R. (2010) Toward a new view of history and process at Crystal River (8CI1). *Southeastern Archaeology* 29 (1): 164–81.

Potter, M. A. (1968) *Ohio's Prehistoric Peoples*. Ohio Historical Society, Columbus, OH.

Quimby, G. I. (1941) *The Goodall Focus: An Analysis of Ten Hopewellian Components in Michigan and Indiana*. Indiana Historical Society Prehistoric Research Series 2: 61–161.

Powell, J. Wesley (1894) Report of the Director. *Twelfth Annual Report of the Bureau of American Ethnology to the Secretary of the Smithsonian Institution 1890-91*.

Prufer, O. H. (1964) The Hopewell complex of Ohio. In Caldwell and Hall (ed.) 1964: 35–83.

Prufer, O. H. (1965) *The McGraw Site: A Study in Hopewellian Dynamics*. Scientific Publications 4, (1). Cleveland Museum of Natural History, Cleveland, OH.

Prufer, O. H. (1968) *Ohio Hopewell Ceramics: An Analysis of the Extant Collections*. Anthropological Paper 33. University of Michigan Museum of Anthropology, Ann Arbor, MI.

Prufer, O. H. (1997) Fort Hill 1964: new data and reflections on Hopewell hilltop enclosures in southern Ohio. In Dancey and Pacheco (ed.) 1997: 311–27.

Putnam, F. W. (1882) Notes on copper objects from North and South America. *Peabody Museum, Fifteenth Annual Report* 3 (2): 83–148.

Putnam, F. W. (1883) Altar mounds in Anderson Township, Ohio. *Science* 1: 348–9.

Putnam, F. W. (1886) Explorations in Ohio. The Marriott Mound, No. 1, and its contents. *Peabody Museum, Eighteenth and Nineteenth Annual Report (1884 and 1885)*: 449–66. Harvard University, Cambridge, MA

Putnam, F. W. (1887a) Report of the curator. *Peabody Museum Sixteenth and Seventeenth Annual Reports (1882 and 1883)*. Harvard University, Cambridge, MA.

Putnam, F. W. (1887b) Explorations of the Harness Mounds in the Scioto Valley, Ohio. *Peabody Museum 18th and 19th Annual Reports (1884-1885)*. Harvard University, Cambridge, MA.

Putnam, F. W. (1890a) Prehistoric remains in the Ohio Valley. *Century Magazine* 39: 698–703.

Putnam, F. W. (1890b) The Serpent Mound of Ohio. *Century Magazine* 39: 871–88.

Putnam, F. W. (1890c) Notice of a singular prehistoric structure at Foster's, Little Miami Valley, Ohio. *Pro-ceedings of the American Association for the Advancement of Science* 39: 389.

Putnam, F. W. (1891) A singular ancient work. *American Antiquarian Society Proceedings* new series 7 (1): 136–7.

Rafferty, J. (1987) The Ingomar Mounds site: internal structure and chronology. *Midcontinental Journal of Archaeology* 12: 147–73.

Rafinesque, C. S. (1824) *Ancient History, or Annals of Kentucky; With a Survey of the Ancient Monuments of North America, With a Tabular View of the Principal Languages and Primitive Nations, of the Whole Earth*. Frankfort, KY.

Railey, J. A. (1996) Woodland cultivators. In *Kentucky Archaeology*, ed. R. B. Lewis: 79–126. University of Kentucky Press, Lexington, KY.

Randall, E. O. (1905) *The Serpent Mound, Adams County, Ohio: Mystery of the Mound and History of the Serpent; Various Theories of the Effigy Mounds and the Mound Builders*. Ohio Archaeological and Historical Society, Columbus, OH.

Randall, E. O. (1908) *The Masterpieces of the Ohio Mound Builders: The Hilltop Fortifications, Including Fort Ancient*. Ohio State Archaeological and Historical Society, Columbus, OH.

Rapp, G., Allert, J., Vitali, V., Jing, Z. and Henrickson, E. (2000) *Determining Geological Sources of Copper Artifacts*. University Press of America, Lanham, MD.

Read, M. C. and Whittlesey, C. (1877) *Antiquities of Ohio. Report of the Committee of the State Archaeological Society. Final Report of the Ohio State Board of Centennial Managers to the General Assembly of the State of Ohio, Part II*: 81–139. Columbus, OH.

Redmond, B. G. (2007) Hopewell on the Sandusky: analysis and description of an inundated Ohio Hopewell mortuary-ceremonial site in north-central Ohio. *North American Archaeologist* 28 (3): 189–332.

Reeves, D. (1936a) Aerial photography and archaeology. *American Antiquity* 2 (2): 102–7.

Reeves, D. (1936b) A newly discovered extension of the Newark Works. *Ohio State Archaeological and Historical Quarterly* 45: 187–93.

Reimer, Paula J., Baillie, M. G. L., Bard, E., Bayliss, A., Beck, J. W., Bertrand, C. J. H., Blackwell, P. G., Buck, C. E., Burr, G. S., Cutler, K. B., Damon, P. E., Edwards, R. L., Fairbanks, R. G., Friedrich, M., Guilderson, T. P., Hogg, A. G., Hughen, K. A., Kromer, B., McCormac, G., Manning, S., Bronk Ramsey, C., Reimer, R. W., Remmele, S., Southon, J. R., Stuiver, M., Talamo, S., Taylor, F. W., Plicht, J. van der and Weyhenmeyer, C. E. (2004) IntCal04 Terrestrial Radiocarbon Age Calibration, 0–26 cal kyr BP. *Radiocarbon* 46: 1029–58.

Richner, J. J. and Bauermeister, A. C. (2011) *An Archeological Inventory and Assessment of 14 Archeological Sites in the*

Everett Area, Boston Township, Summit County, Ohio. Midwest Archeological Center Technical Report 113. Midwest Archeological Center, National Park Service, U. S. Department of Interior, Lincoln, NE.

Richner, J. J. and Volf, W. (2000) Front yard archeology: Hopewell occupation at the Szlay Site. *Hopewell Archeology: The Newsletter of Hopewell Archeology in the Ohio River Valley* 4 (1): 10–11.

Riordan, R. V. (1995) A Construction sequence for a Middle Woodland hilltop enclosure. *Midcontinental Journal of Archaeology* 20: 62–104.

Riordan, R. V. (1996) Core and periphery: the final chapter on Ohio Hopewell. In Pacheco (ed.) 1996: 406–25.

Riordan, R. V. (1998) Boundaries, resistance, and control: enclosing the hilltops in Middle Woodland Ohio. In Mainfort and Sullivan (ed.) 1998: 68–84.

Riordan, R. V. (2006) Altering a Middle Woodland enclosure. In Charles and Buikstra (ed.) 2006: 146–57.

Riordan, R. V. (2007) *Report on the Excavations of the Moorehead Circle at Fort Ancient, 2006.* Wright State University Laboratory of Anthropology, Reports in Anthropology 9, Dayton, OH.

Riordan, R. V. (2009) *Report on the Excavations at the Moorehead Circle at Fort Ancient, 2007.* Wright State University Laboratory of Anthropology, Reports in Anthropology 10, Dayton, OH.

Riordan, R. V. (2010a) Enclosed by stone. In Byers and Wymer (ed.) 2010: 215–29.

Riordan, R. V. (2010b) *Where We Stand: The Moorehead Circle in 2010.* Unpublished paper presented at the 56th Annual Midwest Archaeological Conference, Bloomington, IN.

Ritchie, W. A. (1938) *Certain Recently Explored New York Mounds and Their Probably Relation to the Hopewell Culture.* Rochester Museum of Arts and Sciences, Research Records 4, Rochester, NY.

Ritchie, W. A. (1969) *The Archaeology of New York State* (revised edn). Natural History Press, NY.

Romain, W. F. (1991) Evidence for a basic Hopewell unit of measure. *Ohio Archaeologist* 41 (4): 28–37.

Romain, W. F. (1992) Hopewellian concepts in geometry. *Ohio Archaeologist* 42 (2): 35–50.

Romain, W. F. (2000) *Mysteries of the Hopewell: Astronomers, Geometers, and Magicians of the Eastern Woodlands.* University of Akron Press, Akron, OH.

Romain, W. F. (2004) Journey to the center of the world: astronomy, geometry, and cosmology of the Fort Ancient enclosure. In Connolly and Lepper (ed.) 2004: 66–83.

Romain, W. F. and Burks, J. (2008a) *LiDAR Analysis of Prehistoric Earthworks in Ross County, Ohio.* Ohio Archaeological Council, March 3, 2008 http://www.ohioarchaeology.org/joomla/index.php?option=com_content&task=view&id=233&Itemid=32

Romain, W. F. and Burks, J. (2008b) *LiDAR Imaging of the Great Hopewell Road.* Ohio Archaeological Council, February 4, 2008 http://www.ohioarchaeology.org/joomla/index.php?option=com_content&task=view&id=231&Itemid=32

Ruby, B. J. (1996) *Current Research at Hopewell Culture National Historical Park: Recent Excavations at the Hopeton and Spruce Hill Works, Ross County, Ohio.* Paper presented at the 41st Annual Midwest Archaeological Conference, Beloit, Wisconsin. http://home.comcast.net/~bret.ruby/Documents/Hopeton_and_Spruce_Hill_Current_Research_1996.htm, accessed 7 July 2003.

Ruby, B. J. (1997a) Current research at Hopewell Culture National Historical Park. *Hopewell Archaeology* 2 (2): 1–6.

Ruby, B. J. (1997b) *Beyond the Walls: Recent Research at the Hopeton Works, Hopewell Culture National Historical Park.* Paper presented at the Annual Meeting of the Ohio Archaeological Council, Columbus. http://home.comcast.net/~bret.ruby/Documents/Beyond_the_Walls_Recent_Research_at_Hopeton_OAC_Fall97.htm, accessed July 7, 2003.

Ruby, B. J. (1997c) 1997 Field School excavations at the Hopeton Earthworks. Excerpt from Hopewell Culture National Historical Park's newsletter, *The Falcon,* Fall 1997. http://home.comcast.net/~bret.ruby/Documents/Falcon_Fall_97_Hopeton_Redwing_Fieldschool.htm, accessed July 7, 2003.

Ruby, B. J. (2006) The Mann Phase: Hopewellian community organization in the Wabash Lowland. In Charles and Buikstra (ed.) 2006: 190–205.

Ruby, B. J. (2009) Spruce Hill Earthworks: the 1995–1996 National Park Service investigations. In Lynott (ed.) 2009b: 49–66.

Ruby, B. J. and Lynott, M. (2009) Hopewellian centers in context: investigations in and around the Hopeton Earthworks. In Lynott (ed.) 2009b: 109–24.

Ruby, B. J. and Troy, S. J. (1996) *Hopewellian Centers in Context: Intensive Survey in the Vicinity of the Hopeton Works, Hopewell Culture National Historical Park, Ross County, Ohio.* Unpublished paper presented at the 41st Annual Midwest Archaeological Conference, Beloit, Wisconsin.

Ruby, B. J. and Troy, S. J. (1998) *Shattering the Hopewell Core: A Comparative Analysis of Hopewellian Prepared Core and Blade Industries in South-central Ohio.* Unpublished poster presented at the 63rd Annual Meeting of the Society for American Archaeology, Seattle.

Ruby, B. C, Carr, C. and Charles, D. K. (2005) Community Organizations in the Scioto, Mann and Havanna Hopewell regions: a comparative perspective. In Carr and Case (ed.) 2005: 119–76.

Ruhl, K. C. (1992) Copper earspools from Ohio Hopewell sites. *Midcontinental Journal of Archaeology* 17: 46–79.

Ruhl, K. C. (2005) Hopewellian copper earspools from eastern North America: the social, ritual, and symbolic significance of their contexts and distribution. In Carr and Case (ed.) 2005: 696–713.

Ruhl, K. C., and Seeman, M. F. (1998) Temporal and social implications of Ohio Hopewell copper ear spool design. *American Antiquity* 63: 651–62.

Ryan, T. M. (1975) Semisubterranean structures and their spatial distribution at the Marksville Site (16AV1). *Proceedings of the 31st Southeastern Archaeological Conference* 18: 215–25.

Salisbury, J. H. and Salisbury, C. R. (1862) *Accurate Surveys and Descriptions of the Ancient Earthworks at Newark, Ohio.* Unpublished Manuscript, American Antiquarian Association, Worchester, MA.

Sargent, W. (1799) A Letter from Colonel Winthrop Sargent to Dr. Benjamin Smith Barton, accompanying drawings and some accounts of certain articles, which were taken out of an ancient tumulus, or grave, in the Western Country. *Transactions of the American Philosophical Society* 4: 177–80.

Sassaman, W. H. (1952–4) *Record of Excavation. Fort Hill site, Hi9.* Unpublished fieldnotes on file, Ohio Historical Society, Columbus, OH.

Saurborn, B. S. (1968) *A Re-examination of Mounds 23 and 17, Unit H, Mound City Group National Monument.* Report to the National Park Service, Ohio Historical Society, Columbus. Contract P.O. NER 950–755.

Saunders, J. W., Mandel, R. D., Sampson, C. G., Allen, C. M., Allen, E. T., Bush, D. A., Feathers, J. K., Gremillion, K. J., Hallmark, C. T., Jackson, H. E., Johnson, J. K., Jones, R., Saucier, R. T., Stringer, G. L., and Vidrine, M. F. (2005) Watson Brake, a Middle Archaic mound complex in northeast Louisiana. *American Antiquity* 70 (4): 631–68.

Schilling, T. (2013) The chronology of Monks Mound. *Southeastern Archaeology* 32 (1): 14–28.

Sears, W. H. (1962) The Hopewellian affiliation of certain sites on the Gulf Coast of Florida. *American Antiquity* 28: 5–18.

Sears, W. H. (1982) Fort Center: An Archaeological Site in the Lake Okeechobee Basin. *Ripley P. Bullen Monographs in Archaeology and History* 4. The Florida State Museum, Gainesville, FL.

Seeman, M. F. (1981a) *An Archaeological Survey of the Hopewell Site (33Ro27) and Vicinity, Ross County, Ohio.* Unpublished Report, Department of Sociology and Anthropology, Kent State University, Kent, OH.

Seeman, M. F. (1981b) *Phase I (Literature Search) and Phase II (Locational Survey) Investigations of the Chillicothe Correctional Institute, Chillicothe, Ohio.* Unpublished Report to the Bureau of Prisons, U.S. Department of Justice. Kent State University, Kent, OH.

Seeman, M. F. (1995) When words are not enough: Hopewell interregionalism and the use of material symbols at the GE mound. In *Native American Interactions*, ed. M. S. Nassaney and K. E. Sassaman: 122–43. University of Tennessee Press, Knoxville, TN.

Seeman, M. F. (2011) *Hopewell Time and Materiality.* Unpublished Featured Banquet Presentation, 57th Midwest Archaeological Conference, La Crosse, WI.

Setzler, F. (1933) Pottery of the Hopewell type from Louisiana. *U.S. National Museum, Smithsonian Institution, Proceedings* LXXXII: 1–21.

Shearer, G. L. (2009) *Analysis of Sample from Hopeton Earthwork (MWAC-1022, HOCU-275).* Unpublished Report by McCrone Associates to Midwest Archeological Center, National Park Service, Chillicothe, OH.

Shepherd, H. A. (1887) *Antiquities of the State of Ohio.* John C. Yorston & Co. Cincinnati, OH.

Sherrod, P. C. and Rolingson, M. A. (1987) *Surveyors of the Ancient Mississippi Valley: Modules and Alignments in Prehistoric Mound Sites.* Arkansas Archeological Survey, Research Series 28. Fayetteville, AR.

Shetrone, H. C. (1920) The culture problem in Ohio archaeology, *American Anthropologist* ns 22: 144–72.

Shetrone, H. C. (1925) Exploration of the Ginther Mound; the Miesse Mound. *Ohio State Archaeological and Historical Quarterly* 34: 154–68.

Shetrone, H. C. (1926) Exploration of the Hopewell Group of prehistoric earthworks. *Ohio Archaeological and Historical Quarterly* 40: 1–227.

Shetrone, H. C. (1930) *The Mound Builders.* Appleton-Century, New York.

Shetrone, H. C. and Greenman, E. F. (1931) Explorations of the Seip Group of prehistoric earthworks. *Ohio Archaeological and Historical Society Publications* 40: 343–509.

Sieg, L. and Burks, J. (2010) The land between the mounds: the role of "empty" spaces in the Hopewellian built environment. In Byers and Wymer (ed.) 2010: 56–72.

Sieg, L. E. and Connolly, R. P. (1997) *Report of Investigations at Fort Ancient State Memorial Ohio (33Wa2), Vol. 2, The Gateway 84 Embankment Wall.* Unpublished manuscript on File, Ohio Historical Society, Columbus, OH.

Silverberg, R. (1968) *Mound Builders of Ancient America.* New York Graphic Arts Society, Greenwich, CT.

Smith, B. D. (1978) *Prehistoric Patterns of Human Behavior: A Case Study in the Mississippi Valley.* Academic Press, New York.

Smith, B. D. (1992) *Rivers of Change: Essays on Early Agriculture in Eastern North America.* Smithsonian Institution Press, Washington DC.

Snow, D. (1980) *The Archaeology of New England.* Academic Press, New York.

Snyder, G. G., Shane, L. C. K. and Kapp R. O. (1991) *Palynological Studies Associated with the Mound City Group National Monument, Chillicothe, Ohio.* Unpublished Report on file at Hopewell Culture Natonal Historical Park, Chillicothe, OH.

Spielmann, K. A. (2002) Feasting, craft specialization, and the ritual mode of production. *American Anthropologist* 104: 195–207.

Spielmann, K. A. (2003) *Excavation Report for Unit 6, Hopeton Earthworks, Summer 002.* Midwest Archeological Center, Lincoln, NE.

Spielmann, K. A. (2009) Ohio Hopewell ritual craft production. In Lynott (ed.) 2009b: 179–88.

Spielmann, K. and Burks, J. (2011) *Report on the July 2011 Test Excavations to Evaluate a Possible Post Circle at Seip.* Unpublished Report Prepared for the Ohio Historical Society, Columbus, OH.

Spielmann, K., Burks, J., De Vore, S. L., Ingram, S., Kelly, S., Kruse, M. and Thompson, M. S. (2005) *Field Report for the Arizona State University Archaeological Field School, Summer 2005 Excavations at Seip Earthwork (33Ro40).* Unpublished Report Submitted to the Ohio Historical Society, Columbus, OH.

Squier, E. G. (1847) *Observations on the Aboriginal Monuments of the Mississippi Valley, The Character of the Ancient Earth-Works, and the Structure, contents, and Purposes of the Mounds; With Notices of the minor Remains of Ancient Art.* Bartlett and Welford, New York.

Squier, E. G. (1860) Ancient monuments in the United States. *Harpers New Monthly Magazine* 20: 737–53; 21: 20–36, 165–78.

Squier, E. and Davis, E. (1848) *Ancient Monuments of the Mississippi Valley: Comprising the Results of Extensive Original Surveys and Explorations.* Smithsonian Contributions to Knowledge 1. Smithsonian Institution, Washington, DC.

Staffin, D. (1971) Wolfe Havana Hopewell site. In, Prehistoric Investigations, ed. M. B. McKusick: 53–65. *Report 3, Office of the State Archaeologist*, Iowa City, IA.

Starr, S. F. (1960) *The Archaeology of Hamilton County, Ohio. Journal of the Cincinnati Museum of Natural History* 23(1).

Stevens, E. T. (1870) *Flint Chips. A Guide to Pre-historic Archaeology, as Illustrated by the Collection in the Blackmore Museum, Salisbury.* Bell & Daldy, London.

Stevenson, C. M., Scheetz, B. and Hatch, J. W. (1987) Reply to Hughes. *American Antiquity* 57: 524–5.

Stevenson, C. M., Scheetz, B. and Hatch, J. W. (1992) Reply to Hughes. *American Antiquity* 57: 524–525.

Stevenson, C. M., Abdelrehim, I. and Novak, S. W. (2004) High precison measurement of obsidian hydration layers on artifacts from the Hopewell site using Secondary Ion Mass Spectrometry. *American Antiquity* 69 (3): 555–67.

Stoltman, J. B. (2006) Reconsidering the context of Hopewell interaction in southwestern Wisconsin. In Charles and Buikstra (ed.) 2006: 310–27. University Press of Florida, Gainesville, FL.

Stoltman, J. B. (2012) Petrographic analysis of Mound City pottery. In Mound City: *The Archaeology of a Renown Ohio Hopewell Mound Center*, by J. A. Brown: appendix A, 375–410. Midwest Archeological Center, National Park Service, Special Report 6, Lincoln, NE.

Stoltman, J. B. and Mainfort R. C. Jr. (2002) Minerals and elements: using petrography to reconsisder the findings of Neutron Activation in the compositional analysis of ceramics from Pinson Mounds, Tennessee. *Midcontinental Journal of Archaeology* 27 (1): 2–34.

Stuiver, M., Reimer, P. J., Bard, E., Beck, J. W., Burr, G. S., Hughen, K. A., Kromer, B., McCormac, F. G., Plicht, J. van der and Spurk, M. (1998) 1998 INTCAL98 Radiocarbon Age Calibration, 24000–0 Cal BP. *Radiocarbon* 40: 1041–83.

Stuiver, M. and Reimer, P. J. (1993) Extended ^{14}C data base and revised Calib 3.0 ^{14}C Age calibration program. *Radiocarbon* 35 (1): 215–30.

Sunderhaus, T. S., Riggs, R. and Cowan, F. L. (2001) *The Smith Site: A Small Hopewell Site Overlooking the Stubbs Earthworks.* Ohio Archaeological Council: 1–8, www.ohioarchaeology.org.

Tankersley, K. B. (2007) Archaeological geology of the Turner Site complex, Hamilton County, Ohio. *North American Archaeologist* 28 (4): 271–94.

Taylor, J. L. B. (1929) Some researches in the Illinois River valley near Havana. In *The Cahokia Mounds, Part I, Explorations of 1922, 1923, 1924, and 1927, by W. K. Moorehead*: 65–85. University of Illinois Bulletin 26 (4), Urbana, IL.

Toth, A. (1974) *Archaeology and Ceramics at the Marksville Site.* University of Michigan Museum of Anthropology, Anthropological Papers 56. Ann Arbor, MI.

Thomas, C. (1891) *Catalog of Prehistoric Works East of the Rocky Mountains.* Smithsonian Institution Bureau of Ethnology, Washington, DC.

Thomas, C. (1894) *Report on the Mound Explorations of the Bureau of Ethnology.* Twelfth Annual Report, 1890–1891. Smithsonian Institution, Bureau of Ethnology, Washington, DC.

Thomas, C. (1889a) *The Problem of the Ohio Mounds.* Smithsonian Institution, Bureau of Ethnology, Washington, DC.

Thomas, C. (1889b) *The Circular, Square, and Octagonal Earthworks of Ohio.* Bulletin 10. Smithsonian Institution, Bureau of Ethnology, Washington, DC.

Thomas, C. (1903) *Introduction to the Study of North American Archaeology.* Robert Clarke Company, Cincinnati, OH.

Thompson, V. D. and Pluckhahn, T. J. (2012) Monumentalization and ritual landscapes at Fort Center in the

Lake Okeechobee basin of south Florida. *Journal of Anthropological Archaeology* 31: 49–65.

Thunen, R. C. (1987) Geometric enclosures in the Mid-South: an architectural analysis of enclosure form. In *Middle Woodland Settlement and Ceremonialism in the Mid-South and Lower Mississippi Valley*, edited by R.C. Mainfort, Jr. Mississippi Department of Archives and History, Archaeological Report No. 22: 99–116.

Thunen, R. C. (1998) Defining space: an overview of the Pinson Mounds enclosure. In Mainfort and Sullivan: 57–67. University Press of Florida, Gainesville, FL.

Van Nest, J., Charles, D. K., Buikstra J. E. and Asch, D. L. (2001) Sod blocks in Illinois Hopewell mounds. *American Antiquity* 66 (4): 633–50.

Vescilus, G. S. (1957) Mound 2 at Marksville. *American Antiquity* 32: 416–20.

Volf, W. (1998) *The Szalay Site: Hopewell Occupation in Northeastern Ohio*. Master's thesis, Department of Anthropology, University of Nebraska, Lincoln, NE.

Volf, W. J. (2000) *The Szalay Site: Hopewellian occupation in Northeastern Ohio*. M.A. Thesis, University of Nebraska, Lincoln.

Walter, D. E. and Coleman, K. B.(2001) *A Phase I Cultural Resources Survey for the ROS-104-14.26 (PID 21250) Road Widening in Scioto and Union Townships, Ross County, Ohio*. Unpublished ASC Group Report 1999–1216 ROS–104. Prepared for MS Consultants, Inc., Canton, OH.

Walthall, J. A. (1980) *Prehistoric Indians of the Southeast: Archaeology of Alabama and the Middle South*. University of Alabama Press, Tuscaloosa, AL.

Weaver, S. A., Abrams, E. M., Freter, A. and Sack, D. (2011) Middle Woodland domestic architecture and the issue of sedentism: evidence from the Patton Site (33AT990), Hocking Valley, Ohio. *Journal of Ohio Archaeology* 1: 22–40.

Webb, W. S. and Snow, C. E. (1945) *The Adena People*. Publications of the Department of Anthropology and Archeology 6, 1974 reprint, University of Tennessee Press, Knoxville, TN

Webb, W. S. and Baby, R. (1957) *The Adena People - No 2*. Ohio Historical Society, Columbus, OH.

Wedel, W. (1938) Hopewellian remains near Kansas City, Missouri. *Proceedings of the U.S. National Museum* 86: 99–106. Washington, DC.

Wedel, W. (1943) *Archaeological Investigations in Platte and Clay Counties, Missouri*. United States National Museum Bulletin 183. Smithsonian Institution, Washington, DC.

Weisman, B. R. (1995) *Crystal River, A Ceremonial Mound Center on the Florida Gulf Coast*. Florida Archaeology 8. Florida Bureau of Archaeological Research, Florida Department of State, Tallahassee, FL.

Weymouth, J. W. (1979) *A Magnetic Survey of Seip Mounds and the Harness Site, Ohio*. Unpublished Report on file, Midwest Archeological Center, National Park Service, Lincoln, NE.

Weymouth, J. W. (1996).*Geophysical Surveys on the Overly Tract, Ross County, Ohio and Correlation with Test Excavations*. Unpublished Report on File, National Park Service, Midwest Archeological Center, Lincoln, NE.

Weymouth, J. W. (1997) Final Report on magnetic and resistance surveys of mounds on the Wright–Patterson Air Force Base. In Lynott (ed.) 1997: iv, 1–40.

Weymouth, J. W. (1998) *Three Geophysical Surveys of the Hopeton Earth Works: The Second Season*. Unpublished Report on File, National Park Service, Midwest Archeological Center, Lincoln, NE.

Weymouth, J. W. (2002) *Geophysical Investigations at the Hopeton Earthworks, Ross County, Ohio: The 2002 Season*. Unpublished Report on File, Midwest Archeological Center, National Park Service, Lincoln, NE.

Weymouth, J., Bevan, B. and Dalan R. (2009) Geophysical investigations at the Hopeton Earthworks. In Lynott (ed.) 2009b: 145–58.

Weymouth, J. W. and Nickel, R. K. (1977) A magnetometer survey of the Knife River Indian villages. *Plains Anthropologist* 22, Memoir 13: 104–18.

Whittaker, W. E. and Green, W. (2010) Earth and Middle Woodland earthwork enclosures in Iowa. *North American Archaeologist* 31 (1): 27–57.

Wittry, W. (1969) The American Woodhenge. In *Explorations into Cahokia Archaeology*, ed. M. Fowler: 43–48. Illinois Archaeological Survey Bulletin 7, IL.

Willey G. R. and Sabloff, J. (1974) *A History of American Archaeology*. W.H. Freeman, San Francisco, CA.

Willoughby, C. C. and Hooten, E. A. (1922) *The Turner Group of Earthworks, Hamilton County, Ohio*. Papers of the Peabody Museum 8. Harvard University, Cambridge, MA.

Whittle, A., Healy, F. and Bayliss, A. (2011) *Gathering Time. Dating the Early Neolithic Enclosures of Southern Britain and Ireland*. Oxbow Books, Oxford.

Whittlesey, C. (1851) *Description of Ancient Works in Ohio*. Smithsonian Contributions to Knowledge , Smithsonian Institution, Washington, DC.

Whittlesey, C. (1884) Metrical standard of the mound builders, by the method of even divisiors. *American Associatin for the Advancement of Science, Proceedings* XXXII: 422–5.

Wilson, J. N. (1865) *Copy of a letter to O. C. Marsh*. Unpublished Manuscript, Western Reserve Historical Society, Cleveland, OH.

Wymer, D. A. (2006) *The Paleoethnobotanical Assemblage of the Hopeton Earthworks Research Project, Ross County, Ohio*. Unpublished Report Submitted to National Park Service, Midwest Archaeological Center, Lincoln, NE.

Wyrick, D. (1866) Ancient works near Newark, Licking County, O. In *Atlas of Licking County, Ohio*, Ed. F. W. Beers; Beers, Soule, New York.

Yerkes, R. W. (2005) Bone chemistry, body parts, and growth marks: evaluating Ohio Hopewell and Cahokia Mississippian seasonality, subsistence, ritual, and feasting. *American Antiquity* 70 (2): 241–65.

Yerkes, D. (2006) Middle Woodland settlements and social organization in the Central Ohio Valley. In Charles and Buikstra (ed.) 2006: 50–61.